SO-BIB-468

CONTEMPORARY RELEVANCE OF SRI AUROBINDO

Contemporary Relevance of SRI AUROBINDO

Edited by

KISHORE GANDHI

VIVEK PUBLISHING HOUSE
18-D, Kamla Nagar, Delhi-7

PRINTED IN INDIA

AT ZODIAC PRESS, KASHMERE GATE, DELHI AND PUBLISHED BY L.R. GUPTA FOR VIVEK PUBLISHING HOUSE, 18-D, KAMLA NAGAR, DELHI - 7

BLESSINGS FROM
'THE MOTHER'

blessings

PREFACE

A centenary anthology, these essays by scholars of diverse disciplines bring out the range, consistency and integrality of Sri Aurobindo's living thought and his long labour for a new India and a new world.

Not only a yogi but a poet and critic, not only a patriot and politician but a profound humanist and sociologist, Sri Aurobindo's evolutionary world view, culminating in the Supermind, promises to be a breakthough in history. While recovering a lost wisdom he has also projected a new science or dimension of harmony, of ascent and integration, of evolution and epiphany. The evolution of consciousness is the ultimate in revolution, when Matter shall be the Spirit's willing bride. No less than Marx or Lenin, he has given a new direction and meaning to the socio-political existence in the world. But unlike the Marxian revolution, fragmented in vision and overtaken by events, Sri Aurobindo's clarion call is for a total revolution, a revolution by human consciousness.

Sri Aurobindo's radical social and political philosophy, his theory of education and his vision of the society of the future provide an answer to the contemporary crisis in India and the world.

Sri Aurobindo did not merely live in the empyraen of thought. His actions matched his ideas. His concerns were man and society. He had analyzed the political, social and cultural forces operating in the world with the cool objectivity of a scientist, the sympathy of an artist and the insight of an integral yogi to find out the causes of man's fragmentation and schizophrenic culture in a self-created, insensate, and disturbed world.

The proliferation of nuclear weapons, the threat of over-population and the mass media of communication are symptoms of the malaise that now challenges the very existence of man. Man appears a dweller in pointlessness, discontent, triviality and violence, constantly oppressed and harassed by forces from within and without. All the recent breakthrough in technology and adventure in outer space is inextricably linked with the war economy of the Pentagon, Kremlin and Peking. Should man be proud of such technological projections? Can we really call these histrionic acts as adventures?

The essays reveal his contemporary relevance for the East and the West alike. But the poet and the visionary of the 'life divine' is for ever contemporary. Where there is no vision the people perish. Sri Aurobindo's orchestral mind provides a hope for man and society, for an educated humanity and the civilization we need.

He has written for the race and reality and even a little of it will save.

To be ignorant of him is no longer possible nor safe.

As the volume is a product of collaborative work, the editor wishes to express his gratitude to the many distinguished contributors for their generous and willing co-operation. The editor also records sincerest thanks to Prof. Amrik Singh, Secretary, Inter-University Board, Professor R.C. Pandeya, Dean of Arts, Delhi University, Mr. Devendra Satpathy, M.P., Mr. Edward Sastri, Mr. M.C. Chandy and Miss Nong for their 'visible' and 'invisible' help in the preparation of this book. Acknowledgements are also gratefully made to the following authors and publishers for permitting to use the articles and quotations from their journals and books: *Sri Aurobindo Circle*, Twenty-eighth Annual Number 1972 ("Secular and Non-Secular Elements in Sri Aurobindo's Life and Thought" by K.R. Srinivasa Iyengar; "Is the West Ready for Sri Aurobindo?" by Ruud Lohman), Messrs George Allen and Unwin, (*Prophet of Indian Nationalism: A Study of the Political Thought of Sri Aurobindo Ghosh*, by Dr. Karan Singh), *Newsweek*, November 20, 1972, ("The Neet Great Religion?)", and Sri Aurobindo Centenary Library, Pondicherry.

Thanks to Dada Surendra Mohan Ghose for his constant encouragement, feeling of good will and affection which he gave in abundance. The book is dedicated to him.

New Delhi
December 1972

KISHORE GANDHI

INTRODUCTORY

The age of tribal gods is over. Our loyalty today is a world loyalty, to mankind as a whole. So when we speak of *the India that matters** we are not speaking of the history of a particular people and place—other people, other place—but of certain ideas and insights which are relevant to the human situation, especially in terms of the double crisis of civilization and evolution. These ideas and insights are the shared possession of all men of goodwill and maturity, men who can look before and after, whose minds are capable of finding undiscovered agreements and of reconciling opposites.

The reconciler's role is India's. This is *the India that matters.* In the encounter between civilizations, which Toynbee considers to be one of the most important events of modern history, three stages may be marked: (i) a stage of conflict and misunderstanding; (ii) a stage of accommodation and understandng; and (iii) a yet-unachieved stage of the law of service, sacrifice, and toleration. I say 'yet-unachieved', because as Sri Aurobindo says, "if we define civilization as a harmony of spirit, body and mind, where has that harmony been altogether real? The real and perfect civilization waits to be discovered." The Indian insights might help in that discovery of a real and perfect civilization and an educated humanity.

It is perhaps in this sense that it used to be said that a free India would be a guarantee of world peace. One naturally thinks of the example of Mahatma Gandhi, Gandhi who believed that non-violence gave a new meaning of existence. It was at least a civilized way of containing conflicts. In a world torn by hatred and dissension the only proper thing to do is to pay more attention to the areas we can agree about—even agree to differ.

Here may I place six basic concepts or hypotheses about which there need or should not be much difference? (i) Education is

* Text of Sri Aurobindo Centenary lecture on *India that Matters*, by Sisirkumar Ghose at Sofia University, November 24, 1972.

always education in the context of history, today that context is of the One World and the Future of Man; (ii) dialogue must be kept above political considerations, the thinker's loyalty to truth remains inviolable, he is a world citizen rather than a partisan, politician or even a patriot; (iii) the spirit of dialogue and self-searching must eschew propaganda, which is both bad form and a form of defeat; (iv) there can be in all this no question of forcing another person or group to accept one's view or system, you cannot be forced to be free, a simple error that convicts most dogmatic philosophies and the so-called revolutions that depend more on a violent transfer and maintenance of power than on persuasion; (v) education is not skill but a transformation of motive and character. We must change ourselves before we can change others; (vi) 'All problems of existence are essentially problems of harmony!' Therefore, whatever perpetrates disharmony has lost its right to exist.

These ideas, basic and universal, do not, as you will see, stand for an uncritical tradition or a rigid worship of the past. They only imply a loyalty and sensitiveness to the *philosophia perennis* or the *philosophia totalis*. In fact, the eternal is ever new. *Sanatana iva nitya nutanah.* The Passage to India is really the search for a lost language of wisdom. It is the search or secret of balance between life and soul never made wholly real but perhaps never more necessary than now. This is an adventure of consciousness to which everyone is called, everyone according to one's capacity.

What is the nature or content of this wisdom or spirit of balance? That would take us further afield, into inevitable metaphysical issues. But, after all, metaphysics is that which distinguishes man from the animal kingdom and where this natural hunger is suppressed or perverted, it is a sign that evolution is temporarily working in the reverse. Enough to say that the wisdom is practical. Let one example do: yoga, the science of man's further unfoldment, development or becoming. *Yogah karmashu kaushalam,* yoga is the secret or science of action, says Krishna. That the yogic philosophy or world view has been believed in as well as lived, even on a large-scale, will be evident from what is called the "triple quartette" of Indian culture: (i) the synthesis and gradation of the fourfold objects of life: *kama, artha, dharma* and *moksha;* (ii) the fourfold order of society;

brahmin, kshatriya, vaishya and *shudra;* (iii) the four stages in a man's life: *brahmacharya, garhasthya, vanaprastha* and *prabajya* (the life of the supra-social person). These are of course models and it is not suggested that they are meant for imitation or repetition. But it will be hard to deny that they represent principles which will outlast fashions in thought and in social reconstruction. Whatever system one may live in or prefer, two problems one must in the end face: the problem of old age and death. It would seem that by aiming at the eternal and the immaterial the Indian was able to solve the problem, at least a little better than others.

If the most valuable possession of an age, culture or individual is its image or idea of Man, India always had one: a firm but graduated idea of first principles and the Final End. The idea was based on a profound sense of priorities and discriminations.

According to the Indian thinkers this included a distinction between the permanent (*nitya*) and the fleeting (*a-nitya*), between the good (*shreyas*) and the pleasing (*preyas*), above all, between the real (*sat*) and the unreal (*a-sat*). Briefly, the Indian view held that to rest in the apparent and to mistake it for the real is the one general error, the root of all others. Our earliest prayer has been: *Asato ma sadgamaya, tamaso ma jyotirgamaya, mrityormamritam gamaya,* lead me from the Unreal to te Real, from the Darkness to the Light, from Death to Immortality. The earliest formula of Wisdom promises to be also its last.

To bring this brief list or analysis uptodate we should perhaps mention a few more cautions or discriminations. First, the discrimination between ends and means. (One remembers Capt. Ahab in Melville's *Moby Dick:* All my means are sane, my motives and objects mad.) Second, the distinction between change from Within and change from Without. Third, the distinction between the path of power and the path of Charity. Fourth, the distinction between ignorant and interested activity and non-attached action (*nihshkama karma*). These formulas may look unfamiliar and forbidding, but to neglect or ignore them can be disastrous.

The fact is, our so-called science will never be safe without the oldest of sciences, the science of self (*atma-vidya*), just as our press-button revolution will never endure without the most radical of revolutions, the revolution by consciousness, based on the Higher Self present in all of us, the Self one in all. To hope for a true change of human life without a change of human nature is an irrational proposition, it can never succeed. It is foolish to think that a perfected human world can be created by men or composed of men who are themselves imperfect. In brief, the higher and the lower knowledge, the knowledge of self and the knowledge of things, *para* and *apara vidya*, must come together for the perfect perfection. Ideally, Indian culture stood for this balance, which later ages have lost. It is a serious loss, that explains the gap between knowledge and wisdom, a gap that might one day swallow up our superficial civilization.

The world cannot be saved by Things, by massive manipulation, either by the politicians or by the scientists, or the two working together in an unholy combination. If the present crisis or imbalance is to be met and contained, our science of things and processes needs to be matched by a science of self and reality. Those who are thinking on a planetary scale--the Yogi and the Commissar, shall we say?—should not move in different directions. For the sake of the whole man, technique and transcendence, know-how and know-why, should work together. All exclusiveness must be excluded. Neither the Materialist Denial nor the Refusal of the Ascetic will do. On the contrary, we shall do well to affirm with men like Sri Aurobindo that "Spirit is the soul and reality of that which we sense as Matter; Matter is a form and body of that which we realise as Spirit." The true Indian tradition is integral, an integral humanism. This passion for totality and balance, a passion alike for integration and self-exceeding—providing for all types and aims of life, stages of growth and the complex nature of man —is India's real gift to the life of an evolving humanity. If this is not the solution history has little meaning and disillusionment may be our only destiny.

It is this deeper reading of the human situation, a 'saving knowledge' that is once more surfacing in our world today. To make the best use of it the split between materialism and mysticism should not be allowed to grow wider. As Richard Wilhelm had pointed out long back, East and West are no longer to remain apart. A new consciousness is rising in the West too. My all too brief visit convinces me of the fact. As observers of the contemporary scene have already pointed out, western man is ready for yoga and, may I add, *vice versa?* As Saher put it: "The modern West has the material requisites, Communism has the discipline, and the East its ancient wisdom in the training in mystic illumination. Thus it is not necessary to see doom in the future." Which means, the attempt that India has been making throughout her history she will now have to make under entirely new conditions—the taming of technology and a mechanised collectivity, a new serfdom and orthodoxy where one can exist only by *not* thinking. Without the upward and the inward look the exclusive emphasis on economic and political factors can only lead to a new dark age or Animal Farm.

Janaya divyam janam, create the divine race, said the sages of India, They still do. This is the burden of her song, her date with destiny, the sense of her being, her *raison d'etre*. In Sri Aurobindo's words, this "India of the ages is not dead nor has she spoken her last creative word; she lives and has still something to do for herself and the human peoples." We may put the whole matter thus: "The animal is a living laboratory in which Nature has, it is said, worked out man. Man himself may well be a thinking and living laboratory in whom and with whose conscious co-operation (that is the real sense of yoga, co-operating with your own evolution) she wills to work out the superman, or God." It is to actualise this possibility or breakthrough that India is still there, to weave her future out of her past, a future that may well decide the fate of *homo sapiens* and the world's unborn soul. In the new order or civilisation all life must become yoga, an integral, world-affirming yoga. The New Commandment is: "Be yourself, transform yourself, transcend yourself." Here Indian psychology, a science of the ascent of consciousness, will be useful, if not indispensable. The Self of man is not the body, the life, not even the mind. These are instrumental values, not terminal. To rest content in these intermediate stages is to mistake civilization for culture. For not what we have, not what we are, but what we inwardly become is what matters. To become what we are *Hic labor est*.

This is perhaps the place to say a few words about the crisis in evolution to which we have referred earlier. Whether we call it a creative or an emergent evolution, or the Noosphere, it is clear that an age of profound change or breakthrough is upon us. The challenge is also an opportunity. It is growing clearer that reason by itself—rather what we call reason, for it has many unsuspected, unexplored regions still occult and undeveloped —cannot long maintain the race in its progress. The unaided reason cannot lay down the perfect law of our being and development. This is because the rational or intellectual man is not the last and highest ideal of manhood nor a rational society the last and highest perfection of human life. If we have eyes to see our present predicament only proves the point.

Sri Aurobindo puts it thus: "At present mankind is undergoing an evolutionary crisis in which is concealed a choice of destiny....A stage has been reached in which the human mind has achieved in certain directions an enormous development while in others it stands arrested and bewildered and can no longer find its way....Man has created a system of civilization which has become too big for his limited mental capacity and understanding and his still more limited spiritual and moral capacity and understanding...(and) the destiny of man seems to be heading dangerously, as if impetuously and in spite of itself....into a prolonged confusion and perilous crisis and darkness of violent, shifting incertitude." No wonder ours has been called—rather calls itself—an Age of Anxiety.

This only makes clear once more that "the time grows ripe and the tendency of the world moves towards a new and comprehensive affirmation in thought and in inner and outer experience and its corollary, a new and rich self-fulfilment for the race." In other words, "Yoga must be revealed now because without it mankind cannot take the next step in human evolution." Yoga is not India's monopoly, it belongs to all who can make it their own, provided one is willing to pay the price.

In brief, there is a mighty law of life—individual as well as collective—a great law of human becoming, a body of knowledge and accumulated experience which is the foundation of our faith and of the work in progress: the spiritualisation of the human race. Of course the India of which I have spoken is not, I repeat, a national but a universal idea. It is not a country but the world, the world to be. To this India we all must come, sooner or later.

At its simplest, then, a psychological maturity, a constant intuition of the unity of all life, a purposeful organization of society in keeping with the highest principles, a passionate preoccupation with the ultimate freedom—that is the India that matters (and not what the newspapers report). Who can say that her work is over or ever will be? In a shrinking universe, a global village:

She is the Truth.
Seek her in the Kingdom of Anxiety;
You will come to a great city that has expected your return for years.

To the City without Walls—let us march together to this new exploration where social justice and psychological wisdom are not kept apart, where the relation of reason and spirit, *buddhi* and *bodhi*, are not for ever opposed, where one day Matter may become the Spirit's willing bride. Let us claim the key of this rconciliation between the One and the Many, the within and the without, the social and the supra-social, the past and the present, modernity and tradition, the temporal and the eternal and open the doors to a new unitive life, a life of unity, mutuality and harmony for all mankind. But this cannot be done in a hurry or by shouting slogans. The greatest changes begin in the minds of men, a journey along the razors' edge and with the least noise. If, as is getting clear, we are moving towards another great historic transformation on the world scene, India should matter, a new India and a new world, that is a work of diversified oneness, a consciousness, harmonious self-determination for everybody. When all the rest has failed we may find, hid in ourselves, the key to perfect change. *Yad bahyam tadantaram, yadantaram tad vahya,* as within so without.

To sum up: a new way of thinking is neded if mankind is to survive. From the debris of the past and the dissonances of the present may come—if we will—a new emergence, an apocalypse of awareness , a godhead for ever young and progressive, a divine democracy. This is a new vision of history as epiphany, the revolution of revolutions, for which the world has been waiting, 'the heart of a world where all hearts are one.'

Is this possible? you ask. Yes, it is possible, because it is necessary. Based on a yet-unfound law of love and wisdom (the two are one) and a diminishing of external compulsions, let us do the necessary thing together—move, beyond religion and revolution towards That of which both are shadow reflections, towards a greater tomorrow, a fairer and nobler life for all mankind, and fulfil the dream and effort of the ages. Here is the free man's worship, the freedom that is the knowledge of necessity. In the words of Vesselin Andreyev, is there any other way to save the only things I cherish?

There is a need within the soul of man
The splendours of the surface never sate;
For mind and life and their glory and debate
Are the slow prelude of a greater theme,
A sketch confused of a supernal plan,
A preface to the epic of the Supreme.

'There is a need within the soul of man.' Where there is a need there is also an obligation.

THE CONTRIBUTORS

G.S. Pathak
Vice-President of India

Karan Singh
Union Minister, Tourism and Civil Aviation

V.P. Verma
Professor and Chairman, Department of Political Science, Patna University

Bimla Bhagat
Lady Shri Ram College, Delhi University

Nandini Satpathy
Chief Minister of Orissa

Vivek Bhattacharya
Research Officer, Research and Reference Division, Ministry of I. & B.

D.P. Chattopadhyaya
Union Minister, Health and Family Planning

K.R. Srinivasa Iyengar
Ex-Vice-Chancellor and Vice-President, Sahitya Akademi

Ruud Lohman
Auroville, Pondicherry

Sisirkumar Ghose
Professor and Chairman, Departmeut of English, Vishva-Bharati

S.K. Prasad
Professor and Chairman, Department of English, Magadh University

Nirodbaran
Sri Aurobindo Ashram, Pondicherry

S. Nagarajan
Professor and Chairman, Department of English, Poona University

Aravinda Basu
Sri Aurobindo Professor, Banaras Hindu University

Aster Patel
Sri Aurobindo Ashram, Pondicherry

Y. Masih
Professor and Chairman, Department of Philosophy, Magadh University

V. Madhusudan Reddy
Professor and Chairman Department of Philosophy, Osmania University

R.R. Diwakar
Chairman, Gandhi Peace Foundation

D.S. Kothari
Chairman, University Grants Commission

R. Ramanujam
Correspondent, Newsweek

Kenneth L. Woodward
Religion Editor, Newsweek

CONTENTS

Sri Aurobindo's Vision of Free India

G. S. PATHAK

THE fifteenth of August is the date of Sri Aurobindo's birth as well as the date of birth of Free India. His thoughts and endeavours throughout his life were devoted to the securing of our country's independence and helping India to fulfil her role and destiny—as he put it—in the task of reconstitution of the life of men.

There have been many great *Yuga Purushas* in our sacred land since time immemorial. There have likewise been many heroic and patriotic men and women who have made significant contribution to the country's political emancipation. But there have been few, indeed very few, who attained the highest eminence both in the field of political endeavour and spiritual development. Sri Aurobindo belongs to this rare elite. In the earlier stages he dedicated himself wholly to the work of rousing the people from their somnolence and apathy and creating in their hearts and minds a consciousness of their birthright and yearning for political freedom. After some years the nation witnessed the emergence of Sri Aurobindo the seer and yogi who declared that humanity was in the process of an evolution towards attaining cosmic consciousness and experiencing in this world the light, joy and power immanent in it.

Sri Aurobindo's was a golden life, brilliant, pure and packed with high achievement. He shone at every stage of his life, shed lustre on the events of his day and not only illumined the history of his times but left for future generations a rare treasure of thought. He demonstrated what heights man can reach by leading an intense life with definite goals. He was modern and was steeped in what was best in Western civilization. His life also predominantly represented truly, delicately and beautifully all that has been the best in our millennial past.

The formative years of his life were spent in England. It was there that he started his education at the early age of seven. Very soon he acquired proficiency in a remarkable degree in Latin, Greek, English, French, Spanish and Italian. He was recognised during his scholastic career as a student with rare ability. He returned to India at the age of twenty equipped with deep knowledge of Western literature and philosophy but with no knowledge of Indian languages, even of his own mother tongue, Bengali, which he learnt later. Sanskrit he learnt on his own. In England he had imbibed ideas of freedom from the great events in world history like the American Revolution. It is said that Mazzini's life haunted him. The result was that when he took a Professorship in Baroda College he worked also as a revolutionary of an extreme type. He had a burning patriotism and was ready to undergo any suffering for his country's cause. While in Bengal where he came after giving up his Professorship at Baroda, he plunged into more active political work at a time when the Indian National Congress had developed very little spirit and used to petition to the British Government for political concessions. He was perhaps the first politician in India who had the courage to declare that nothing short of absolute independence should be the goal of the nation. In this his views coincided with those of Lokamanya Tilak. He had no truck with the moderates and criticised even Gokhale.

His concept of nationalism was of a very high order. According to him nationalism was simply the passionate aspiration for the realisation of the Divine Unity in the nation. He envisioned that in the idea of nationalism which India would place before the world there would be an essential equality between man and man. He asserted that we could rationally expect our society to reshape itself in the full and perfect spirit of the Vedantic gospel of equality.

Personalities like Sri Aurobindo are always far ahead of their times. He was socialist in his outlook. He affirmed that socialism was not a European concept but that it was essentially Asiatic and especially Indian. He believed that socialistic democracy was the only true democracy. "Socialism", according to him, "seeks to free human society from the tyranny of wealth, it aims at bringing about such social conditions as will ensure equal comforts and conveniences of life for all the members of society." He said: "The duty of a citizen is strictly speaking a socialistic duty—Freedom is the end of both patriotism and socialism. The all-round well-being of man is the aspiration of both".

Sri Aurobindo was a social reformer. His views about the caste system were based on the original concept of caste as found in the philosophy of life embodied in our ancient books. He wrote: "The baser ideas underlying the degenerate perversions of the original caste system, the mental attitude which bases them on a false foundation of caste, pride and arrogance, of a divinely ordained superiority depending on the accident of birth, of a fixed and intolerant inequality, are inconsistent with the supreme teaching of basic spirit of Hinduism which sees the one invariable and indivisible divinity in every individual being".

In the evolution of the mind and spirit, he reached the pinnacle of achievement in the seclusion of Pondicherry. The highest glory that human life can attain is to understand the Truth, understand the Self and one's relation with the Maker. That became the aim of his intense life thenceforward. He resorted to experimental spirituality and practised Yoga according to a peculiar pattern evolved by himself. He called it "Integral" or *Purna Yoga*. The process of learning it is difficult. Indeed true Yoga requires first unlearning a crowd of so-called imperative habits which we have inherited from our animal evolution. The real learning comes only after this unlearning process ends. He experienced "great Psychic rhythms which exceed the brief pulsations of a single human life". He realised that Yoga was the state of perfect equilibrium. He explored the Self and felt that there is nothing more wonderful in this creation than the Heaven within man. His faith was that in the political battle as in the spiritual, one must search within oneself and not outside or elsewhere for the causes of our misfortunes and of the calamities of the world. This is a truth which should be a lesson of enduring value to all who are concerned with the evolution of national life as well as international life.

Sri Aurobindo was a great writer, an eminent philosopher and a poet of rare distinction. Indeed the most fascinating part of his work was his exposition of Vedic texts and Upanishadic teachings and in particular of the *Gita*. His discovery of the lost meanings of certain concepts of Vedantic literature was unique, and his application of the Vedantic philosophy to practical life was superb. According to him, the man of spiritual realisation lives and acts and behaves, in all ways of his being and acting —and it is said in the *Gita* "he lives and moves in Me"—as if he dwells in the Divine. When he realised the spiritual existence, he would be living inwardly a divine life and its reflection would fall on the outer acts of his existence. Sri Aurobindo believed that the true Self must be realised within, if true life is to be realised in the world and Nature. He pointed out that to arrive at the creation of a world which shall be the true environment of a divine living is the final object that Force of Nature has set before us. The individual being has to find himself his true existence; he can do this only by going inward, by living within and from within. He speaks of "the full delight of being"—a delight which is intrinsic, self-existent, automatic, not dependent on things outside itself. This is the type of bliss that comes from the practice of spirituality.

Sri Aurobindo believed in evolution which according to him, is an unfolding of the Consciousness. He regarded the growth of Consciousness as "the supreme secret of life, the master key to earthly evolution." Out of matter came plant, out of plant came animal, out of pure animal came man, and out of man will inevitably come Superman. "The Superman will be born when man has risen above his mind and emerged into the Supramental Consciousness". Indeed, Intuition, inspiration and revelation are pointers to the development of Supramental Consciousness. Sri Aurobindo regarded these as the "faint beginnings and distant echoes" of that higher consciousness which the Supermind will possess.

Through his great mystic powers, Sri Aurobindo acquired the ability to probe into the future. He was able to see coming events. In a message given by him on August 15, 1947, he said, "Indeed almost all the world movements which I hoped to see fulfilled in my life-time, though at that time they looked like impossible dreams, I can observe on this day either approaching fruition or initiated and on the way to their achievement. . . . I have always held and said that India was arising, not to serve her own material interests only, to achieve expansion, greatness, power and prosperity—though these too she must not neglect—and certainly not like others to acquire domination of other peoples, but to live also for God and the world as a helper.... of the whole human race. Those aims and ideals were in their natural order: a revolution which would achieve India's freedom and her unity; the resurgence and liberation of Asia and her return to the great role which she had played in the progress of human civilization; the rise of a new, a greater, brighter and nobler life for mankind which for its entire realisation would rest outwardly on an international unification of the separate existence of the peoples...." He foresaw that "a new spirit of oneness will take hold of the human race" and that "the world is moving towards a greater development of the principles of state control over the life of the community...." In another context he declares, "the indwelling deity who presides over the destiny of the race has raised in man's mind and heart the idea, the hope of a new order which will replace the old unsatisfactory order, and substitute for it conditions of the world's life which will in the end have a reasonable chance of establishing permanent peace and well-being." We are witnessing the gradual fulfilment of Sri Aurobindo's prophecy about India and it is our fervent hope that his prophecy about the future of the human race will also be some day fulfilled.

In the troubled days through which we are passing we are fortified by the certainty that through Sri Aurobindo's blessings and spiritual guidance, India will fulfil her destiny, and also make her contribution towards peace in the world.

Sri Aurobindo : Man and Superman

KISHORE GANDHI

Sri Aurobindo is one of the most spectacular evolutionary and revolutionary thinkers that the world has ever produced. He combines in his vision the alacrity of the West along with illumination of the East. Evaluated in its totality he transcends the narrow territorial loyalties and emerges as a powerful exponent of a consciousness of the human unity.

SPEAKING during the historic trial of Sri Aurobindo for sedition in the court of English Judge Beachcroft in 1909, Desbandhu Chittaranjan Das described his personality in the following prophetic words:

> "Long after the controversy will be hushed in silence, long after this turmoil, this agitation will have ceased, long after he is dead and gone, he will be looked upon as the poet of patriotism, as the prophet of nationalism and the lover of humanity. Long after he is dead and gone, his words will be echoed and re-echoed, not only in India, but across distant seas and lands."[1]

Sri Aurobindo's extraordinary achievements had not merely brought C.R. Das's dream to fruition but when we look at his

1. Quoted by Sisir Kumar Mitra, *Resurgent India*, Bombay, 1963, p. 366.

theory of spiritualism, his radical nationalism and his brilliant exposition of the ideal of human unity, his personality transcends the estimate of C.R. Das. Gifted with highly perceptive and original mind he foresaw that man was being threatened with a crisis—an evolutionary crisis and looking before and after and pining for what is not. Man was in search of a teacher who could give him a revelation, a faith and take a leap into the future.

Sri Aurobindo—the 'Prophet of Supernature' and 'Pilgrim of Eternity' never wanted to leave humanity in despair. He was deeply concerned with human affairs and human possibilities and he used his gifts to enrich man, to keep alight humanity's sense of responsibility for its own and the world's destiny. He surveyed the political, social and cultural forces operating at that time with the cool objectivity of a scientist and the sympathy of an artist to find out the causes of man's fragmentation and schizophrenic culture in a divided, insensate, disturbed and confused world. The proliferation of nuclear weapons, the threat of overpopulation and the mass media of communication had challenged the very existence of man. Man was dwelling in pointlessness, triviality and topicality, constantly oppressed and harassed by these forces some within and some without.

Man had become proud and vain due to his staggering technological advancement and adventure in the outer space. Was it an adventure,—an adventure in gearing the war economy of the Pentagon, Kremlin and Peking.? Had not this adventure made him completely restless and was he not "wandering in the Valley of False Glimmer, the labyrinths of illusion, unreality and appearance"? Was he not preparing his self-destruction?

Sri Aurobindo after a long *sadhana* found the clue to the solution of this crisis in the spiritual evolution of man. He believed in the adventure of consciousness. He affirmed that 'if the doors of perception were cleansed, everything will appear to man as it is, infinite'. He was always opening doors—doors through which not only he but all the rest of us might pass to enter on new kinds of experiences, new ways of thinking, new possibilities of living. Unlike the partial revolution envisaged by Marx, Sri Aurobindo calls for a total revolution—a spiritual or supreme revolution because the material is the only reflex. If Marx gave the clarion call, Proletariat of all nations, unite!

Sri Aurobindo said: Youth of all nations, unite! and now Auroville, the Dawn city's call is "Children of all nations, unite! You have nothing to lose except fear, insecurity and mental unhappiness". He believed in the inner revolution involving the complete transmutation and transformation of the individual because he was convinced that the present egoistic consciousness was responsible for most of our ills and difficulties. He was deeply convinced and fully affirmed that a new step in the evolution or the ascent and descent of consciousness is not only possible but inevitable.

Sri Aurobindo found that there were insuperable forces obstructing the advancement of this consciousness. He grew up in a climate when India was being exploited both politically and economically by the British. He did not like the idea of remaining a passive and silent spectator when the tragic drama was being enacted on his motherland. His deep study of the political and historical forces had convinced him that without freedom—freedom of the individual man and for each nationality —healthy self-expression will not be possible. In the *Bande Mataram,* he wrote: "The primary requisite for national progress, national reform, is the free habit of free and healthy national thought and action which is impossible in a state of servitude. Political freedom is the life-breath of a nation".

During his stay in England he was deeply influenced by the world revolutionary movements which left an indelible imprint on his highly rich and sensitive mind. The revolutionary and mighty personalities of Joan of Arc, Robespierre, Danton, Mazzini and Napoleon had made a profound impact on him and he longed to imbibe their spirit of self-confidence, self-sacrifice and dedication to the just cause. Imbued with revolutionary ideas he could not tolerate the mendicant policy of prayer, petition and protest followed by the moderates for the emancipation of the country. His hatred of foreign rule was as intense as the feeling of a son who sees a monster sitting on the breast of his mother and sucking her blood with a dagger in his hand.

Sri Aurobindo directed his entire energies to awakening the nation which had become sluggish and infused in it a profound love for the motherland. He gave a new meaning and direction to the concept of nationalism and planted the seeds of revolution and extremism in the country's politics. He was the first political thinker and strategist who felt the urgency of radicalizing the national movement; the first leader who recognized the necessity of the active involvement of the masses in the movement; the pioneer political tactician to evolve and employ the methods of boycott, swadeshi and passive resistance in the Freedom Movement. He did not hesitate at the use of force when his country was humiliated and crushed by an alien aggressor. For him the deliverance of the motherland from the foreign rule was of supreme importance and to achieve this objective all means were admissible including the use of force. He believed that India must get independence for the benefit of mankind because he had firm faith that India was destined to play a major role towards the promotion of peace and international understanding. In his "Open Letter to My Countrymen" in 1909, he wrote: "Our ideal of patriotism proceeds on the basis of love and brotherhood and it looks beyond the unity of the nations and envisages the ultimate unity of mankind. But it is a unity of brothers, equals and free men that we seek, not the unity of master and serf, of devourer and devoured."[2] He had elaborated his concept of oneness and the ideal of human unity in his various writings. The conception of East and West did not disturb him and he strongly affirmed that "all human beings are of the same divine origin and meant to manifest upon earth, the unity of this origin". He believed in the united notions as against the united nations. He was a true reconciler to the end. In a message to America in 1949, he wrote:

> "It has been customary to dwell on the division and difference between these two sections of the human family (the East and the West) and even oppose them to each other; but, for myself I would rather be disposed to dwell on oneness and unity than on division and difference....There is a common hope, a common destiny, both spiritual and material, for which both are needed as co-workers....East and West could be reconciled in the pursuit of the highest and largest ideal. Spirit embraces Matter and Matter finds its own true reality and the hidden Reality in all things is the Spirit."[3]

2. *Speeches*, p. 142.
3. *Sri Aurobindo, on Himself*, Sri Aurobindo Birth Centenary, Library, Pondicherry, 1972, vol. 26, pp. 413-416.

Sri Aurobindo was a sociologist who visualised a society of the future—a society of the perfect people living in peace, enjoying bliss and harmony with the environment. He believed in the individual transformation and social transformation or perfection of the individual and perfection of the race. Auroville —the city of Dawn—has been conceived in the light of Sri Aurobindo's vision of the future society. It looks forward to the creation of a new world, a new community, a new humanity, a new society expressing and embodying the new consciousness. It was in 1954 that the Mother revealed to the world her inspiring Dream for the future:

> "There should be somewhere upon earth a place that no nation could claim as its sole property, a place where all could live freely as citizens of the world obeying one single authority, that of supreme Truth, a place of peace, concord, harmony, where all the fighting instincts of man would be used exclusively to conquer the causes of his sufferings and miseries, to surmount his weakness and ignorance, to triumph over his limitations and incapacities; a place where the needs of the spirit and the care for progress would get precedence over the satisfaction of desires and passions, the seeking for material pleasures and enjoyment...."
>
> "The earth is certainly not ready to realize such an ideal, for mankind does not yet possess the necessary knowledge to understand and accept it nor the indispensible conscious force to execute it...."
>
> "Yet, this dream is on the way of becoming a reality. This is exactly what we are seeking to do at the Ashram of Sri Aurobindo on a small-scale....little by little we advance towards our goal which, we hope, one day we shall be able to hold before the world as a practical and effective means of coming out of the present chaos in order to be born into a more true, more harmonious new life."[4]

Auroville, the dream city, was formally inaugurated on the 28th

---

4. *Auroville*, Pondicherry, p. 1.

February, 1968 with a view to achieving the spirit of human unity, the unitive consciousness, 'the inner integration of the four sectors of our existence, individual and collective, inner and outer.' It is an answer to the challenge of our time: truth or abyss.

Above all, Sri Aurobindo was a great spiritualist—the seeker after the invisible and the infinite and his entire life had been a *sadhana,* a divine experiment. He was in quest of actualising the dream of ages, of bringing out the kingdom of Heaven on Earth, the Life Divine. Though his interest in spirituality dated back to his formative years of growth, it gradually matured at Baroda and Alipore jail and witnessed its fruition at Pondicherry where he spent forty years of uninterrupted life in *sadhana.* His philosophy has a universal appeal and is free from any sectarian or dogmatic approach. It is based on human experiences because it emerged as a result of his own experiments with the working powers of his consciousness.

In considering Sri Aurobindo's achievement one is again and again struck by the amazing versatility of his genius. It is difficult to assess his life and work that is wider than the universe. He was a writer par excellence and perhaps the most accomplished scholar who was able to take all the knowledge for his province. His intellect in both its span and depth covered an astonishing range of subjects. But what is most important he was able to integrate this range of fact and idea and to give it a comprehensive vision of man and of his unique possibilities. He was well steeped in Western classical and Indian Literature and was almost the most versatile, the most brilliant and the most extraordinary thinker and writer of the time. His journalistic writings, his prose, poetry and drama, his speeches and letters and conversations which covered a period of about sixty years have few parallels in the history of the creative spirit:

"What was written for the *Indu Prakash* in the first flush of political idealism soon after his return to India from England in 1893: what was penned in the heat of active political involvement as editorial or special article, for the *Bande Mataram, Karma Yogin* or *Dharma*: what was put into the mouth of a dramatic character in consonance with the imperatives of his imaginative creation: what was spoken in a climate of debate or controversy, or even of relaxation among an assembled group of admirers and disciples: what was recorded whether in prose or in verse—after the plentitude of mystic experience or spiritual realization: all have their distinguishing yet limiting features. On a first few indeed, the writings and the utterances are not all of a piece. Aphorisms, epigrams, thoughts, glimpses—at one end, massive sequences, global sweeps of thought like *The Life Divine, The Synthesis of Yoga, The Human Cycle, The Foundation of Indian Culture* and *the Ideal of Human Unity*—at the other end: and, in between, all intensities of expression, all varieties of form, all ranges of experience—mysticism and religion, poetry and philosophy, education and yoga, psychology and sociology, war and peace and human unity, all is grist that comes to the mill."[5]

The assessment of Sri Aurobindo's life and work has been brilliantly done by his contemporaries. Looking at his contributions in the *Bande Mataram,* Bipin Chandra Pal remarked: "This paper at once secured for itself a recognised position in Indian journalism. The hand of the master (Sri Aurobindo) was in it, from the very beginning....From a tutor of a few youths he thus became the teacher of the whole nation....His only care is for his country—the Mother as he always calls her. His only recognised obligations are to her. Nationalism.... is with Aravinda a supreme passion of his soul".[6] K.N. Katju said: "Sri Aurobindo has been to us like a star of freedom."[7] S.K. Ratcliffe wrote: "We know Aurobindo Ghose only as a revolutionary nationalist and editor of a flaming newspaper which struck a ringing new note in Indian daily journalism."[8] Brahmabandhab Upadhyaya said "Our Aurobindo is a rare phenomenon in the world. In him resides the *sattwic* divine beauty, snow-clad, resplendent. Great and vast. Vast in the vastness of his heart. Great in the glory of his own self, his *swadharma* as a Hindu. A man so pure and complete—a fire-

5. K.R. Srinivasa Iyengar, "Secular and Non-Secular Elements in Sri Aurobindo's Life and Thought," *Sri Aurobindo Circle*, Pondicherry, 1972, pp. 41-42.
6. Quoted by Sisir Kumar Mitra, *op. cit.*, p. 362.
7. *Ibid.*
8. *Ibid.*

charged thunder, yet tender and delicate as the lotus-leaf. A man rich in knowledge, self-lost in meditation, you can nowhere find his like in the three worlds. When such a one worships the Mother, Swaraj is now no far-off event."[9]

Tagore paid him a glowing tribute:

> "Rabindranath, O Aurobindo, bows to thee !
> O friend, my country's friend, O Voice incarnate, free,
> Of India's soul."

Henry W. Nevinson, an English M.P. who visited India in 1907 remarked in his book entitled *The New Spirit in India* that "grave with intensity, careless of fate or opinion, and one of the most silent of men I have known, Arabindo was of the stuff that dreamers are made of, but dreamers who act their dreams, indifferent to the means[10]" J. Ramsay MacDonald met Sri Aurobindo. "To his question, What is your conception of the end which is being worked by our Indian administration?', Sri Aurobindo replied, 'A free and Independent India.'"[11] He was truly one of the greatest sons of India and indeed one who had a unique message for the entire mankind.

Despite his staggering contributions in various fields, opinions are sharply divided about his subtle and elusive personality ranging from adulation to disparagement. After nearly half a century of speculation, thinkers are unable to find a means of explaining the most curious aspect of this strange man. The often posed question which still remains to be answered: "What was the precise nature of the task which called him away from active politics into seclusion" when the country still needed him on the active front. In *The History of Freedom Movement,* Dr. Tara Chand writes, "The circumstances of his flight and subsequent life have given rise to speculation of not altogether complimentary nature. The prophet of Karma Yoga of the *Bhagwad Gita* had become an adept in Yoga without the Karma".[12] The historians consider him little better than a spent force and useless

---

9. *Ibid.*
10. *Ibid.*
11. *Ibid.*, p. 363.
12. Tara Chand, *History of Freedom Movement*, Delhi.

for the country and the world at large. They divide his personality into two parts—the Master Spirit and the Master Yogi with all sorts of flowering compliments and adulations for the first part of his life and work and accusations for the second phase. "Dissection whether of a great poem or of a great yogi's life and thought, can hardly ever prove edifying and can never lead to illumination."[13] Dr. Tara Chand further writes: "It must be admitted that besides issue of books and statements, the forty years were otherwise sterile from the point of view of history for while during this period India was engaged in a fierce struggle 'to do or die', this lustrous genius whose magic words had once stirred India from the mountains to the seas was immersed in his lonely quest in the almost complete isolation of his Ashram very much like an ancient immersed in a cave in the Himalayas."[14] True this mystery has all the ingredients of a paradox and so various theories have been put forth to explain this out. But incidently, they have illuminated confusion instead of clarifying the truth. In fact these historians and thinkers know little about him and "even the little they perhaps do is often not correct, mixed, as it mostly is, with the false and legendary".[15]

A flashback at the Freedom Movement reveals an interesting phenomenon, that the war against foreign domination was fought on dual planes—that of force and that of idea. The movement was nurtured and sustained by the powerful ideological base. The two-fold search for freedom within and without is not unusual. "All human uprisings have shown similar dual features. The French Revolution of 1789 was preceded by the philosophies of Voltaire, Rousseau, Diderot and the Encyclopaedists. The Bolshevic Revolution of Russia in 1917 was preceded by the writings of Marx, Engels and Lenin. Even the more limited movement of Germany and Italian unification had their literary precursors—Goethe, Hegel, and others in Germany and Mazzini in Italy".[16] In more recent times the revolution in Turkey and Arabia had the backing of rich philosophical thought. Exactly in the same way, India's Freedom Movement

---

13. K.R. Srinivasa Iyengar, *op. cit.*, p. 42.
14. Tara Chand, *op. cit.*
15. Sisir Kumar Ghose, *The Poetry of Sri Aurobindo*. Calcutta, 1969, p. 2.
16. Tara Chand, *op. cit.*

was nurtured and grew on India's rich philosophical and spiritual tradition and its manifestation took place through the following personalities: B.G. Tilak, Sri Aurobindo, C.R. Das, M.K. Gandhi, Pandit Nehru, Maulana Abul Kalam Azad and Muhammad Iqbal. The most striking feature which emerges from the study of Sri Aurobindo's life and work at Pondicherry is that in the midst of his *sadhana* he never withdrew from his political activities. The political battle which Sri Aurobindo fought earlier on both the planes became only philosophical in character. There was a shift in emphasis from the plane of action to the plane of thought. Like Voltaire, Rousseau and Goethe he silently through internal force prepared the nation for Independence and vigorously pursued and worked for the achievement of Asian resurgence and the world union based on mutual understanding, love and order.

When Sri Aurobindo came to Pondicherry he did not have any intention of staying there permanently. He went there to do *sadhana* to transform himself and to give a fierce battle with a renewed vigour and a force against British imperialism. In a diary dated March 30, 1924, it is noted : "When Sri Aurobindo came to Pondicherry the idea was that the *sadhana* might take about six months after which time all those who were here would go back and restart the work. Then one year passed and yet Sri Aurobindo did not go back. Then a period of four years was put down as time-limit. In the meantime, the first World War intervened."[17]

With the passage of time Sri Aurobindo was deeply convinced that India is destined to get freedom with or without him and so he decided to pursue more vigorously the task which he had undertaken—the liberation of the entire mankind. In 1917, B. Shiva Rao who was building up a campaign in favour of Home Rule movement, met Sri Aurobindo in Pondicherry. During the course of discussion, Sri Aurobindo told him that "Mrs. Besant was absolutely right in preaching home rule for India as well as in her unqualified support of the Allies in the first World War against Germany."[18] But Gandhiji and many other Congress leaders on the political forefront declared such a move to be

17. Quoted by A.B. Purani, *The Life of Sri Aurobindo*, Pondicherry, 1964, p. 154.
18. *Ibid.*, p. 171.

premature. We can well imagine the price which the country had to pay for Gandhi's lack of far-sightedness and judgment at that decisive psychological moment. In 1918, when the British Government announced the Montagu Chelmsford Reforms, Mrs. Annie Besant wrote an urgent letter to Sri Aurobindo seeking his opinion about the Reforms. Sri Aurobindo sent her an article signed : "An Indian Nationalist" for publication in which he described the Reforms as "a Chinese Puzzle" and a "great shadow." Tilak wanted him back in the country's politics and requested him through Baptista to accept the editorship of the paper started by the Socialist Democratic Party of Bombay. But Sri Aurobindo could not answer him in the affirmative because of certain compelling circumstances. However, Sri Aurobindo's reply is revealing because it throws a great deal of light on his political attitude at that time. In his reply he stated :

> "....the importance of politics at the present time is very great. But my line and intention of political activity would differ considerably from anything now current in the field. I entered into political action and continued it from 1903 to 1910 with one aim and one alone, to get into the mind of the people a settled will for freedom and the necessity of a struggle to achieve it in place of the futile ambling Congress methods till then in vogue. That is now done and the Amritsar Congress is the seal upon it .there is the will and plenty of strong and able leaders to guide it. I consider that inspite of the inadequacy of the Reforms, the will to self-determination, if the country keeps its present temper, as I have no doubt it will, is bound to prevail before long. What preoccupies me now is the question what it is going to do with its self-determination, how will it use its freedom, on what lines is it going to determine its future ? You may ask why not come out and help, myself, so far as I can, in giving a lead ? But my mind has a habit of running inconveniently ahead of the time,—some might say, out of time altogether into the world of the ideal. Your party, you say, is going to be a social democratic party. Now I believe in something which might be called social democracy, but not in any of the forms now current, and I am not altogether

> in love with the European kind, however great an improvement it may be on the past. I hold that India having a spirit of her own and a governing temperament proper to her own civilization, should in politics as in everything else, strike out her own original path and not stumble in the wake of Europe."[19]

This letter is ample proof of Sri Aurobindo's deep concern for and involvement in the country's political developments. He foresaw the country's Independence and desired that it should evolve its own political and social institutions after independence instead of imitating the European models. Alas ! the country did not bother to take note of his warning and is consequently paying a heavy cost.

Lajpat Rai, C.R. Das and many other nationalist leaders visited Sri Aurobindo at Pondicherry and requested him to return to British India to guide the destiny of the country. He could not accede to their request but discussed with them in great deal the line of action they had to follow. He categorically opposed the malicious British design of 'divide and rule'. He was sane enough to foresee that the separate representation of the Muslims in the Assemblies and Corporations and the acceptance of communal principles by the Congress would make the Muslims permanently a separate entity. He opposed tooth and nail the attitude of Gandhiji on Khilafat Movement.

Dr. Munje wanted Sri Aurobindo to preside over the session of the Indian National Congress at Nagpur but he could not accept this offer. In reply, he stated :

> "As I have already wired to you, I find myself unable to accept your offer of the Presidentship of the Nagpur session....but have definitely commenced another kind of work with a spiritual basis, a work of spiritual, social, cultural and economic reconstruction of an almost revolutionary kind, and am even making or at least supervising a sort of practical or laboratory experiment in that sense which needs all the attention and energy that I can have to spare...I have taken it up as my mission for the rest of my life."[20]

---

19. *Sri Aurobindo on Himself*, Sri Aurobindo Birth Centenary, Library, Pondicherry, 1972, Vol. 26, pp. 430-31.
20. *Ibid.*, pp. 432-33.

On the outbreak of the Second World War, he issued a declaration :

"We feel that not only is this a battle waged in just self-defence...but that it is a defence of the civilization and its highest attained social, cultural and spiritual values, and of the whole future of humanity. To this cause, our support and sympathy will be unswerving whatever may happen; we look forward to the victory of Britain and, as the eventual result, an era of peace and union among the nations and a better and more secure world order".[21]

In March, 1942, Sir Stafford Cripps brought an offer from the British Government seeking India's co-operation in war effort. Sri Aurobindo did not consider the Cripps proposal to be perfect but felt that in the circumstances its acceptance would surely help the country. He sent his personal message to the Congress Working Committee at Delhi advising them the acceptance of this offer. Sri Aurobindo's advice was not heeded due to lack of far-sightedness and political immaturity on the part of our leaders and consequently we had to bear the cross—the partition of the country and colossal human sufferings and bloodshed.

Later when India emerged as an Independent nation—on what happened to be his birthday—he openly wrote against the division of the country. The logical progression of events during the post-independence period has unfolded the basic truth to humanity that the division of the country was more a political contrivance suited to vested interests than the culmination and fulfilment of the popular demand—the Vision of Greater India. The two-nation theory—an imperialist design and contrivance aimed at shattering the cultural link of the country, soon broke into pieces. The emergence of Bangladesh as an Independent nation is a clear demonstration of this fact and has partly brought Sri Aurobindo's prophecy to fruition. Sri Aurobindo's message of fifteenth August, 1947, is an important political document and it set forth five dreams, profoundly pur-

---

21. *Ibid.*, p. 393.

poseful and prophetic. This day has a great significance for the country because it marks the end of an old era, the beginning of a new age. It signifies the entry into the comity of nations of a new power with untold potentialities which has a great part to play in determining the political, social, cultural and spiritual future of humanity.

"The first of these dreams was a revolutionary movement which would create a free and united India. India today is free but she has not achieved unity. At one moment it almost seemed as if in the very act of liberation she would fall back into the chaos of separate States which preceded the British conquest. But fortunately it now seems probable that this danger will be averted and a large and powerful, though not yet a complete union will be established. Also, the wisely drastic policy of the Constituent Assembly has made it probable that the problem of the depressed classes will be solved without schism or fissure. But the old communal division into Hindus and Muslims seems now to have hardened into a permanent political division of the country. It is to be hoped that this settled fact will not be accepted as settled for ever or as anything more than temporary expedient. For if it lasts, India may be seriously weakened, even crippled: civil strife may remain always possible, possible even a new invasion and foreign conquest. India's internal development and prosperity may be impeded, her position among the nations weakened, her destiny impaired or even frustrated. This must not be; the partition must go. Let us hope that that may come about naturally, by an increasing recognition of the necessity not only of peace and concord but of common action, by the practice of common action and the creation of means for that purpose. In this way unity may finally come about under whatever form—the exact form may have a pragmatic but not a fundamental importance. But by whatever means, in whatever way, the division must go; unity must and will be achieved, for it is necessary for the greatness of India's future."

"Another dream was for the resurgence and liberation of the peoples of Asia and her return to her great role in the progress of human civilization. Asia has arisen; large parts are now quite free or are at this moment being liberated: its other still subject or partly subject parts are moving through whatever struggles towards freedom. Only a little has to be done and that will be done today or tomorrow. There India has her part to play and has begun to play it with an energy and ability which already indicate the measure of her possibilities and the place she can take in the council of the nations."

"The third dream was a world-union forming the outer basis of a fairer, brighter and nobler life for all mankind. That unification of the human world is under way; there is an imperfect initiation organised but struggling against tremendous difficulties. But the momentum is there and it must inevitably increase and conquer. Here too India has begun to play a prominent part and, if she can develop that larger statesmanship which is not limited by the present facts and immediate possibilities but looks into the future and brings it nearer, her presence may make all the difference between a slow and timid and a bold and swift development. A catastrophe may intervene and interrupt or destroy what is being done, but even then the final result is sure. For unification is a necessity of Nature, an inevitable movement. Its necessity for the nations is also clear, for without it the freedom of the small nations may be at any moment in peril and the life even of the large and powerful nations insecure. The unification is therefore to the interests of all, and only human imbecility and stupid selfishness can prevent it; but these cannot stand for ever against the necessity of Nature and the Divine Will. But an outward basis is not enough; there must grow up an international spirit and outlook, international forms and institutions must appear, perhaps such developments as dual or multilateral citizenship, willed interchange or voluntary fusion of cultures. Nationalism will have fulfilled itself and lost its militancy and would no longer find these things incompatible with self-preservation and the integrality of its outlook. A new spirit of oneness will take hold of the human race."

"Another dream, the spiritual gift of India to the world has already begun. India's spirituality is entering Europe and America in an ever-increasing measure. That movement will grow; amid the disasters of the time more and more eyes are turning towards her with hope and there is even an increasing resort not only to her teachings, but to her psychic and spiritual practice."

"The final dream was a step in evolution which would raise man to a higher and larger consciousness and begin the solution of the problems which have perplexed and vexed him since he first began to think and to dream of individual perfection and a perfect society. This is still a personal hope and an idea, an ideal which has begun to take hold both in India and in the West on forward-looking minds. The difficulties in the way are more formidable than in any other field of endeavour, but difficulties were made to be overcome and if the Supreme Will is there, they will be overcome. Here too, if this evolution is to take place, since it must proceed through a growth of the spirit and the inner consciousness the initiative can come from India and, although the scope must be universal, the central movement may be hers."[22]

In the *Ideal of Human Unity,* Sri Aurobindo has analysed the political predicament of the world and warned humanity of the impending threat of China and of Communist ideology to entire Asia. From the foregoing study we can conclusively establish that Sri Aurobindo remained actively committed to the political development of the country. Of course, in the later phase of his life, he changed his strategy and concentrated more on the human problems to attain the ideals of the individual perfection and an orderly society.

II

Sri Aurobindo, the man, strange and still unfathomed compels a special interest. To trace the evolution and mark the contours of the development of such a complex personality is truly an adventurous task. He never approved of the idea of writing his autobiography or biography because it did not tally with his line of thinking or temperament. In this context his letter to his disciple Dilip Kumar Roy is revealing: "No one can write about my life because it has not been on the surface for man to see."[23] On another occasion when requested to give his consent to a disciple for helping a writer of his biography, he wrote in his inimitable way, "I do not want to be murdered by my own disciple in cold print."[24] About his biography he said: "To write my biography is impossible. The idea is quite wrong.

22. *Ibid.*, pp. 404-406.
23. Quoted by A.B. Purani, *op. cit.*, p. 1.
24. *Ibid.*

Who could write it? Not only in my case but in that of poets, philosophers and yogis it is no use attempting a biography, because they do not live in their external life. Their real life is inner and how can anyone else know that life? It is different with men of action like Napoleon or Julius Caesar, men who develop themselves through action.[25] Truly, the problem of structuring and probing into such an inner life, so rich and complex, presents innumerable difficulties. Granted that we cannot perceive the inner recesses of his mind but to mark the "outward life" is a no less difficult a task on account of his versatility and multi-faceted personality. He was a teacher, a scholar, a poet, a political revolutionary, an indologist, a psychologist, a literary critic, a translator and a powerful interpreter and exponent of the Upanishadic thought. There is no aspect of life and knowledge that he did not comment upon. But all these difficulties need not dismay us, because A.B. Purani's, *The Life of Sri Aurobindo,* K.R. Srinivasa Iyengar's, *Sri Aurobindo* and R.R. Diwakar's, *A Mahayogi* are some of the pioneering and well-documented biographical works which are available with us and our task is therefore not very difficult.

Broadly speaking, there are three stages in the evolution of Sri Aurobindo's life and work. The first begins with his entry into St. Paul School, West Kensington, London, in 1884 and culminates in 1893. This was a period of preparation, a period of learning, thinking and experimenting. During this period many diverse influences operated on his sensitive mind stretching from the deliberate isolation from the Indian environment to the complete identification with the country's vibrations and its milieu. The second period though very brief (1895-1910), was extraordinarily significant from the historical and political point of view. It was during this period that he shone like a brilliant meteor and created a powerful impression on the youth. He exploded the myth of the Congress Party and criticised their policy of protest, prayer and petition and laid the firm foundation of militant and radical nationalism. He formulated the concept of *Purna Swaraj* and initiated the application of boycott and passive resistance—the unique weapons for the achievement of the country's independence. The third phase (1910-1950), was

25. *Ibid.*, p. 209.

more dramatic and psychological because when he was at the height of glory and virtually the leader of the nation, he went to Pondicherry. He spent the last forty years in meditation and contemplation in search of solutions to the ultimate problems which have afflicted humanity. He wrote profusely and worked calmly and silently in exploring the greater truths of life. But this need not be understood as a complete withdrawal from political activities which he persistently pursued till the end of his life. He identified politics with spirituality and raised it to a level where it could be cleansed of its vitalistic and egoistic associations.

III

Aurobindo was born on August 15, 1872, in Calcutta. He was the third son of Dr. Krishnadhan Ghose and Shrimati Swaran Lata Devi. His father belonged to the well-known Ghoses of Konnagar in District Hoogly, Bengal. Dr. Ghose was a Civil Surgeon and he had obtained his advanced medical education in England. His mother was the daughter of Rajnarayan Bose, the grandfather of Indian nationalism. Dr. Ghose was a man of exceptional ability and was imbued with a great admiration for European values and way of life. Yet, he was fully aware of the injustice and exploitation of the British administrators in India and felt strongly that they were the cause of all indignities and humiliations to which his countrymen were being subjected. He was deeply touched by ailing humanity and he resolved to dedicate his life to the service of the people. He had a generous and lovable temperament and once a Christian missionary exclaimed to Rajnarayan: "I have never seen such a sweet face as his!"

Dr. Ghose was so much anglicised in habits, ideas and ideals that he had no faith in the existing system of education in India. He was determined to give his children entirely European education and did his best to keep them aloof from the Indian way of life. At the age of five, Aurobindo was admitted to Loretto Convent School, Darjeeling established by missionaries to educate primarily the children of European officials. Details of his school days are lacking[26]. However, Aurobindo in

26. Lotika Basu, *Indian Writers of English Verse*, p. 101. "In the shadow of the Himalayas, in the sight of the wonderful snow-capped

one of his Evening Talks referred to the dream which he remembered to have experienced in Darjeeling. Evidently it suggests that Aurobindo was a dreamy and contemplative child from the beginning:

"I was lying down one day when I saw suddenly a greatness rushing into me and enveloping me and the whole universe. After that I had a great *Tamas* always hanging on to me all through my stay in England. I believe that darkness had something to do with *Tamas* that came upon me. It left me only when I was coming back to India."[27]

At the age of seven Aurobindo was taken to England along with his brothers, Benoybhushan and Manmohan. Dr. Ghose placed them with an English family—the Drewetts, who were his friends—with strict instructions that they should not be allowed to make the acquaintance of any Indian or undergo any Indian influence. Deliberately, they were brought up in such a climate that they "grew up in an entire ignorance of India, her people, her religion and her culture." Mr. Drewett taught him history, geography, arithmetic and French. The Drewett family cultivated in him a keen sensitivity and deep love for English and classical literature. He read the Bible, Shakespeare, Shelley and Keats at home. At the age of eleven, he had started writing English poetry and a year or two later experimented with Latin and Greek verse.

There was a widespread rumour that Aurobindo was converted to Christianity and the registration of his name at St. Paul and even at Cambridge as Aravinda Ackroyd Ghose would evidently confirm such a suspicion. We do know for certain that Mr. Drewett's mother wished to see the Ghose brothers converted but her son did not share her zeal. Aurobindo has himself described his conversion:

"There was once a meeting of non-conformist ministers at Cumberland when we were in England. The old lady in whose house we dwelt, i.e. Mrs. Drewett, took me there. After

---

peaks, even in their native land they were brought up in alien surroundings."

27. *Evening Talks*, 10.3.1943.

the prayers were over all nearly dispersed, but devout people remained a little longer and it was at that time that conversions were made. I was feeling completely bored. Then a minister approached me and asked me some questions. I did not give any reply. Then they all shouted 'he is saved, he is saved', and began to pray for me and offer thanks to God. I did not know what it was all about. Then the minister came to me and asked me to pray. I was not in the habit of praying. But somehow I did it in the manner in which children recite their prayers before going to sleep in order to keep up an appearance. That was the only thing that happened. I did not attend the Church regularly. I was about ten at that time."[28]

After his education under the Drewetts for five years, he was admitted to St. Paul School in London, at the age of thirteen. The Head Master was greatly impressed by his proficiency in Latin and Greek and took a keen interest in him. Aurobindo was getting conscious of his mission when he was a boy living in a foreign country. A powerful feeling began to grow in him that "a period of general upheaval and revolutionary changes was coming in the world and that he himself was destined to play a part in it." His attention was now drawn to India and this feeling soon developed into the idea of the liberation of his country. But it took concrete shape only four years later.

From St. Paul School, Aurobindo proceeded to King's College, Cambridge with a senior classical scholarship of the value of £80 per year. He mainly engaged himself in the study of English Literature, French Literature and the History of Europe. He passed the first part of the classics Tripos in the first division and won several prizes for Greek, English and Latin verses. A letter to his father reveals the mark he had made at that university. "Last night I was invited to coffee with one of the dons and in his room I met the great O.B. otherswise Oscar Browning, who is the feature par excellence of King. He was extremely flattering and passing from the subject of Cotillions to that of scholarship," he said to me:

"I suppose you know you passed an extraordinarily high

---

28. Quoted by A.B. Purani, *op. cit.*, pp. 7-8.

examination. I have examined papers at thirteen examinations and I have never during that time seen such excellent papers as yours....As, for your essay, it was wonderful. In this essay (a comparison between Shakespeare and Milton), I indulged my oriental tastes to the top of their bent, it overflowed with rich and tropical imagery, it abounded in antitheses and epigrams and it expressed my real feeling without restraint or reservation. I thought myself that it was the best thing I have ever done, but at school it would have been condemned as extraordinarily Asiatic and bombastic. The great O.B. afterwards asked me where my rooms were and when I had answered he said: 'That wretched hole!' (and) then turning to Mahaffy: How rude we are to our scholars! We get great minds to come down here and then shut them up in that box. I suppose it is to keep their pride down."[29]

Aurobindo simultaneously worked for the I.C.S. and passed the competitive examination with distinction. His father had great hopes of him as also of his brothers. As he wrote to Jogendra Bose, his brother-in-law:

"The three sons I have produced, I have made giants of them. I may not, but you will live to be proud of three nephews who will adorn your country and shed lustre on your name.... Ara, I hope, will yet glorify his country by a brilliant administration. I shall not live to see it, but remember this letter if you do...."[30]

It was a remarkable prophecy but curiously it fulfilled itself in a manner which the father had never anticipated. Aurobindo instead of clearing the I.C.S. deliberately failed to complete the riding requirement. As he himself put it he felt no call for the I.C.S. and was seeking some way to escape the bondage.

It should not be assumed that in England, Aurobindo had an easy and comfortable time. The remittances from his father became irregular and then almost stopped. The years of his

---

29. *Ibid.*, p. 23. Letter of Sri Aurobindo to his father, K. D. Ghose December 2, 1890.
30. *Ibid.*, p. 22. Letter from Dr. K.D. Ghose to Jogendra Bose, Khulna, December 2, 1891.

study were often spent in momentary difficulties: "during a whole year a slice or two of sandwich, bread and butter and a cup of tea in the morning and in the evening a penny saveloy formed the only food of the scholar." At time, he could not stir out for fear of creditors. It was only when a few tradesmen threatened to take legal action against him that Prothero managed to extract from his father enough money to pay some tradesmen who would otherwise have put him into the country court. On seeing the living place of Aurobindo, let us recall the great O.B.'s comments: "That wretched hole! (and) then turning to Mahaffy: How rude we are to our scholars. We get great minds to come down here and then shut them up in that box."

Since Aurobindo had deliberately rejected the Indian Civil Service, he decided to return to his motherland. But the question: what was he going to do? What were his prospects in India? Fortunately, an excellent opportunity presented itself. The Maharaja of Gaekwar was in England and James Cotton brought to his notice the name of Aurobindo. The Maharaja was greatly impressed by Aurobindo's scholastic achievements and offered him a job carrying a salary of Rs. 200. Aurobindo accepted the offer and set sail for India in February, 1893. This brings to an end the first phase of his career.

It would be misleading to believe that at Cambridge, Aurobindo spent his formative years completely cut off from his country and its problems. His father may have sent him to England to protect him from all native influences but in later years himself began sending clippings of Bengali newspapers describing the atrocities committed by the Britishers in India. He thus kindled in him a love for his motherland and a hatred for its foreign masters. While still in England, Aurobindo began to play an active part in an underground society of Indian Students, the *Lotus and Dagger* which aimed at promoting the national Independence. He also became an active member of the *Indian Majlis* in England and delivered many fiery and revolutionary speeches.

Before Aurobindo could reach India, he lost his father who died under tragic circumstances. The news of Aurobindo's rejection of the I.C.S. came as a shock to him and the rumour that Aurobindo's steamer had sunk near Lisbon and his son had drowned proved too much for him.

Aurobindo had spent fourteen years in England and he was so much immersed in the culture of the West that he did not know even his mother tongue. Dinendra Kumar Roy, a novelist was appointed to make him acquire the working knowledge of Bengali. His tutor was taken aback in his first meeting with him. But soon he discovered that Aurobindo "was not an ordinary mortal but was a man of destiny." Despite the entirely foreign milieu in which he was brought up he did not lose his identity and came out of that environment "all untouched, intact, true to his own self, in every way as true Indian as could be wished for."

IV

The year 1893 in which Aurobindo returned home has great significance in the history of India. Though this significance is based on certain coincidences, these coincidences are so significant in the history of human thought that we cannot completely isolate them while interpreting the chain of events. It is in this year that Swami Vivekananda first goes out to the West; Annie Besant arrives in India; Gandhi sails for South Africa to prepare himself for the political struggle. Another significant fact calls for our attention. On arrival at Apollo Bunder in Bombay, Aurobindo experiences a flash and a sudden sensation of deep calm and silence within him. He writes:

> "Since I set foot on the Indian soil on the Apollo Bunder in Bombay, I began to have spiritual experiences, but these were not divorced from this world but had an inner and infinite bearing on it, such as a feeling of the infinite pervading material space and the immanent inhabiting material objects and bodies. At the same time I found myself entering supraphysical world and planes with influences and an effect from them upon the material plane."[31]

Aurobindo joined the Baroda Service in 1893 and he worked in various departments: settlement department, stamps and revenue department and secretariat. He soon fami-

---

31. *On Yoga*, Tom I. p. 129.

liarized himself with the administrative work. The Maharaja was so much impressed by his administrative ability and his proficiency in the English language that he began to seek his assistance for important correspondence, speeches and in the preparation of various kinds of documents. He also taught the Maharaja the exact and minute details of English Grammar. Once he was sent to Ooty to prepare a summary of an important case and the Maharaja also took him to Kashmir as his private secretary. But soon Aurobindo became disenchanted with this dull and mechanical administrative work. How could he enjoy such a job which did not involve any creativity?

Aurobindo took up a job in Baroda College and was soon appointed as a Professor of English Literature. His life in Baroda was pre-eminently a preparation for his future work. He remained deeply absorbed most of his time in study and writing. He delved deep into the motives and sources of Indian thought and culture. He also studied Indian languages and his intellectual equipment helped him greatly in mastering Indian thought and literature. He was profoundly influenced by the inspiring writings of Bankim Chandra Chatterjee and Michael Madhusudan Dutt. Thus most of the scholarship which manifested subsequently in his writings was acquired during this period of intense *Jnana-yoga*. He had never been able to devote himself to literature and intellectual pursuits with the same concentrated vision as when he was at Baroda. He also wrote a number of poems and translated some portions of the *Ramayana* and the *Mahabharata*. Datta who had himself translated these epics was amazed on seeing some of Aurobindo's translation: "Reading these poems of yours I feel sorry that I wasted my time in translation. Had I known these earlier, I would not have printed mine." His extensive study of the Hindu classics "strengthened his intellectual predilections towards religion". It was at Baroda that the spiritual element in his thinking gradually grew and took a definite shape. He began to show a marked inclination in spirituality. He had the first experience of trance in 1893; followed by another experience in 1901 and during his visit to Kashmir he had still another spiritual experience of the vacant infinite. His meeting with Lele facilitated the growth of his mind towards spirituality. Lele guided him in spiritual practices and experiences.

Aurobindo was a remarkable teacher and gave inspiring lectures to the students. His dynamic personality inspired many youths. Many of those who served the country under Tilak's leadership were Aurobindo's students at Baroda College. The English Principal said to C.R. Reddy, "'So you met Aurobindo Ghose. Did you notice his eyes? There is a mystic fire and light in them. They penetrate into the beyond....'If Joan of Arc heard heavenly voices, Aurobindo probably sees heavenly visions'".[32] K.M. Munshi who was Aurobindo's student at Baroda paid him a glowing tribute. Dinendra Kumar Roy who helped him learn Bengali wrote:

> "Among the student community Aurobindo was regarded as a god. More than the English Principal of the College, this Indian professor was the object of their trust and respect. His ways of teaching had a charm for them....As long as I stayed with him, I could not think of him except as a devoted *brahmacarin* and a self-denying *sannyasin* with a heart weighted with other's sorrows. The acquisition of knowledge seemed to have been the only concern of his life. And to achieve this he remained immersed in severe *tapasya.* amid the din and bustle of the busy world....Living with him day and night, the more intimately I got to know him, the more I understood that Aurobindo was not of this earth; a god he was, descended from Heaven. He alone could say why God had made him Bengali and banished him to ill-fated India."[33]

It is necessary to throw some light on the type of life which he led at Baroda. He could well afford the necessary comforts of life but he was born a non-attached soul. The houses in which he lived were often far from comfortable; "even a poorly paid clerk would have resented the iron cot which was his bed at night. In biting winter he did not use quilts; in the gruelling heat he did not suffer from any special discomfort." His cooks and servants could not have worked for more than a day with any other master, but never a word of censure or show of ill temper disfigured Aurobindo.

---

32. Quoted by Sisir Kumar Mitra, *op.cit.*, pp. 350-51.
33. *Ibid.*, p. 351.

It was at Baroda that Aurobindo married, in 1901, a charming and beautiful lady, Mrinalini Devi. His correspondence with his wife in Bengali is a valuable document because it provides us a glimpse into his passionate love for his country and his profound and comprehensive understanding of the motherland. It also provides an extraordinary clue to the decisive and psychological change occurring in his personality. Writing to his wife, Aurobindo spoke of the path which he had chosen—surely a Promethean way and he reminded her of the sufferings and pangs of separation which she would have to bear for marrying him. It was here that he spoke of the three insanities that possessed his being:

"I have three madnesses. Firstly, it is my firm faith that whatever virtue, talent, the higher education and knowledge and the wealth which God has given me belongs to Him. I have the right to spend only as much as is needed for the maintenance of the family and on what is absolutely necessary. Whatever remains should be returned to the Divine....In these hard days, the whole country is like a dependent at your doors, I have thirty crores of brothers and sisters in this country....They must be helped...."

"The second folly has recently taken hold of me;...If the Divine is there, then there must be a way of experiencing His existence, of realising His presence; however hard the path I have taken a firm resolution to follow it...."

"The third folly is this: Whereas others regard the country as an inert object, and know it as the plains, the fields, the forests, the mountains and rivers I look upon my country as the mother, I worship her and adore her as the mother. What would a son do when a demon sitting on the breast of his mother is drinking her blood? Would he sit down content to take his meals, and go on enjoying himself in the company of his wife and children or would he, rather, run to the rescue of his mother?...We have come to the world to do God's work, let us begin it."[34]

---

34. Quoted by A.B. Purani, *op. cit.*, pp. 88-91.

The emergence and maturation of Aurobindo's revolutionary political philosophy took place during his stay in Baroda. He was convinced of the basic fact that India's salvation lay not in blindly imitating the institutions of the West, but in understanding and vigorously following the principles of its own identity. He wanted to translate his political ideas into action. At a time when Gokhale could say, "only men outside lunatic asylum could think or talk of independence....there is no alternative to British rule, not only now but for a long time to come."[35] Aurobindo impelled by this awareness for the need for Liberty, pointed to *Purna Swaraj* as his country's prime goal.

Aurobindo launched a series of articles in the *Indu Prakash,* published under the caption of "New Lamps for Old" which manifested his revolutionary political philosophy and flaming nationalism. These articles created a great sensation and stir in the whole country. He exposed categorically the hollowness and futility of the policy of 'protest, petition and prayer' pursued by the Indian National Congress. He also directed his energies to mobilise strong public opinion against the British rule in India. Imbued with profound idealism and burning as he did for a bold and forward drive, he was planning to prepare the country for armed rebellion: his political programme of action.

Though in the beginning he had built up high hopes in the Congress, soon his expectations were belied. The Congress within eight years of its existence pitched from its noble height into ignominious abyss:

> "Our actual enemy is not the force exterior to ourselves, but our crying weakness, our cowardice, our purblind sentimentalism...I say, of the Congress, then, this...that its aims are mistaken, that the spirit in which it proceeds towards their accomplishment is not a spirit of sincerity and whole heartedness and the methods it has chosen are not the right methods and the leaders in whom it trusts, not the right sort of men to be leaders,—in brief, that we are at present the blind led, if not by the blind, at any rate, by the one-eyed."[36]

---

35. *Speeches*, p. 1148.
36. *The Indu Prakash*, August 28, 1893.

The Congress which included within its fold only the middle class anglicised intelligentsia had started speaking of the blessing of British rule in India to mislead the public. Aurobindo wrote:

"There was too a little too much talk about the blessing of British rule, and the inscrutable providence which has laid us in the maternal or more properly the step maternal bosom of just and benevolent England. Yet more appalling was the general timidity of the Congress, its glossing over of hard names, its disinclination to tell the direct truth, its fear of too deeply displeasing our masters."[37]

Exclusively a middle class organ, the Congress of course had secured a few seats for the self-seekers in the Legislative Assemblies and Councils but could hardly achieve anything for the country's liberation. He exposed the hypocrisy, selfishness and dualistic approach of the Congress Party and called for the active involvement of the masses to strengthen the movement. Aurobindo wrote:

"...Mr. Pherozshah assures us that the awakening of the masses from their ignorance and misery is entirely unimportant ....now that the middle class is proved deficient in sincerity, power and judgment—with that proletariat resides, whether we like it or not, our sole assurance of hope, our sole chance in the future."[38]

Further he wrote:

"Yet the proletariat is, as I have striven to show, the real key of the situation...he is a very great potential force, and whoever succeeds in understanding and eliciting his strength, becomes by the very fact master of the future."[39]

Aurobindo was a trenchant critic of his countrymen who had developed love for the British people and their way of life. He had exposed not only the bankruptcy of their institutions

37. *Ibid*, August 7, 1893.
38. *Ibid.*, December 4, 1893.
39. *Ibid.*, March 6, 1894.

but also their mental make up. There was nothing extraordinary or unique about their character. They were ordinary people—'philistines with the narrow hearts and commercial habits of mind.' It was sheer imbecility to glorify them and imitate their way of life. They had not been able to evolve permanent and stable institutions like Athens and France. Aurobindo reminded his countrymen that our institutions approximated more to Athenian and French institutions than the British. It was sheer nonsense and stupidity to look to the West for physical, moral and spiritual strength for the regeneration of the country's spirit. He insisted that we should seek and draw inspiration from the ancient sources. However, Aurobindo was fascinated by Japan's marvellous progress, the clue to which he found in the unique synthesis of modern scientific thought and Eastern spirituality. He strongly insisted that India should follow the strategy of Japan for achieving her objectives rather than imitate the sterile and mechanical political institutions of the West.

In *The Prophet of Indian Nationalism*, Dr. Karan Singh has correctly pointed out that Aurobindo was a profound political theoretician and at the same time a clever and discerning strategist and tactician. Thus his political programme can be analysed under two broad headings: theoretical aproach to the problem of India's Independence and the concrete measure which he undertook to implement those ideals for the liberation of the country. His practical programme covered a three-fold task: an open armed insurrection; effective public propaganda and mass opinion against British rule in India. He wanted to pursue his three-fold task vigorously and with complete sincerity. He chalked out a comprehensive programme of setting up secret youth societies for imparting integrated training and inspiring them with love of the motherland. The *modus operandi* of the programme was "that centres were to be established in every town and eventually in every village. Societies of young men were to be set up with various ostensible objects, cultural, intellectual or moral and those already existing were to be won over for revolutionary use. Young men were to be trained in activities which might be helpful for ultimate military action, such as riding, physical training atheletics of various kinds, drill and organised movement." Aurobindo and

Bipin Chander Pal from Bengal, Bal Gangadhar Tilak from Maharashtra and Lala Lajpat Rai from Punjab became the leaders of these youth organisations in the country. They inspired the youngmen by the revolutionary political ideas of Mazzini, Garibaldi and exhortation from Swami Vivekananda.

Aurobindo set up a revolutionary committee in Bengal and sister Nivedita, a disciple of Swami Vivekananda also became a member of the committee to work for the revolutionary cause. She was one of the revolutionary leaders: "She was open, frank, talked openly of revolutionary plans to everybody. There was no concealing on her part. Whenever she used to speak on revolution, it was her very soul, her true personality that came out, her whole mind and life expressed themselves. Yoga apart, revolutionary work was the one that was intended for her. She was all fire." Her book *Kali the Mother* is very inspiring and filled with revolutionary ideas. It is said that "Swami Vivekananda himself had ideas of political work and of revolution. Once he had a vision which corresponded to something like the Maniktala Garden revolutionary centre."[40] Vivekananda is believed to have told a co-worker of Nivedita:

> "...I have travelled all over India for organising revolution, manufacturing guns, etc....I have made friendship with Sir Hiram Maxim (maker of the Maxim gun). But India is in putrefaction. So I want a band of workers who would, as *brahmacarins* educate the people and revitalise the country."[41]

A close look at the historical perspective of the Freedom Movement reveals that Aurobindo, in his radical political programme, effectively made use of all these weapons: non-cooperation, boycott and swadeshi (or economic self-sufficiency through indigenous industry) for the achievement of the country's independence. His political philosophy contains the use of

---

40. Quoted by Sisir Kumar Mitra, *op. cit.*, p. 135.
"Talks with Sri Aurobindo" recorded by Nirodbaran of which a Bengali version published in book form contains this talk dated 21.1.1939.
41. R.C. Majumdar, *History of Freedom Movement in India*, Vol. 1, pp. 463-64.

violence and non-violence depending on the situation and circumstances.

In 1905, Aurobindo wrote *Bhawani Mandir,* which was his revolutionary manifesto. This pamphlet was widely circulated and was little better than "a packet of revolutionary dynamite." Taking the cue, perhaps from Bankim Chandra's *Ananda Math* Aurobindo wanted to establish in a mountainous seclusion a temple consecrated to Bhawani, the Divine Mother, with a school attached which would train a new kind of selfless workers who would work for the liberation of their motherland. The accent in this pamphlet was on the nation, the nation's reviving strength, the nation's hope of regeneration. It was a stirring call for the resurgence of the national spirit. It was here that Aurobindo had expressed his philosophy of radical nationalism. To inspire the young revolutionaries he gave a new interpretation, a new meaning and a new dimension to the concept of nationalism. He wrote:

> "India, the ancient Mother, is indeed striving to be reborn, striving with agony and tears, but she strives in vain. What ails her, she who is after all so vast and might be so strong? There is surely some enormous defect, something vital is wanting in us....which we must strive to acquire before all others, is strength—strength physical, strength mental, strength moral, but above all strength spiritual which is the one inexhaustible and imperishable source of all the others. If we have strength everything else will be added to us easily and naturally...."

> "If India is to survive, she must be made young again. Rushing and billowing streams of energy must be poured into her: her soul must become, as it was in the old times; like the surges, vast, puissant, calm or turbulent at will, an ocean of action or of force...."

> "For what is a nation? What is our mother country? It is not a piece of earth, nor a figure of speech, nor a fiction of the mind. It is a mighty *Shakti,* composed of the Shaktis of all the millions of units that make up the nation....The *Shakti* we call India, *Bhawani Bharati*, is the living unity of the Shaktis

of three hundred million people...."

"India can not perish, our race cannot become extinct, because among all the divisions of mankind it is to India that is reserved the highest and the most splendid destiny, the most essential to the future of the human race. It is she who must send forth from herself the future religion of the entire world, the eternal religion which is to harmonize all religion, science and philosophies and make mankind one soul. In the sphere of morality, likewise, it is her mission to purge barbarism (mlecchahood) out of humanity and to aryanise the world. In order to do this, she must first rearyanise herself. India's need of drawing from the fountains of religions far greater....we have to create strength where it did not exist before; we have to change our natures, and become new men with new hearts; to be born again...."[42]

Aurobindo was deliberately using religious images and concepts familiar to Hindus and Hinduism to transform a pure intellectual movement into a mass movement. He openly began advocating the use of violence to retaliate against the various cruelties committed by the British Government. Through his revolutionary activities he intended to set ablaze a countrywide passion for freedom. He believed that in the absence of overwhelming military organisation guerrilla warfare accompanied by general resistance and revolt might be effective. Aurobindo wanted to propagate his revolutionary ideas on a wider scale and on more pragmatic lines to prepare the youths for organised action. At the suggestion of Barin, Aurobindo started a Bengali paper entitled *Yugantar* which began to publish articles on open revolt and on the conduct of guerrilla warfare. "A tiny spark, it blew into a flame and burnt its way into the hearts of the people. Young and old, none could do without reading it, the first thing in the morning. In the words of Upendranath Bandyopadhyaya...the *Yugantar* sold like hot cakes. One thousand and five thousand—ten—twenty thousand copies every week—that was how the sale leapt up in the course of a year."[43] The British Government became psychologically perturbed and

42. Quoted by A.B. Purani, *op. cit.*, pp. 76-81.
43. Sisir Kumar Mitra, *op. cit.*, p. 358.

was determined to crush the spirit of revolt by adopting the policy of *divide et impera*—a stab in the heart of a race.

In 1905, Lord Curzon recommended the partition of Bengal—a deliberate malicious political strategy—to crush the growing solidarity of Bengali nationalism and to create the communal problem in the country. Aurobindo wrote: "Here is our great opportunity. Push on the anti-Partition agitation with utmost force. Lots of workers will emerge from it."[44] He published an article on 'No compromise' which was widely received. He considered the Partition "as the greatest blessing that had ever happened to India." No other measure, said he, "could have stirred national feeling so deeply or roused it so suddenly from the lethargy of previous years."

Aurobindo was planting the seeds of revolution and extremism in the country's politics. He gave a call to the students for dynamising in them a will to freedom. The students openly defied the Government order and left their studies to take an active part in the political movement of the country. The song of 'Bande Mataram' was on the lips of every patriot and became a powerful force behind the resurgent movement. B.C. Pal started *Bande Mataram* which became the organ of the nationalist party and Aurobindo expounded his ideas and ideals through this paper. Stressing the urgency of India's Independence and its unique role which it is destined to paly for the survival of humanity and expansion of human consciousness, Aurobindo wrote in *Bande Mataram* "that it was not only for her own sake, that India must be free, but for all humanity." India is destined to spearhead the next phase of human evolution, because it is her *swadharma,* or essential nature to guide the world on the spiritual path. It was in *Bande Mataram* that Aurobindo formulated his conception of *Swaraj.* "Swaraj is not the colonial form of Government. It means the fulfilment of our national life. That is what we seek, that is why God has sent us into the world to fulfil Him by fulfilling ourselves in our individual life, in the family, in the community, in the nation, in the humanity". Aurobindo's only slogan at that time was: "India must have a *swaraj.* She must have *swaraj* in order to live; she must have *swaraj* in order to live well and happily, she must have *swaraj* in order to live

44. *Ibid.*, p. 356.

for the world, not as a slave for the material benefit of a single purse-proud and selfish nation, but as a free people for the spiritual and intellectual benefit of the human race."[45] It was his firm convictiont that no real development was possible in India, be it economic, social, administrative or any other, unless she obtained her freedom from foreign rulers. Unlike other thinkers of India, Aurobindo believed that political freedom was the *sine qua non* of all other progress in India."

Aurobindo's political strategy was so unique that it created a powerful impact on the youth of the country. The feeling of nationalism spread throughout the country and "electrified the masses of India". The Nationalist party became a potential force in the country and came into open confrontation with the moderate group of the Congress. Gopal Krishna Gokhale in his presidential address to the Congress remarked: "The question that is uppermost in the minds of us all at this moment is the partition of Bengal...a cruel wrong has been inflicted on our Bengali brethren and the whole country has been stirred to the deepest depths of sorrow and resentment as had never been the case before." But the moderates were never serious about the cause of the country's independence. In the meanwhile, Aurobindo launched a movement of passive resistance: "Just as 'No representation, No taxation', was the watchword of the American constitutional agitation in the eighteenth century, so 'No control, No co-operation' should be the watchword of our lawful agitation. For constitution we have none—in the twentieth—we sum up this refusal of co-operation in the convenient word of 'Boycott', refusal of co-operation in the industrial exploitation of our country, in government, in judicial administration, in the details of official intercourse."[46]

The extremist group because of their hectic activities became a very powerful force in the country and had the sympathy and support of the masses. They decided to throw the moderates out of the Congress organisation. In the Calcutta session they decided to propose the name of Tilak for presidentship of the Congress. The moderates sent a telegram to Dadabhai Naoroji to save the situation from the impending crisis. The extremist

45. *Ibid.*, pp. 359-60
46. *Ibid.*, p. 360.

group exerted a tremendous pressure on the moderates and compelled them to pass a resolution on complete boycott, swadeshi and national education. It was decided to hold the next meeting at Nagpur but soon the moderate group foresaw that they would not be able to muster so much strength at Nagpur since the place was dominated by the extremists, so they shifted the venue of the session to Surat. At the Surat session Aurobindo and Tilak played a predominant role in spearheading the split in the Congress. The election of the President became crucial. The moderates proposed the name of Rash Behari Ghose and the extremist proposed that of Lala Lajpat Rai. Tilak was not permitted to speak on the stage and when he insisted on it suddenly a fiasco ensued, shoes and chairs were freely hurled from both the sides. Describing the Surat session, R.R. Diwakar wrote:

> "The Surat Congress ended in a fiasco but made history. The result was that the Moderates continued to possess the body of the Congress while the spirit went out along with the Extremists. For the next ten years Indian nationalism flourished outside the pacifist precints of the national organisation. . . . it completely routed the Moderates who later continued their existence outside the Congress as a small and not very influential coterie. They ceased to be a political force in the country."[47]

Thus did Surat session "signalise on the one hand the end of moderatism in Indian politics and, on the other a further accentuation of the forward programme of the New Party, which the country had already accepted with enthusiasm as an effective plan of action."[48]

After the Surat Session Aurobindo addressed several meetings in which he explained the reasons for the split in the party. Meanwhile the terrorist activities spread throughout the country The Government was convinced that the man behind the entire movement was no other than Aurobindo. The spirit of nationlism was all-pervasive. Those were the days when it was bliss to be alive for the vision of Free and greater India. "The New

---

47. R.R. Diwakar, *Mahayogi Sri Aurobindo* Bombay, 1967, p. 69.
48. Quoted by Sisir Kumar Mitra, *op. cit.*, pp. 363-64.

Nationalism" wrote Sri Aurobindo, "is a call for the men of faith, men who dare and do impossibilities, the men of extremes, the prophets, martyrs, the crusaders and rebels, the desperate adventurers and reckless doers, the kshatriyas, the samurai, the initiators of revolutions. It is the right of the new India."[49]

Alarmed by the terrorist activities the Government adopted violent and repressive measures against the radical element in the Indian Congress. Pointing out the excesses of the administration, Lord Morley wrote to Lord Minto and asked him to exercise restraint in dealing with the situation: "I must confess to you that I am watching with the deepest concern and dismay the thundering sentences that are being passed for sedition, etc. We must keep order, but excess of severity is not the path to order, on the contrary, it is a path to the bomb." The Chief Presidency Magistrate, Calcutta, Kingsford, was a ruthless administrator and used to inflict brutal punishment on the political workers. The young revolutionaries decided to murder him for his criminal imbecilities. It was on April 30, 1908, that two youths threw a bomb at a carriage thinking mistakenly that Kingsford was travelling in it. As a result of this incident two innocent ladies, Mrs. Kennedy and her daughter, were killed.

The Government was very much disturbed and launched widespread searches and arrests within a few days after this tragic episode. On May 2, 1908, a police party raided the garden and unearthed many bombs and weapons. Aurobindo and forty other people connected with the Maniktolla garden episode were arrested. The arrest of Aurobindo created a great stir throughout the country. The wave of discontent and indignation against the cruelty and the callousness of the British rule in India became widespread. *Amrit Bazar Patrika* in its editorial remarked: "But why were they (Aurobindo and others) pounced upon in this mysterious manner, handcuffed and then dragged before the Police Commissioner? Where was the necessity for this outrage?...It served no other purpose than that of wantonly outraging public feeling."

Sarojini Ghose issued an appeal to all the countrymen for contribution to engage an able counsel for his defence in the Court : "My countrymen are aware that my

49. *Ibid.*, p. 365.

brother Aurobindo Ghose stands accused of a grave offence. But I believe, and I have reason to think that the vast majority of my ountrymen believe, that he is quite innocent. I think if he is defended by an able counsel, he is sure to be acquitted. But as he has taken a vow of poverty in the service of the Motherland, he has no means to engage the service of an eminent barrister-at-law. I am, therefore, under the painful necessity of appealing to the public spirit and generosity of my countrymen on his behalf. I know all my countrymen do not hold the same political opinion as he. But I feel some delicacy in saying that probably there are few Indians who do not appreciate his great attainments, his self-sacrifice, his single-minded devotion to the country's cause and the high spirituality of his character. These embolden me, a woman to stand before every son and daughter of India for help to defend a brother—my brother and theirs too."[50]

Then followed the historic trial of Aurobindo in the court of C.B. Beachcroft, Additional Session Judge who was his contemporary at Cambrdige. Chittaranjan Das who came forward to defend his case abandoned everything and spent days and nights to save Aurobindo. Norton, Chief Prosecutor, employed all sorts of antics and perverted logic to implicate Aurobindo in this case. In the *Life and Time of C.R. Das* we find that "in this case 206 witnesses were examined, 4,000 documents were filed and the exhibits, consisting of bombs, revolvers, ammunitions, detonators, fuses, poisonous acids and other explosive materials, numbered 5,000."[51]

The statement of Aurobindo read by Chittaranjan Das during the course of his defence reveals his strength of character and sincerity of purpose:

"The whole of my case before you is this. If it is suggested that I preached the ideal of freedom to my country which is against the law, I plead guilty to the charge. If it is an offence to preach the ideal of freedom, I admit having done it. I have never disputed it. I have adopted the principle of the political philosophy of the West and I have assimilated that

50. Quoted by A.B. Purani, *op. cit.*, pp. 122-23.
51. Quoted by Karan Singh, *op. cit.*, p. 136.

to the immortal teachings of Vedantism."

"I felt I was called upon to preach to my country to make them realise that India had a mission to perform in the comity of the nations."

"If this is my fault you can chain me, imprison me, but you will never get out of me a denial of that charge. I venture to submit that under no section of the law do I come for preaching the ideal of freedom, and with regard to the deeds with which I have been charged, I submit there is no evidence on the record and it is absolutely inconsistent with everything that I taught, that I wrote and with every tendency of my mind discovered in the evidence."[52]

Chittaranjan Das made a prophetic and passionate appeal to the court in defence of Aurobindo. His prophecy was that Aurobindo would be remembered in history as the poet of patriotism, the prophet of nationalism and the lover of humanity. His speech for the defence was spread over eight days and is a "masterpiece of forensic eloquence".

"The time has come for you, Sir, to consider your judgment and for you, gentlemen, to consider your verdict. I appeal to you, Sir, in the name of all the traditions of the English Bench that forms the most glorious chapter of English history. I appeal to you in the name of all that is noble, of all the thousand principles of law which have emanated from the English Bench, and I appeal to you in the name of the distinguished judges who have administered the Law in such a manner as to compel not only obedience but the respect of all those in whose cases they had administered the Law. I appeal to you in the name of the glorious chapter of English history and let it not be said that an English judge forgets to vindicate justice."[53]

Then turning to the Indian Jury, Chittaranjan Das addressed in these words:

---

52. Navajata, *Sri Aurobindo*, Delhi, 1972, p. 30.
53. Quoted by *Ibid.*, p. 31.

"To you gentlemen, I appeal in the name of the very ideal that Arabinda preached and in the name of all the traditions of our country; and let it not be said that two of his own countrymen were overcome by passions and prejudices and yielded to the clamour of the moment."[54]

On hearing the passionate appeal of Chittaranjan Das the court pronounced its judgment: "I find Naren Bakshi, Sailendra Kumar Sen, Nolini Kanta Gupta, Purna Chandra Sen, Bijoy Kumar Nag, Kunja Lall Shaba, Hemendra Nath Ghose, Dharini Nath Gupta, Birendra Nath Ghose, Bijoy Bhattacharji, Hem Chandra Sen, Probhash Chanda De, Dindoyal Bose, Nikhileswar Roy Maulik, Deba Brata Bose, Arabinda Ghose, not guilty under sections 121, 121A and 122 and all accused persons not guilty under 123. —C.B. Beachcroft."[55]

Soon after his acquittal in the Alipore Bomb Case, Sri Aurobindo delivered an eloquent Uttarpara speech which is intensely revealing. "It shows clearly that it was during his confinement in jail that the decisive psychologicl break with active politics came as the result of a transcending of politics and progression into a deeper and wider sphere of spiritual activity."[56] As he puts it:

"When I was arrested and hurried to the Lal Bazar Hajat, I was shaken in faith for a while, for I could not look into the heart of His intention. Therefore I faltered for a moment and cried out in my heart to Him, 'What is this that has happened to me? I believed that I had mission to work for the people of my country and until that work was done I should have Thy protection. Why then am I here and on such a charge? A day passed and a second day and a third, when a voice came to me from within 'wait and see'. Then I grew calm and waited; I was taken from Lal Bazar to Alipur and was placed for one month in a solitary cell apart from other men. There I waited day and night for the voice of God within me, to know what He had to say to me, to learn what I had to do. In this seclusion the earliest realization, the first lesson came to me. I remembered then that a month or more before

54. *Ibid.*, pp. 31-32.
55. *Ibid.*
56. Karan Singh, *op. cit.*, p. 137.

> my arrest a call had come to me to put aside all activity, to go into seclusion and look into myself, so that I might enter into closer communion with Him. I was weak and could not accept the call. My work was dear to me and in the pride of my heart I thought that unless I was there it would suffer or even fail and cease; therefore I would not leave it. It seemed to me that He spoke to me again and said: 'The bonds you had not the strength to break, I have broken for you, because it was not my will nor was it ever my intention that that should continue. I have had another thing for you to do and it is for that I have brought you here, to teach you what you could not learn for yourself and to train you for my work.'"[57]

It was a dual trial both at the mundane and the spiritual level. The jail brought a final crisis in Sri Aurobindo's life and opened a new voyage to self-progression. Prison life gave him an opportunity for seclusion to contemplate and meditate without any aberration from the outside world. His imprisonment afforded him the silence and one-pointedness needed to realize Oneness. Sri Aurobindo wrote: "I was hearing constantly the voice of Vivekananda speaking to me for a fortnight in the jail in my solitary meditation and felt his presence,...The voice spoke only on a special and limited but very important field of spiritual experience and it ceased as soon as it finished saying all that it had to say on the subject."[58]

In *Kara Kahini* (Tales of the Prison House), Sri Aurobindo has left an account of his process of self-discovery. His entire life in jail was for him 'Ashram life': "Long and hard had I striven", he wrote, "to have a direct vision of Narayana in the heart; high-hopes had I cherished to have the Lord of the universe, the Purushottama, as friend and master. But a thousand and one pulls of the world, bonds of various activities, and the massed obscurities of ignorance stood in the way. At length the God of all grace and bliss put away those obstacles with a single wave of his hand and cleared the way, showed me the Yogashram and himself stayed with me in the small cell of *sadhana*, as Friend and *Guru*. ...The one result of the wrath of the British Government was

---

57. *Speeches*, pp. 51-66.
58. Quoted by A.B. Purani, *op. cit.*, p. 129.

attainment of God'"[59]

Sri Aurobindo's companions in jail remained completely unnerved on account of his serene and all pervasive influence: "death on the gallows or transportation for life" did not bother them at all. A European warder remarked: "Look here, the man's going to be hanged, and he laughs". His companion replied, "Yes, I know, they all laugh at death." Sri Aurobindo had expressed their adventuring spirit and sacrificing zeal in the following words:

> "'Let me speak about the boys—my co-accused, my companions in danger. From their bearing in court I could well perceive that a new age had dawned over Bengal, children of a new mould were on the lap of the Mother....A glance at these boys gave one the impression as if men of different culture, high-souled, indomitable heroes of another epoch, had now returned to India. That frank, fearless look, those manly accents, that carefree cheerful laughter, the same forcefulness of spirit, unshaken even in such grave danger, the same light heart, the absence of sadness, of worry or of anguish were the marks not of the Indians sunk in ignorance and inertia but of a new age, a new race, a new stream of activity. If they were murderers, one must say that the monster's shade of murder had not fallen over their nature; of cruelty, fanaticism, brutality, there was no trace in them.'"[60]

On his release from jail, Sri Aurobindo felt that it was the command of God to work for the all-round development of the nation 'both in the inner and outer spheres of life'. But the climate was not conducive because depression and feeling of helplessness was all pervasive on the political scene of the country. On account of the severely repressive measures which the Government had taken most of the top leaders had been jailed or deported, some had chosen self-exile for the time being. "The storm that swept had scattered over the country, had scattered them far and wide." Though the people's spirit was in the lowest ebb, Sri Aurobindo continued his work uninterruptedly. He once

---

59. Quoted by Sisir Kumar Mitra, *op. cit.*, p. 366.
60. *Ibid.*, p. 367.

more plunged into political activity. The experience of jail gave him a great power of endurance and strengthened his will and faith.

He launched two new publications the *Karmayogin*, an English weekly, and the *Dharma* a Bengali counterpart to propagate his views to build up an effective opinion against the British rule. The response of these publications was quite encouraging. He did not merely discuss the political situation in the country but there was plenty of spiritual exposition too.

The Government was greatly disturbed over Sri Aurobindo's revolutionary activities and decided to deport him. On knowing this he warned the Government that the removal of the individual would never stop the wheels of the Time spirit from taking its destined course. Sister Nivedita suggested to Sri Aurobindo that he should now leave India and work from outside. He also began to realize that the political destiny of the nation would reach its end without him but the long spiritual evolution of humanity was awaiting him. He received a command from above and an inner voice for undertaking a deeper *sadhana* to explore the mysteries of self within. A greater world the Traveller must explore. Thus his celebrated journey towards self-progression or a voyage to self commences with his departure to Pondicherry. It also witnesses the end of the second phase of his career.

V

The third phase of Sri Aurobindo's life is the most extraordinary and fruitful in the spiritual history of the world. He went to Pondicherry to fathom the bottom of the cosmos, to redisocver for himself and for the world, the soul of India. His apparent exit from the political scene created a great stir in the country and all sorts of stories were fabricated to explain this inexplicable mystery. It was believed that Sri Aurobindo was disenchanted on account of his bitter experiences in jail and consequently ran away to Pondicherry. But this explanation is absolutely nonsense.

In retrospect we find that Sri Aurobindo went to Pondicherry not because of any threat of the British Court but because of an answer to an imperative need to pursue the path of yoga. Here is his own explanation:

> "I did not leave politics because I felt I could do nothing more there; such an idea was very far from me. I came away because I did not want anything to interfere with my *Yoga* and because I got a very distinct *Adesh* in the matter....I knew from within that the work I had begun there was destined to be carried forward, on lines I had foreseen, by others, and that the ultimate triumph of the movement I had initiated was sure without my personal action or presence. There was not the least motive of despair or sense of futility behind my withdrawal."[61]

Sri Aurobindo's last political will and testament which was published in the *Karmayogin* under the caption of 'An Open Letter to my Countrymen' on July 31, 1909, is most revealing as it throws some light on his exit to Pondicherry. He wrote:

> "All great movements wait for their God-sent leader, the willing channel of His force, and only when he comes more forward triumphantly to their fulfilment. The men who have led hitherto have been strong men of high gifts and commanding genius, great enough to be the protagonists of any other movement, but even they were not sufficient to fulfil one which is the chief current of a world-wide revoluton. Therefore the Nationalist Party, custodians of the future, must wait for the man who is to come."[62]

Before coming to Pondicherry on 4th April, 1910, Sri Aurobindo stayed for some time at Chandernagore. Moni, Bijoy, Saurin and Nolini were his companions at Pondicherry. In the beginning they stayed at the house of Shankar Chetty. They lived through hard times because they did not have enough money. Moti Lal Roy extended some financial assistance but that was not sufficient for their living. Sri Aurobindo was not permitted by the British administration to pursue his work uninterruptedly.

---

61. Quoted by A.B. Purani, *op. cit.*, p. 139.
62. Quoted by Karan Singh, *op. cit.*, p. 142. He had rightly observed that perhaps this was a reference to Gandhiji, who was destined to lead the Nationalists to the final victory.

Many attempts were made by the British C.I.D. to implicate him in some fabricated conspiracy case or kidnap him from there. But all these attempts were in vain.

On March 29, 1914 two distinguished visitors Paul and Mirra Richard, or the Mother as she is now called, arrived in Pondicherry in quest of spiritual light. She had her spiritual urges right from her childhood and was looking forward to a teacher who could guide her activities and with whom she could collaborate for carrying out her mission. At the very first meeting she recognised him as the Being who had been guiding her in her *sadhana* and whom she used to call Sri Krishna. She wrote in her diary: "It matters not if there are hundreds of beings plunged in the densest ignorance. He whom we saw yesterday is on earth, his presence is enough to prove that a day will come when the darkness shall be transformed into light, when Thy reign shall be, indeed, established upon earth."[63]
Paul and Mirra Richard suggested to Sri Aurobindo to start a philosophical magazine to give to the world his grand synthesis of knowledge and yogic experiences in terms of rational exposition. To realize this objective they started the *Arya* which appeared in English, and the *Revue de Grande Synthese,* which appeared in French. Among other things, the *Arya* serialized *The Life Divine, The Synthesis of Yoga, The Human Cycle, The Ideal of Human Unity, The Secret of Vedas, The Foundation of Indian Culture, The Philosophy of Upanishads, The Essays on the Gita* and *The War and Self Determination.*

The First World War broke out in 1914. Mirra Richard left Pondicherry for France on February 22, 1915. From France she went to Japan and she also met there Rabindranath Tagore who invited her to take charge of Santiniketan. But she could not accede to his request because she was aware that her future work lay with Sri Aurobindo. During this period Sri Aurobindo and Mirra Richard exchanged with each other many letters which are highly philosophical and show their deep concern for humanity.

She returned to Pondicherry on April 24, 1920. In 1921 they started collective meditation. In 1922 the Mother took charge of the entire management of the house. The member-

---

63. Quoted by Navajata, *op. cit.*, p. 60.

ship in the Ashram began to increase and she became the guiding spirit of the Ashram. People from all over the world began to come to Pondicherry and some of them settled there. It is a world community and the inmates are from America, France, Germany, China, Japan, and other countries.

From 1910 to 1950 Sri Aurobindo remained involved in exploring the mysteries of human becoming or the evolution of the spirit of man and society: "The method by which the involved evolves is evolution. Evolution is not self-explicable, but has to refer to an original involution, a plunge into the inconscience. Life is the first step of that release of Consciousness, mind is the second, but the evolution has not ended with mind and man, both of which are obviously transitional terms or incomplete. A release into something greater, a consciousness which is spiritual and supramental, a mutation into men that will be gnostic beings, self-fulfilled, is the next step ahead."[64]

But there are many psychological difficulties in this process. Sri Aurobindo does not minimise the risk and "he holds on to a brighter hope." In his own words: "As there has been established on earth a mental Consciousness and Power which shapes a race of mental beings and take up into itself all of earthly nature that is ready for the change, so now there will be established on earth a gnostic Consciousness and Power which will shape a race of gnostic spiritual beings and take up into itself all of earth nature that is ready for this new transformation."[65] The vision of the transformation of the individual, society and human race is the main achievement of Sri Aurobindo's long labour. In other words, his basic problem was how to transform the individual and society to establish their harmonious relationship with the environment. Sri Aurobindo found the clue to the solution of the problem in the Integral Yoga: "Yoga must now be revealed to mankind because without it mankind cannot take the next step in the human evolution....In reality there is nothing hidden or mystic about Yoga."[66]

The basic distinction between other Yogas and Sri Aurobindo's Yoga is that while others advocate 'the path to the Beyond leading to the spirit and, in the end, away from life' Sri Aurobindo's

64. Sisir Kumar Ghose, *op. cit.*, p. 21.
65. *Ibid.*
66. Ibid.

Yoga is a double movement of ascent and descent; one rises to higher and higher levels of consciousness, but at the same time one brings down their power, not only into the mind and life, but in the end even into the body." Sri Aurobindo believed that his Yoga is the method of actualizing the potentialities of self, of opening new doors of Consciousness, of realizing the kingdom of Heaven on Earth, the Life Divine. He was always opening doors—doors through which not only he but all the rest of us might pass, to enter on new kinds of experiences, new ways of thinking, new possibilities of living. In *The Life Divine*, he has himself summed up his philosophy of life:

> "The ascent to the Divine Life is the human journey, the Work of works, the acceptable sacrifice. This alone is man's business in the world and the justification of his existence without which he would be only an insect crawling among other ephemeral insects on a speck of surface mud and water which has managed to form itself amid the appalling immensities of the physical universe.'[67]

From the foregoing discussion, it emerges that Sri Aurobindo was not merely a writer, a prophet of nationalism, a political thinker and strategist, but also a poet of the descent of new consciousness and above all a sociologist who worked and looked forward to the emergence of a new society—society of the Future.

Looking up at the narrative part it took India four decades to bring to fruition his dream of *Purna Swaraj,* and within three years he departed leaving his countrymen with the still greater challenge of helping to realize a new phase of human consciousness.[68]

---

67. *Life Divine.*
68. See the discussion on his political activities during this phase of life on pp. 13—22.

Towards an Assessment of Sri Aurobindo as a Political Thinker

KARAN SINGH

A broad assessment of Sri Aurobindo's contribution to modern Indian political thought beginning with his return from England in 1893 and leaving for Pondicherry in 1910 would show four characteristics:

1. His concept of spiritual nationalism and the divinity of the Motherland, which imparted a religious or esoteric significance to the movement for India's liberation;
2. His exposition of the ideal of complete freedom from foreign rule, and his role in radicalizing the national movement;
3. His contribution to the theory of boycott and passive resistance, as also to the use of force, if necessary, to achieve freedom;
4. His vision of the broader role that India was destined to play in world affairs, and his enlightened ideal of human unity that must ultimately transcend mere national development.

Let us deal with each of these, briefly.

We may take first his concept of spiritual nationalism and the divinity of the Motherland. The bedrock of his political theory, it underlies all his writings in this field. The divinity of the Motherland is, of course, a concept that has existed since the dawn of history. In the earliest religious texts, not only of India but of other ancient civilizations, the earth—particularly that portion of it occupied by the tribe or society in question—was worshipped as the sustainer, nourisher and supporter of all life and prosperity. The Vedas contain numerous hymns in adoraton of the earth, and the worship of *prithvi* is one of the basic rituals in Hindu religious ceremonies. This tradition has continued unbroken in India right down to modern times, when Bankim Chandra Chatterjee in his *Ananda Math* created the 'Bande Mataram' glorifying the divinity of the Motherland. Sri Aurobindo's contribution lay in taking up this mystic and religious concept, adapting it to the political requirements of India at the turn of the century, and turning it into a dynamo of strength and inspiration. His exposition of the religion of nationalism and the heroic spirit of utter self-sacrifice and immolation at the feet of Mother India was unsurpassed for its deeply-felt eloquence. Brief though his political career was, he defined the essence of spiritual nationalism in a manner which, for power and passion, has perhaps never been equalled. He thus imparted a new dimension to the national movement, lifting it above the purely material plane and placing before it an inspired and inspiring spiritual ideal. It was his *Bhawani Mandir* that became the gospel of the Indian revolutionaries, and it was with a smile and the cry of "Bande Mataram" on their lips that thousands of patriots faced repression and even death at the hands of their foreign rulers. His concept of the whole National movement is beautifully summed up in his own words: "The strength of the new movement in India lies in its supreme idealism. It is not a mere economic movement though, it openly strives for the economic resurrection of the country. It is not a mere political movement, though it has boldly declared itself for absolute political independence. It is an intensely spiritual movement having for its object not simply the development of economic emancipation in every sense of the term of the Indian manhood and womanhood."[1] Sri Aurobindo's own contribution to the creation of this 'supreme idealism' was considerable.

His second characteristic achievement as a political thinker lay in his exposition of the ideal of complete freedom from foreign rule and his role in radicalizing the national movement. Despite the brevity of his political career, Sri Aurobindo did enough to infuse a new spirit into the movement and thus to help change the very complexion of politics in the country. As early as

1. The Bedrock of Indian Nationalism', *Bande Mataram*, weekly edition, June 14, 1908.

1893-94, himself barely out of his teens, in 'New Lamps for Old', he had laid out a radical philosophy of politics and revealed an astute insight amazing in one so young. Later his tireless dedicated activity helped to galvanize the people especially of Bengal, during the anti-partition agitation. The key to his great influence upon men and events is to be found in the fact that he laid before the people a worthwhile ideal, the ideal of *Purna Swaraj*, or complete independence. He had the courage to declare this openly, not as a favour from the alien rulers but as the inalienable birthright of India. His concept of the divinity of the Motherland led directly and inevitably to the demand for her complete emancipation from foreign rule, and Sri Aurobindo preached this doctrine with immense patriotic fervour. Not only did he powerfully advocate the ideal of independence, he also effectively demolished the cautious and constricted political position of the moderates. Pouring scorn and biting sarcasm upon the 'mendicant' policies of the moderates, his writings went a long way towards isolating them from the support of public opinion and making the Indian mind receptive to a more radical political programme.

It must be mentioned that Sri Aurobindo was one of the first Indian leaders to recognize the absolute necessity of generating mass enthusiasm and participation in the national cause, of getting the support of all the varied constituents of the Indian body politic, in other words, of democratizing the whole movement. This has not been sufficiently recognised. As early as 1893 he clearly enunciated this populist view, and trenchantly criticized the Congress for remaining a confined and narrow organization without any mass support. He is thus one of the earliest democrats on the modern Indian scene.

Another facet of his thought which enabled him to impart fesh spirit into the national movement was his stress on the necessity for suffering by the 'children' before their Mother could be liberated. Unlike the prim and correct conservatives who thought that the British would, out of their own *noblesse oblige,* grant India a rationed freedom by instalment, Sri Aurobindo knew and stressed clearly the necessity for a 'purification by blood and fire' before the goal could be attained. His stress on the goal of complete independence, his theory of the divinity of the Motherland and the most religious character of the liberation movement, and his emphasis upon the necessity of suffering and sacrifice to achieve the goal, all combined to impart a charismatic, revolutionary spirit to the national movement against British domination. His flaming advocacy of India's right to be free swept aside the more modest goals of the moderates and left them without public support.

Yet another factor in his thought which helped to revitalize the spirit of India was his profound reappraisal of the springs of Indian culture, the abiding sources of her spiritual heritage. His writings, combining as they did startling erudition with flaming patriotic fervour, caused a stir among the intelligentsia. As expositions they are models, of mystical faith and rational commentary. Of all the great leaders of the Radical movement, Sri Aurobindo's literary talent was by far the most impressive. This enabled him effectively to transmit his dream of the future India to receptive and anxious minds. At the same time his forceful writing helped to break the myth of British cultural superiority so assiduously fostered by the foreign rulers. His contribution towards creating a climate of revolutionary nationalism in India directed at securing her complete independence from foreign rule was very substantial. He was indeed, as Tagore so eloquently put it, the 'Voice incarnate, free, of India's soul'.

Here a word may be added about the criticism levelled against Sri Aurobindo and other Radical leaders that they neglected the important issue of social reform. It is true that they did not lay much emphasis upon this aspect of public life which has now assumed so much significance, but this was not because they considered social reform unimportant. It was rather because they were convinced of the primary necessity of securing political independence before a really effective scheme of social reform could be attempted with any hope of success. They recognized the importance of such reform, but felt that it could not precede political independence. To attempt social reform before becoming independent would not only be to put the cart before the horse, but also to fritter away energies that could more usefully be yoked to the national movement itself. It was this view and not any aversion to social reform *per se*, that led Sri Aurobindo to attack the moderate leadership for thier misplaced obsession with social problems.

We may turn now to his contribution to the theory of boycott and passive resistance. As his writings reveal, he was not only a theorist but a masterly political tactician. His voluminous writings on boycott (sadly nelgected) contain a comprehensive exposition of the theory in its many aspects. At the same time he made concrete suggestions about the positive steps that must accompany boycott if it was to be really effective. Thus, along with his theory of economic boycott, he postulated the necessity of swadeshi; along with educational boycott he put forward his views on national education; along with judicial boycott he stressed the necessity for national arbitration courts; along with executive boycott he expounded the importance of national organisation; and as the sanction behind the whole boycott theory he placed the concept of social boycott. It needs to be emphasized that Sri Aurobindo was one of those rare thinkers whose thought was not confined only to the theoretical implications of a problem but who, apparently withdrawn, was in touch with life and who tested his theories against the actual demands of practical politics. He was a practical visionary.

A word may be said here about his advocacy of force and violence, if necessary, in the struggle against foreign domination. This is sometimes levelled against him as a criticism, and it is said he was really an anarchist and a terrorist. As for his being an anarchist, the proposition can be dismissed out of hand as absurd. He sought to replace British rule not by anarchy but by national rule. Regarding his terrorism, there is now little doubt that he was not only closely in touch with secret revolutionary groups throughout the country but, in Bengal, was for a considerable time their secret leader and inspirer. This charge, if such it can be termed, is one which is fully in consonance with his basic political theory as he put it: Which son, if his mother was being crushed and humiliated by an alien aggressor, would hesitate to use every means, including force and violence, to effect her deliverance? For Sri Aurobindo the deliverance of the Motherland from foreign rule was the one over-riding consideration. To this end all means were admissible, including violence, especially when the foreigners themselves were in India as the result of forcible conquest.

Finally, we come to his ideal of human unity and of India's

role in the international community. Although his latter exposition of this concept took place mainly after 1910, even in the 1893-1910 period it is both hinted at and sometimes clearly brought out in his political writings. Among the theoretical compulsions behind Sri Aurobindo's political goal of complete independence was the undying conviction that India must be free not for herself alone, but for the good of entire mankind. He felt that India had a spiritual message which was urgently needed in the world of the twentieth century, in fact that she was destined to lead mankind up the next step of spiritual evolution. This was one of the reasons why he was so adamant that the political goal should be nothing less than complete independence, since only then could India fulfil her truc destiny or *swadharma* in the broader international community. This, it may be added, was one of the major motives of the Indian Renaissance.

At a time when India was firmly and securely under British rule, and the prospect of her becoming, free appeared extremely dim, it is a tribute to Sri Aurobindo's breadth of vision that he was able clearly to foresee her destiny as a free nation, and to stress the importance of the contribution that she must make to the world community. In his celebrated 'Open Letter to My Countrymen', written in 1909, he says:

> "Our ideal of patriotism proceeds on the basis of love and brotherhood and it looks beyond the unity of the nation and envisages the ultimate unity of mankind. But it is a unity of brothers, equals and free men that we seek, not the unity of master and serf, of devourer and devoured."[2]

This lofty idealism in a way forecast the importance that free India has given to the maintenance of world peace, and the special role she has played therein. Sri Aurobindo's nationalism never descended into chauvinism or obscurantist revivalism. He always placed it in a broader, international context, and even in the white heat of political controversy he never lost sight of

---

2. *Speeches*, p. 142. In his political writings Sri Aurobindo lays great stress upon this broader aspect of Indian nationalism. See, for example, Editorials in the *Bande Mataram* on 'The Asiatic Role' (April 12, 1908), 'The New Ideal' (April 12, 1908), 'Ideals Face to Face' (May 3, 1908), 'The Bedrock of Indian Nationalism' (June 4, 1908).

his ideal of human unity which far transcended local problems and had for its goal the reconciliation of all conflicts in a spiritual development. The theme recurs in almost all his writings, from the early passion of *Bhawani Mandir* and *Bande Mataram* to the mature reflections of his later monumental works such as *The Ideal of Human Unity, The Human Cycle, Essays on the Gita* and *The Life Divine,* and must be classed as one of his major contributions to modern Indian political theory. Although at the time he wrote the idea had mainly an academic interest, as India was then not free, yet it had the effect of raising the tone of the national movement and placing before it an ideal more elevated than that of national independence. That his ideal of human unity has to some extent been realized is a tribute to Sri Aurobindo's wisdom; that it has still not been fully translated into action is the measure of mankind's failure to rise to its full stature.

Sri Aurobindo thus emerges as a political thinker of unusual importance in modern Indian political thought. He was largely responsible for imparting an esoteric and spiritual significance to the national movement, for placing before it the inspiring ideal of complete independence, for invigorating the spirit of India by a reassessment of the true bases of her great cultural heritage, for expounding a practical system whereby the goal of independence could be achieved, and for placing the whole movement in the broader context of internationalism and the ideal of human unity. For a person so averse to propaganda to have done all this in the short period of hardly five years of active political life is an achievement of no mean importance. Sri Aurobindo must be counted among the great builders of modern India, as one who contributed nobly towards laying the foundations for the edifice of national freedom which Mahatma Gandhi and others later reared. Even after 1910 his interest in Indian freedom remained undiminished, and he lived to see the fruition of his work when India finally achieved Independence on his seventy-fifth birthday, the fifteenth of August, 1947. As he himself said, it was more than a fortuitous accident.

The Political Philosophy Of Sri Aurobindo

V.P. VARMA

A many-sided genius, Sri Aurobindo (1872-1950) was a poet, metaphysician, yogi, teacher, writer, and above all, a social and political philosopher. *The Ideal of Human Unity* and *The Human Cycle* are his significant contributions to the domain of political philosophy.[1] Sri Aurobindo had deep and abiding interest in politics. From the days of his studentship in England when he had joined a secret society called "The Dagger and the Lotus" till the end, he had profound concern for politicis. Not only was he a foremost leader of the extremist school of political thought and action, but even after his retirement in 1910 from active politics, he was making political pronouncements and issuing statements. Influential leaders of that time like Lala Lajpat Rai and C.R. Das met him in Pondicherry to find out his reactions to the various political developments in the country. In his independence day message, Sri Aurobindo had categorically affirmed his undiminished faith in a free and united India, implying thereby his non-acceptance of the partition of the country. He prognosticated and warned his countrymen against the catastrophe of Chinese imperialistic excesses, in case Tibet was surrendered to the Chinese.

Ordinarily, there is supposed to exist some contradiction bet-between Yoga as the dedicated pursuit of a contemplative life and politics as concerned with power, mundane values and hectic activities. There is some antithesis between them if we equate politics with the Machiavellian pursuit of political power by taking recourse to instruments of force, chicanery, manipulation and fraud. If we believe with Hobbes that politics is the relentless

1. For details see V. P. Varma, *The Political Philosophy of Sri Aurobindo.* Bombay, 1960.

and remorseless institution of centralized sovereign omnicompetence then certainly there is a contradiction between politics and a higher spiritual life. If we think that politics means joining the caravan of one's country's army for the suppression of other weaker peoples, then, of course, the philosopher will remain confined to his sanctuary, and not have to do anything with this sordid glorification of national interest and egoism at the cost of moral values and principles. Sri Aurobindo conceived of the life of the Indian politician during the early years of the twentieth century as an adventure in the higher life because the latter had to identify himself with nobler pursuits for the redemption of the honour of the motherland.[2] Even as a Yogi he formulated the gospel of the spiritualized society and the gnostic community where audacious coercion will be replaced by the higher law of spiritual management of the affairs of men.

Sri Aurobindo was a political philosopher in three senses. First, on the basis of idealistic and spiritual metaphysics he had attempted the construction of a system of political thought. He had taken as his starting point those metaphysical propositions of spiritual idealism, evolution and supramental transformation which he had developed in *The Savitri*, *The Life Divine*, *The Synthesis of Yoga, Essays on the Gita* and other works, and attempted to draw their social and political implications in *The Ideal of Human Unity* and *The Human Cycle*.

Secondly, even when Sri Aurobindo was a political leader his actions and political speeches were permeated with philosophical principles. His *Speeches, The Doctrine of Passive Resis-*

2. Cf. Sri Aurobindo, *Savitri*, Book VII, Canto 6, p. 174.
Thou hast come down into a struggling world,
To aid a blind and suffering mortal race,
To open to light the eyes that could not see,
To bring down bliss into the heart of grief,
To make thy life a bridge 'twixt earth and heaven;
If thou wouldst save the toiling universe,
The vast universal suffering feel as thine:
Thou must bear the sorrow that thou claim'st to heal;
The day-bringer must walk in darkest night,
He who would save the world must share its pain.
If he knows not grief,
How shall he find grief's cure?
If far he walks above mortality's head,
How shall the mortal reach that too high path?"

tance, Dharma Aur Jatiyata, The Ideal of the Karmayogin and his numerous editorials in the *Bande Mataram* breathe a spirit of philosophical idealism and there is present in them a spiritual call.

Thirdly, even in his metaphysical and esoteric treatises, Sri Aurobindo never loses sight of the world and its problems and the technics of their solution.[3] Politics is concerned with the authoritative administration and organisation of the affairs and resources of human society and even at the height of his supernal flights Sri Aurobindo never forgets the world. He is vitally concerned with the creation of a non-coercive socio-political order founded on peace, spiritual legitimacy, participation based on communion, mutuality and fraternity.

The most important contribution of Sri Aurobindo as a political philosopher is his advocacy of a responsible, constitutional and popular system of government in India entirely free from alien control. He formulated this ideal for the country in the pages of the *Bande Mataram* in 1907. This bold assertion of the political aspirations of the country was indeed remarkable specially at a time when other leaders like Ranade and Gokhale were passionate believers in the divine dispensation of India's membership in the British imperial system.[4] Twenty-two years earlier than the Lahore session of 1929, when the Indian National Congress accepted the goal of complete independence, Sri Aurobindo in his prophetic utterances stressed the notion of perfect democratic *Swaraj*. This challenging and defying ideal was set forth at a time when the national soul was sezied with a great predicament. This notion of absolute democratic *Swaraj* appears to be a richer and fuller concept than the Wilsonian and the Bolshevic notions of self-determination. Self-determination signifies freedom and national autonomy from imperial domination and despotic control. But Sri Aurobindo contemplated a complete remaking of India's fully autonomous political

---

3. *Letters, Second Series*, p. 68. "....both the Mother and myself have had one side of the mind as positive and as insistent on practical results and more so than any Russell can be."

4. In an article entitled "Swaraj" (Feb. 23, 1908), Sri Aurobindo, is eloquent over "Swaraj without any limitation or reservation". *On Nationalism*, p. 61.

existence on the basis of her recovered soul.[5]

But although Sri Aurobindo was a triumphant champion of the full and absolute independence of the country he, always in his latter writings, is careful to warn against the degeneration of assertive self-determination into a blind imperialistic and fascistic chauvinism which is concerned with an irrational glorification of the national ego. He is always careful to distinguish his romantic theory of the soul of the nation[6] which stresses spiritual ideals, from the fascistic irrationalism which exalts instincts, blind passions of conquest, absolutism of the state,[7] party and leader, and racial superiority.

Sri Aurobindo's championship of the ideal of responsible and constitutional government of India and the entire elimination of British imperial control, was a call for the Indianization of the political movement. He wanted to root the freedom movement in the hearts and the heritage of the people. Hence from 1908 onwards he stressed that India's freedom was destined to fructify because only a free country could broadcast the message of the *Vedas*, the *Upanishads*,[8] the *Yoga*, the *Gita*, the *Puranas* and *Tantra* to the world. The *Vedic* and Vedantic teachers had incalculated the supreme gospel of spiritual freedom; Buddha, Nanak, Chaitanya, Kabir, Tukaram and other saints were heralds of the notion of social freedom; the message of

---

5. *On Nationalism*, p. 39. "Nationalism is an *avatar* and cannot be slain. Nationalism is a divinely appointed *sakti* of the Eternal and must do its God-given work before it returns to the bosom of the Universal Energy from which it come".
6. Cf. *The Volksgeist*.
7. Although, in a sense, both Hegel and Sri Aurobindo accept the rationality of the state, there are some important differences between their positions. To Hegel, rationality is opposed to the romanticist emphasis on feelings and subjective emotions. But to Sri Aurobindo, the rational stage of human evolution is opposed to the preceding infra-rational stage. Rationality, to him, only signifies ordering and mechanical efficiency while, in Hegel's view, rationality postulates universality.
8. According to Sri Aurobindo, (*Dharma Aur Jatiyata* (in Hindi), p. 48, the roots of monism, nominalism, realism, evolutionism, positivism, hedonism and utilitarianism could be traced in the Upanishads. But contrary to the teachings of Samkara, Deussen and Vivekananda, Sri Aurobindo *Aravinda Mandira Men* (in Hindi), p. 51, regarded that the Vedic gnosis was at a higher level than that of the Upanishads.

political freedom was the third basic component of the testament of liberty. India was the "chosen" land of God for spreading the message of spiritual emancipation.[9] *Swaraj* has been revealed to the nation in order that through political freedom India would regain her spiritual freedom and make her spiritual deliverance available to the world. The gospel of a "National, Pan Indian" *Swaraj*[10] was no exotic ideal, suddenly accepted in the days of Curzonian frustrations. *Swaraj* was the political culmination of the centripetal tendency in Indian history which is associated with the career and exploits of Sri Krishna, Chandragupta, Asoka, the Gupta emperors, Shivaji, Bajirao and other great Indian heroes. Hence at a time when the political leaders of the moderate school were drinking to their heart's content at the fountain of Burke, Bentham, Mill and Spencer, and were quoting Gladstone and Morley, Sri Aurobindo along with Tilak pleaded that the national movement should be thoroughly rooted in the philosophical and cultural heritage of the country.[11] Thus, by advocating complete independence for India he hurled a signal to stop to the 'Occidentalizers'.

Furthermore, Sri Aurobindo stressed the need of moral training for the leaders and followers if this great ideal was to be realized. Political movements, to obtain success, must be informed with profound philosophic and moral ideals and visions. Behind the Maratha empire of Shivaji lay the idealism of Ramadas and it may be said that behind the French Revolution lay the teachings of Rousseau, Diderot and Voltaire. But mere verbal adherence to ideals is not enough. The goddess of liberty requires great sufferings and is only pleased when individuals and nations are ready to sacrifice their all for her sake. To bask in the sunshine of liberty one has to give up the charms and plea-

9. *On Nationalism*, pp. 62-65.

10. *Ibid.*, p. 87.

11. *On Nationalism*, pp. 51-52, Sri Aurobindo earnestly pleaded that a vital and robust Indian nationalism could not neglect any section of the people. The Hindu masses, the "slumbering mass of Islam", the shopkeepers, artisans, peasants, "the submerged classes" and even the tribal population had to be brought within the comprehensive fold of nationalism.

sures of a complacent easy-going existence.[12] India was matched against the imperial might of a foreign European power, and Indians with their apathy, torpor, inertia and ease could not hope to eliminate the British merely by writing bombastic editorials and indulging in heroic and melodramatic orations. If liberty was the ideal to be realized there had to be cultivated a robust heart which would be steeled against all fears, trials and persecutions.[13] For the sake of realizing the freedom of the nation there had to be developed the readiness not only to sacrifice money and family ties but even to mount the gallows. Hence Sri Aurobindo always stressed that suffering was essential because without undergoing it the nation could never be free. Even sufferings and humiliations at the hands of the imperialistic aggressors were in the divine dialectic for training India in the path of self-reliant nationhood.

As a social philosopher, Sri Aurobindo recognised the evils of the caste system as it was operating in contemporary India. Caste was based on the negation of democratic rights and was a neutralization of the older Vedantic gospel of equality. It is true, however, that he did not devote his attention and energies at any extensive level to the eradication of the evils of the caste. Like Tilak, he believed that the immediate concern of the country was the elimination of foreign rule. Thus, political liberation was the uppermost concern of the Nationalist Party to which he belonged. But there is no doubt that he was very much aware of the evils the caste organisation was perpetrating on Indian society. As a philosopher of Indian history, Sri Aurobindo acknowledged that the old *varna* organisation was based on functional differentiation and specialization of skill. The old

12. Cf. Sri Aurobindo's statement, (*The Human Cycle* (Indian ed.), pp. 120-121), that because of aesthetic immersion divorced from ethical impulse, the Renaissance (a) weakened Italy and (b) called forth the Reformation.

13. *Letters, Second Series,* p. 77 "My whole life has been a struggle with hard realities, from hardships and starvation in England and constant dangers and fierce difficulties to the far greater difficulties continually cropping up here in Pondicherry, external and internal. My life has been a battle from its early years and is still a battle: the fact that I wage it now from a room upstairs and by spiritual means as well as others that are external makes no difference to its character."

social structure was founded upon functional specialization and was never a scheme for the selfish distribution of privileges, power and property. It was a scheme of social organisation wherein specific *varna* had specific duties to perform. Sri Aurobindo pointed out that while the European class structure was oriented towards the distribution of powers and rights and was based on economic criteria, the old Hindu *varna* system was based on the recognition of moral and psychological differentiations of individuals and groups and was a scheme for the distribution of duties. It did not sanction any concept of the humiliation of the lower strata. In ancient India as well as in medieval times towering personalities flourished who had Sudra antecedents. People like Vidura, Chokha Mela and the Chandala who taught Shankaracharya,[14] are examples of the fact that the ancient social system of *varna* was based upon the recognition that all groups and individuals were participants in the cosmic body of one God-*Virat Purusha.* In the ancient Indian system, heredity did enter into the structure but entered into it as a subordinate element. Hence it is clear that in the scheme of ancient values, the caste did perform a necessary function.

But the recognition of the merits of the system does not amount to a blindness towards recognising its perversions and degeneration as operating in the contemporary Indian society. Caste represented loss of flexibility and the exaltation of lifeless social standards. The purely mateial criteria of occupation and birth had become the leading factors resulting in the neglect of the moral, psychological and spiritual qualifications which were supposed to determine one's *varna.* Sri Aurobindo was a merciless denouncer "of the caste arrogance, exclusiveness and superiority"[15] which had led to national degeneration. It was essential to bring transformation in this social system. When some of the revivalists and conservative defenders of the *status quo* charged Sri Aurobindo with incorporating notions of socialism, he candidly pointed out that even socialism in its fundamental roots was an old Asiatic conception rather than a European infiltration. Socialism was a means for providing some kind of leisure and peace for the development

---

14. *On Nationalism,* p. 20.
15. *Ibid.,* p. 21.

of the human personality. He acknowledged even in his early writings in 1907 that without socialism, democracy would merely remain a tendency that would never reach its fulfilment. It would only be a " a rule of the masses by a small aristocratic and monied class with the consent and votes of the artisan classes over the rest. Socialistic democracy is the only true democracy..."[16] Sri Aurobindo recognised that the goal of ancient Hindu philosophy as well as the original intention of the *varna* was some kind of a socialistic democracy based on equal and harmonious distribution of functions[17] but caste as operating in the country did pose a serious problem. It was difficult to acknowledge that a caste-governed society could be the field for the realisation of equality and liberty. Hence Sri Aurobindo denounced monopoly in all its forms including social oligarchy.

The second important contribution of Sri Aurobindo to political science is his stress on freedom. He is an advocate of full political freedom for all nations; he wants the betterment of the economic life of the people; he is an opponent of political and economic imperialism and is a trenchant critic of coercive authoritarianism. His attachment to the concept of liberty is deep and profound. But never would he equate liberty with bohemian libertarianism, particularistic, egoistic and sensationalistic satisfaction or an anarchical display of arbitrary self-will. He is categorical in his statement that freedom can be enjoyed only in the context of subservience to the moral and spiritual laws which essentially are the laws of God.[18] Like some of the Vedic sages he adheres to the concept of *Rita*—immanental

---

16 *Ibid.*, p. 22.

17. Sri Aurobindo was never a champion of absolute equality. He says, *(The National Value of Art*, p. 11 :*)* "Only a few, the rare aristocrats of the earth can really and truly think...the aristocracy of knowledge, undisturbed insight and intellectual ability. It emerges, though it has not yet emerged, and in any future management of human society this natural inequality will play an important part".

18. *War and Self-Determination*, p. 35. "...true freedom is only possible if we live in the infinite, live, as the Vedanta bids us, in and from our self-existent being...", *ibid.* p. 48. "the kingdom of God within and in the race is the basis on which man must come in the end to the possession of himself..."

cosmic laws of good and truth.[19] Like Gautam Buddha he believes in Dharma—primordial laws which lead to the triumph of good over evil. Unless the commandments and promulgations of God are accepted there can be no freedom, no *Swaraj*. Hence like Tilak, Rabindranath and Gandhi,[20] Sri Aurobindo also states that only the subjugation of the passions of the lower self[21] can lead one to the enjoyment of genuine *Swaraj*.[22]

Sri Aurobindo accepts the moral and spiritual approach to freedom and he pleads for the incorporation of a superior transforming power in democracy, socialism, communism, anarchism and humanism. He does recognise the educational and political good conferred on the community by the practices of the democratic formula, but asserts that democracy is bound to degenerate into oligarchy and plutocracy unless those in control of the decision-making centres of power exercise legitimate authority in consonance with moral and spiritual criteria. The socialist ideal of the enhancement of the economic resources and opportunities for all through the formation of a free association of procedures cannot be brought into existence unless socialism undergoes a moral and spiritual transmutation. Sri Aurobindo is in sympathy with the communist crusade against exploitation, expropriation, suppression of the proletariat and the transformation of the state machine into an agent for serving the good of the capitalists. But he is definite that

19. Discussing the question of "predetermination and free will", Sri Aurobindo, *(The Isha Upanishad*, pp. 64-65*)*, points out that viewed by itself the realm of Vijnana would seem to be a state of predetermination, the realm of Virat, if taken separately, would be one of law and predetermination, while viewed by itself the realm of Manishi would be a state of plasticity and free will.
20. *Letters, Second Series,* for Sri Aurobindo's comments on Gandhi's views regarding "change of religion" (pp. 588-89), "equality and hierarchy" of caste (pp. 590-92), and "evolution beyond knowledge" (pp. 592-94). In *Aravinda Mandira Men* (In Hindi, p. 74), Gandhi's *sadhanu* is regarded as being rooted in morality.
21. *The Synthesis of Yoga,* Vol. 1, pp. 64-65. Sri Aurobindo points out that the Gita enunciates the cultivation of "wide equal oneness of the spirit", which represents a higher ideal than indifference and resignation or the stoic notion of detachment and aloofness. See also *Gita Ki Bhumika* (In Hindi, pp. 115-116).
22. *Thoughts and Glimpses,* p. 25, : "Freedom is the law of being in its illimitable unity, secret master of all Nature".

communism in action has meant dictatorship of an authoritarian party and proletarian imperialism.[23] He is positive that the good society cannot be born in blood. Unmoralized and unregenerated force can never be the midwife of the new society. Anarchism will degenerate into vitalistic excesses and assassinations of political rivals unless it is informed with a moral and spiritual purpose. Humanism is a formula advocated by some people who do not believe in the spiritual laws of God and at the same time are not ready to reduce man to a physico-chemical conglomeration. But humanism, so long as it is content to boost the empirical man with his contemporary aspirations and affections, can never be a permanent solution. Humanism is to be preferred as an antidote to dictatorship and coercive domination as practised in some imperial systems, but the true aim is not to perpetuate the blundering egoistic[24] man as he exists today but to chasten his passions and make of him a better man so that he can render service for the betterment of society. Thus, although Sri Aurobindo accepts some of the merits of each of these five political concepts—democracy, socialism, communism, anarchism and humanism, he pleads for a transformation of the empirical ego of man.[25] Thus, alone, can the divine society based on spiritual gnoses be realized on earth. Just as Plato, St. Augustine and Fichte propounded the idealistic synthesis of philosophic consciousness and political rulership, so also Sri Aurobindo teaches the transformation[26] of the present political

23. *War and Self-Determination*, p. 37 : "The earliest use of liberty and democracy by the emancipated proletariat has been the crude forceful tyranny of an ill-organised labour oligarchy over a quite disorganised peasantry and an impotently recalcitrant bourgeoisie.
24. Sri Aurobindo, *(The Isha Upanishad*, pp. 104-105*)*, holds that Savita dispels the evil dream of egoism.
25. According to Sri Aurobindo, *(The Renaissance in India*, p. 59*)*, the drift of the notions of Nietzsche, Bergson and James "is much too externally pragmatic and vitalistic to be genuinely assimilable by the Indian spirit...".
26. In *The Synthesis of Yoga* (Pondicherry, 1955), p. 55. Sri Aurobindo refers to the "integralisation of a widely perfect spiritual existence" as a "consummation being no other than the kingdom of heaven within reproduced in the kingdom of heaven without." In the *Hymns to Mystic Fire* (1st ed., p. XLI), expounding the Vedic notions of transformation he says that *Agni*, representing knowledge stands for Ascent and Indra, representing mind, stands for Descent.

system based on passions, coercion and perversity into politics founded on mutuality, equality, reciprocity, spontaneous co-operation, harmony[27], love and goodwill.[28]

The third important political contribution of Sri Aurobindo is the theory of a World State. The retention of armed sovereign states is undoubtedly a great danger to world peace. Hence eventual renunciation of sovereignty is essential. But the nation-states may not and will not agree to that proposition. Hence Sri Aurobindo in the first stage pleads for a world confederation. But in the second stage, he is committed to the ideal of a world state. In the case of the United States of America, the transformation of the confederation into the federal form of government was easy and since 1789 the American federation is continuing. But in th case of the formation of a world state the transition will not be so easy because many diverse countries and cultures are concerned and they will very grudgingly accept the renunciation of even a part of sovereignty. But the abandonment of sovereign egoism is essential if humanity has to escape the devastations of nuclear annihilation. The uncontrolled ambitions of nation-states have to be tamed so that the ideal of human unity whose religious foundations appear in Buddhism and Christianity[29] can be made a political reality. The transformation of nationalism into some form of a bigger and comprehensive world organisation is the imperative need of the hour.[30]

27. Sri Aurobindo, *(The Isha Upanishad*, p. 21*)*. "The result of the separation is the inability to enter into harmony and oneness with the universe and a consequent inability to possess and enjoy it."
28. *War and Self-Determination*, p. 30 : "Only when his race knows God and lives in the Divine, will the ideal sense of his strivings begin to unfold itself and the kingdom be founded, "*rajyam samriddham*."
29. P. A. Sorokin, *(Social Philosophies of an Age of Crisis*, pp. 122-27*)*, finds the notions of "one world" in the Gospel of St. John. Also Schubart, *(Europa und die seele des Ostens)*. Cf. Hilaire Belloc, *Crisis of Our Civilization*, pp. 6, 235. Belloc held against Gibbon, Freeman, Carlyle and Macaulay that Catholicism was a creative force in Europe and hoped that only the Catholic philosophy could initiate the curbing of monopoly, usury and abuses of private property.
30. *Messages*, First Series, p. 8 : "...international forms and institutions must appear, perhaps such developments as dual or multilateral citizenship, willed interchange or voluntary fusion of cultures."

It is also in the divine dialectic and efforts have to be made for the realization of this great aim. Nationalism is important but it is only a stage and not the terminus. Human unity founded on the moral aspirations of old prophets and a spiritual awareness of the potentialities of mankind is the next stage of evolution[31] and it alone can safeguard human dignity, moral rectitude, and cultural heritage.

---

31. *Savitri*, Book VII, Canto VI, p. 178 and Book XI, Canto I, p. 334 :
"This world is a vast unbroken totality,
A deep solidarity joins its contrary powers.

* * *

A key turned in a mystic lock of Time
But where the silence of the gods had passed,
A greater harmony from the stillness born
Surprised with joy and sweetness yearning hearts,
An ecstasy and a laughter and a cry.
A power leaned down, a happiness found its home
Over wide earth brooded the infinite bliss."

Sri Aurobindo : The Prophet of Renascent India

BIMLA BHAGAT

WRITING to his wife on 30th August, 1905, Sri Aurobindo spoke of the three insanities that possessed his being:

"My first insanity consists in my firm belief that the qualifications, the genius, the higher education, the learning, and the wealth that the Lord has given me, all belong to Him. We have a right to spend only as much as is required for the upkeep of the family and as much as is absolutely needed. What remains ought to be rendered back to the Lord...."

"My second madness which has recently taken hold of me is, happen what may, I must see God face to face, whatever the means....Whom I love and to Whom I pray that I may devote my life...."

"My third madness is with regard to Mother India. Other people look upon their country as some material thing, consisting of vast plains, fields, forests, mountains and rivers. I look upon India as my Mother, I am devoted to her, I worship her".[1]

In a sense the first madness—the conviction that he was born for a mission—was a necessary condition for the other two, and these were to govern Sri Aurobindo's thought right to his

1. Quoted by R.R. Diwakar, *Mahayogi Sri Aurobindo*, Bombay, 1957, pp. 145-47.

end. The two might seem to us discrete—the soul's quest for God and the service of one's Motherland but for Sri Aurobindo they were two sides of the same coin. What distinguished India for him, as we shall see, was its preoccupation with the spiritual goal of union with God, and he who wished to follow the dictates of his great Mother must train his mind on that ultimate goal.

As the letter I have just quoted implies, the madness for India chronologically came first. Looking back in retrospect in the early sixties, Jawaharlal Nehru was to remark, "It is extraordinary that a person who had spent fourteen of the most formative years of his life, from the age of 7 to 21, cut off from India and steeped in the European classics and the England of his day, should have become, in later years, the brilliant champion of Indian nationalism based on the philosophic and the spiritual background of Indian thought."[2] Strangely enough, what Nehru overlooked was that his own career exhibited a rather similar pattern. Sri Aurobindo, however, provided a more extreme example. Born in the home of a fervent Anglophile, his entire education from his early years was pursued under English teachers and the young Sri Aurobindo was even kept innocent of his mother tongue. Unlike Nehru he was not only a master of the English language, but was proficient in the classical languages of Europe and conversant with the classical background of the Western way of life. But in spite of all this, Aurobindo realised that one's own country, one's own native tradition, could provide something that an alien one, however, well mastered, could not. As is well-known, he decided to forego the ICS, and preferred to become a college teacher, using his time for a systematic and extensive study of Indian languages and of the Indian tradition.

With each passing year he grew more convinced of the truth that India's salvation lay not in blindly imitating the West, but in understanding and vigorously pursuing the law of its own identity. For any healthy development one needed faith in one's own identity and the freedom to pursue its logic. Liberty "is the first condition of life," Sri Aurobindo was to declare, and his active participation in the Indian National Movement can be best understood as an effort to translate this into a political reality.

---

2. "Foreword", Karan Singh, *Prophet of Indian Nationalism*, London, 1963, p. 7.

At a time when Gokhale could say, "only men outside lunatic asylums could think or talk of independence...there is no alternative to British rule, not only now but for a long time to come."[3] Sri Aurobindo, impelled by this awareness for the need for liberty, pointed to *Puran Swaraj* as his country's prime goal. "All expectations of moral regeneration which leaves freedom out of the count is a dream," he declared. "First freedom, then regeneration....To recover possession of the State is therefore the first business of the awakened Indian consciousness."[4] In fact both Gandhi and Nehru were to arrive at this conclusion after many years of social and political activity. Sri Aurobindo, however, on account of his remarkable capacity to go to first principles, began his work in the field of politics on this very assumption. "The primary requisite for national progress, national reform, is the free habit of free and healthy national thought and action which is impossible in a state of servitude. Political freedom is the life-breath of a nation," he affirmed, and "to attempt social reform, educational reform, industrial expansion, the moral improvement of the race without aiming first and foremost at political freedom is the very height of ignorance and futility".[5]

Sri Aurobindo's contribution to the Indian National Movement has been examined at some length by scholars. There are, however, a point or two to which I would like to draw attention to bring out the individuality of his approach. The first of these involves the transformation of the belief that India had a distinct spiritual identity of its own into the concept of a great Mother who sustained her children amid much suffering and whom her children must serve with all their strength in order to rescue her from her oppressors. To speak of one's country as though it were a mother was in itself not new. It was, in fact, conventional enough. But Sri Aurobindo was to give the concept a wholly new vitality because for him it was not merely a convention but a fact of experience, something that was in a sense literally true. The variety and uniqueness of India's topography, its languages, arts, cultures, peoples, the glory of its past and the pain of its present, were all factors that bound one to it. But the sap that

3. Quoted by Karan Singh, *op. cit.* p. 79.
4. Quoted by S.K. Mitra, *Sri Aurobindo and Indian Freedom*, Madras, 1948, p. 48.
5. *Bande Mataram*, 9th April, 1907.

kept alive one's love for one's country and ensured that it remained pure must be "the realisation of the Motherhood of God in the country, the vision of the Mother, the perpetual contemplation, adoration and service of the Mother."[6] Accordingly, in Sri Aurobindo's case, patriotism got assimilated into a form of mother-worship of the kind Ramakrishna had helped to popularise. For the British, in the words of the Rowlatt Committee, it may have come to represent "a remarkable instance of the perversion of religious ideals to political purposes"[7]! but it was precisely such a conviction that enabled Sri Aurobindo to give to nationalism a spiritual character and make it, as we shall see later, a necessary step on the road to internationalism.

The second point has to do with what we may term the ethics of the struggle for national independence. Students of the Indian National Movement, as also Karan Singh and Diwakar, have shown how Sri Aurobindo had anticipated Gandhi's programme of non-cooperation, passive resistance and swadeshi by well over a decade. In fact Sri Aurobindo's contributions to the *Bande Mataram* from 9th to 23rd April, 1907, collected subsequently under the title, *The Doctrine of Passive Resistance,* represent the first full and detailed discussion of the philosophy of non-violent, passive resistance or, as Sri Aurobindo called it, "defensive resistance", and its special application to the Indian situation. However far-fetched Sri Aurobindo's analysis may have seemed at the time, Gandhiji was to develop the national movement on the lines he had suggested. History, in his very life-time, was to prove him right. The important thing to which I wish to draw attention, however, is not the relationship with Gandhiji but the difference. Gandhiji was to virtually make a creed of *Ahimsa*. Sri Aurobindo's approach was, however, not absolute on this point. He argued in favour of it on two counts: first, he felt, such passive resistance demanded a kind of spiritual strength and inner discipline—"soul force"—which the people of India possessed as a part of their native tradition. Second, the British Empire, on account of the conditions of modern technology, possessed a military strength that was difficult to overcome by an unarmed nation. The British were able to govern and exploit India on account of

---

6. *The Doctrine of Passive Resistance*, Pondicherry, 1952, pp. 83-84.
7. Quoted by Karan Singh, *op. cit*., p. 101.

the cooperation of the Indian people themselves, he argued. If this cooperation were denied to them and their goods were boycotted, their strength would be greatly undermined as also their will to continue to govern the country:

> "We are dissatisfied with the fiscal and economic conditions of British rule in India, with the foreign exploitation of the country....Accordingly we refuse to help the process of exploitation and impoverishment in our capacity as consumers, we refuse henceforth to purchase foreign and especially British goods or to condone their purchase by others. By an organised and relentless boycott of British goods, we propose to render the further exploitation of the country impossible".[8]

I have already remarked on Sri Aurobindo's capacity in viewing any issue to go to its very roots. Nowhere is this gift more apparent than in his analysis of the problems of India's liberation. He points simultaneously to the source of British power—namely, the cooperation of the Indians themselves—and to their prime incentive for conquering and continuing in India—namely their interests as a trading nation. Having analysed the problems this far, he proposes a mode of political action which would deny the British the local support on which they relied and the profit incentive which had brought them out to India and encouraged them to stay on.

Sri Aurobindo's *Open Letter to My Countrymen,* written shortly after his release from Alipore jail in 1909, covers the entire ground. In fact, it contains all the basic tenets of the Gandhian philosophy of political action, but with a difference: passive resistance for Sri Aurobindo is only a means, one of many, for attaining the chosen goal. A great admirer of the *Gita*, Sri Aurobindo did not rule out the use of violence and force to secure an end that was just and right. In this he was nearer to the ancient tradition than was Gandhiji. The Vedic approach, more clearly than any other great religious tradition, has maintained that there can be no single code or ethic that can cover all human situations. As Lord Krishna's message to Arjuna underlines, each situation dictates its own ethic or dharma, and

---

8. *The Doctrine of Passive Resistance*, pp. 36-37.

the greatness of the Indian tradition may be said to lie in clearly recognising this principle and taking a comprehensive view of things. It was in the spirit of this tradition that Vivekananda remarked, "Buddha ruined us and so did Christ ruin Greece and Rome" by preaching to all men an ethic of pacifism which should have been meant only for the *sannyasin* or the spiritual seeker.[9] Sri Aurobindo was very clear on this point and repeatedly insisted that a nation must not undermine its manhood by an overemphasis on pacifism. It was on acount of this that he attacked the approach of the moderates to the issue of political reform. "We desire to put an end to petitioning." he argued, "until such a strength is created in the country that a petition will only be a courteous form of demand."[10] Passive resistance had much to recommend it in the Indian context. Even so,

> "There is a limit, however, to passive resistance. So long as the action of the executive is peaceful and within the rules of the fight, the passive resister scrupulously maintains his attitude of passivity, but he is not bound to do so a moment beyond. To submit to illegal or violent methods of coercion, to accept outrage and hooliganism as part of the legal procedure of the country, is to be guilty of cowardice, and by dwarfing national manhood, to sin against the divinity within ourselves and the divinity in our motherland".

None could see more clearly than Sri Aurobindo the immense relevance of passive resistance as a political weapon in the Indian context, and yet no one had less use for it if it became an instrument of the weak, a philosophy that made for a nation of pacifists.

> "Passive resistance cannot build up a strong and great nation unless it is masculine, bold and ardent in its spirit and ready at any moment and at the slightest notice to supplement itself with active resistance. We do not want to develop a nation of women who know only to suffer and not how to strike".[11]

---

9. *Collected Works*, Vol. V, Calcutta, p. 357.
10. *The Doctrine of Passive Resistance*, p. 73.
11. *Ibid.*, pp. 62-65.

Just as Lord Krishna had directed his energies in helping Arjuna to overcome his pacifist scruples, Sri Aurobindo addressed himself to the moderates in the Indian National Movement and sought to radicalise them. Passive resistance was, for him, a means, not an end. Considered as almost an end in the Gandhian fashion, it meant for him an inevitable undermining of the will, manhood, and dignity of a nation. And so while he preached in public a mass movement based on passive resistance, in private he associated with secret societies based on a philosophy of terror and violence by a band of select political *sannyasins* in order to undermine the morale of the British in the country. He thus anticipated at once the two great philosophies of revolution that have dominated the modern world, those represented by Gandhi and Martin Luther King on the one hand, and by Mao Tse-Tung and Che Guevera on the other.

Gandhi showed what could be made by the instrument of passive resistance whose application Sri Aurobindo had defined, while Mao Tse-Tung relying on the mode of violence, showed how a people in spite of every obstacle could win back their unity and power. It is indeed interesting to observe how in Sri Aurobindo's own life-time the two great nations of Asia, India and China, renewed themselves by relying on one or the other of the two philosophies of political action that he had defined. To us they may seem mutually contradictory, but that the two could be combined and made to complement each other as Sri Aurobindo envisaged, has been borne out by the recent traumatic events across our eastern borders. Passive resistance under the leadership of Mujibur Rahman built up a momentum in East Bengal even greater than that generated by Gandhi in British India. But on the 25th March 1971, faced by unprecedented brutality and coercion, it became transformed overnight into a movement of "aggressive resistance" of guerrilla warfare and violence.

II

"....I have always held and said that India was arising, not to serve her own material interests only, to achieve expansion, greatness, power and prosperity—though these too she must not neglect—and certainly not like others to acquire domination of other peoples, but to live also for God and the world as a helper and leader of the whole human race".

More markedly than any other great leader of the Indian National Movement, Sri Aurobindo was a nationalist in the interests of internationalism, being convinced that India must be great not so much for its own sake as for that of the world. When on emerging from the Alipore jail, he addressed the first public meeting at Uttarpara (30th May, 1909), it was such a conviction that inflamed his words. During his confinement he had been vouchsafed a vision of God's purposes, and he now shared the divine message he had received with his countrymen:

> "When you go forth, speak to your nation always this word, that it is for the *Sanatana Dharma* that they arise, it is for the world and not for themselves that they arise. I am giving them freedom for the service of the world. When therefore it is said that India shall rise, it is the *Sanatana Dharma* that shall rise. When it is said that India shall be great, it is the *Sanatana Dharma* that shall be great. When it is said that India shall expand and extend herself, it is *Sanatana Dharma* that shall extend itself over the world."[12]

What Sri Aurobindo made of the spiritual message, the *Sanatana Dharma* that India could offer to the world and the synthesis it could help to effect form a subject too complex and too large for a full discussion here.[13] At best one can only point briefly to some of the more obvious features of his work. He had already realised while in Alipore jail the uniqueness of the Vedantic philosophy and its relevance to the modern world. As he declared at Uttarpara, the religion developed in India:

> "....is the one religion that can triumph over materialism by including and anticipating the discoveries of science and the speculations of philosophy. It is the one religion which impresses on mankind the closeness of God to us and embrace in its compass all the possible means by which man can

12. *Uttarpara Speech*, Pondicherry, 1968, pp. 16-17.
13. For a recent discussion of the subject I may refer the reader to K. D. Sethna's, *The Vision and Work of Sri Aurobindo*, Pondicherry, 1968.

approach God. It is the one religion which insists every movement on the truth which all religions acknowledge, that He is in all men and all things and that in Him we move and have our being. It is the one religion which enables us not only to understand and believe this truth but to realise it with every part of our being".[14]

If from 1905 to 1910 he was to concentrate on the problem of India's political emancipation, defining its nature and solution, on retiring to Pondicherry thereafter he was to focus on the mission that India must fulfil once it was free and independent.[15] When Albert Schweitzer came to speak of *Indian Thought and Its Development,* he noted in it a marked tendency towards "life-negation." Vivekananda, to some extent, had sought to reinterpret the Vedantic religion as one which affirmed life rather than denied it. Sri Aurobindo was to carry such an effort infinitely further.[16] Vivekananda may on occasion have decried the materialism of the West: for Sri Aurobindo, however, material fulfilment was a necessary step in a process that led to the final spiritual fulfilment. As he put it in an article in *Arya* (15th Sept. 1914), :

"The whole trend of modern thought and modern endeavour revealed itself to the observant eye as a large conscious effort of Nature in man to effect a general level of intellectual

---

14. *Uttarpara Speech*, pp. 18-19.
15. When Sri Aurobindo first moved to Pondicherry, many thought it represented a sudden shift in his life, a kind of break—even a betrayal of the mission with which he had started out. But he was essentially a *jnanin*, and having analysed the problem of India's freedom and having shown the road that led to liberation, he needed to stand apart from the thick of the struggle in order to crystallise and define the task which his country must take up once it was free.
16. If there was anyone who repeatedly anticipated Sri Aurobindo on various issues facing India, it was Vivekananda. The relationship between the two is well worth examining. It is significant to recall in this connection, that at Alipore, according to Sri Aurobindo himself, he was "hearing constantly the voice of Vivekananda speaking to me for a fortnight in the jail in my solitary meditation." Quoted by, A.B. Purani, *The Life of Sri Aurobindo*, Pondicherry, 1964, p. 129.

equipment, capacity, and further possibility of universalising the opportunities which modern civilisation affords for the mental life. Even the preoccupation of the European intellect, the protagonist of this tendency, with material Nature and the externals of existence, is a necessary part of the effort. It seeks to prepare a sufficient basis in man's physical being and vital energies and in his material environment for his full mental possibilities....It may even be said that the supra-physical can only be really mastered in its fullness, when we keep our feet firmly on the physical".

As evident from the above, Sri Aurobindo brought to bear an evolutionary perspective in treating of the subject in hand. He may have derived it from his education in the West, but the Indian doctrine of transmigration had already used it in a spiritual context. Sri Aurobindo applied the concept to the spiritual life of a whole nation, in fact of the human race. If the two wisdoms of East and West could be synthesised, he was convinced there could be a great leap forward in man's spiritual evolution. In *The Human Cycle, The Ideal of Human Unity, The Life Divine, The Synthesis of Yoga* and his numerous essays on the Superman, Sri Aurobindo dwelt on this tantalising new possibility. This in fact constituted the last and the greatest of his five dreams. As he recorded in his message for the fifteenth of August, 1947:

> "The final dream was a step in evolution which would raise man to a higher and larger consciousness and begin the solution of the problems which have perplexed and vexed him since he first began to think and to dream of individual perfection and a perfect society. This is still a personal hope and an idea, an ideal which has begun to take hold both in India and in the West on forward-looking minds....Here too, if this evolution is to take place, since it must proceed through a growth of the spirit and the inner consciousness the initiative can come from India and, although the scope must be universal, the central movement may be hers".[17]

---

17. Quoted by Karan Singh, p. 157.

The new phase in evolution, Sri Aurobindo heralded, was to be one which denied nothing, which assimilated every energy within the make-up of man to his higher development. Vivekananda had insisted on the need to integrate *Bhakti*, *Karma* and *Jnana* for the fullest attainment of the Self. Sri Aurobindo was to try out all the forms of Yoga, as Ramakrishna had tried out all the great religions of Man, and was to go even further. He turned to the tradition of Tantra and included its discoveries as well into his syncretic Yoga. The rational and the irrational, the physical and the intellectual were all manifestations of the One Life, and their energies had to be brought into harmony and harnessed to the one goal. If Vivekananda had criticised Buddhism for emasculating Indian society, Sri Aurobindo extended the same criticism to Shankara. By insisting on the sensory world as illusion, Shankara had denied the reality of the world of body and of intellect and had deprived the Vedantic religion of a basis in daily experience. "The perception of the spiritualised mind that the universe is an unreal dream can have no more absolute value to us, Sri Aurobindo declared, "than the perception of the materialised mind that God and the Beyond are an illusory idea." If the Reality was One as Advaitism affirmed, it was a contradiction in terms to speak of a principle of unreality working within it. "An Omnipresent reality is the Brahman, not an omnipresent cause of persistent illusion." (AW, XVIII, pp. 35, 30) "The real Monism", according to Sri Aurobindo :

> "is that which admits all things as the one Brahman and does not seek to bisect Its existence into two incompatible entities, an eternal Truth and an eternal Falsehood, Brahman and not-Brahman, Self and not-Self, a real Self and an unreal yet perpetual Maya. If it be true that the Self alone exists, it must be also true that all is the Self. And if this Self, God or Brahman is no helpless state, no bounded power, no limited personality, but the self-conscient All, there must be some good and inherent reason in it for the manifestation, to discover which we must proceed on the hypothesis of some potency, some wisdom, some truth of being in all that is manifested."[18]

18. *Sri Aurobindo, The Life Divine,* Sri Aurobindo Birth Centenary Library, Pondicherry, Volume XVIII, 1972, p. 31.

Sri Aurobindo's vision of the coming of the Superman may seem to us no more than an idealist's dream. But then the vision of an independent India seemed no less far-fetched when he first gave utterance to it. Idealist he certainly was, but with a difference. Like the Lord of the *Upanishads* his idealism was rooted on earth. Just as he was not content to announce the goal of freedom but went on to spell out the practical means for its realisation; so too it was not enough for him to speak of the world-wide propagation of a new spiritual awareness : he discussed at length the socio-political changes which it dictated. Sri Aurobindo saw the various aspects of life as complementing and supporting one another, and in his case a concern for the spiritual meant equally a concern for the social and the political planes of action. According to him a subterranean divine purpose was always at work and man was its chosen instrument on earth. This purpose manifested itself through a proces of socio-political and spiritual evolution, and Sri Aurobindo saw a movement towards greater and still greater unity as of the essence of this evolution. On the spiritual side, India had realised its purpose more fully than the rest of the world which had experimented with doctrainaire creeds that were, according to Sri Aurobindo, doomed from the first to ephemerality. It had been the cradle of the *Sanatana Dharma*, the eternal and universal religion which was to be the religion of the future. On the socio-political side, scholars and historians had generally regarded India as something of a failure. Its polity had been too loose and the centrifugal forces it embraced too great for it to hold together as a single viable unit. Sri Aurobindo, however, was to regard this quite differently. For him the Indian approach to polity was a counterpart of its approach to religion. It did not seek to impose an artificial unity from without. "The inner spirit is indeed one," India had realised, "but more than any other the spiritual life insists on freedom and variation in its self-expression and means of development." (AW, XV, p. 554). And so "the whole life of ancient India retained even in the time of the great kingdoms and empires its first principle and essential working and its social polity remained fundamentally a complex system of self-determined and self-governing communal bodies."[19]

---

19. *The Spirit and Form of Indian Phlity*, Pondicherry, 1947, p. 58.

India had never sought to impose unity from without. It had desisted from the temptation to let its centripetal tendency fulfil itself by destroying and levelling down the centrifugal forces obstructing its path. Instead it had been content to let a subterranean sense of spiritual unity develop and mature gradually on the assumption that the mechanical means for its outer political realisation would follow in due course. It had, in other words, in preference to a centralised militaristic authority, relied upon :

"...a spiritual oneness which would create a psychological oneness not dependent upon any intellectual or outward uniformity and compel a oneness of life not bound up with its mechanical means of unification, but ready always to enrich its secure unity by a free inner variation and a freely varied outer self-expression."[20]

India may have arrived at a political realisation of its sense of nationhood after a prolonged and slow process,[21] but as in religion, it could offer a new approach in politics. Unity was the law of nature, and in our times it had become almost a necessity if the race was not to become extinct. There could be two approaches to the problem :

"There is likely to be either a centralised World-State or a looser world union which may be either a close federation or a simple confederacy of the peoples for the common ends of mankind. The last form is the most desirable, because it gives sufficient scope for the principle of variation which is necessary for the free play of life and the healthy progress of the race".[22]

If the world was to escape the tyranny of some neo-Nazism

---

20. *Sri Aurobindo, Social and politichl Thought, op. cit.*, Vol. XV, p. 555.
21. The division of India at the time of Independence from Aurobindo's viewpoint represented a partial thwarting of this purpose. The rejection of the two-nation theory implied by the emergence of Bangla Desh would seem to represent an important step forward in the direction of a spiritual unification.
22. *Sri Aurobindo, Social and political Thought, op. cit.*, Vol. XV, p. 551.

or the nightmare of Orwell's 1984, it must turn to the example of India and evolve an international polity that aimed at unity without any sacrifice of local variation or of minority interests, or any attempt at outward standardisation.

We have seen how Sri Aurobindo was put in mind of his dream of a new phase in man's spiritual evolution when celebrating India's independence and his own seventy-fifth birthday. In line with his syncretic approach to human problems—spiritual and political—he put yet another significance into the date of his country's independence :

> "The third dream was a world-union forming the outer basis of a fairer, brighter and nobler life for all mankind. That unification of the human world is underway; there is an imperfect initiation organised but struggling against tremendous difficulties. But the momentum is there and it must inevitably increase and conquer. Here too India has begun to play a prominent part and, if she can develop that larger statesmanship which is not limited by the present facts and immediate possibilities but looks into the future and brings it nearer, her presence may make all the difference between a slow and timid and a bold and swift development."[23]

Sri Aurobindo lived to see his first great dream, that of national liberation, for which he worked so feverishly until 1910, fulfilled. Will we be able to live up to his challenge and see even partially the fulfilment of his other great dreams—that of the approaching advent of the superman and that of a world unity achieved without any sacrifice of variety and liberty—for which free India was the Lord's chosen instrument—the dreams which led him to the life of a recluse in Pondicherry from 1910 till his death forty years later, is the question of questions that each of us as Indians must ask ourselves.

---

23. Quoted by Karan Singh, p. 156.

Sri Aurobindo in the Vanguard of Freedom Struggle

NANDINI SATPATHY

THE post-Independence historians in their critical evaluations of freedom movement have sometimes explicitly and more often by implications proclaimed that India achieved her independence through the unique weapons of non-violence and non-cooperation. In *The History of Freedom Movement*, Dr. Tara Chand has maintained the same thesis by stating that the attainment of the freedom of India was a 'unique phenomenon', being displayed in the ethical character of the national stuggle. It was unprecedented in the history of mankind because "where-similar struggles have been accompanied with bloodshed, the movement in India, though intense and accompanied with much suffering, was non-violent" (*vide* preface, p. XII). The soundness of this judgment inevitably invites certain fundamental questions about the efficacy of ethical and non-violent techniques which were employed in the freedom movement. A close flashback at the history of freedom movement reveals that during the whole course of the struggle for Independence the cult of non-violence and the philosophy of the bomb ran *pari pasu*. It is a fact that Indian freedom movement commenced as a purely peaceful and evolutionary ethical fight confined to the constitutional limits but with the march of time the perspective changed and the movement culminated into an open revolt against the continuation of British rule in India.

Before the entry of Sri Aurobindo on the political front of the country the Congress Party was dominated by the moderates. They were the interpreters of the popular mind to the British

Government and that of the Government to the people and their motto was: patience and infinite patience. Sri Aurobindo's analysis of the political climate in the country after his return from England in 1893 led him to believe that the situation was completely depressing and the country's prestige was at the lowest ebb. He plunged actively into the country's political activities and his goal was nothing less than complete freedom from foreign domination. Imbued with revolutionary ideas he attempted to inject revolutionary spirit in the country's politics and advocated the concept of radical nationalism. He was a militant, aggressive, the leader par excellence, and for him the reality of politics was paramount. He was a born strategist and wanted to transform the style of politics in the sub-continent. He vociferously criticised the policies of the moderates and formulated a positive programme of political action. There was a vital difference in his concepts and techniques from that of moderates who believed in the mendicant policy of prayer, petition and protest. He launched a series of articles published in the *Indu Prakash,* under the caption of 'Old Lamp for the New' in which he exposed their sluggishness, insincerity and hollowness. He wrote: "I say of Congress, then this—that its aims are mistaken, the spirit in which it proceeds towards their accomplishment is not a spirit of sincerity and whole-heartedness, and that the methods it has chosen are not the right methods, and the leaders in whom it trusts are not the right sort of men to be leaders, in brief, that we are at present the blind led, if not by the blind, at any rate by the one-eyed." He decried the inherent weakness of the moderates for their insane appreciation of the blessing of British rule in India and urged for the active involvement of the masses in the country's Independence movement. Critising Congress he pointed out that "it is a middle class organ, selfish and disingenuous in its public action and hollow in its profession of a large and disinterested patriotism." He believed that "middle class has proved deficient in sincerity, power and judgment—with the proletariat resides, whether we like it or not, our sole assurance of hope, our sole chance in future." They are the real key of the situation.

The key to the understanding of Sri Aurobindo's political philosophy lies in his all-embracing vision of spirituality. He aimed at spiritualising the politics and imparting the process of this identification, a much wider meaning and a greater functional significance. In *Bhawani Mandir,* which is considered to be his revolutionary manifesto he gave a new meaning and interpretation to the concept of nationalism. It is both an acknowledgement of national degradation and a stirring call for the resurgence of India. He wrote: "India cannot perish, our race cannot become extinct because among all the divisions of mankind it is to India that is reserved the highest and the most splendid destiny, the most essential to the future of the human race. It is she who must send forth herself the future religion of the entire world, the eternal religion which is to harmonise all religion, science and philosophies and make mankind one soul—the greatest and most wonderful work ever given to a race". These ideas of Sri Aurobindo says Marquis Zetland "seem indeed to have been the mainspring behind Sri Aurobindo's activities in support of the revolutionary movement, for in the same pamphlet we catch sight of the idea which was to form the core of the philosophy which was to formulate later on during the long years of his retirement from the world."

Sri Aurobindo wanted to set ablaze a countrywide passion for freedom. He aimed at preparing the country for an armed rebellion. In 1905 the partition of Bengal took place and he wrote to his revolutionary group: "Here is our great opportunity. Push on the anti-Partition agitation with utmost force. Lots of workers will emerge from it."

Sri Aurobindo aimed at establishing the secret societies of revolutionaries throughout the country for imparting integrated training to the youth of India. In Bengal he set up a revolutionary society and sister Nivedita, a disciple of Vivekananda became an active member to shape and carry out the activities of the secret society. In the *Bande Mataram,* he gave expression to his revolutionary ideas and formulated his conception of *Purna Swaraj.* He wrote: "India must have Swaraj in order to live; she must have Swaraj in order to live well and happily; she must have Swaraj in order to live for the world, not as a slave for the material and political benefit of a single purse-proud and selfish nation, but as a free people for the spiritual and intellectual benefit of the human race. India is the guru of the nations, the physician of the human soul in its profounder maladies; she is destined once more to new-mould the life of the world and restore the peace of the human spirit. But Swaraj is the necessary condition of her work and before she can do the work, she must fulfil the condition."

Sri Aurobindo's programme of radical nationalism and his political goal of complete Independence was accepted throughout the country and he became an acknowledged leader of the country. At the Surat session of the Congress the extremist group of the Congress led by Sri Aurobindo, Tilak and Lajpat Rai came into open confrontation with the moderates. "It signalized the end of moderatism in the Congress and further accentuation of the forward programme of the new party". Sri Aurobindo was not merely a political theorist but a strategist of considerable importance. Not only he expressed his revolutionary ideas through journalism but he did secret work for an armed resurrection. Two young revolutionaries belonging to his secret society planned to kill Kingsford because he was inflicting heavy punishment on the political workers. But it so happened that they killed by mistake two innocent British ladies. On this tragic incident the British Government was greatly alarmed and started widespread searches and arrests. Sri Aurobindo was arrested along with many other revolutionaries. He was kept in Alipore Jail. It was at Alipore Jail that the transformation of his personality took place. He heard the voices of Swami Vivekananda who gave him the clue in the direction of Supermind. Chittaranjan Das took up the defence of Sri Aurobindo in the court of law and he was acquitted on May 5, 1909. Immediately after his release he gave an eloquent Uttarpara speech which shows predominance of spiritual elements in his thinking. It gives us a clue to the line of action which he was going to undertake.

In 1910 Sri Aurobindo at the command of inner imperative left for Pondicherry to find a clue to the solution of the problems which have bewildered and vexed humanity since man began to dream of a perfect individual and a perfect society. But it need not be assumed that he left politics completely and remained involved only in spiritual experiment. He simply changed his strategy because he silently but with a spiritual force prepared the country for Independence. When India became free on 15th August, 1947, he gave a message to the nation which is an important political document. He mentioned his involvement in certain world movements: "India's freedom and unity, Asia's resurgence, world union, the overflow of India's spirituality to Europe and America, and finally a step in evolution which would raise man to a higher and larger consciousness leading to the individual perfection and a perfect society".

Sri Aurobindo was an exponent of the ideal of human unity. The problem of East and West did not disturb him, rather he combined in his vision the alacrity of the West along with the illumination of the East. In his message of August 11, 1949, Sri Aurobindo said : "East and West have the same human nature, a common human destiny, the same aspiration after a greater perfection, the same seeking after something higher than itself... East and West have always met and mixed or less closely, they have powerfully influenced each other and at the presentday are under an increasing compulsion of nature and fate to do so more than ever before." He was a reconciler to the end.

Sri Aurobindo has got great contemporary relevance for India and the world. The youth of the East is disillusioned with the idea of old passivity, poverty and mere pretence of spirituality and is in a challenging mood. The youth of the West is also beset with innumerable challenges—the challenge posed by materialism and affluent society. This crisis is an evolutionary crisis which can be solved on a global basis. Sri Aurobindo's writings provide an answer to this challenge.

The Yogi in the Prison Cell

VIVEK BHATTACHARYA

THE trial of Sri Aurobindo forms an important epoch in the political and spiritual history of India. It is of tremendous significance in arousing public opinion throughout the length and breadth of India. It contributed a new approach to 'life divine' beyond political emancipation. It is of equal importance in the history of Indian philosophy. It turned a prince among patriots a saint. The man who defended Sri Aurobindo--a selfless patriot dedicated to the cause of freedom struggle—had an equal transformation in the life, so long restricted only to worldly goods and wisdom. Deshbandhu Chittaranjan Das was yet a budding barrister with the full promise of a versatile genius. Sri Aurobindo turned a *rishi* and Chittaranjan a prophet. Chittaranjan yet to be known affectionately to the people as Deshbandhu had certainly a great far sight. He could forsee the greatness and promise of the Man he was defending and it is indeed a miracle yet to be solved the way he piloted through the whole case. He left everything else to save Sri Aurobindo.

It is indeed yet to be studied how the two master minds acted and reacted during the trial period. May 4, 1908 to May 5, 1909 was the most significant period in the life of Sri Aurobindo. It was during this period that he was an under trial prisoner. The prison life opened a new world before the Master. He had already begun the yogas four years before. The meditation in the prison cell was a turning phase to his spiritual realisation. It was here that he discovered the foundations of his *sadhana*.

The allegation by some British loyalists that Sri Aurobindo used to recite the *Gita* before the under trial terrorists in the jail was wrong. Sri Aurobindo did not know them personally. These young patriots used to keep themselves busy in talking and singing. Sri Aurobindo passed his time in deep meditation, completely unconcerned about the surroundings. It is recorded, "Among the people around him some knew that Sri Aurobindo was doing some yoga but they had no idea of the kind of *sadhana*." Sri Aurobindo himself describes his prison life in the following words : "I spent the first part of my imprisonment in Alipore jail in a solitary cell and again after the assassination of Noren Gossain to the last days of the trial when all the Alipore case prisoners were, similarly lodged each in his own cell. In between for a short time all were put together. There is no truth behind the statement that while I was meditating they gathered around me, that I recited the *Gita* to them and they sang verses, or that they put questions to me on spiritual matters and received instructions from me."

In fact, very few people had been knowing about the yoga practices of Sri Aurobindo. He had been doing it almost secretly. Not before the historic Uttarpara speech did anybody know about the power of this secret ascetic. The saint admitted for the first time before the public about his spiritual realisation. He said : "I was carrying on my yoga during these days learning to do so in the midst of much noise and clamour but apart and in silence and without any participation of others in it. My yoga begun in 1904 had always been personal and apart, those around me knew I was a *Sadhak* but they new little more as I kept all that went on in me to myself. It was only after my release that for the first time I spoke at Uttarpara publicly about my spiritual experiences."

Sri Aurobindo did not practise yoga for mere salvation. In his own words "I wanted to do yoga for work, for action, not for *Sannyasa* or *Nirvana*—but after years of spiritual effort I had failed to find the way and it was for that I had asked to meet him (Lele Vishnu Bhaskar who taught him yoga, popularly known as Lele Maharaj)". His first answer was, "It would be easy for you as you are a poet." Sri Aurobindo was not satisfied with the progress of spiritual pursuit due to yoga practices all these four years. He regularly practised *Pranayam* but thought the real bliss was yet to come. "After four years of *Pranayam* and other practices of my own, with no other result than an increased health and out-flow of energy, a great out-flow of poetic creation, a limited power of subtle sight (turminous patterns and figures etc.) mostly with the waking eye, I had a complete arrest and was at a loss." As was the case of Sri Ramakrishna Paramahansa who got his training of *Nirvikalpa Samadhi* from Totapuri, so too Sri Aurobindo had similar experience from the training he luckily received from Lele Maharaj. Lele Maharaj taught him according to the highest thought of the *Gita* (Chapter VI, Sloka 25) not to think of anything, (but one thought of the Brahman ?) *Na kinchidapi chintayet* but of the mind alone. This leads to full concentration of the mind. Sri Aurobindo practised this deeply in solitude in the prison cell. "I had never heard before of thoughts coming visibly into the mind from outside but did not think either of questioning the truth or the possibility; I simply sat down and did it...My mind became silent..., I saw one thought and then another coming in a concrete way from outside. I flung them way before they could enter; in three days I was free." (Sri Aurobindo on Himself). This was exactly the experience of Sri Ramakrishna when he was asked by Totapuri to concentrate on a point between the two eye-lids thereby meaning the same idea as expressed by Lele Maharaj. His time of realization of the heavenly bliss by attaining the *Nirvikalpa Samadhi* was also the same !

Sri Aurobindo was ever indebted to Lele Maharaj whom he regarded nothing less than a preceptor. It was this saintly man who taught him deep meditation. That is not all. It was Lele Maharaj who told him in advance that whenever he would have any problem—be it of any nature, a voice will come to Sri Aurobindo from within and guide him in every step. That did happen and Sri Aurobindo not only realised this miraculous experience but he left himself entirely at the guidance of this inner voice. That happened later on in every step of his historic career.

It is indeed interesting to record that over a month before his arrest in connection with the Alipore conspiracy case Sri Aurobindo had an intuition. "A call had come to me", he recorded. It was a call to lead a life of seclusion, solitude and deep meditation. It was a divine call to leave everything and be in tune with infinity. It came to him at a time when he was leading the busiest life. A full *Karma Yogin* that he was, he did not take that call so seriously. And the saint himself tells us that because of 'ego' (*ahang jnan*) he perhaps could not leave out all the works immediately. He thought who would complete them if he left them undone ? After a few days' stay in the prison cell he realised this was predestined. This was only a process, a device that was necessary to 'educate' him to go ahead with the philosophy of renunciation i.e. the *Gita*. Sri Ramakrishna Paramahansa gave perhaps the easiest interpretation of this most significant epic. He said if you read the word *Gita* in the reverse direction you find its inner most meaning and that is *tagi* i.e. renunciation. Sri Aurobindo was deeply absorbed in the study of this masterpiece of Indian philosophy and according to his own statements, for the first time he realised that those who are destined to carry on divine works cannot do anything on their own. They have to surrender themselves completely in the hands of God. They must give up their desire, their own approaches to a programme of work. They must work as a tool in the hands of God. The result of the work has to be taken sportingly without any grudge. Whether success or failure, the result will have to be faced with equal reaction of mind.

One day a miracle happened. This was perhaps the first of his numerous miraculous experiences in the prison cell. A divine feeling was there and the saint felt the existence of God in everything surrounding him. He was in great ecstacy. This is how he himself recorded the experience later on. It was published in *The Hindu*—fifty years ago from November 8 to November 15, 1909: Sri Aurobindo writes, "During my solitary confinement Dr. Daly and the Assistant Jail Superintendent used to come into the cell almost daily, and indulged in a little talk. I do not know the reason why I excited their compassion and sympathy form the very beginning. I would not talk much but only replied to their queries. I used to listen to them in silence and made but little comment."

"They, however, would still come to me. One day Dr. Daly observed, 'I have asked the Jail Superintendent through the Assistant Superintendent to give you permission to have a constitutional outside your cell; otherwise, your mind and body will suffer'. From the next day I could walk about in the open from ten minutes to one or two hours."

"I enjoyed this very much; on one side lay the Jail workshops and on the other the cowshed and between them I paraded as if in my own independent territory. Then I repeated the soul stirring verses of the Upanishads, or watched the inmates of the prison working or passing by. I tried to see God in every man moving before me, even every tree, wall, bird and beast. I muttered the *Mantra*, 'God is in every metal and in the earth and mud'. I realised it very successfully and became lost in thought until the prison ceased to be prison to me".

The saint realised the inner meanings of the message of the Upanishads—*Ekamebadvitiyam* (one and only one that He is) and *Sarbang Khalvidong Brahmah* (Brahma pervades everything). God is omnipresent, omnipotent and omnicient. This was a fulfilment of an earlier preliminary similar experience that peeped into the mind of the Master in an experiment carried in the training process by Lele Maharaj. Basudeva pervades everything, Sri Aurobindo realised *Basudevah*, *Sarbamiti*. His illustrious Bengali biographer Principal Pramada Ranjan Ghosh tells us how the Master reacted to the feeling. "The tree on his head was no longer a mere tree. It seemed Basudeva, Sri Krishna had spread the shade on his head. Even the prisoners in the jail—some of whom were thieves and dacoits—seemed to him as the embodiment of Basudeva".

This brought a revolutionary change in Sri Aurobindo's outlook. A transition came. He switched from a princely patriot to a mysterious yogi. His heart was yearning for transcendental peace and life divine. By peace he meant "a calm deepened into something that is very positive amounting almost to a tranquil waveless *Ananda*. Peace is more positive than calm; there can be a negative calm which is merely an absence of disturbance or trouble, but peace is always something positive bringing not merely a release as calm does but a certain happiness or *Ananda* of itself". "In peace there is besides the sense of stillness, a harmony that gives a feeling of liberation and full satisfaction.

Of course, Sri Aurobindo has also said that even those who have no peace can march ahead: "One can go forward even if there is not peace—quietitude and concentration are necessary. Peace is necessary for the higher States to develop.

"Peace, purity and silence can be felt in all material things—for the Divine self is there in all". But will this peace stay in one's mind permanently? Heavenly bliss comes to seekers of Truth but it does not linger long. It stays on only when one reaches the stage of renunciation—*tyagat sukham anantaram.* Sri Aurobindo tells us, "Peace and joy can be there permanently, but the condition of this permanence is that one should have the constant contact or indwelling of the Divine, and this comes naturally not to the outer mind or vital but to the inner soul or psychic being. Therefore one who wants his *yoga* to be a path of peace or joy must be prepared to dwell in his soul rather than in his outer mental or emotional nature."

Here one should try to understand the significance of renunciation as experimented by the Master. It is here again that great similarity is clearly seen between the explanation of Sri Aurobindo and Sri Ramakrishna Paramahansa. To both Gita is the source of wisdom. Both said renunciation was the ultimate process to peace from their personal realization and successful experiment. Said Sri Aurobindo, "Renunciation must be for us an instrument and not an object; nor can it be the only or the chief instrument since our object is the fulfilment of the Divine in the human being, a positive aim which cannot be reached by negative means. It must be a renunciation of all that is other than and opposed to the divine self-fulfilment and a progressive renunciation of all that is lesser or only a partial achievement".

Renunciation should be indifference to material desire, explained Sri Ramakrishna. To an ordinary *griht* his famous advice was to lead the life of *Pankal* fish which lives in dirty mud without getting the touch of it. Unattachment to wordly material and inward concentration leads one to the divinity, he said. Sri Aurobindo said, "Our renunciation must obviously be an inward renunciation of attachment, and the craving of desire in the senses and the heart, of self-will in the thought and action and of egoism in the centre of consciousness."

This inward renunciation was exactly what Sri Ramakrishna pleaded his disciples and followers to practise. Sri Aurobindo gives us a positive approach to life when he says, "By renunciation we seize upon the falsehoods, pluck up their roots and cast them out of our way so that they shall no longer hamper by their persistence, their resistance or their recurrence the happy and harmonious growth of our divine living".

Sri Aurobindo showed complete indifference to his prison life. He was even completely unconcerned about his trial and who would defend him? Who would finance the case? And finally even when the trial started he left everything to the lawyer keeping himself aloof from the whole case.

The details of the trial form an important chapter in the legal, political and spiritual history of the world. Some of the salient features of the trial may be narrated in brief.

On May 4, 1908 police arrested Sri Aurobindo after a search at his Grey Street residence. The report that he was handcuffed was wrong. According to his own statement "Hand cuffed—no, tied with a rope; this was taken off on the protest of Bhupen Bose, the Congress Moderate Leader." Simultaneously his brother Barin Ghosh, Ullaskar Dutt, Indra Bhusan and Upendra Nath Banerjee were taken to jail from Sri Aurobindo's Murari Pukur Bagan residence. Prafulla Chaki was arrested the next day. He committed suicide by shooting himself to avoid interrogation by police. The case was brought before Mr. Birley on May 9.

Aurobindo's sister Sarojini Ghosh issued an appeal to raise funds for the defence.

Sri Aurobindo's brother Barin Ghosh started a secret society at their ancestral garden house at Murari Pukur Road. They collected some selfless princely patriots who were given training in guerrilla battle. He was also collecting arms for the cause.

In December 1907 and April 1908 two cases of violence took place at Narayangarh and Chandernagar. An attempt was made on the life of Sir Andrew Frazer, the Govenor of Bengal by throwing a bomb at the train in which he was travelling via Narayangarh near Khargpur. In the latter case the target was the Mayor of Chandernagar. Both the attempts proved abortive.

Kingsford was a tyrant. He used to punish the Swadeshi Movement volunteers ruthlessly. He became extremely unpopular by giving a judgment of publicly caning a young volunteer of 14—Sushil Chandra Sen. One day Khudi Ram Bose and Prafulla Chaki followed Kingsford at Mazaffarpur. They threw a grenade at a car which was entering Kingsford's bungalow. Unfortunately, for them Kingsford was not there. Two innocent ladies—Mrs. and Miss Kenedy were killed by mistake. This took place on April 30. Khudi Ram was arrested and hanged later. Prafulla Chaki killed himself. They were the forerunners of terrorist movement in India. Both of them belonged to the secret society of Barin Ghosh. So the search and the arrests followed. The main charge against Sri Aurobindo was that the Government thought that he was the brain behind the whole terrorist movement.

It was mainly because of the series of articles published in *Bande Mataram* under the series "Passive Resistance', two unpublished articles "The Morality of Boycott" and "What is extremism", letters to his wife and "Sweet Letter". In the judgment some of the passages were quoted. The judge said: "There are passages in 'Morality of Boycott' which taken by themselves certainly indicate support of the use of violent methods."

Sri Aurobindo had written: "The object of the nationalist is to build up the nation. The nationalist has a deep respect for law, because without it the nation cannot attain proper development. But the law must be in accordance with the wish of the nation. If it is not, it is not moral; and if immoral, it should be broken. The nationalist is not afraid of anarchy and suffering".

The judge recorded his opinion in the following words: "As an essay the article is a splendid piece of writing. The danger lies in the effect it might have on ill-balanced and impressionable minds. The fact that neither of these articles was published is again a point in Aurobindo's favour."

The *sadhana* that the great yogi practised in the prison cell was not an ordinary one. It was certainly not for mere personal salvation. It was a significant experiment in a scientific modern manner. Sri Aurobindo himself explains the meaning of the type of *sadhana* he preached and practised. He preached little. His practice is the ideal to his followers and to humanity.

What is this *sadhana* ? Why practise it ? How to practise ? Sri Aurobindo says, "*sadhana* is the opening of the consciousness to the Divine, the change of the present consciousness to the psychic and spiritual consciousness. In this yoga it means also the offering of all consciousness and its activities to the Divine for possession and use by the Divine and for transformation."

In the prison cell Sri Aurobindo was completely unconcerned

with his own trial. There is an interesting anecdote, about Sri Ramakrishna's influence on Sri Aurobindo. A friend of Sri Aurobindo belonging to the Ramakrishna order brought some earth from Sri Ramakrishna's hut. He had deep faith in the greatness of Sri Ramakrishna. Sri Aurobindo himself tells us about the incident. Says Sri Aurobindo, "The earth was brought to me by a young man connected with the Ramakrishna Mission and I kept it; it was there in my room where the police came to arrest me." It was just May 1908.

The case was committed to session in the court of Mr. Beachcroft. On October 19, 1908, about four thousand exhibits were produced; objects constituting the evidence exceeded four hundred. More than two hundred witnesses were examined. The case lasted upto April 13, 1909. Meanwhile, the approver Narendra Goswami was assassinated by Kanailal Dutt. He was hanged in jail on September 14. It may be mentioned here that Mr. Beachcroft was Sri Aurobindo's contemporary in Cambridge. Both passed the I.C.S. examination together, Sri Aurobindo topping in Greek literature. Beachcroft secured the next position.

The whole idea behind the trial of Sri Aurobindo was to substantiate the theory that whereas Barin Ghosh was the ring leader behind the terrorist movement in India, the brain was Sri Aurobindo. There is no doubt that the Government left no stones unturned to substantiate the theory. The Government lawyer Mr Norton was paid a thousand rupees a day! Chittaranjan Das took up the case as the defending lawyer.

In the meantime, Sri Aurobindo's father-in-law had earlier employed one lawyer—Byomkesh Chakravarty in the court of the Magistrate. Chittaranjan appeared in the Sessions court of Beachcroft. It is said, when Sri Aurobindo heard that C.R. Das had taken up the case, he (Sri Aurobindo) observed, "Narayan himself has come to defend me."

For one full year Chittaranjan conducted the case with religious zeal. He maintained his family by borrowing money. Persons who saw him at that time described him as a saint, deeply devoted to meditation! He forgot sleep. Cihttaranjan observed later on that he thought as if he had been arrested himself.

Sri Aurobindo could not give even instructions to Chittaranjan.

Describes his biographer Purani: "He hardly attended to the evidence or the conduct of the case. C.R. Das was at last engaged to defend Sri Aurobindo. Sri Aurobindo was guided by an inner voice to leave the defence completely in his charge. His view of life was thus undergoing a radical change in jail. In the beginning of the *sadhana* the idea was to take the Divine help in the mission that he had undertaken, but the nature of the experiences during the jail life completely changed his outlook. He decided to dedicate himself entirely to the spiritual life and his outer life thenceforward became a part of his *sadhana* and its results. The field of action also enlarged enormously afterwards, from the service of the country and its freedom it became a worldwide work touching intimately the future of humanity".

Sri Aurobindo left himself entirely in the hands of the divine power. He could not help it. In spite of his efforts he could not do otherwise. That was the state of his spiritual experiences. He did not want to give written instruction to Chittaranjan Das for the defence in the court. But his inner voice resisted. Sri Aurobindo tells us: "I still thought it necessary to write instructions. Then all that was put from me and I had the message from within. This is the man who will save you from the snares put round your feet. Put aside these papers. It is not you who will instruct him. I will instruct him."

"I am in the nation and its uprising and I am Vasudeva, I am Narayana and what I will, shall be, not what others will, what I choose to bring about, no human power can stay."

Here it should be made very clear that Sri Aurobindo did not choose the spiritual path just for his personal salvation. His love for his country did not diminish a bit. What he felt in the jail was the presence of the omnipresent almighty God in whose hands he was only an instrument. About his unstinted devotion to his Motherland his prayers speak for themselves. Sri Aurobindo's constant prayers were, "If Thou art, then thou knowest my heart. Thou knowest that I do not ask for *Mukti*, I do not ask for anything which others ask for. I ask for strength to uplift this nation, I ask only to be allowed to live and work for this people whom I love and to whom I pray that I may devote my life." (For details please read Sri Aurobindo's historic speech at Uttarpara dated May 30, 1909).

Chittaranjan knew his responsibility. The minimum punishment for sedition for a man who is considered to be the brain behind the terrorist movement was death. He left everything else. He lost himself in defence of Sri Aurobindo. That became his dream—his meditation. He forgot even his personal minimum requirements of food, sleep and rest. His income dwindled down. He, in fact, incurred a debt of more than fifty thousand rupees during one year.

As already stated, Justice Beachcroft was dealing with the case. He used to play tennis with the Maharaja of Natore who was his great pal. The Maharaja used to wait for Beachcroft rather impatiently. Once he asked him, "Well, how is it that now-a-days you are so absent-minded and erratic at the game?" Beachcroft said with a smile, "Ask your friend, C.R. Das. He pins me to the chair right from morning to the dusk."

Once Beachcroft lost his temper and remarked, "You (i.e. C.R. Das) are talking nonsense"!

It was a crowded court.

Chittaranjan retorted, "You are on the Bench, Sir, and that language should not come from your mouth. Had you been anywhere else, I would have given the proper answer."

Concluding his arguments in defence of Sri Aurobindo, C.R. Das observed: "Do not think that this court will be the final judge of the case in which you have accused Sri Aurobindo. In the greater court of the annals of mankind, the points and counterpoints of today, this class of ideological thoughts, will get lost in the mundane darkness of time. This excitement of today will not stir any man yet unborn. But the man who is standing before you as an accused will command homage and tribute, as a martyr searching for TRUTH eternal, dedicated sage for the prosperity of humanity."

How true was the prophecy. The man whom the foreign rulers accused of conspiracy to wage war against the king and collecting arms for the same object turned one of the greatest *Yogis* of modern times. It has been truly described as "*a cause celebre*" memorable in the annals of India's freedom movement."

Chittaranjan won the battle. Sri Aurobindo took an altogether new path. He devoted his life to deep *Yogic* practices and found divinity in life.

After his release Sri Aurobindo was accorded a hearty felicitation at Uttarpara near Calcutta. There Sri Aurobindo observed:

"Then something happened which I had not expected. The arrangements which had been made for my defence were suddenly changed and another counsel stood there to defend me. He became unexpectedly a friend of mine, but I did not know he was coming. You have all heard the name of the man who put away from him all other thoughts and abandoned all his practice, who woke up half the night day after day for months and broke his health to save me—Chittaranjan Das. When I saw him I was satisfied."

Chittaranjan's genius won the case. Indeed he fought out each argument of the prosecution with superb skill and in all the cases turned the tables on their face. He proved that many of the evidences were forged. The 'Sweet Letter' reported to have been written by Barin was proved to be a forged one. Chittaranjan raised some fundamental questions from the point of common family relationship in a Bengali house. Why should Barin address Sri Aurobindo as Dear Dada? Sri Aurobindo always was addressed as "Sejda". Why should Barin put his full signature in a personal letter to his brother. Even Europeans do not put their full signatures in such cases.

About the letters from Sri Aurobindo to Mrinalini too, the Judge had to admit, "viewing it in an unprejudiced way there is nothing in it that really calls for explanation." Above all Chittaranjan pleaded categorically that patriotism is not a crime. If patriotism be a crime, Sri Aurobindo is certainly guilty of that crime, he told the Court. In the final judgment Beachcroft observed, "Taking all the evidence together I am of opinion that it falls short of such proof as would justify me in finding him guilty of so serious a charge."

That was the judgment of Beachcroft. But what is the judgment of the ordinary Indian about the mystic saint? To the ordinary man he gave, besides the path of transcendental peace, more importantly and fundamentally the message of deep love for Mother India. The idea of patriotism has hardly any parallel in history. It reminds one remarkably of the messages of Swami Vivekananda. There are many passages so similar in thoughts. Swami Vivekananda said, "for the next fifty years this alone shall be our Great Goddess—Mother India. Let us forget everything else." Sri Aurobindo wrote, "There are times in a nation's history when providence places before it one work, one aim to which everything else, however high and noble in itself, had to be sacrificed. Such a time has now arrived for our Motherland when nothing is dearer than her service, when everything else is to be directed to that end. If you will study, study for her sake; train yourself body and mind and soul for her service, work so that she may prosper; suffer so that she may rejoice. All is contained in that one single advice." This is the message of Sri Aurobindo to his countrymen particularly the youth of modern India.

Sri Aurobindo is the ideal of modern youth. Freedom from slavery does not mean freedom to act in any way one likes. Obedience is the key-note to perfection in life. Forgiveness and tolerance are necessary qualifications to lead a peaceful and harmonious life. "It is deficiency of psychic perception and spiritual discrimination that makes people ignore the importance of obedience", says Sri Aurobindo.

He pleads the youth to lead the life of a *Karma Yogin*, leaving carefully the evil of egoism. "To be free from all egoistic motive, careful of truth in speech and action, void of self-will and self-assertion, watchful in all things, is the condition for being a fearless servant." Sri Aurobindo says further, "All should be done quietly from within—working, speaking, reading, writing as part of the real consciousness—not with the dispersed and unquiet, movement of the ordinary consciousness." Sri Aurobindo says, "The work here is a field and an opportunity for the *Karmayoga* part of the Integral yoga, for learning to work in the true yogic way, dedication through service, practical selflessness, obedience, scrupulousness, discipline, setting the Divine and the Divine's work first and oneself last, harmony, patience, forbearanace. One must universalise oneself and allow harmonious unegoistic action. Afterwards a truer and higher order can come in from above."

Indian youth hardly ever heard such a commanding guidance except perhaps from the Swami with the flaming tongue—known to the world as Vivekananda!

Integral Sociology of Sri Aurobindo

D.P. CHATTOPADHYAYA

HERE we propose to delineate the main conceptual characteristics of Sri Aurobindo's Integral Sociology* with a stress particularly on its methodological aspect. The treatment of the subject is mainly expository and only incidentally critical. To clarify his position this will be compared with and contrasted from some concepts of sociology which had been very influential during the second half of the nineteenth century and the first quarter of this century. A brief rerference to contemporary theories of sociology has been felt necessary because they constitute the background of our exposition and criticism of Sri Aurobindo's thought on the matter. We would round off our argument by highlighting the sociological points of similarity between Marx and Sri Aurobindo notwithstanding their philosophical difference. It may be mentioned in this connection that we have used the term sociology in an extended sense.

The foremost thing which is required to understand a thinker and his ideas is that one must get into his method. Every man has his character, style and method. The method of a thinker reveals his perspective, indicates his field of interest and also its contents. The fact that a man chooses a particular field of study rather than another indicates further a personal-cum-valuational component of his character. There is nothing wrong or surprising in the personal factor being present in the choice of

* This paper is the first chapter of my forthcoming book, *Integral Sociology of Sri Aurobindo*. Being a part of the whole, some limitations of the paper will be obvious to the reader.

a thinker's field of study. However strange it might sound, there is always an *irremediable personal element*, bias or prejudice or both, which a thinker brings to bear upon his study. Of Shakespeare's mind Hazlitt says that "it had no one peculiar bias or exclusive excellence more than another." We wonder if any modern social psychologist would accept without reservation this otherwise admirable characterization of Shakespeare's mind.

Sri Aurobindo's treatment and interpretation of human nature is altogether different from that of the modern empirical psychologists. They have interpreted human nature in terms of external factors. But he has recommended a depth psychology or spiritual psychology which includes introspective or phenomenological studies of both the individual mind and the group mind.

II

Broadly speaking, Sri Aurobindo's ideas, though metaphysical in origin, are sociological in formulations. He characterizes one of his major works, *The Human Cycle*, as a psychology of social development. Whatever term he may use to designate the ideas of his sociological theory, there is no doubt that they are subsumable under the discipline of sociology.

The origin of sociology may be traced back to four subjects; political philosophy, philosophy of history, biological theories of evolution, and the movement for socio-political reforms. Except the third one, all other subjects are fairly old. These subjects, though distinct, have influenced one another all along. Auguste Comte, known as the founder of sociology as a distinct discipline, approaches the science from the point of view of philosophy of history. Hegel is admittedly against the ideas of approaching history by way of Nature. Nature, he says, has no history; it merely repeats its cycle. Historical process is spiral and creative, or dialectical, as he puts it. For Hegel the difference between higher and lower organisms is merely logical and not temporal, and thus he does away with the idea of evolution.[1] The positivist's revolt against Hegelian rationalism was strongly supported by John Stuart Mill, a consistent admirer of Auguste

---

1. R.C. Collingwood, *The Idea of History*, pp. 114-15.

Comte.

Before the social Darwinians who exploited most the notion of natural evolution was Herbert Spencer. Spencer defines sociology as "the study of evolution in its most complex forms." In points of change from homogeneity to heterogeneity, increasing integration, definiteness, multiformity and coherence, social evolution is fulfilling the formula of evolution at large. Sociology for him is the *science of super-organic evolution*, engaged in empirical study of the growth, structure, functions and products of the human society.[2] True that Spencer follows Comte in doing away with the Hegelian distinction between the processes of social and natural evolution, but he lacks the latter's insight in the philosophy of history. Whilc Comte approaches sociology from the standpoint of philosophy of history, Spencer does it from that of biological and anthropological theories of evolution.

The publication of Darwin's *The Origin of Species* in 1859 marks the beginning of gradual disappearance of the difference between the static or scientific and the changing or historical view of nature. Darwinian notions of *Natural Selection* and the *Struggle for Existence* had been extensively and often extravagantly used by the social Darwinians like Ludwig Gumplowicz, Gustav Ratzenhofer and Franz Oppenheimer. All of them accept social conflicts as the analogue of the struggle for existence in the sphere of socio-cultural life. They attribute a sort of causal agency to it. Conflict, according to them, is the cause of social development. The implication of this view is obviously dangerous. Certainly all conflicts are not conducive to social development and, therefore, positive encouragement of conflict should not be accepted as a matter of policy.

Darwin's scientific method in general and his notion of the struggle for existence in particular had an important influence on Karl Marx. But the latter never accepts the former's belief that human society is an extension of biological evolution, nor does he accept the Hegelian contention that social development is autonomous and has nothing to do with the natural process. Biological pattern of man's nature is only one constituent of his character, which has in it other equally, if not more, important constituents. The constituent or factor which shapes human

2. H. Spencer, *Principles of Sociology*, pp. 617-18.

nature most decisively is said to be economic. Quite unlike the unintelligent animals man is not helpless against the biological and physical forces of nature. But his autonomy or freedom has its limits—limit is set, broadly speaking, by the historical conditions amidst which he is obliged to live and have his being. Man is essentially a historical agent. Marxian sociology studies the inter-relations of the different productive forces working within definite historical contexts and tries to lay bare the laws of economic development. It is basically these laws in terms of which, Marx thinks, the continuity of the developing social process is to be interpreted. Non-economic factors are said to be relatively unimportant and have to be explained in terms of the economic ones.

In spite of Hegel's strong and unmistakable influence upon Marx, his sociology is largely based on his own independent study and creative assimilation of past history, classical economic ideas and contemporary industrial society. Vico also influenced him through Hegel and other German idealists. But while he accepts the historical kernel of the Vician and Hegelian theories, he rejects most of their ideas on the ground that they are highly speculative and not borne out by historical facts. Every theoretical discipline, he insists, must be tested in practice. To the unity of theory and practice he attaches great importance. It is from Comte, St. Simon, Fourier and Owen that he inherited the practical zeal for social and political reforms. His insistence on *practical test* of theoretical truth is to be traced to the positivist tradition of Comte and Mill. But it has to be admitted that he is neither an ideal visionary nor a utilitarian of the Millian type. He was deeply interested in political philosophy, philosophy of history, the movements for socio-political reforms, and biological and anthropological theories of evolution, the factors responsible for the growth of the comparatively new discipline, sociology.

In the field of anthropological sociology, Lewis Henry Morgan is undoubtedly a pioneer. He regards sociology as a systematic study of the correlation between the successive stages of social evolution and the corresponding degrees in the technological advancement. *Gentes, phratries* and *tribes* are, according to him "the instrumentalities by means of which ancient society was organized and held together." Both Marx and Engels have been considerably influenced by his anthropological researches and conclusions based on them. He clearly anticipates Marx when he says that there is a definite relation between the different forms of family and the ownership of property, on the one hand, and different stages of human progress from savagery through barbarism to civilization, on the other. Morgan's conclusions have found favour also with McIennan, Briffault and Malinowski. But it has been rejected, among others, by Lowie and Evans-Pritchard.

The hypothesis of evolution has been differently used by different groups of sociologists. Spencer, Schafle, Lilenfeld and others have tried to verify it in the light of the findings of working anthropologists and biologists. Tylor thinks that it is more easily verifiable in the study of culture. Both Durkheim and Tarde attach great importance to the study of cultural data in sociology. What is common to all these thinkers is *love for facts.* This helped them to avoid empty philosophical speculation. *Fact-fetish* and *empty speculation* prove almost equally pernicious trends in theory-construction.

But in spite of them the spirit of philosophy lingered long in the domain of sociology. Georg Simmel and Paul Barth take sociology as a sort of philosophy of history. Historical sociology alone, they think, can establish the philosophy of history on the firm foundation of scientific method and historical accuracy. They think that there are some underlying causal laws to connect and account for the constant patterns of historical phenomena. One observes the same view in the writings of Karl Lamprecht as well. These thinkers try to bring sociology close to a sort of naturalism highlighting the influence of biophysical nature on human activities.

Hobhouse is one of those sociologists, who tries to steer a middle way between philosophical speculation, on the one hand, and dry-as-dust positivism, on the other. In spite of his own significant contribution to philosophy as a critic of contemporary idealism, he is never in favour of treating sociology as a branch of philosophy. Both Durkheim and Hobhouse try to treat sociology as an autonomous discipline. According to Hobhouse, sociology is to be studied under two heads—social philosophy and social science. The former would be mainly an analysis of values and the latter of study of facts. Values are quite independent of facts; they are realized in facts and through social evolution. "Social development and ethical development," says Hobhouse, "are at the end same."[3] He holds that "Social Philosophy and Social Science are legitimate methods of investigating social phenomena." As a critic of positivism he points out that a social fact has to be clearly distinguished from a bare physical fact. He defines social fact in terms of purpose (but not Divine purpose). Ginsberg writes:

> "His method was to examine and classify the forms of mental activity, social groupings, and institutions, and to disentangle principles governing their evolution. These studies led him to formulate a theory of development as consisting in the extension of harmony through a series of syntheses, affected by the liberation of elements originally in conflict and building up of structures of varying degrees of plasticity, scale and coherence."

The consideration of value is conspicuous by its absence in Marx's thought. Presumably it is due to his pro-naturalistic bias in favour of facts and the belief that values may be explained in terms of facts. By contrast we find that the question of value and that of purpose occupy a central position in the scheme of Hobhouse's thought. In Marx's theory man has little importance outside or independently of his class context. Further, he thinks that inter-class relationship is *determined by inevitable historical laws.* In other words, man's position in a class is not his choice. Hobhouse, on the contrary, highlights the view that social evolution proceeds by stages and marks the development of consciousness and self-consciousness under resultant control of mind over the conditions of life. While Marx takes pains to show how human mind is determined by its circumstances, productive relationship and class context based there upon, Hobhouse emphasizes the fact that human mind has been continuously shaping the course of history.

Marx interprets social evolution primarily in terms of *conflict* and *contradiction.* Hobhouse asserts that "mere conflict and contradiction cannot lead to anything."[4] Society, according to the latter, moves through a series of syntheses and not

3. L. T. Hobhouse, *Social Development*, p. 89.
4. *Ibid.*

antitheses as alleged by Marx. Hobhouse attaches great importance to the concept of harmony. He has been very much influenced, as we said before, by Spencer's evolutionary and organic view of nature. But he rejects Spencer's naturalistic suggestion that society moves automatically and independently of human will. Spencer credits human will only with the capacity to hinder and not to promote social progress, which is said to be a mechanical process governed and guided by its own inherent laws.

Hobhouse's debt to Hegel is also considerable. The ideas of the presence of consciousness in the process of evolution and the *purposive realization* of that consciousness through evolution were unmistakably Hegelian. We are told that there was a time when Hobhouse was opposed to the purposive interpretation of evolution; but his empirical study of concerned facts subsequently persuaded him to change his view. He is a rationalist of a sort, certainly not of the classical sort. To him empirical study is no less important than the role and function of reason.

> "Reason is a principle of harmony pervaded through experience and working it into an organic whole. So understood, reason is supreme in the mind simply as that which embraces every element of experience, inter-connects every feeling and thought, takes account impartially of every suggestion and every impulse, and weaves of them on a tissue which is never ossified but always plastic and recipient. It is a conscious expression of that harmony which dominates the entire evolution of mind, and rationality of the process is the best guarantee of its ultimate success."[5]

The method of Hobhouse is *inductive* and *evolutionary*. He takes over the most up-to-date findings of the special sciences, organizes them in terms of a hypothesis and then tests it rigorously, desiring all the time to develop a consilient system. He differed from his contemporary idealist thinkers mainly on the ground that while they were in favour of accepting extravagant speculative principles, he insisted on testable theories. He claims that his theory of evolution, unlike the Hegelian one, is borne out by

---

5. L.T. Hobhouse, *Development and Purpose*, p. xxix.

and based upon sociological and anthropological facts.

III

Sri Aurobindo's concept of sociology is in a sense very unorthodox. True that many of his conclusions are strikingly similar to those arrived at by other contemporary sociologists, but his method has a striking originality of its own. Consistent with his philosophical position of Integral Monoism, he develops what we propose to call a system of *Integral Sociology*.

Sri Aurobindo speaks of the necessity of avoiding two extremes. In the name of spiritualism one should not ignore empirical findings and soar to the height of empty speculation or transcendental abstractions, and in the name of empiricism one should not resort to fact-fetish. In other words, he advises us to avoid two negations, transcendental abstractionism and crass empiricism. Sri Aurobindo is against that type of history and sociology which concentrate on external data, laws, institutions, rites, customs and economic factors. He is an evolutionist and the true significance of it cannot be obtained merely from the scientific account (s) of the human past. To get to the depth of social life we must try to realize the spiritual future of mankind in the cycles of Nature. A proper understanding of our social life demands that we should shift the emphasis from external data to internal data of our lived life. Society is more rooted in spiritual reality than what is indicated by its surface movements. Sri Aurobindo is in favour of stressing the course of evolution from within. Man is key to the understanding of his own spiritual cycles in the course of Nature.

Sri Aurobindo differs from the objectivists and materialists like Marxists who affirm that social existence is based on our natural existence and that it has to be explained in terms of economic necessity (or motivation). Sometimes he goes to the length of suggesting that economic, historical, institutional and other approaches to society are indeed very 'futile'. These hypotheses can at best successfully arrange, classify and organize social phenomena but fail to produce dependable and tested theory. Classification and organization of social phenomena throw little light on their genesis, existence, duration and transition from one stage to another. The rationale of chance lies deep in the process of change, is not generally exhibited by its surface movements and is to be therefore discovered by a sort of 'subjectivist' method. To understand social process we are advised to take proper account of the influence, importance and modes of working of human thoughts. Thoughts and ideas of man mould his history more than anything else. We have to lay bare the potent secrets and all determining laws of social life. But this is not an easy task. And, therefore, we are generally more interested in a relatively easy task, i.e. collection and classification of superficial sociological data. It is on the basis of this external data that "we advance hasty generalizations and make absolute systems which are positively announced today to be abandoned perforce tomorrow." Collection and classification, however careful they might be, of external facts of social existence leads us at best to certain generalizations which are only "secondary rules and practical bye-laws (and) which help us to tide over the difficulties of the moment and to organize empirically without understanding them." Organization is not understanding. This inability on our part to go deep into the laws of social evolution is attributed by Sri Aurobindo to the incapacity of our main instrument, *Reason*. Reason works with commendable facility and rapidity. But it lacks profundity and *consequently* has to remain satisfied only with the *whats* and *hows* of the surface movements of society and cannot get to their *whys*.

> "Sociology does not help us, for it only gives us the general theory of the past and the external conditions under which communities have survived. History teaches us nothing, is a confused torrent of events and personalities or a kaleidoscope of changing institutions. We do not seize the real sense of all this change and this continual streaming forward of human life in the channel of time. What we do seize are current or recurrent phenomena, facile generalizations and partial ideas. And all this happens because of our whole thought and action with regard to our collective life is shallow and empirical; it does not seek for, it does not base itself on a firm, profound and complete knowledge."[6]

---

6. *The Ideal of Human Unity*, p. 2.

The very idea of complete knowledge is very vague. It becomes even more vague in the context of collective life. Every piece of knowledge is a sort of answer to a given question or solution to a felt problem. It has its limit and is *partial*. Sociological hypotheses are framed in order to explain (and, in some cases, to tackle) *specific* social problems. Because of its relation to a specific problem or difficulty (theoretical or practical or both) a hypothesis is bound to be aspective or partial and cannot be exhaustive and complete. Social phenomena are of interest to us in between their ends, past and present, and have to be explained in terms of both to what they are due and what will be due to them. Both ground and consequence are of importance for proper understanding of social phenomena.

What Sri Aurobindo means is the inadequacy of causal explanation in history and sociology. What we really need in Integral Sociology is teleological or purposive explanation. Unless we know the purpose of man in the world, we cannot fully understand his thoughts and actions, which are being continuously influenced, either consciously or unconsciously by it. The concept of human purpose itself may be understood in two different (but *may* be related) ways, in an autonomous or secular way and also in the larger context of divine purpose. Human context is said to be an open context—open to the larger context of the divine itself. That is how Sri Aurobindo takes it. For methodological convenience some sociologists prefer to study the complexity of human phenomena within a closed context as if it can be satisfactorily understood without reference to the distant past and the distant future and what lies deep in it. Besides, facile generalizations of the modern sociologist tend to ignore the complexity of human situation. In order to achieve theoretical simplicity he ignores the real human complexity, and that exposes his theory to frequent falsification.

IV

Broadly speaking there are two different methods of going beyond the given data. One is called deductive or more accurately, *hypothetico deductive,* and the other *inductive*. The latter has its different forms, enumerative induction and induction per simple enumeration. On the basis of careful study of a set of data obtained in a closed system, it has been argued, we may go well beyond the system and tentatively formulate some general principles which will hold good in other closed systems *of the same type*. Florian Znaniecki tells us that this method of enumerative induction has been extensively and profitably used, among others, by Spencer in his *Principles of Sociology* and/or Westermarck in his *Origin and Development of Moral Ideas*. This method of enumerative induction is not to be confused with the method of induction per simple enumeration. While the latter is a sort of summary or inventory of some things and or properties and does not enable us to go beyond the given, the former, however limited and reliable might be its scope, provide an inferential passage from the known to the unknown. It has often been argued against induction in general, and enumerative induction in particular, that either it is summative and therefore extremely restrictive in its scope or it is not induction at all. Without a non-inductive postulate induction cannot help us to go beyond the limits of observation. Induction, strictly speaking, is an *aimless* summary and is not of any intellectual or scientific significance. Observation or, more broadly speaking, experience assumes significance only in the light of some hypothesis or theory. It is only in terms of a general truth that particular pieces of information become *meaningfully* related and testable. Individual and isolated bits of observations are neither testable nor of any scientific worth. To surmount the difficulties of enumerative induction logicians have often spoken of and emphasized the superiority of an eliminative induction over enumerative induction. While enumerative induction relies mainly on the method of agreement, eliminative induction does so on the method of difference. In scientific investigation disconfirmation is more important than confirmation. Exclusive reliance on confirmation encourages the development of only those theories which hold good within a *closed* system. The search of disconfirming instances tends to take a theory beyond the bounds of a closed system. The notion of scientific 'induction' is more closely akin to elimination than to enumeration. Scientific inference has always a non-inductive or theoretical component in it and is not inductive as it is ordinarily understood.

Another method which has often been resorted to in sociological research to surmount the difficulties associated with the closed-system theories is known as *comparative method.*

The Darwinian tradition is said to have provided sociology with successful application of the comparative method by which various conclusions arrived at by different social sciences have been successfully verified. Attempts have been made in social anthropology and also in historical sociology to establish the ambitious hypothesis that societies or cultures and institutions continually evolve and pass through a series of stages, rhythms, or forms. It is stated that the 'life' of macro-sociological units like culture is strikingly analogous to the life of biological species. The Darwinians have been obviously over-impressed by the biological analogy. The marriage institution, to take an example, is claimed to have *universally* passed through the phases of promiscuity, group-marriage, clan, gens and individual family, in that order. On the basis of his studies of some isolated tribes the anthropologist frames the provisional hypothesis that the marriage institution in *all* tribes is marked by some or all of the phases, depending upon the stages of their evolution. Through comparison of relevant institutional data obtainable from different and independent tribal societies the Darwinian tries to establish his evolutionary hypothesis. But it is to be remembered that meaningful comparison itself presupposes a hypothesis. Data become comparable in terms of, and also converge upon, a given hypothesis. The plausibility of comparative method as used by Darwinians depends upon the tenability or otherwise of the Darwinian theory of evolution itself. So it has been often pointed out that the relation between the Darwinian comparative method and the Darwinian theory of evolution is viciously circular. Unless we can explain or understand the succession of different phases of the marriage institution in a given order in terms of the theory of evolution, we perhaps cannot cite definite rhythms or phases in different historical series to prove the necessary character of the evolutionary hypothesis. In other words, the proof must not take the probandum for granted. If the consequence is surreptitiously assumed in the antecedents then the proposition is logically worthless. Morgan's theory of marriage institution has been challenged precisely on this score. Critics have pointed out that careless users of the comparative method have taken *incidental resemblances for essential similarities.*

An *incidental* character of the comparative method is its emphasis on *genetic approach.* By genetic approach we mean the attempt to explain the subsequent phases of the human cycle by its antecedent ones. This incidental character of comparative method is at times regarded as an essential feature of historical sociology. The least that may be safely claimed in this connection is that the relation between comparative method and genetic approach is not antithetical.

One should not lose sight of the limits of genetic method. Nobody denies the importance of *origin* and details in sociological study. On the contrary most of us agree that the forms of primitive society throw light on the obscure beginning of subsequent development of different socio-political forms, but to insist that all types of society, modern and medieval, must be explained in terms of the earliest forms of society is to ignore the *qualitative characteristics* found in relatively modern forms of society. Secondly, the proponents of genetic approach forget that we cannot adequately explain a form of society or an institution merely by tracing its origin. The past *whats* of a form of society do not necessarily provide its *why.*

Reacting rather rashly to this criticism of genetic method some sociologists say that every form of society is to be explained in terms of its *attending* circumstances and *not* by relating it to its antecedents. If genetic method encourages a sort of reductionism, one might say, circumstantial explanation tends to make history worthless. The present cannot be reduced to the past, nor can it be completely isolated from that. Highlighting this point as a criticism of both the genetic mode of explanation and the circumstantial one evolutionists like Sri Aurobindo claim that explanation in terms of evolution can steer a clear way in between the two.

But this approach may not commend itself to many modern sociologists. They would say, if comparative-genetic method commits us to illicit and ambitious generalizations, and if circumstantial explanation encourages a sort of static and insular outlook, there is still another method different from the evolutionary one to avoid the difficulties. If *abstraction* is combined with *comparison,* then, it is claimed, we may scientifically compare different forms of society in their respective cycles without being landed in indefensible and highly general laws of social evolution. Morgan's analysis in *Ancient Society* is cited as an example of what may be achieved by judicious combination of comparative and abstractionist strategies.

To start with, Morgan carefully observes the external conditions under which some Indian tribes of North America evolved. He first notes the fundamental but external conditions of a given tribe in the course of its development and then tries to see how they compare, favourably or unfavourably, with similar conditions attending the development of other spatially separated local tribes. Morgan studies these societies *individually* and not as elements of a class. Then he assumes hypothetically, resorting to the strategy of abstraction, that the more general and fundamental conditions of development should be universal, i.e. found in different classes of tribes in the different parts of the world. Then he tries to test his hypothesis by applying it to some primitive tribes *other than* the Indian ones. This is the method which is termed *analytic induction* by Znaniecki, and he regards it scientific and finds it very useful.

Applying the method of analytic induction, aided by comparison and abstraction, Morgan arrives at the conclusion : "civilization must be regarded as an accident of circumstances the result of a series of fortuitous circumstances."[7] This is the typical conclusion of empirical sociologists and historians. And Sri Aurobindo's attack is directed against this view.

It is well known that Marx has been deeply impressed by Morgan's research findings and conclusions. He thinks that his general theory of materialistic interpretation of history is being substantially corroborated by Morgan's works. Engels tells us that Marx "planned to present the result of Morgan's researches in connection with the conclusions arrived at by his own."[8] Morgan's view that social relations are chief determinants of human history has been highly commended and gratefully acknowledged in the Marxist quarters.

Social relations, says Marx, are expressive of the relations obtained in between the conflicting classes of a definite system of production. The relations of production are stated to be

7. H. L. Morgan, *Ancient Society*, Indian Edition, p. 563.
8. F. Engels, *The Origin of the Family, Private Property and the State*, (Preface to the first edition).

the foundation of all other relations—legal, political, cultural and so on. The basic structure of society consists of inter-class economic relationships and which operate more or less independently of the will of the people concerned. Consequently, it is argued, super-structural phenomena and processes are to be explained in terms of basic structural relationships and not human ideas or ideals. To put it in Marx's own language: "it is not the consciousness of men that determines their existence, but, on the contrary, their existence determines their consciousness."[9] Those who, like Sri Aurobindo, take the trouble of tracing 'the so-called general progress of the human mind' in order to explain social phenomena, are regarded by Marx as essentially mistaken. He criticizes them for taking an upside down view of historical explanation. Social progress is due neither to the human mind nor to the divine mind nor to the combination of either. Society is a network of productive relationships. "The anatomy of the civil society is to be sought in political economy." And it is for the political economist to study the contradictions involved in productive relationships which account for conflict, movement and change.

Marx's method is marked by abstraction. The first step of abstraction is betrayed by his aim to study the *anatomy* of society rather than the society itself in which he is obviously more interested. The second step of abstraction is clear from the fact that in spite of his interest in different fields or levels of history, he concentrates on economic history or, to be more precise, on the economic structure of the capitalist society, and that too within a very limited set of conditions obtained in England in the mid-nineteenth century. Further, it may be pointed out that, Marx implicitly assumes that the conditions of the capitalist mode of production of that time and of that place would remain more or less constant over a long period of time and in different societies. And this assumption has been repeatedly questioned and criticized later on. Thirdly, from a variety of productive relationships Marx chooses only the capital-labour relationship and decides to explain the others in terms of it. Understood through all these levels of abstractions, human beings lose their *basic* identity in the world of Marx's

---

9. Karl Marx, *The Critique of Political Economy*, (Preface).

theory. "Individuals are dealt with," he writes in the preface to the *Capital,* "only in so far as they are the personifications of economic categories, embodiments of particular class and class interests." Marx is of course aware that individuals are not how they are *dealt* with in theory. To classify and organize the vast and extremely complex facts of social life, abstraction is indeed necessary. But the point is that excessive abstraction projects a deformed and distorted picture of social reality. In fairness to Marx it is also to be admitted that his abstract economic categories may at least partially be corroborated by historical and sociological findings. He does not borrow a priori these categories from some speculative social philosophy. That is all right. But his belief in the constancy of class antagonism down the epochs of history is nothing more than a speculative hypothesis and has been repeatedly falsified by the historical findings of different times and places. It is to be remembered that this belief is essential to the tenability of his theory of history. Partly discounting Marx's claim that class struggle is a universal character of history the critic may point out that he was over-impressed by some particular phases of European History. History may be interpreted in a very general way in terms of class-struggle, but this key concept of Marx does not help us to explain all phases of human history. There is a clear distinction between interpretation and explanation, and it seems that Marx is either not aware of it or does not attach sufficient importance to it. The resulting confusion is there.

To understand the abstract approach and speculative sweep of Marx one should bear in mind his grounding in classical economics in general and Hegel in particular. Hegel wrote in his *Philosophy of History*: in the "process of scientific understanding, it is of importance that the essential should be disentangled and brought into relief in contrast with the so-called non-essential. But in order to render this possible we must know what is essential." For Marx the 'essential' is capital-labour conflict and in terms of this basic concept designating a constant dialectical process he tries to explain all other less essential and non-essential social processes, phenomena and relationships. In defence of Marx it has often been said that Marx is *not* a reductionist and that he does not propose to level down all non-economic factors to the economic ones. Marx never asserts that the relation between economic categories and other categories is unilateral; on the contrary, he speaks of dialectical relation between the two, one influencing the other in turn. But Marx is never tired of asserting that the economic factors are more influential than the rest.

A careful Marxist would not deny, for instance, that individuals are partly responsible for creating the social circumstances under which they are obliged to live. This is what Marx has in his mind when he says that the *forms* of economic relations of today become our *fetters* tomorrow. Obviously, that man does not like to find himself in fetters, shows that social relations are to a great extent independent of his likes and dislikes and determined by certain *laws of history*. This is *historical inevitability*, an important corollary of economic determinism and economic interpretation of history. The *form-fetter contradiction* is being continuously created and resolved by the *necessary* and dialectical process of history. Whatever might be the Marxist's argument in defence of the role of man in history, it cannot be denied that he does not quite see how and to what extent human ideas shape the course of history. However impressive might be the Marxist's frequent reference to history and sociology, it is difficult to admit that this is enough to undo the miseffects of his extravagant use of abstract and over-simplified economic categories.

When I say all this about Marx I do not like to detract one's attention in the least from the great contribution he has made to human thought. He is perhaps the ablest spokesman of his time. I do not know of any other social philosopher who could see through the anatomy of the capitalist economy as clearly as he did. Eager to get to the anatomy of the capitalist economy Marx relatively ignores a lot of other very related and important things, particularly the influence of human ideas and ideals in history. The broad sweep and wide sympathy of his mind obviously could not save him from his abstract economic bias. Whitehead says:

> "Every age produces people with clear logical intellects and with the most praiseworthy grasp of the importance of some sphere of human experience, who have elaborated, or inherited, a scheme of thought which exactly fits those experiences

which claim their interest. Such people are apt resolutely to ignore, or to extend away, all evidences which confuse their scheme with contradictory instances. What they cannot fit in is for them nonsense. An unflinching determination to take the whole evidence into account is the only method of preservation againt the fluctuating extremes of fashionable opinion. This advice seems so easy, and is in fact so difficult to follow."[10]

Following Aristotle it has been often said that the truth of a thing lies somewhere in between the extreme views about it. Ordinarily I take this adage to be true. But I doubt very much whether it is always the case. The Marxist says that the propellant force of history is *contradiction* or *struggle*. Some others like Hobhouse have struck a quite different note when they asserted that history moves through a series of syntheses and that the main trait of history is *harmony* and not contradiction.

V

At this stage we may perhaps profitably look into Hobhouse's concept of sociology. According to him, there are two important aspects of sociology, social philosophy and social science. The former is mainly concerned with analysis of *values,* and the latter with study of *facts*. Whether fact and value are independent of one another is a perennial problem of philosophy. Evolutionists like Hobhouse in their bid to reject value-fact dualism speak of a sort of purposive harmony between the two. It is said that values are being realized in facts through social evolution and by human instrumentation. "Social development and ethical development are at the end same." Proper investigation of a social phenomenon should be carried on at two levels, factual and valuational. "Social philosophy and social science," to use Hobhouse's own language, "are legitimate methods of investigating social phenomena." So far as the factual component of a social phenomenon is concerned there is no methodological problem for the pro-naturalist. The problem arises in respect of the

10. A. N. Whitehead, *Science and the Modern World*, p. 232.

valuational component. For the pro-naturalist points out that value as understood (*not* defined) by the idealists is not amenable to scientific methodological treatment. If the so-called scientific methodologist does not know how to deal with value, one wonders, whether that in itself may be regarded as a good reason for excluding the question of value from the domain of sociology. Hobhouse's position on the point is very clear. Social fact is quite different from *physical fact.* It has no definite spatio-temporal locus. It is essentially (but not exclusively) mental and that explains the *possibility* of its relation with value. The value-fact dualism presupposes a physicialist notion of social fact. The main defining character of a social phenomenon is purpose. Physical facts are identified or identifiable more or less definitely in a space-time co-ordinate. Social phenomena are indicated in terms of some or other purpose. Referring to Hobhouse's method Ginsberg observes that its main aim:

> "was to examine and classify the forms of mental activity, social groupings and institutions and to disentangle evolution. These studies led him to formulate a theory of development as consisting in the extension of harmony through a series of syntheses, effected by the liberation of elements originally in conflict and building up of structures of varying degrees of plasticity, scale and coherence."

The consideration of value or purpose in Marx's writings is conspicuous by its absence. Whenever it is discussed there it is discussed as an external adjunct or character of a fact, physical or mental. In Marx's theory man is an "ensemble of social relations," subordinate to the productive technique and more a creature than a creator of his circumstances. In other words, man, according to him, is a product of social evolution marked by certain definite productive relationships. Hobhouse, on the other hand, holds that social evolution proceeds gradually and by stages and is marked by the development of consciousness and self-consciousness, and the resultant control of mind over the conditions of life. While Marx explains social evolution in terms of conflict and contradiction, Hobhouse asserts that "mere conflict and contradiction cannot lead to anything." The key concept of Hobhouse's sociology is *harmony*.

Hobhouse has been largely influenced by Spencer's evolutionary and organic conceptions of Nature. But he rejects the latter's suggestion that society moves automatically and that this movement has nothing to do with human will, which, given freedom, can play only a negative role and hinder the progress of society. According to Spencer, the main features of the evolutionary process are progressive differentiation and better adjustment. Social growth, says Hobhouse, exhibits correlation and harmony of different factors like fact and value.

Hobhouse's debt to Hegel is also unmistakable. His accent on *harmony* reminds one of Hegel's notion of *synthesis*. While Marx and his followers highlight the Hegelian notion of *antithesis*, Hobhouse emphasizes the notion of synthesis. Of course it has to be admitted that both Marx and Hobhouse have assimilated the legacy of Hegel in a very creative way. Marx claims to have put Hegel upside down, meaning thereby that while Hegel tried to explain the external world in terms of consciousness, he has succeeded in showing that the case is just the other way round, i.e. consciousness is determined and explained by the external world. Hobhouse rejects the talk of dichotomy between the 'external' and the 'internal', between the world within and the world without. He thinks that the relation between the two is more intimate than what is indicated by the proponents of the dialectical method. Their relation is stated to be *essentially harmonious* and only *incidentally antithetical*.

VI

About the obvious objects of experience philosphers generally do not quarrel. Their controversy centres on or around some subtly formulated issues regarding the relative status, meaning and value of things which we uncritically take for granted on the basis of our pre-reflective experience. No philosopher in his senses would deny, for instance, that conflicts and contradictions are there in the social life. The controversy is over the question: whether contradiction or conflict is incidental or essential to the process of social evolution.

Sri Aurobindo has his own answer to the question. His emphasis is neither on contradiction nor on harmony. He does not subscribe to the Hegelian theory of dialectics either. He is an integralist, and his method is called integral method. According to him, elements of harmony and those of contradiction are both integral to the process of evolution. The scale of evolution, from the material and the vital to the mental and the spiritual, is marked by gradual increase of integration and progressive decrease of contradiction. The traits of opposition, differentiation and contradiction are very clear in the natural world, in the physical and the chemical processes and compositions. The same is not the case with the human world, the mental and the spiritual phenomena, their formations and transformations. Socio-political evolution is an integral part and extension of natural evolution.

Nature is secret *God.* And *Man* is the middle-term in between God and Nature. That is how Sri Aurobindo defines the relation between the three main terms of different stages of evolution. Man is both drawn towards Nature and withdrawn from it due to the forces of God from above. Man is, in a very important sense, natural—the conscious part of Nature, yet "he possesses a power of turning his mind and will upon Nature and a possibility of governing her movement, even of varying from the course she dictates to him."[11]

Man is integral to (but not supreme in) the scheme of things of God. He is here to realize the purpose of the Divine. He is engaged in realizing the 'ideal of human unity' through association and union, and strife and opposition. Social evolution is the development of the integral relation between three terms—*individual, community* and *mankind.* "Each seeks its own fulfilment and satisfaction," but Nature requires them to follow "the law of liberty and harmony rather than the law of discord and regimentation, compulsion and adjustments and strife." To follow correctly the law of liberty and harmony and avoid that of conflict and contradiction man must know his *destiny* first and should also master the means to realize it freely. The more he is conscious of his common (or community) self the more he knows the aim of his own life and gets the power to realize it.

Sri Aurobindo raises the question : how best can man know

---

11. *The Ideal of Human Unity,* p. 174.

and realize the aim of his life. Should he rely on *reason*, which is almost universally glorified as supremely necessary instrument for the discovery of truth, or should he fall back upon the intuitive *resources* of his *spiritual mind*? Frankly speaking, while Sri Aurobindo gives reason its due, he is never tired of exposing the hollowness of its lofty claims.

Reason is stated to be incapable of appropriately grasping and tackling with the object of knowledge, for, it is intrinsically *differential*, while the object we seek to realize in knowledge is integral. His critique of *reason as a method* is a moving plea for integral knowledge, pointing out the inadequacy and shortcomings of rational knowledge. "The coils and zigzags of Nature are too deep to be fathomed by the plummet of reason".

Sri Aurobindo favours the psychological approach to sociology. It is to be remembered in this connection that by *psychology* Sri Aurobindo does not mean ordinary *empirical psychology*. His notion of *integral psychology* is quite different in character. It is based on introspection, insight, and realization and not on generalized or quantified experimental and observational data. Not by looking at the things but rather by looking *through* them that he wants to get to the truth or rationale of the problems to be explained. In the name of science he is not in favour of following the 'objective' approach, which is capable of studying and explaining only what is observable or presentable to sense-experience. The objective approach, he fears, leads to a sort of crass empiricism or positivisim. Deeper truths elude the inspection of eyes and lie beyond the reach of senses. It is on this ground that he strongly advocates the 'subjective' method. Here again he cautions us against a false sort of subjectivity—subjectivity which is fed by and is based upon sense-data. True subjectivity is spiritual and at that level the mind can work and carry on its search for truth more or less independently of what is sensible and the sense-mind.

Sri Aurobindo's subjective-psychological approach towards human history and its main elements, individual, community, and mankind, remind one of the phenomenological approach of Dilthey and Lamprecht. Sri Aurobindo has evidently been influenced particularly by the latter. Anti-naturalist philosophers draw a line of distinction between what is natural and what is historical and they attach great importance to it. Those who deny it profess a sort of empiricism or naturalism, trying to reduce everything to the terms of sense-experience or to the mechanical laws of Nature. In Sri Aurobindo's integral sociology the concept of Nature occupies a very important position. But it clashes both with empiricism and naturalism as ordinarly understood. He rejects the dichotomy between Nature, on the one hand, and Society and History, on the other. We cannot properly understand our socio-political life unless we get to the rationale of the forces of Nature working in and around us.

In other words, circumstantial and objective analysis and explanation of social events are not very illuminating. The proper *meaning* of an event cannot be fully grasped in terms of its relations with its *actual* circumstances or conditions. Most of the available sociological theories regarding the place of man in society are found to have been offered mainly in terms of the physical, vital and intellectual conditions of his life. Sri Aurobindo thinks that these approaches are unsatisfactory on several scores. First, as it has been already pointed out, this approach is superficial, external and does not get us to the depth of the true explanatory conditions. Secondly, it does not tell us how the *potentiality* of a particular event or phenomenon shapes its *actual* perceptible characteristics. This unsatisfactoriness is attributed by Sri Aurobindo to the inherent limitations of the role of reason in our life. Pre-occupied with the actualities of our social life, reason, because of its mechanical character, cannot inform and intimate us correctly the immense *possibility* that lies within us and ahead of us. Our understanding of *man in society* cannot be satisfactory unless we can grasp his Spiritual destiny in the future cycles of Nature. Placed in between Natural base and Spiritual destiny, *man as a phenomenon* is to be studied with reference to what is behind him and particularly what lies ahead of him. Nature's natural man, according to Sri Aurobindo, is a growing God.

Like Hobhouse Sri Aurobindo thinks that social evolution represents a 'progressive self-realization and self-fulfilment of the values and potentialities' of the individual. Man is a sort of evolving value. He is more a promise than an achievement. His true significance cannot be adequately brought about only by analysing and classifying the factual conditions of his life.

In this respect Sri Aurobindo's approach to man and what is human is quite different from the Marxist's. Sri Aurobindo seems to accept Hobhoue's basic position that society moves forward mainly through syntheses and that contradiction and conflict are only incidental and instrumental in character. In this respect too his difference from Marx is very clear.

Sri Aurobindo's method of sociology has a peculiarity of its own. It not only differs from the Dialectical Method of Hegel and is inconsistent with the Dialectical Materialism of Marx, it clashes also with structuralism, functionalism, structural-functionalism, and other accepted methods of sociology and anthropology. His main argument against structuralism may be developed somewhat along the lines of his opposition to external and objective approach. Just by correlating a social phenomenon or an institution to its *actual* structure or theorized frame of reference one cannot explain it satisfactorily. Structural relations reveal at best some prominent and actual traits of what is to be explained. He points out further that merely by indicating the function performed by an institution in a particular context we cannot rationally claim to have explained it adequately either. After all *function* is not *purpose*. The distinction between the two must not be overlooked. Function has a distinct positivist connotation and is more or less indifferent to the human purpose which is being progressively realized in history and society. Even a judicious and careful combination of structuralism and functionalism is not enough to meet Sri Aurobindo's objections against external approach to sociology. minimizing the influence of ideas and ideals on history and ignoring the significance of spiritual destiny or potentiality of man and mankind.

Sri Aurobindo is consistently against misplaced concreteness and wild historical analogies. He says that the modern age should not be understood through old ideas,[12] nor the old age through modern ideas.[13] One age must not be telescoped into another. To support a particular theory of history or sociology we are not entitled to refer to events and trends out of their context. The individuality of historical perspectives should be borne

12. *The Human Cycle.*, pp. 28-29.
13. *The Ideal of Human Unity.*, p. 176.

in mind. The more we get into the depth of a social phenomenon and its human root, the more difficult it becomes for us to tear it off its appropriate context and use it as a supporting evidence for a theory based on things of other times and other places. Sri Aurobindo is in favour of *studying society* mainly through *man*. For he regards the former as an expression of the latter. To him depth psychology is a key to the understanding of sociology and history. Here again his difference from the Marxist's approach is unmistakable. While Marx thinks that man is more a creature than a creator of society and that he is mainly to be explained by his social circumstances. Sri Aurobindo takes pains to rebut this thesis and establish the view that man is destined to orient, regulate and progressively establish his control over the attending circumstances of his life.

Looking at the divergence of views expressed by Karl Marx and Sri Aurobindo one must not think that they have nothing in common. They share many fundamental ideas in common. First, they have expressed in different ways their profound and studied *concern for the alienated man* in an age dominated by matter, machine and money. Humanism and a profound moral appeal are there in the core of their social philosophies. Secondly, their approach is *essentially historical,* based of course on their own *individual* interpretation of history. Thirdly, both of them are *historical determinists* and have tried to show that history of different societies exhibits a general pattern marked by certain predictable rhythms. Fourthly, they subscribe to the doctrine of *methodological holism.*[14] Finally, both of them profoundly impressed by the doctrine of *anarchism,* have visualized the future of human society in terms of statelessness and 'complete' individual freedom. It goes without saying that the formulation of their views, arguments to establish their points and method of deriving conclusions are quite independent.

One may or may not agree with what Sri Aurobindo has said on Man and his spiritual destiny, but one who has gone carefully through his works is bound to be impressed by the sweep of his integral outlook, the perceptiveness of his mind, style and subtlety of expression, and the broad conclusions which are

---

14. D. P. Chattopadhyaya, *Individuals and Societies : A Methodological Inquiry*, Calcutta, 1967.

being progressively borne out by later events. In spite of the fact that some of the disciples of Marx tried to portray him as a prophet of the doom of capitalism, and in spite of all that has happened in the world in the last hundred years or so, a critical thinker cannot accept the Marxist claim that history has consistently corroborated Marx's theory.[15] Nor can he accept the view advocated by some of the devotees of Sri Aurobindo, viz. that he is a prophet. Personally I do not believe in prophecy. Man, being finite, can only predict what is likely to happen, but cannot prophesy the future course of events. Finite and fallible man cannot usurp the role and power of God who never fails. A sound and scientific method should be based on this basic truth regarding human nature and ability.

---

15. K. R. Popper, *Poverty of Historicism*, London, 1961.

Secular and Non-Secular Elements in Sri Aurobindo's Life and Thought

K.R. SRINIVASA IYENGER

SRI Aurobindo's life was not lived on the surface for men to observe, analyse or generalise about: dates and entrances and exists, prosecutions and court-trials and acquittals, confabulations and conferences and confrontations, these 'facts' of his outer life were certainly *not* his real life: on the other hand, his inner life was a universe vast and full, crowded with multitudinous events, although coalescing into a transcendent unity—

"His soul must be wider than the universe
And feel eternity as its very stuff,
Rejecting the moment's personality,...
In the calm infinity it has become."[1]

How is the biographer or historian to seize this 'life' that is "wider than the universe" or pluck and exhibit the heart of the mystery?

Again, Sri Aurobindo's 'thought' was spread out in prose and drama, in speeches and letters and conversations, over a period of about sixty years, and the *Collected Centenary Edition* of his *Works* is expected to cover some thirty large volumes. What was written for the *Indu Prakash* in the first flush of political idealism soon after his return to India from England in 1893: what was penned in the heat of active political involvement, as

1. *Savitri*, 1954, p. 610.

editorial or special article, for the *Bande Mataram, Karmayogin* or *Dharma:* what was put into the mouth of a dramatic character in consonance with the imperatives of his imaginative creation: what was spoken in a climate of debate or controversy, or even of relaxation among an assembled group of admirers and disciples: what was recorded—whether in prose or in verse—after the plenitudes of mystic experience or spiritual realisation: all have their distinguishing yet limiting features. On a first view, indeed, the writings and the utterances are not all of a piece. Aphorisms, epigrams, 'thoughts', 'glimpses'—at one end; massive sequences, global sweeps of thought like *The Life Divine, The Synthesis of Yoga, The Human Cycle, The Foundations of Indian Culture* and *The Ideal of Human Unity*—at the other end: and, in between, all intensities of expression, all varieties of form, all ranges of experience—mysticism and religion, poetry and philosophy, education and Yoga, psychology and sociology, war and peace and human unity, all is grist that comes to the mill, and any "division by dichotomy"—'secular' and 'non-secular' elements in Sri Aurobindo's life and thought—could prove to be an utterly frustrating exercise. I did not choose the subject; it was given to me. Dissection, whether of a great poem or of a great Yogi's 'life and thought', can hardly ever prove edifying and can never lead to illumination. But analytical inquiry and salubrious seminarism have their kick too, and perhaps—while not exactly acquiescing in the validity of the implied antithesis between 'secular' and 'non-secular'—one might nevertheless make a cautious approach to the given problem.

In 1905, soon after his involvement in nationalist politics and secret revolutionary activity, Sri Aurobindo wrote *Bhavani Mandir,* which became presently the Bible of the young revolutionaries. The pamphlet was secretly, if also widely, criculated; and, in the eyes of the bureaucracy, *Bhavani Mandir* was little better than a packet of revolutionary dynamite. It could be read as a plea for the establishment of a Temple for Bhavani, Bhavani Bharati, Mother of India, and for the organisation of a religious order of political *Sannyasins*—taking the cue, perhaps, from Bankim Chandra's *Ananda Math.* Politics and religion: an explosive concatenation! On closer scrutiny, however, the accent in the pamphlet would seem to be on something larger, something more inclusive:

> "We have to create strength where it did not exist before; we have to change our natures, and become new men with new hearts, to be born again. There is no scientific process, no machinery for that. Strength can only be created by drawing it from the internal and inexhaustible reservoirs of the Spirit, from that *Adya-Shakti* of the Eternal which is the fountain of all new existence. To be born again means nothing but to revive the Brahma within us, and that is a spiritual process...."
> "We need a nucleus of men in whom the Shakti is developed to its uttermost extent, in whom it fills every corner of the personality and overflows to fertilize the earth. These, having the fire of Bhavani in their hearts and brains, will go forth and carry the flame to every nook and cranny of our land...."
> "Come then, hearken to the call of the Mother....You who feel Her stirring within you, fling off the black veil of self, break down the imprisoning walls of indolence, help Her each as you feel impelled, with your bodies or with your intellect or with your speech or with your wealth or with your prayers and worship, each man according to his capacity. Draw not back, for against those who were called and heard Her not She may well be wroth in the day of Her coming; but to those who help Her advent even a little, how radiant with beauty and kindness will be the face of their Mother's...."[2]

The language of religion is apparently used, but the emphasis is on the nation, the nation's reviving strength, the nation's hope of regeneration; and the allegiance is to be offered ultimately at the altar of no "fragment of land bounded by seas and hills, but the whole earth with her teeming millions". Hindu names are given but more as symbols of the spiritual realities behind the religious facades. 'Bhavani' is no mere Hindu goddess but is a symbol signifying Infinite Energy, Love, Strength, Power, Knowledge; and Knowledge is "the great *so-ham,* the mighty formula of the Vedanta", and to revive the Brahma within us is "a spiritual process". If 'secular' is to be concerned with the affairs of *this* world (rather than with a world to come, a transcendent world) and if 'religious' is to have a feeling for a superhuman Power controlling human destinies, the Aurobindonian integral

---

2. A.B. Purani, *The Life of Sri Aurobindo: 1872-1926* (1964), pp. 81ff.

view locates the unfolding Godhead *within* man and looks forward to the establishment of only an *earthly* Paradise.

It was not long after *Bhavani Mandir* was written that Sri Aurobindo indited in Bengali the powerfully charged *Durga Stotra,* a passionate appeal to the veiled indwelling *Shakti* to make Herself manifest. It is both an acknowledgement of the present plight of national degradation and a stirring call for the resurgence of the spirit, the reawakening of India's puissant purpose; and, perhaps, it is as relevant today as it was sixty-years ago:

> "Mother Durga! India lies low in selfishness and fearfulness and littleness. Make us great, make our efforts great, our hearts vast, make us true to our resolve. May we no longer desire the small, void of energy, given to laziness, stricken with fear...."
>
> "Mother Durga! Slay the enemy within, then root out all obstacles outside. May the noble heroic mighty Indian race, supreme in love and unity, truth and strength, arts and letters, force and knowledge ever dwell in its holy woodlands, its fertile fields, under its sky-scraping hills, along the banks of its pure-streaming rivers. This is our prayer at the feet of the Mother. Make thyself manifest".[3]

Has it the outer cast of a religious hymn? The favour is no doubt there, but what is invoked is no sectarian deity but the home-of-all womb-of-all—the Power that is everywhere and hence can become manifest in this land too, and being latent in everything can come out into the open in everyone of us as Aspiration the Mother of Radiances dawns in the narrow horizons of the mind, fills, illumines and vibrates "the multiple strings of life".[4]

Throughout Sri Aurobindo's political period—a matter of four or five years—there is this attempt to charge the 'secular' activity of politics with the deeper urgencies of religion. He used images and concepts familiar to Hindus and Hinduism, but on a closer look it would be found that these have no narrow credal, dogmatic or ritualistic limitation but only a wide-arching, enriching and

3. *Sri Aurobindo Mandir Annual*, 1967, pp. 5-6.
4. "Hymn to the Mother of Radiances" in *The Hour of God* (May 1970), p. 5.

all-embracing spiritual connotation. While Sri Aurobindo did not make 'religion' and 'politics' incompatible with one another, he also raised both to a level where they would be cleansed of their vitalistic and egoistic associations. Thus in an article in the *Bande Mataram* on 2 August 1907, he wrote:

"No artificial or ceremonial ways of preparing the soul can approach in effectiveness the spiritual process of merging one's hopes, desires, and one's very life in a wider individuality such as that of one's nation. The very foundation of the *Gita* is Sri Krishna's exhortation to Arujna to forget his petty affections for a greater good."

Three months later (9 November 1907), in an article on "Politics and Spirituality", Sri Aurobindo returned to the theme, ridiculed the view that spirituality was associated with cowardice, and added:

"Spiritual energy is not on this earth a thing apart but reposes and draws upon physical energies....It was an ebb in the spiritual sentiment which resulted in a complete physical nervousness with Arjuna on the eve of the great battle of Kurukshetra, and one spiritual ideal worked out in the *Gita* is that if you allow any physical timidity to intervene between you and your duty, all spiritual possibility is gone."

More than four months later (28 March 1908), in an article on "Spirituality and Nationalism", Sri Aurobindo referred to the unique example of Ramakrishna Paramahamsa, who had been able in his own extraordinary life to re-enact the inner drama of *all* religions, thereby exemplifying their oneness in the spirit. A 'religion of man' was possible, although it was still only an ideal to be realised in the future. India's resurgence, however, held out the hope that the possible would become the actuality:

"Sri Ramakrishna gave to India the final message of Hinduism to the world. A new era dates from his birth, an era in which the people of the earth will be lifted for a while into communion with God and spirituality become the dominant note of religious life. What Christianity failed to do, what

> Mahomedanism strove to accomplish in times as yet unripe, what Buddhism half accomplished for a brief period and among a limited number of men, Hinduism as summed up in the life of Sri Ramakrishna has attempted for all the world. This is the reason of India's resurgence....The movement of which the first outbreak was political will end in a spiritual consummation."

But, of course, Sri Aurobindo was not unaware of Hindu-Muslim "differences" generally keeping the communities apart and occasionally exploding in riots. Writing after the East Bengal communal riots in the *Bande Mataram* of 25 May 1907, Sri Aurobindo stressed "the seriousness and true nature of the Mahomedan problem which our older politicians have always tried to belittle or ignore". The rioter, whether Hindu or Mahomedan, was but a disturber of the peace, and force should be met by force and there could be no parleying with the engineers of communal strife. In the larger life of the nation, as Sri Aurobindo wrote in the *Karmayogin* in 1910, it would be suicidal to treat "Hindu and Mahomedan as permanently separate units", for that must preclude "the growth of a single and indivisible Indian nation". Sri Aurobindo also saw clearly that the Hindu-Muslim problem asked, not for a settlement in terms of political horse-trading, but for a spiritual solution. As he wrote in the *Karmayogin:*

> "Hindu-Mahomedan unity cannot be effected by political adjustment or Congress flatteries. It must be sought deeper down, in the heart and in the mind, for where the causes of disunion are, there the remedies must be sought....We shall do well to remember...that love compels love and that strength conciliates the strong. We must strive to remove the causes of misunderstanding by a better mutual knowledge and sympathy; we must extend the unfaltering love of the patriot to our Mussulman brother remembering that in him too Narayan dwells and to him too our Mother has given a permanent place in her bosom; but we must cease to approach him falsely or flatter out of a selfish weakness and cowardice."

And he concluded by setting forth the editorial policy of the paper:

> "We shall make it a main part of our work to place Muhammad and Islam in a new light before our readers, to spread juster views of Mahomedan history and civilisation, to appreciate the Mussulman's place in our national development and the means of harmonising his communal life with our own."[5]

The 'spiritual' includes and exceeds both 'religious' and 'secular' and the Muslim is the Hindu's brother because the Divine dwells in them both. The hucksterings of the political mart—separate electorates, weightage, reservations, veto—might in the end prove a fiasco after all, but the unitive ground of the spirit can easily absorb the shocks of all adverse circumstances. What was needed was a genuine effort at understanding, a change of heart, a clearing of the mist of mutual suspicion. As early as 4 September 1907, Sri Aurobindo had warned against "the introduction of a Hindu-Mahomedan dualism" into the Council Chamber proposed by Morley, but the warning was not heeded, and the Dragon's teeth were to do their work unimpeded and accomplish the tragic partition of India forty years later.

The 'spiritual' as the solvent of both 'secular' and 'non-secular' (or 'religious') was one distinguishing feature of Sri Aurobindo's thought before his retirement to Pondicherry in April 1910. Another was his evolutionary view of religion. In his play, *Perseus the Deliverer* (originally published in the *Bande Mataram* in 1907), religious belief and worship moves from Poseidon to Pallas Athene. It is a dialectic, in fact, Poseidon being matched by Pallas, Polydaon the blood-thirsty priest by Andromeda the maiden, and Poseidon's sea-monster by Pallas' champion, Perseus with his aegis and the Medusa head. After the destruction of the monster and the death of the priest, Perseus announces the change from the old religion to the new:

> "let the shrine
> That looked out from earth's breast into the sunlight,
> Be cleansed of its red memory of blood,
> And the dread Form that lived within its precincts
> Transfigure into a bright compassionate God...

---

5. Reprinted in the *Advent*, Vol. XXV, No. 2 (April 1968), pp. 19-20.

In your human image of her deity
A light of reason and calm celestial force
And a wise tranquil government of life,
Order and beauty and harmonious thoughts
And, ruling the waves of impulse, high-throned will
Incorporate in marble, the carved and white
Ideal of a young uplifted race."[6]

In another play, too, the posthumously published *Eric* (1960), there is likewise a decisive movement from Thor (and Odin) to Freya, Mother of Heaven, and the spirit of compassion, love and Grace."[7]

An even more significant transformation is dramatised in the symbolistic epic, *Savitri,* that was begun at Baroda but revised later, and almost completed during the last years at Pondicherry. Here the change is not from the sovereignty of one god to that of another; it rather involves the transformation of one god into another—a radical outer and inner change. After *Savitri's* overthrow of Death, the Dark becomes Light indeed:

"One whom her soul had faced as Death and Night
A sum of all sweetness gathered into his limbs
And blinded her heart to the beauty of the suns.
Transfigured was the formidable shape....
A secret splendour rose revealed to sight
Where once the vast embodied Void had stood.
Night the dim mask had grown a wonderful face."[8]

The change, the transformation has to come, in thought and action alike, and it has to be a total revolutionary change, both inner and outer. As one might say, it is the rabid 'communalist' that must shed his imperfect adhesions and grow into the Nationalist; and it is the fire-eating Nationalist that must outgrow his chauvinistic loyalties, grow wings of global understanding, and change into the internationalist, the true apostle of human unity.

---

6. *Collected Poems and Plays*, Vol. I, p. 305.
7. *Eric* (1960), p. 74.
8. *Savitri*, p. 762.

After his year (1908-9) in the Alipur prison, Sri Aurobindo returned to 'civilisation' illumined by his prison-experiences, notably his vision of the godhead in everybody and in all things. In his Uttarpara speech (30 May 1909), and in his articles in the *Karmayogin* and *Dharma,* he spoke not so much as the 'prophet of nationalism' but as the 'lover of humanity'—both phrases were used by C.R. Das in the inspired peroration of his speech in defence of Sri Aurobindo in the Alipur bomb case—and he spoke, not of Hinduism, but of *Sanatana Dharma,* the Eternal Religion, that was a phenomenon, of 'becoming' in historic time. Human knowledge and power have had to go through a 'natural' stage dominated by the life-impulses and an intermediate stage dominated by the reasoning intelligence, but the last and highest stage of spiritual self-governance is yet to come. In our age of science, transitional man has either to accomplish this difficult ascent towards the heights, change himself, change society or the human aggregate, and change the global human polity—or fall into the abyss prepared by his own advanced technology. In one of his important contributions to the *Karmayogin,* Sri Aurobindo spelt out what he meant by *Sanatana Dharma*:

> "[It is] that wider Hinduism which is not a dogma or combination of dogmas but a law of life, which is not a social framework but the spirit of a past and future social evolution, which rejects nothing but insists on testing and experiencing everything and when tested and experienced turning it to the soul's use, in this Hinduism we find the basis of the future world-religion. This *sanatana dharma* has many scriptures, *Veda, Vedanta, Gita, Upanishad, Darshana, Purana, Tantra,* nor could it reject the *Bible* or the *Koran*; but its real, most authoritative scripture is in the heart in which the Eternal has His dwelling. It is in our inner spiritual experiences that we shall find the proof and source of the world's Scriptures, the law of knowledge, love and conduct, the basis and inspiration of *Karmayoga.*"[9]

In another article in the same series, Sri Aurobindo spoke of the three elements in all life—"the fixed and permanent spirit, the

9. *The Ideal of the Karmayogin* (Seventh Edition, 1950), pp. 6-7.

developing yet constant soul and the brittle changeable body"[10]—and it was clear therefore that our evolutionary endeavour should be conducted in consonance with the nature of these elements. Outer forms could be changed when necessary, the inner soul must evolve continually, but all should be grounded on the Spirit.

Ten months after his acquittal in the Alipur case, Sri Aurobindo suddenly decided to take himself away from Calcutta. First he spent a few weeks at Chandernagore, then he left for Pondicherry and arrived there on 4 April 1910. Other self-exiled Indian patriots too were there—notably V.V.S. Aiyar and Subramania Bharati—but Sri Aurobindo had not just sought political asylum at Pondicherry, but rather a "cave of *Tapasya*". The experience of Divine Omnipresence and of overhead planes of consciousness at the Alipur jail had brought about a profound change in his outlook: his commitment to the cause of Indian independence had grown vast new dimensions: but while he kept a close watch on happenings in India and the world, he dropped all outer participation in public affairs. The years of "silent *Yoga*", the "god's labour" of writing simultaneously a number of prose sequences for the *Arya,* the coming of the disciples, the establishment and growth of the *Ashram* were all events on a plane other than the political. He didn't exactly withdraw from life, he only explored its deeper possibilities; he didn't try to establish a new religion, he only strove to mobilise the secret sustaining power behind all religions. As he wrote to C.R. Das in November 1922, he felt more than ever convinced that "the true basis of work and life is the spiritual". On the basis of personal realisation, he knew that a new consciousness—a consciousness that is power also at the same time—could be won through *Yoga*, and it is this consciousness that should be turned on life to remould and perfect it. In the long and chequered course of earth-history and human history, various attempts have been made to change outer nature, the structure of society, and the ways of the individual and collective man. But only the "spiritual revolution" can really touch the heart of the problem. As Sri Aurobindo wrote in *The Life Divine:*

---

10. *Ibid.*, p. 32.

"...the solution of the problem which spirituality offers is not a solution by external means, though these also have to be used, but by an inner change, a transformation of the consciousness and nature....Spirituality cannot be called upon to deal with life by a non-spiritual method or attempt to cure its ills by other panaceas, the political, social or other mechanical remedies which the mind is constantly attempting and which have always failed....Only a spiritual change, an evolution of his being from the superficial mental towards the deeper spiritual consciousness, can make a real and effective difference."[11]

Life on this earth must still mean—that is, even after the "spiritual revolution"—inhabiting and making the most of the physical body, using the vital impulses and the powers of the mind and the heart to the best purpose, but all would be leavened by the infusion of the spiritual consciousness. The point is eloquently made in *The Synthesis of Yoga:*

"The divinising of the normal material life of man and of his great secular attempt of mental and moral self-culture in the individual and the race by this integralisation of a widely perfect spiritual existence would thus be the crown alike of our individual and of our common effort. Such a consummation being no other than the kingdom of heaven within reproduced in the kingdom of heaven without, would be also the true fulfilment of the great dream cherished in different terms by the world's religions."[12]

Here in a couple of sentences Sri Aurobindo shows how the 'secular' and the 'religious' could—and indeed should—be gathered into the richer integral unity and puissance of the 'spiritual'. Body, life, mind are nothing, less than nothing; it is the degree of their rapport with the Spirit that gives them their power and purpose. And a complete and total rapport must mean the transformation of the ordinary to the spiritual, the mundane to the Divine.

---

11. *The Life Divine*, (International Centre of Education Collection, 1960), pp. 52-53.
12. *The Synthesis of Yoga* (1955), p. 55.

In June 1916, when both *The Life Divine* and *The Synthesis of Yoga* were appearing serially in the *Arya*, Sri Aurobindo wrote to Madame Mirra Richard (now known as the Mother) that "an absolute equality of the mind and heart and a clear purity and calm strength in all the members of the being" were the essential conditions for the desired climb of consciousness. The sense of others and a sense of the unity of all things and the attendant feeling of rapture are the foundations on which the great work of self-transformation and world-transformation should be reared: "It is then that in the One we must see the Master and His Power,—Krishna and Kali as I name them using the terms of our Indian religions." There is thus both a static and a dynamic side to the perception and consciousness of "unity": the static *wills*, the dynamic *executes;* the unity of Knowledge governs the action of the sovereign Power of Consciousness. When 'Krishna, Kali' and other Hindu names are used they do not credally confine but define symbolistically certain spiritual powers or phenomena within the experience of all religions. Actually, in the writings of the *Arya* period and after, Sri Aurobindo brings in such names but seldom, and invariably the discussion is freed seraphically from the taint of the credal, the dogmatic or the sheerly religionistic. Speculating about the future society, Sri Aurobindo writes in *The Human Cycle:*

> "It is a spiritual, an inner freedom that can alone create a perfect human order. It is a spiritual, a greater than the rational enlightenment that can alone illumine the vital nature of man and impose harmony on its self-seekings, antagonisms and discords...it means that no machinery invented by the reason can perfect either the individual or the collective man; an inner change is needed in human nature...if this is not the solution, then there is no solution; if this is not the way, there is no way for the human kind."[13]

Equality, freedom, harmony, unity are what man and society long for, but there is an inveterate enemy barring the way: "That enemy, the enemy of all real religion, is human egoism, the egoism of the individual, the egoism of class

13. *The Human Cycle, The Ideal of Human Unity, War and Self-Determination* (1962), pp. 295-97.

and nation."[14] Eighteenth-century Europe pinned its faith on the ideals of liberty, equality and brotherhood; but as these are verily three "godheads" of the soul "they cannot really be achieved through the external machinery of society or by man so long as he lives only in the individual and the communal ego."[15] Is there, then, no hope for humanity? Perhaps "a spiritual religion of humanity" may yet be able to redeem the time not an Esperanto-religion, not a fabrication of shreds and patches, not a "system, a thing of creed and intellectual belief and dogma and outward rite", but a religion unfalteringly centered in the Spirit:

> "The inner spirit is indeed one, but more than any other the spiritual life insists on freedom and variation in its self-expression and means of development. A religion of humanity means the growing realisation that there is a secret Spirit, a divine Reality, in which we are all one, that humanity is its highest present vehicle on earth, that the human race and the human being are the means by which it will progressively reveal itself here. It implies a growing attempt to live out this knowldge and bring about a kindgom of this divine Spirit upon earth....A spiritual oneness which would create a psychological oneness not dependent upon any intellectual or outward uniformity and compel a oneness of life not bound up with its mechanical means of unification, but ready always to enrich its secure unity by a free inner variation and a freely varied outer self-expressions, this would be the basis for a higher type of human existence."[16]

In his own *Ashram* at Pondicherry, there are people with diverse, racial, religious, cultural and social backgrounds, and they adopt as their means of self-expression a variety of literary, artistic, industrial, agricultural, managerial or educational pursuits. There are no specific forms of prayer or worship, no prescribed scripture, no catechism, no bundle of dogmas, no body of ritual. No doubt Sri Aurobindo is for his disciples the Master, and his

14. *Ibid.*, p. 761.
15. *Ibid.*, p. 763.
16. *Ibid.*, pp. 775-56.

major writings not only provide a conspectus of all knowledge, they also offer guidelines to the *sadhaka* of integral *Yoga*. On the other hand, Sri Aurobindo is quite emphatic that the *Guru* and the *Shastra* are really within:

> "As the supreme *Shastra* of the integral *Yoga* is the eternal *Veda* secret in the heart of every man, so its supreme Guide and Teacher is the inner Guide 'the World-Teacher' *jagad-guru,* secret within us."[17]

Spiritual sovereignty is thus lodged *within,* and it is out of this that the godheads of freedom, harmony, brotherhood and creative unity have to make themselves manifest in our terrestrial life. Everywhere in Sri Aurobindo's later writings we are hit by the blaze of this revelation, the steady light that dispels the clouds of unknowing, the Sunrise that dissolves the mists of all false dichotomies and differentiations, the heart-warming Radiance that cures all egoistic retreats and rejections. In the following passage, for example, Sri Aurobindo presents in an extreme form what may be taken to be the old religious and the new materialistic (or, say, the 'non-secular' and the 'secular') points of view, and also states the inclusive and enfranchising *Vedantic* (or 'spiritual') gospel:

> "Mediaeval Christianity said to the race, 'Man, thou art in thy earthly life an evil thing and a worm before God; renounce then egoism, live for a future state and submit thyself to God and His priest'. The results were not over-good for humanity. Modern knowledge says to the race, 'Man, thou art an ephemeral animal and no more to Nature than the ant and the earthworm, a transitory speck only in the universe. Live then for the State and submit thyself antlike to the trained administrator and the scientific expert'. Will this gospel succeed any better than the other?'
>
> "Vedanta says rather, 'Man, thou art of one nature and substance with God, one soul with thy fellow-men. Awake and progress then to thy utter divinity, live for God in thyself and in others.' This gospel, which was given only to the

17. *The Synthesis of Yoga,* p. 68.

few, must not be offered to all mankind for its deliverance."[18]

The integral—the unitive—the spiritual view is projected also in these aphorisms:

"Life, Life, Life, I hear the passions cry; God, God, God, is the soul's answer. Unless thou seest and lovest Life as God only, then is Life itself a sealed joy to thee".[19]

"I should love my neighbour not because he is in the neighbourhood,—for what is there in neighbourhood and distance? nor because the religions tell me he is my brother,—for where is the root of that brotherhood? but because he is myself. Neighbourhood and distance affect the body, the heart goes beyond them. Brotherhood is of blood or country or religion or humanity, but when self-interest clamours what becomes of this brotherhood? It is only by living in God and turning mind and heart and body into the image of his universal unity that that deep, disinterested and unassailable love becomes possible".[20]

An end to all dichotomies, then: first, station yourself in the Spirit, then all shall be added unto you.

Perhaps a prophetic vision, perhaps only a waking dream,—this notion of the spiritual or divinised man. But in Sri Aurobindo's life, vision and experience coalesced in terms of progressive realisation, and in *Savitri*, the great creative work of the culminating phase of his *sadhana*, he projected this vision as Reality unfolding as the preordained conclusion of the human adventure now in a process of fulfilment:

"Man shall desire to climb to his own heights.
The truth above shall wake a neither truth;
Even the dumb earth become a sentient force.
The Spirit's tops and Nature's base shall draw
Near to the secret of their separate truth
And know each other as one deity.

18. *Thoughts and Aphorisms* (1968), pp. 52-3.
19. *Ibid.*, p. 115.
20. *Ibid.*, pp. 126-7.

The Spirit shall look out through Matter's gaze
And Matter shall reveal the Spirit's face....
This earth shall stir with impulses sublime,
Humanity awake to deepest self
Nature the hidden godhead recognise....
The Spirit shall take up the human play,
This earthly life become the life divine".[21]

21. *Savitri,* pp. 796, 798.

Is the West Ready For Sri Aurobindo?

RUUD LOHMAN

Is the West ready for a new and higher consciousness, for a "leap towards the future", for giving up its mental constructions and vital cravings, in order to open itself to the Divine? Is there something growing already behind the screen, under the surface, something seeking a way out, groping for means and forms of manifestation ? Is there a hidden power for transformation, working mostly invisibly but breaking through in glimpses? Or must the West simply be broken down, collapse under its own weight? Is it waste material, an evolutionary failure?

"The West". A rather vague term. West of what? Of the East? Or rather a specific way in which evolution developed in a part of the world. A rational way, a mental way, highly specialised, fragmented, technical, with a high degree of mastery over some aspects of Nature and with skills of production and needs of consumption as no culture before has ever shown. A mental structure, a solid building, with a huge amount of vital stuff, sure, but even this built in a smooth mental way. An enormous brain providing solutions for all the old needs of mankind: for security, status, possession, recreation, information.

Is the West ready for Sri Aurobindo? Is this huge machinery an evolutionary force, able to breakthrough its own limitations and borders into a possibility for man and culture to go beyond themselves? Either the future will tell, or a highly developed consciousness, knowing both the West's surface and God's depths, may point it out to us. If lesser men venture to express their opinion we may consider this as an exercise in sensitivity and in sharpening the consciousness. Living close to the Mother makes one see more shades of colour in a flower, hear more nuances in music, and should make one able to distinguish finer gradations in evaluating a situation, a culture or an age. And one of the enjoyments in reading Sri Aurobindo's works is the discovery of how he continuously experiences the Truth even in the heart of the lie, the Light where we only see darkness.

"The West" is a culture, an age, but "the West" is also human beings with their own way of feeling, thinking, aspiring, being—fathers and mothers and children, teachers and workers, artists and scientists and spiritualists. On both levels we may ask the question: is the West ready for Sri Aurobindo? We will consider these two levels, of the culture as a totality and of the individuals, and then proceed to a medium level, the level of some movements, some groups, tendencies, new waves, sets of ideas and experiences, which are partly consequences of the main stream of the culture and partly reactions and corrections to it. Here we will ask the same question again.

The culture as such is an abstraction. When one applies a typology to compare cultures or ages one leaves necessarily many opposing tendencies out of the picture, as well as many individuals and groups who refuse to conform. But still, we should first ask: is "the Western culture", taken as an abstraction, ready for Sri Aurobindo? The answer which suggests itself is: absolutely speaking NO, relatively speaking YES.

In *The Human Cycle* Sri Aurobindo describes the situation of different cultures with the help of several, more or less coinciding, sometimes parallel, sometimes overlapping typologies. He begins with an exposition of how human society progresses through five distinct psychological stages, outflowering into a sixth and final one: symbolic, typal, conventional, individualist or rational, subjective and, ultimately the spiritual age. In other chapters of the same book Sri Aurobindo takes the reason as medium of reference and then speaks about three types of societies or ages: the infrarational, the rational, the suprarational. In other places again he takes as point of comparison the way in which a culture succeeds in ordering the various levels of collective consciousness —physical, vital, mental, psychic—and speaks of barbarism, culture or civilisation and spirituality as the three phases through which a collectivity evolves. Sri Aurobindo utilises in his analysis the rational ordering of life, a culture determined by reason, and its outflowering in science, as the medium-term, the necessary transition. "The West" as an abstraction clearly belongs to this type, as a half-way resting place between the obscure infrarational beginnings of culture and its ultimate culmination in the spiritual age.

Taken isolatedly this rational phase of the cycle of culture is different from and closed to the spiritual influences. Things made exclusive, constructed into a "type", become a kind of caricature, in which their basic elements are overstressed for the sake of having a "clean" type. The West, then, as a type in this sense, is a system bent upon itself, self-sufficient, finding in its rational ordering of life the full satisfaction of being. It has no need for powers and influences which go beyond the rational field from which it derives its essence. Science and technology are its powerful instruments, the clothes it wears. Whatever comes up from deep down in the collective nature, vital and physical tendencies, are either made to fit in—one makes an industry out of it—or excluded and rejected. As a closed system and a self-sufficient totality—and therefore as long as it remains as it is—"The West" seems *not* open for subjectivity, even less for spirituality. Allowing these higher tendencies to influence its rational system would undermine the system itself and is therefore not tolerated.

The rational type of culture, however, is not an eternal and absolute ordering. It is partly a reaction, as Sri Aurobindo describes, to a previous conventional and rigid type, partly a preparation for new sets of values. Seen from the high point of view, from where cultures and ages appear to evolve one out of the other and move towards a divine ordering of things, no absolute type exists. Then we may ask the question: how soon is the rational society going to break open towards the future? And: are there any signs of an impending opening to the future? No rigid measures can be applied. Speaking about India Sri Aurobindo shows how it is not absolutely necessary for a culture to bear the full weight of the rational age in all its extremes. India may well go through it very rapidly, taking up on its way the positive elements of reason and then immediately moving into the subjective age, as a preparation for its emergence into the spiritual age. But he also clearly shows how the West bears in itself the seeds of its own destruction. The reason is not the ultimate instrument of Nature and when it does not succeed in dealing efficiently with the irrational in man and society, it necessarily has a limited existence. Many of the foresights of Sri Aurobindo have come true in the meantime and many of us who have gone through the educational, technological or in industrial institutions know that they cannot last. Developments in evolution used to go slow. A typal or conventional society managed to safeguard its existence for many a century. The rational culture is a swift-moving one. It comes into existence within a lifetime, flowers for a century or two and crumbles down, collapses again within another lifetime.

Speaking about the individual *sadhana* Sri Aurobindo indicates that "mental silence" does not mean that one has never used his mental instrument, but, on the contrary, that one first knows how to use it to the full before one can go beyond it. If we apply this principle to the collectivity, we might even say: because the West has used the rational on such a tremendous scale and with such a fanatic vigour, it is more ready for going beyond itself than, may be, any other culture which is not yet awakened to the rational, but still half slumbers in the subrational.

Relatively speaking, the West seems to make itself up to get ready for Sri Aurobindio. We may well witness first its going through the dark night of downfall, failure and large-scale doubt. But that, we know, is how Nature prepares a new dawn.

On the level of the individual, abstractions cannot be made. We would have to look behind the surafce personality of each and every individual to analyse the situation of the West on this basic level. A possibility open to us is to speak from experience, however shallow. It seems, then, that especially in the last few years, many people in the West, young ones, but also older ones, suddenly or in a gradual process, have grown to look through the mental machinery which makes up their culture. From the all-pervading atmosphere of intensive search, the success of books that discuss new aspects of being, the multitudes that visit lectures and symposia on the problems of life, the conclusion can be derived that underneath, deep down in the hearts and minds something is growing, something is being taken apart and something new is fighting its way up.

The impression created by this massive search is that many people are waiting for something to happen, waiting for someone to come. Many feel lonely in their search, give up old securities without finding new ones, and they wait for a direction, for a clear light to follow. More and more persons experience the weight of the institutionalised culture as a burden on their souls and they wait for somebody who can take the burden off.

We cannot approach this individual level in a quantitative way, but qualitatively speaking the air seems to be full of expectation. We would say : many are making themselves ready, unconsciously or consciously, for their guru. On this level of the individual we might even answer our question "Is the West ready for Sri Aurobindo?" with "Yes, Sri Aurobindo is ready for them; the time is on hand and they are waiting, waiting for him without knowing who he is."

It is on the medium level that new things first find their more collective expression. It brings people with similar ideas together, but it does not influence yet the culture as such. Always, in every phase of culture, there exist numerous groups, withdrawn from the mainstream of the culture, protesting against it, working for a new structure, experimenting with alternatives: religious groups, orders and sects; political organisations, cells and movements; mystical, occult, spiritual societies; groups inspired by other cultures or religions. For each one we would have to answer the question about the readiness for Sri Aurobindo separately. We will not even try.

What we intend to go into are some new movements, more recent ones, those which have come into existence as a reaction or correction to the mainstream of culture which we call "The West"; those groups which take a step out of the mental, rational sphere and plunge into fields which are, in the West, relatively undiscovered and unknown. The patterns are multifarious and not clear and balanced yet. Many experiments are going on, interesting ones, dangerous ones. Among these groups, tendencies, experiments, we may find the ones that are getting ready for Sri Aurobindo. A systematic report is not possible yet. We just mention a few of the main characteristics.

The most discussed—and criticized—group is "the youth". They represent a tendency, a movement, outside the general culture, but through their influence and their number are almost in the heart of it. With the same zeal both a very positive and very negative picture of them can be given. The mood of each report depends on the position of the observer with regard to the framework of the culture. Very generally speaking, they step collectively outside the domain of the rational mind. The criticism, "They are out of their mind", may be quite true. And so they step out of the way of their fathers and teachers and governments and industries and positions and successful futures. But then, where do they go from there, from the secure, collective path? Here the real trouble starts. They cannot but go into regions of their being where they are at a loss, not being prepared for them, not being coached by any existing teaching. And they can only experiment for themselves and on themselves. And we know how vast the regions above and below and behind the surface mind are, how dangerous without sufficient guidance, patience and discipline. These groups have nothing of it, and they have also lost the security of the old mental way. They are nowhere and everywhere, travelling and hitch-hiking into obscure, occult, mystical regions of their being. The "soular" institutions fail in giving guidance, being at a loss themselves. Is it a surprise that quite a few of the poor wanderers run the risk of finding artificial gurus—mind-destroying drugs and soul-destroying teachings? Each half-luminous and every obscure region of our being has got its prophets and they cling to them hoping for light. And who can synthesize for them, integrate or select? Who is there to show them a way out into the real, the higher regions, the way towards divine perfection? As long as this is not done, they keep mixing up high and low, so-called spirituality and so-called mysticism with a tremendous amount of vital, physical and sexual stuff. Without discernment and discipline it really is difficult!

And the paradox of the situation is this: they reject their fathers and governments and any authority and guidance. And—they desperately seek for guidance and authority. Wouldn't many of them be ready for Sri Aurobindo?

A rational culture tends to develop into a verbal culture. Committees, meetings, boards, classes, lectures, words. People are getting bored, deaf. And in the very heart of the culture, —in information-centres, in schools, factories, managing bodies, churches, organisations—a tendency is growing rapidly to do away with the supremacy of the word and to experiment with new ways of communicating. One discovers one has never really listened to one's partner in the dialogue, always covering up the other's intentions and feelings with one's own preconceived and massive feelings and thoughts. One discovers through new group-dynamic methods, the thickness of the wall each one has built around himself, around his culturally determined ego. One experiences new dimensions within oneself, as a source for living within and communicating from within. There seems to grow, in many spheres of Western life, a conviction, and experience, of how the culture has estranged man from the creative sources of his personality, alienated him from what he really is. And so many movements, methods, schools, sprout up which develop ways and techniques to help groups and individuals to re-establish the real communication, with their fellowmen, and implicitly or explicitly with Nature and God.

This field is vast and the experiments are undertaken on different levels. Many criticisms can be brought against them. Who are the teachers, to which level of depth have they themselves grown; are not many of the new methods and techniques new mental ways rather than real processes of growth; into what —in the West unknown—regions of the human being do the schools and movements throw their groups; are the new socio-psychologies on which they base themselves able to really guide; is it not the blind leading the blind? Certainly the dangers are tremendous. But happily this does not stop the experiments. Happily, because it seems to give a real opening, in the very heart of the culture, for a subjective age. And this, we know, may lead to what Sri Aurobindo calls the Spiritual Age. The trends may be summarised under the title of "non-verbal communication". They all stem out of the desire to go beyond the verbal and mental level, to pierce through the veils and plunge into some deeper layer, behind the surface; to dig towards the creative depths of personality.

We mention a few of the various trends within this non-verbal communication movement.

"Sensitivity training" is becoming the fashion and is being used now on all levels of society. One is taught to become sensitive to the below surface parts of oneself and others. Breaking through one's own surface being causes a crisis of disintegration in many participants. For many persons (especially for the "types": the manager, the pastor, the professor) this is a hard but crucial experience.

What the "sensitivity training" aims at on an individual level becomes a shared experience in "group work methods". Here one learns how to handle the below surface factors as a group to accomplish a collective task and develop a group consciousness. Group work searches for the "collective personality" and tries to open closed personalities for something greater that goes on in the groups in which they take part. The groups serve as a kind of laboratory, in which the tendencies one meets in the culture at large are reflected in an intensive way. A first fruit of group dynamic methods often is the tearing off of masks and revealing the barriers one puts up in oneself for communicating with oneself and the others. And one sometimes experiences that the same applies to one's relationship towards the Divine.

In "ecstasy groups" one experiments with the awareness on the body level. Being tired of communicating on the almost exclusively verbal level one wants to extend the relationships to the physical and sensual levels. It is like "getting to the cells" and to communicate with hands and feet and the whole body instead of only with mind and mouth. Nudity, touch, dance and music become means of relating and expressing. One learns to give up the easy protection and defences one builds around oneself and comes in contact with aspects of personality which the culture has tried to suppress.

"Peak experience groups" aim at contact with the transcendental reality through mystical and religious means. Here one searches for the depths and the heights of the being and tries to reach the luminous dimensions of reality in cosmic experiences. When some of the above-mentioned techniques are used in existing religious groups one sometimes reaches far behind the traditional, typical "religious" elements, and manages to find a firm stand on depths that really matter.

This great variety of experiments is getting the support of new psychologies. Especially hopeful with respect to a breakthrough in Western culture is a new group of psychologies which call themselves "the third force". After the long domination of the analytic and the behavioural psychologies which deal with either the sick or the determined personality, a psychology of the healthy person, the creative person is in the process of being developed. Interesting to note is how many of the psychologists of this "third force" look towards the East in order to be able to cope with the unexpected treasures they discover in the depth of a healthy, a full grown, a realised person. Western sciences hardly have words to describe these dimensions, an awareness of which is new for the West. Great stress is being laid nowadays on the different levels of consciousness.

Only when these new experiments turn towards spirituality will they really be fruitful and creative. Now they may be considered as signs of the dawn of a new age. Unguided by the higher Light they run many a risk and cause considerable frustrations. Our conclusion with regard to them is twofold:

firstly, they show how parts of the Western, verbal, technical, mental culture are making themselves ready for the future, breaking down some of its mental barriers and sharpening its collective ears to hear and understand the prophets of the future when they come;

secondly, the new ways of communicating and the group dynamic methods should be raised towards higher levels. Then they really may be powers of progress towards a new age. Groups oriented to spirituality should experiment with these methods in order to transform them into "spiritual group dynamics". Would this not be a task for Auroville? When these methods could be purified, intensified, spiritualised, and then given back to where they came from, to the West, the readiness for "some" future may become a readiness for the Spiritual Age, towards which Sri Aurobindo and the Mother are the sure guides.

Is "the West" ready for Sri Aurobindo? Sri Aurobindo and the Mother have their own ways of working on the answers. Humbly and respectfully we may only be happy to see their influence so strongly working in that part of the world that could be such a power for the better, once it has opened its inmost heart towards the Divine. And in the meantime, what better can we do to prepare the West than living up to the divine ideals Sri Aurobindo and the Mother put before us!

The Poet Sri Aurobindo

SISIRKUMAR GHOSE

SRI Aurobindo is little known as a poet, too little. The world outside has heard of him as a political revolutionary, later as a yogi and a thinker. But as a poet ? Opinion is sharply divided. In the controversy few have cared to see the object as it is.

But Sri Aurobindo who was not given to making claims for himself consistently held that he was first and foremost a poet. He also looked upon poetry as a voice of life, a rhythmic voyage of self-discovery. In his critical writings, especially in *The Future Poetry,* he places poetry, fairly and squarely, at the centre of human knowledge and activities, as the leader of the inner journey. In *The Creative Experiment*, Bowra had let fall a suggestion that has for the most part gone unheeded: 'In the self modern poetry has a subject which demands the highest standards of truth.' It is the range and quality, the standard of truth, the truth of man *on many levels*, that distinguishes Sri Aurobindo's adventure of consciousness. This is especially true of his later poetry, which opens a new chapter in recovery and symbolic vision. Here is the poetry of tomorrow and a hope for man. In terms of existence-clarification there is no poet who is not a little superficial by the side of his massive vision and incomparable inwardness, as in *Savitri.* But to see the poetry as it is, it is necessary to clear one's mind of cant.

Sri Aurobindo's works in other areas and mediums have earned their legitimate place in the cultural landscape. We have tried to show, following the poet, that the heart of the matter is in his poetry, of vision, prayer, totality, poetry as a factor in the human becoming, as the essence of man's manhood. The Return of the Rishi, as the ancient voyants of India were called, may be the answer to the modern chaos and insufficiency of vision which passes for poetry today. Sri Aurobindo is the proof and the challenge.

The question is still asked: Is Sri Aurobindo a poet and poet of what sort? There are reasons for reservation. Leader in more fields than one, his successive role as a revolutionary, a nationalist, a thinker, above all, as a yogi and mystic, has tended to throw his work as a poet to the background. Also there exists a feeling that no Indian can or should write poetry in English. Add to this the poet's own indifference and aversion to publicity. It is sad but true his *Collected Poems and Plays* (1942), has long been out of print. But the real difficulty lies in the nature of the poetry itself, in the fact that in his maturer utterances Sri Aurobindo has spoken almost exclusively of inner states and subtle ranges of the being never easy to grasp, much less to judge. Not unaware of the situation, in a letter he had written: "This is the real stumbling-block of mystic poetry....The mystic feels real and present, even ever present to his experience, intimate to his being, truths which to the ordinary reader are intellectual abstractions or metaphysical speculations. He is writing of experiences that are foreign to the ordinary mentality." No wonder if such a poet now and then looks a little *passé*, to stand outside the mainstream of modern poetry or what has imposed itself as the mainstream. On the contrary, if poetry and the other arts are an index of a psychological growth or becoming of man, Sri Aurobindo is as modern as tomorrow. To a true inward view his essential poetry points to that break-through in consciousness which is the heart of the poetic as well as the human evolution. But to see it for what it is we must come to it without presuppositions, and with a certain capacity for experience and inwardness. Else what with the values—rather disvalues—of a sensate culture, we shall be but "an insect crawling among other ephemeral insects on a speck of surface mud and water which has managed to form itself amid the appalling immensities of the physical universe".[1] A lien on our manhood, it is poetry alone that can make us something other than the lord of flies.

The modern consciousness has lost its centre. In fact, that

1. *The Life Divine.*

would seem to be its *raison d'être*. The Age of Anxiety is also an age of eager, sometimes unconventional experiments in form—or formlessness, a cover for a tortured and confused seeking for intensity and wholeness. But integration is always from above or within. This is where a good many of our poets and intellectuals reveal their insufficiency. Placed by the side of their sophisticated stances, of the disinherited mind as it calls itself, Sri Aurobindo speaks almost a new tongue, an Orphic voice of such sanity and serenity. While it is not unfamiliar with our agonies, real or pretended, it also points to the remedy within, a change of consciousness. His archetype is one who could drink the poison[2] of the world and yet be whole. The poet is like his own Shiva :

A face on the cold dire mountain peaks.
Grand and still, its lines white and austere
Match with the unmeasured snowy streaks
Cutting heaven, implacable and sheer.

A moon-ray on the forehead blue and pale
Stretched afar its finger of still light.
Illumining emptiness. Stern and male
Mask of peace, indifferent in might !

But, as Sri Aurobindo has repeatedly pointed out, the adequacy of poetry does not depend wholly on the tone or level of its inspiration much less its philosophical affiliation. The question of formal adequacy is important and never to be denied. As we shall see, his own poetry of the middle period suffers, now and then, from a doctrinal or philosophical weightage, comes dangerously close to being criticism of life. But this is not the whole of Sri Aurobindo or Sri Aurobindo at his most Aurobindean.

From scale to scale, the poetry is full of surprises, and its dwelling place is not merely on inaccessible, spiritual heights. For instance, it cannot be remembered too often that, early and late, Sri Aurobindo is a poet of love. Indeed, after reading

---

2. Baudelaire's phrase that we must drink poison in order to be whole has been repeated by the *avant garde* in self-defence. It may be doubted how many survive the fatal draught.

Savitri, one might say, *the* poet of love. This is how Narad, the divine sage, describes Savitri :

> Who is this that comes, the bride,
> The flame-born, and round her illumined head
> Pouring their lights her hymeneal pomps
> Move flashing about her ? From what green glimmer of glades
> Retreating into dewy silences
> Or half-seen verge of waters moon-betrayed
> Brings thou this glory of enchanted eyes ?...
> What feet of gods, what ravishing flutes of heaven
> Have thrilled high melodies round, from near and far
> Approaching through the soft and revelling air,
> Which still surprised thou hearest ? They have fed
> Thy silence on some red strange-ecstasied fruit
> And thou hast trod the dim moon-peaks of bliss....
> Thou comest like a silver deer through groves
> Of coral flowers and buds of glowing dreams,
> Or fleest like a wind-goddess through leaves,
> Or reamest, O ruby-eyed and snow-winged dove,
> Flitting through thickets of thy pure desires
> In the unwounded beauty of thy soul.

Or, an earlier description of the heroine:

> As in a mystic and dynamic dance
> A priestess of immaculate ecstasies
> Inspired and ruled from Truth's revealing vault
> Moves in some prophet cavern of the gods,
> A heart of silence in the hands of joy
> Inhabited with rich creative beats
> A body like a parable of dawn
> That seemed a niche for veiled divinity
> Or golden temple door to things beyond....
> At once she was the stillness and the word,
> A continent of self-diffusing peace,
> An ocean of untrembling virgin fire.

For all the 'immaculate ecstasies' the poet is not unfamiliar with *Angst,* not only his own but of the race, of the human condition.

A wayfarer along the razor's edge:

In menacing tracts, in tortured solitudes
Companionless he roamed through desolate ways
Where the red wolf waits by the fordless stream
And Death's black eagles scream to the precipice
And met the hounds of bale who hunt men's hearts
Baying across the veldts of Destiny.
In footless battlefields of the Abyss,
Fought shadowy combats in mute eyeless depths,
And bore the fierce inner wounds that are slow to heal.

In "A God's Labour" he has told us more simply, with a touch of confession perhaps;

He who would bring the heavens here
Must himself descend into clay
And the burden of earthly nature bear
And tread the dolorous way.

Yoga is not anti-life. That too one could learn from the poet, the last of the Rishis, as Romain Rolland once described him. The poet is always a symbol, the highest point of contemporary consciousness. A representative man, or "deputy of the aspiring world", he invites us to the possibility of a transforming experience or knowledge, the knowledge by which we become what we are. Sri Aurobindo's essential poetry is a natural fruit of his interior life or inward grace. A gift appropriate to the giver, it is in effect the recovery of our buried self. Reading it we learn over and again that :

To these high-raised dominions of the Self
Too far from our surface nature's postal routes,
Too lofty for our mortal lives to breathe
Deep in us are responsive elements.

This short essay is addressed to the responsive elements, the *sahridays* or the likeminded who are willing to explore and encounter man's ultimate poetry in the dominions of the Self. Sri Aurobindo's peak poetry is for those who are not afraid to be;

> One with the Eternal, lost in his infinity,
> Drowned in the Absolute, found in the Godhead,
> Swan of the supreme and spaceless ether winged
> wandering through the universe,
> Spirit immortal.

II

Sri Aurobindo's first book of verse, *Songs to Myrtilla* (1895), was written mostly between eighteen and twenty, a few, like "A Rose of Women" and "To the Cuckoo" even earlier. Fine and fluent, and quite English, here are the opening lines of the cuckoo poem:

> Sounds of the wakening world, the year's increase,
> Passage of wind and all his dewy powers
> With breath and laughter of new-bathed flowers
> And that deep light of heaven above the trees
> Awake mid leaves that muse in peace
> Sweet noise of birds, but most in heavenly showers
> The cuckoo's voice pervades the hours.

As in most young men's poems, a stylised fancy and a melancholy note are frequent. The occasions are no doubt appropriate. Here are two examples :

> I saw you mid the rose trees, O white rose,
> Linger a moment, then the dusk defeat,
> My eyes, and listening, heard your footsteps fade
> On the sad leaves of the autumnal glade...

> Hearken, Edith, to the sea....
> Not we the first nor we alone
> Heard the mighty ocean moan.

A few are translations and adaptations from the Greek and the Bengali. Two groups of poems stand out : the political poems (an interest which survives yoga, one might say) and the tributes. Most of the political poems were about Ireland and her tragic hero, Parnell :

And he who raised her from forlorn life
Loosening the fountains of that mighty strife,
Where sits he ? On what high foreshadowing throne
Guarded by grateful hearts ? Beneath this stone
He lies : this guerdon only Ireland gave.
A broken heart and an unhonoured grave.

Among tributes may be mentioned the one on Goethe and the other, a sonnet, on his grand-father, Rajnarayan Basu :

A perfect face amid barbarian faces,
A perfect voice of sweet and serious rhyme,
Traveller with calm, inimitable paces,
Critic with judgment absolute to all time
A complete strength when men were maimed and weak,
German obscured the spirit of a Greek.

The sonnet has a gravity and sustained movement unusual among juvenilia :

Not in annihilation lost, nor given
To darkness, art thou fled from us and light,
O strong and sentient spirit ; no mere heaven
Of ancient joys, no silence eremite
Received thee ; but the omnipresent Thought
Of which thou wast a part and earthy hour,
Took back its gift. Into that splendour caught
Thou hast not lost any special brightness. Power
Remains with thee and the genial force
Unseen for blinding light, not darkly lurks :
As when a sacred river in its course
Dives into ocean, there its strength abides
Not less because with vastness wed and works
Unnoticed in the grandeur of the tides.

But in "Envoi" the young poet bids adieu to the foreign fields, the Hellenic Muses and announces his return home :

Pale poems, weak poems....
In Sicilian olive groves no more
Or seldom must my footprints now be seen,
Nor tread Athenian lanes, nor yet explore
Parnassus or thy voiceful shores, O Hippocrene.
Me from here lotus throne Saraswati
Has called to regions of eternal snow
And Ganges pacing to the southern sea,
Ganges upon whose shores the flowers of Eden blow.

He seems unaccountably severe with himself. In any case, 'the flowers of Eden' betrays the classicist. But true to his words, the regions of eternal snow do appear in the poems that follow. With this difference that against the snowy background is displayed the oldest theme known to mankind—love, deathless love.

III

These narrative poems, of heroic and romantic love, are adaptations from the Sanskrit, which he was quick to learn. Part of a young man's dream, they reveal a side of his sensibility too little known. The Urvasie theme has been an old favourite of the Indian poets. In the Aurobindean version it is passion more than penance that is a felt quality, the passion for love and the passion for beauty. The King, Pururavus, who prays to the silent Himalayas: "Give her back to me, O mountain, give her back" later finds the object of his adoration, abandoned on the cold hillside, a lily mishandled:

Perfect she lay amid her tresses,
Like a mishandled lily luminous,
As she had fallen. From the lucid robe
One shoulder gleamed and golden breast left bare,
Divinely lifting, one gold arm was flung
A warm rich splendour exquisitely outlined
Against the dazzling whiteness, and her face
Was as a fallen moon among the snows.

But the fallen moon is no doll. The meeting of lovers provides one of the most glowing passages in the poem, *Urvasie:*

She a leaf
Before a gust among the nearing trees
Cowered. But, all a sea of mighty joy
Rushing and swallowing up the golden sand,
With a great cry and glad Pururavus
Seized her and caught her to his bosom thrilled,
Clinging and shuddering. All her wonderful hair
Loosened and the wind seized and bore it streaming
Over the shoulder of Pururavus
And on his cheeks a softness. She o'erborne,
Panting with inarticulate murmurs lay,
Like a slim tree half seen through driving hail,
Her naked arms clasping his neck, her cheek
And golden throat averted, and wide trouble
In her large eyes bewildered with their bliss.
With her sweet limbs all his, feeling her breasts
Tumultuous up against his beating heart,
He kissed the glorious mouth of heaven's desire.
So clung they two as shipwrecked in a surge.
Then strong Pururavus, with golden eyes,
Mastering hers, cried tremulous : "O beloved,
O miser of thy rich and happy voice,
One word, one word, to tell me that thou lovest."
And Urvasie, all broken on his bosom,
Her godhead in his passion lost, moaned out,
From her imprisoned breasts, "My lord ! My love!"

If this is not love poetry, where is love poetry to be found ? The companion poem, *Love and Death,* is in some ways more youthful. The hero is "boyish Ruru", Priyumbada is young to the point of being *ingenue*. But what an esctasy of young love, "fresh and new!"

As a bright bird comes flying
From airy extravagances to his own home,
And breasts his mate, and feels her all his goal,
So...came Ruru back to his white-bosomed girl,
Strong-winged to pleasure, She all fresh and new
Rose to him, and he plunged into her charm.

Soon after, bitten by a serpent, she dies. In search of her Ruru has to go to the underworld. For all the youthfulness the descent into death's kingdom is real and menacing: "then with a prone wide sound/All ocean hollowing drew him swiftly in, /Curving with monstrous menace over him":

He down the gulf where the loud waves collapsed
Descending, saw with floating hair arise
The daughters of the sea in pale green light
A million mystic breasts suddenly bare,
And came beneath the flood and stunned beheld
A mute stupendous march of waters race
To reach some viewless pit beneath the world.

The Lord of Death demands a final sacrifice before Priyumbada can be returned to earth, the expected price :

Thou must render to the Immutable
Total all thy fruit-bearing years, then she
Re-blossoms.

Ruru chooses, unhesitatingly. This brings Priyumbada back to life.

But suddenly a bloom, a fragrance...
Then twixt brief sobbing laughetr and blissful tears,
Clinging with all her limbs to him, "O love,
The green, green world ! The warm sunlight !"

Both *Urvasie* and *Love and Death,* point to the author's enduring concern which he has phrased, elsewhere, a little differently, as "Earth and Love and Doom". Between these early sensuous exercises and the 'inner epic' of his maturity he has come a long way—from romance to Reality.

IV

His next book of verse, *Poems* (1905), deals with a different world. We are faced with the problem of belief, and soliloquies and debates abound. The mood and manner of these writings explain why in certain minds Sri Aurobindo is equated with "The Philosopher as Poet". An unequal volume, there are however, exceptions to the philosophising mood. For instance, in a poem like "Who" he sings with such gaiety and buoyancy.

In the strength of a man, in the beauty of a woman
In the laugh of a boy, in the blush of a girl,
The hand that set Jupiter spinning through Heaven,
Spends all its cunning to fashion a curl.

These are His works and His veils and His shadows,
But where is He then ? by what name is He known ?
Is He Brahma or Vishnu? a man or a woman ?
Bodied or bodiless ? twain or alone ?

All music is the sound of His laughter,
All beauty the smile of His passionate bliss;
Our lives are His heart-beats, our raptures the bridal
Of Radha and Krishna, our love is their kiss.

Though the Vaishnava note is obvious the poem is not weighed down by any kind of dogma or doctrine. In the next poem, "A Vision of Science" —three Angels strive in the bosom of the distracted poet. The most powerful, and Philistinian, happens to be the Angel of Science.

Wide were the victories of the Angel proud
Who conquered now and in her praise were loud
The nations....

But the Angel of Religion poses the inevitable, unanswerable question :

Thou hast forgot
The Sphinx that waits for man beside the way.
All questions thou mayest answer, but one day
Her question shall await thee. That reply
As all we must; for they who cannot die.
She slays them and their mangled bodies lie
Upon the highways of eternity.

Last comes the third Angel, "veiled, vague, remote". As she touches the poet's eyes "the mornings of the future rise". A supporting voice decides the issue and all doubts are, apparently and for the nonce, resolved :

Know thyself infinite....
For Thou, O Splendour, art myself concealed—
And thy grey cells contain me not, the stars
I out measure and older than the elements are.
Whether on earth or far beyond the Sun,
I, sublime, clouded, am the Eternal One.

This is solution of a kind no doubt but perhaps not sufficiently dramatised, not the very voice of vision. Quite different, and more adequate, energetic and moving, is "The Vedantin's Prayer". Strong, sinewy, it has the real Aryan vigour :

Spirit Supreme
Who musest in the silence of the heart.
Eternal gleam,
Thou only art !
Ah, wherefore with this darkness am I veiled,
My sunlit part
By clouds assailed ?
Why am I thus disfigured by desire,
Distracted, haled,
Scorched by the fire
Of fitful passions, from the peace out-thrust
Into the gyre
Of every gust ?
Betrayed by grief, o'ertaken with dismay
Surprised by lust ?

The male voice has true sublimity and one is not surprised when the poet seeks solace in the message of the sea :

O grey wild sea,
Thou hast a message, thunderer, for me....
I come, O sea,
To measure my enormous soul with thee.

But the solutions and prayers are only occasional. For a more complete picture or statement we should go to "The Rishi". With the help of an argument, a new feature, the poet reconstructs an imaginary encounter between King Manu, a seeker of old, and the Rishi of the Pole. In the poem Manu's search has received perhaps less attention than the Rishi's idealised moralising :

But while thou livest perfectly fulfil
Thy part, conceive
Earth as thy stage, thyself the actor strong,
The drama His.
Work, love and know,—so shall the spirit win
Immortal bliss.
Work, but the fruits to God alone belong,
Who only is.

The unexceptional statement is not perhaps the highest poetic truth. Though K.D. Sethna thinks, rather thought, that the poem's "scriptural magnificence" and opening portions have no parallel it is to be valued more as a document than as a poem. Obviously the poet is both Manu and the Rishi who says : "I could not hold the bliss,/The force for men/My brother."

One feels an increase of the individual accent in "In the Moonlight". Characteristically the poet's mind is "rife with thoughts of the infinite" rather than with romantic musings. Realistic details like "the bullock's jingling tune" and "the frog's harsh discord in the ringing pools" are easily allowed. All the while the sad old debate goes on: "Two genii in the dubous heart of man/Wrestle and strive to win unhampered ground." As usual, the genie of materialism or science seems to have the upper hand. The gospel according to nineteenth-century science follows:

Our lives are but a transitory breath:
Mean pismires in the sad and dying age
Of a more glorious planet, on the edge
Of bitter pain we await eternal death....
The inner you
So cherished is a dream that shall depart

Of course the poem cannot be allowed to end like that. Science is forced to admit her limitations. There arises a new hope, a hint of an apocalypse, at the end:

> Through chemistry she seeks the source of life,
> Nor knows the mighty laws she has found,
> Are Nature's bye-laws only, meant to ground
> A grandiose freedom building peace by strife.
>
> It comes at last, the day foreseen of old,
> What John of Patmos saw, what Shelley dreamed,
> Vision and vain imagination deemed,
> The City of Delight, the Age of Gold.

In the next poem we are in a different world. Intellectual debates and idealised solutions left behind, the locale of *Baji Prabhou* is not the Himalayas or the moonlight or the tortured mind of modern Hamlets but the scorching Deccan plateaus, a background of battle, harsh:

> A noon of Deccan with its tyrant glare
> Oppressed the earth, the hills stood deep in haze,
> And sheltering a thirst the fields glared up
> Longing for water in courses long parched
> Imprisoned by a bronze and brilliant sky,
> Sought an escape for the wide trance of heat.

He chooses an epical episode from Mahratta history, Baji Prabhou's defence of gorge against the superior and overwhelming Moghul army. There can be little doubt that the choice of theme, including the tribute to Bhabani, "the goddess formidable who watches over India till the end", was expressive of the poet's own intense nationalism. The martial mood is also reflected in the free translation of "Vidula", from the *Mahabharata,* in which the queen mother upbraids her faltering son, Sanjoy, to take up arms against the enemy: "Wake for victory, Sanjoy: Warrior, wake! I have laboured to provoke the will, the strength of thy heart within."

One may wonder how, in *Nine Poems,* the same poet was writing, at about the same time, the invocation to the "Mother of Dreams" a poem part aesthetic, part symbolic, link between the world of dreams and of the visionary:

Goddess Supreme, Mother of Dreams, by the ivory doors
When thou standest,
Who are they that come down unto men in thy visions
That troop, group upon group, down the path of the shadows slanting?....
What then are these lands and these golden sands and these seas more radiant than earth can imagine?
Thine is the shadow in which visions are made, sped by thy hands from celestial lands come to the souls that rejoice for ever
In thy dream-worlds we pass, or look in the magic glass, then beyond these we climb out of Space and Time to the path of the divine endeavour.

Musical and rich with the hints of the occult, there is just a touch, may be, of the languorous about the poem, an unusual note in Sri Aurobindo. But, at the end, "the divine endeavour" is not forgotten, an endeavour to which he would devote his entire energies. In some sense the shorter poems are better. For instance, "An Image'. Fresh from meeting Helen, Paris is moving to bottle. To him both are like bridals, a dream or a dance, red with the beauty of blood:

Joyous as ever, Paris led them glancing in armour,
Brilliant with gold, like a bridegroom, playing with death and the battle
Even as apart in his chamber he played with his beautiful Helen,
Touching her body rejoiced with a low and lyrical laughter,
So he laughed as he smote his foemen. Round him the arrows
Round him the spears of the Argives sang like voices of maidens
Trilling the anthem of bridal bliss, the chant hymeneal;
Round him the warriors fell like flowers strewn at a bridal.
Red with the beauty of blood.

The key poem in this volume is no doubt "Ahana". The Argument tells us: "Ahana, the Dawn of God, descends in the world where amid the strife and trouble of mortality the Hunters of Joy, the Seekers after Knowledge, the Climbers in the quest of Power, are toiling up the slopes for waiting in the valleys. As she stands on the mountains of the East, voices of the hunters of joy are the first to greet her". The Argument prepares us for the pattern in which the familiar features of reason's rubrics of the mysteries of life are repeated. These are the voices of negation according to which "Vain in the passion to divinise manhood.... None can exceed himself. ..Shun the light of the ideal and chimera....curb heart's impatience, bind they desires down, pause from self-vexing." But the passion to divinise manhood is an evolving theme in the Aurobindean imagination, and we are not surprised to hear:

Two are the ends of existence, two are the dreams of the Mother;
Heaven unchanging, earth with her time-beats yearn to each other,
Earth-souls needing the touch of heaven's peace to recapture,
Heaven needing earth's passion to quiver its peace into rapture.

Later the statement rises into the form of prayer, of anguish and adoration:
Flower of Beautitude! living shape of the Bliss of Brahman !
Art thou not she who shall bring into life and time the eternal?...

Vision delightful, alone on the peaks whom the silences cover,
Vision of bliss, stoop down to mortality, lean to thy lover.

At last Ahana answers, calling the aspiring souls to Brindavan, Krishna's kingdom:

Come then to Brindavan, soul of the joyous; faster and faster
Follow the dance I shall teach thee with Shyama for slave and
    master....
Then shalt thou know what the dance meant, fathom the song
    and the singer,
Hear behind thunder its rhymes, touched by lightning thrill to
    his finger,
Brindavan's rustle shalt understand and Yamuna's laughter,

Take thy place in the *Ras* and thy share of the ecstasy after.

This provides a kind of climax, though the cascades of rhetoric coming before do not seem wholly to belong. One has a feeling, again, that instead of the drama of seeking we have been presented with an allegory, (This is more than made up for *Savitri* with its astounding exploration of the inner worlds). A kind of "bridge linking up Sri Aurobindo's earlier with his more recent poetry", with its fluency and finesse, ardour and argument, all, or nearly all, of Sri Aurobindo is here—except that intense vision and rhythm, the sheer spirit touch of the later poems. For that we have to wait a little longer.

V

When, years later, out of "the great mass of poems written during the twenties and thirties" a few short ones, like *Six poems* (1934), *Transformation and Other Poems, Poems Past and Present* were published, the change and impact were unmistakable. If there had ever been any doubt about the quality and direction of the Aurobindean muse, his role and rank as a poet, these poems dispel that effectively. Every bit authentic, they carry their own authority. Incidentally, they are also a proof of his theory of poetry, not that the poems were written to illustrate any theory.

What is that distinguishes these poems above all others? The secret is to be found in the new stance, a poise of consciousness and a wholly changed form and content unlike anything before, except perhaps, in brief hints. Here is a new world of insight and experience, of unknown or little known modes of the being. If, as many believe, the best works of literary, plastic and musical arts give us more than pleasure, something significant about the nature of ultimate reality, the value of Aurobindean poetry should be self-evident. The series of the later poems is an enlargement of awareness. Here is one, for instance, *"Nirvana"*, Setting forth a state of superior cognition in simple words, the poem is part of a tradition richer, and more normal than what the sophisticated *avatars* of the narrow view will achieve through their complex indirections. The language of wisdom can do without trappings.

All is abolished but the mute Alone.
The mind from thought released, the heart from grief,
Grow inexistent, now beyond belief;
There is no I, no Nature, known-unknown....

A silent unnamed emptiness content
Either to fade in the Unknowable
Or thrill with the luminous seas of the Infinite.

Here is what he has elsewhere called the poetry of 'open realisation'. This and other poems are beautiful in the sense in which Santayana described beauty as a contemplation of the essential. We may call it pure poetry with a difference, poetry born of a superior organisation of consciousness, that is a purification of the language of consciousness. This is the new creation, arising out of "Trance", a tender epiphany:

My mind is awake in a stirless trance,
    Hushed my heart, a burden of delight;
Dispelled is the senses' flicker-dance,
    Mute the body aureate with light.
O star of creation, pure and free,
    Halo-moon of ecstasy unknown,
Storm-breath of the soul-change yet to be,
    Ocean self enraptured and alone!

The trance state is not an escape from reality, as the popular mind loves to think of insight. On the contrary, it relates to potentialities which are the province of true poetry. Liberation is a power for life and a value. Yoga is the art of living. So in "Jivanmukta" we are told:

Only to help God's forces to waiting Nature,
To help with wide-winged Peace her tormented labour
    And heal with joy her ancient sorrow,
    Casting down light on the inconscient darkness

He acts and lives. Vain things are mind's smaller motives
To one whose soul enjoys for its high possession
    Infinity and the sempiternal
    All his guide and beloved and refuge.

Such a poet has no wish to escape into an unchanging beyond. To a student of life the earth herself reveals her unsuspected 'deeper power':

> I, Earth, have a deeper power than heaven;
> My lonely sorrow surpasses its rose-joys
> A red and bitter seed of the raptures seven;
> My dumbness fills with echoes of a far Voice
> By me the last finite, yearning, strives
> To reach the last infinity's unknown,
> The Eternal is broken into fleeting lives
> And Godhead pent in the mire and stone.

But he is not earth-bound either. In golden privacies, on wings of inspiration the poet moves into other fields of awareness. The poetic consciousness is always an explorer. To it are opened worlds of experience of which logic can make no sense. But memory lingers and we cherish these glimpses of a vaster self.

> At last he wakes to a memory of Self:
> He sees within the face of deity....
> She seemed to her remembering witness soul
> To trace again a journey often made.

The poem "Thought the Paraclete" describes one such complete experience or movement:

> As some bright archagel in vision flies
> Plunged in dream-caught spirit immensities,
> Past the long green creates of the seas of life,
> Past the orange skies of the mystic mind
> Flew my thought self-lost in the vasts of God.
> Sleepless wide great glimmering wings of wind
> Bore the gold-red seeking of feet that trod
> Space and Time's mute vanishing ends. The face
> Lustred, pale-blue-lined of the hippogriff
> Eremite, sole, daring the bourne less ways,
> Over world-bare summits of being
> Gleaned, the deep twilights of the world-abyss

Failed below. Sun-realms of supernal seeing,
Crimson-white mooned oceans of pauseless bliss
Drew its vague heart-yearning with voices sweet.
Hungering, large-souled to surprise the uncounted
Secrets white-fire-veiled to the lost Beyond.
Crossing power-swept silences rapture- stunned,
Climbing high far ethers eternal-sunned,
Thought the great-winged wanderer paracelete
Disappeared slow-singing in a flame-word rune
Self was lost, lone, limitless, nude, immune.

This is not a voyage to nowhere, but evidence of that enlarged awareness and coherent symbolism known to ancient seekers. If the poem sounds occult or subjective that cannot be helped. Whatever it is, it is real, as real as "The Other Earth", where

Fire-importunities of scarlet bloom
And bright suddennesses of wings in a golden air,
Strange bird and animal forms like memories cast
On the rapt silence on unearthly woods,
Calm faces of the gods on backgrounds vast
Bringing the marvel of the infinitudes,
Through glimmering veils of wonder and delight
World after world bursts on the awakened sight.

As symbolic poetry "The Bird of Fire" is immediately impressive. The world it evokes is more true and imperishable than any "Grecian Urn" existence. We quote only the first and the last two lines, though this is to do violence to the poem:

Gold-white wings a throb in the vastness, the bird of flame went glimmering over a sunfire curve to the haze of the west,
Skimming, a messenger-sail, the sapphire-summer waste of a soundless, wayless burning sea.
Now in the eve of the waning world the colour and splendour returning drift through a blue-flicker air back to my breast,
Flame and shimmer staining the rapture-white foam-vest of the waters of Eternity....

Rich and red is thy breast, O bird, like the blood of a soul
climbing the hard crag-teeth world, wounded and nude,
A ruby of flame-petalled love in the silver-gold alter-vase
of moon-edged night and rising day.
O Flame who art Time's last boon of the sacrifice, offering-flower
held by the finite's god's to the Infinite,
O marvel bird with the burning wings of light and the unbarred
lids that look beyond all space,
One strange leap of thy mystic stress breaking the barriers of mind
and life, arrives at its luminous term thy flight;
Invading the secret clasp of the Silence and crimson Fire
thou frontest eyes in a timeless Face.

Instead of seeking shelter behind our incapacity for the symbolic mode of perception we should be grateful for these revelations, hewn from the silence of the Ineffable. To read the later poetry of Sri Aurobindo is to witness the reintegration of Man, to participate in a ritual in which aesthetics and spirituality join hands.

Another indisputable achievement is "Rose of God". As poetry of prayer and vision, of poetry as a variation of the sacred name, it has few equals. The first two lines in each stanza describe the Divine Ground or Nature, the upper hemisphere or *parardha* of mystical philosophy, while the third and fourth are cast in the form of prayers from below. The whole thing rises to a crescendo in the final stanza. One of the most magical and potent poems to be written by Sri Aurobindo, here to the root symbols of a lost tradition, language and experiences, never wholly lost, bloom for ever:

Rose of God, vermilion stain on the sapphires of heaven,
Rose of Bliss, fire-sweet, seven-tinged with the ecstasies seven!
Leap up in our heart of humanhood, O miracle, O flame,
Passion-flower of the Nameless, bud of the mystical Name.

Rose of God, great wisdom-bloom on the summits of being,
Rose of Light, immaculate core of the ultimate seeing.
Live in the mind of our earthhood, O golden Mystery flower,
Sun on the head of the Timeless, guest of the marvellous Hour.

Rose of God, demask force of Infinity, red icon of might,
Rose of Power, with thy diamond halo piercing the night!
Ablaze in the will of the mortal, design the wonder of thy plan,
Image of Immortality, outbreak of the Godhead in man.

Rose of God, smitten purple with the incarnate divine Desire,
Rose of Life, crowded with petals, colours lyre!
Transform the body of the mortal like a sweet and magical
 rhyme,
Bridge our earthhood and heavenhood, make deathless the
 children of time.

Rose of God, like a blush of raptue on Eternity's face,
Rose of love, ruby-depth of all being, fire-passion of Grace!
Awake from the heart of the yearning that sobs in Nature's abyss!
Make earth the home of the Wonderful and life Beautitude's kiss.

The poem defines the term and end of Aurobindean poetry as well as of his yoga: it is the "outbreak of the Godhead in man". In his adventure of consciousness poetry is Sri Aurobindo's chosen strategy. If, as Middlcton Murry once said, we require from the highest poetry that it should not merely thrill us but also still us what better proof can we point to than these poems where "the passion of a bliss yet to be sweeps from Infinity's sea?"

In Apendix B there are some poems in quantitative metres. The titles are self-explanatory, "Ocean Stillness", "Trance in Waiting", "Soul's Scene", etc. Most of these poems refute the charge, now and then heard against Sri Aurobindo. that his poems are wanting in music. Let a few examples do. First, "The Dream Boat".

Who was it that came to me in a boat made of dream-fire
 With his flame-brow and his sun-gold body?
Melted was the silence into a sweet secret murmur,
 "Do you come now? Is the heart's fire ready?"

Hidden in the recesses of the heart something shuddered,
 It recalled all that the life's joy cherished,
Imaged the felicity that it must leave lost for ever,
 And the boat passed and the gold-god vanished.

Now within the hollowness of the world's breast inhabits—
    For the love died and the old joy ended—
Void of a felicity that has fled, gone for ever,
    And the gold god and the dream boat come not.

But the poetry is not confined to gold gods and dream boats. The fearful symmetry is not overlooked. "The Tiger and the Deer" is a brilliant proof. Here is the entire poem:

Brilliant, crouching, slouching, what crept through the green
    heart of the forest,
Gleaming eyes and mighty chest and soft soundless paws of
    grandeur and murder?
The wind slipped through the leaves as if afraid lest its voice
    and the noise of its steps perturb the pitiless Splendour,
Hardly daring to breathe. But the great beast crouched and
    crept, and crept and crouched, a last time, noiseless fatal,
Till suddenly death leaped on the beautiful wild deer as it drank
And it fell and, torn, died remembering its mate left sole in
    the deep woodland,—
Destroyed, the mild harmless beauty by the strong cruel beauty
    in Nature
But a day may come when the tiger crouches and leaps no more
    in the dangerous heart of the forest,
As the mammoth shakes no more the plains of Asia;
Still then shall the beautiful wild deer drink from the coolness
    of great pools in the leaves' shadow.
The mighty perish in their might;
The slain survive the slayer.

Perhaps the moral comes a little pat! But the same witness like gaze may turn upward and inward, to peaks of silence. And then we have a kind of poetry whose authenticity needs no argument. Here are waters of restoration for the dry moderns. Reading Sri Aurobindo we too may move:

Into the Silence, into the Silence,
Arise, O Spirit immortal,
Away from the turning Wheel, breaking the magical Circle
Ascend, single and deathless:

Care no more for the whispers and the shoutings in the darkness
Pass from the sphere of the grey and the little,
Leaving the cry and the struggle,
Into the Silence for ever.

Here is poetry in a new key. Only the insensitive will try to have a *cordon sanitaire* for its own safety. *The Times Literary Supplement*, usually guarded about Aurobindean poetry, had come upon the truth when its reviewer said that Sri Aurobindo writes as though he was standing among the stars, with the constellations for companions. Yes, but the star-gazer has his feet firmly on the ground, and is no stranger to the abyss or 'the inner war without escape'.

VI

Poems Past and Present (1946) is a record mostly of spiritual experiences and a further proof of the kind of writing he had hinted at in *The Future Poetry*. A lyric with a difference, the opening poem, *Musa Spiritus*, is a sample of the new manner, of prayer and invocations:

O Word, concealed in the upper fire,
Thou who hast lingered through centuries,
Descend from thy rapt white desire,
Plunge through gold eternities....
Break the seals of Matter's sleep.
Break the trance of unseen height...
O Muse of the Silences, the widenest make
In the unplumbed stillness that hears thy voice.

The spiritual muse resides in no shut heavens. The poet is a mediator between the upper fire and matter's sleep down below. In another poem we hear:

The Light was still around me
When I came back to earth
Bringing the Immortal's knowledge
Into man's cave of birth.

Bride of Fire, a companion piece, reminds of the earlier *Rose of God.* A poem of holy love, the first two lines of the opening stanza comprise a prayer or an act, while the third and fourth set fourth the conditions of the embodiment:

> Bride of the fire, clasp me now close,—
> Bride of the Fire!
> I have shed the bloom of the earthly rose,
> I have slain desire.

So it is that the final prayer finds its piercing note and the fire changes into a living sun:

> Voice of Infinity, sound in my heart,
> Call of the One!
> Stamp there thy radiance, never to part,
> O living Sun.

The Blue Bird, a symbolic intermediary, knows its role. Agent of grace:

> I bring the bliss of the Eternal's face
> And the boon of the spirit's sight....
> My song is rapture's mystic art,
> My flight immortal will.

Such rapture is never without a ransom. *A God's Labour* speaks of the Promethean Passion "to bring the fire to man."*

> He who would bring the heavens here
> Must descend himself into clay
> And the burden of earthly nature bear
> And tread the dolorous way.
>
> Coercing my godhead I have come down
> Here on the sordid earth,
> Ignorant, labouring, human grown
> Twixt the gates of death and birth.

* See "My whole life has been a struggle with hard realities from hardships, starvation in England and constant dangers and fierce difficulties... My life has been a battle from its early years..."

I have laboured and suffered in Matter's night
To bring the fire to Man;
But the hate of hell and human spite
Are my need since the world began.

My gaping wounds are a thousand and one
And the Titan kings assail,
But I canot rest till my task is done
And wrought the eternal will.

It is only after the inner war has been fought to a finish that the poet—always a giver—can utter the formula of peace and victory. In a kind of final gesture and courtesy he leaves his undying dream which is nothing other than "the living truth of you."

The gulf twixt the depths and heights is bridged
And its golden waters pour
Down the sapphire mountain rainbow-ridged
And glimmer from shore to shore....
There shall move on the earth embodied and fair
The living truth of you.

Is not this, after all, the function of the poet and of poetry—to provide man with his 'living truth' which can be earned only by bridging the depths and the heights? Sri Aurobindo's later poetry has no other theme, a theme with endless variations.

A posthumous publication of forty-eight poems, mostly sonnets, *Last Poems* (1953) was among the last to be written by him. In 1967 came *More Poems*, it contained some early works, a few fragments as well as political poems and sonnets. Rarely has the sonnet been put to such wide use as in Sri Aurobindo, as a vehicle of ontological discourse inspired by "some greater voice and mightier vision". Some may feel that these poems lack in a certain vital vividness, but this is more than made up for by their inner character (which is the reason why they cannot be 'vital') and consistency. The vitality is of a different kind, portion of the unitive consciousness:

A tranquil heart is sympathy with all,
A will one-pointed wide imperial.

Poem after poem reveals the same tranquil stance which nothing can disturb. "The small self is dead." What we hear is the living voice of the tranquil self, *santa,* one in all, "a close identity."

All eyes that look on me are my eyes;
The one heart that beats within all breasts is mine.
The world's happiness flows through me like wine,
Its million sorrows are my agonies....

I contain the whole world in my soul's embrace,
I see my own body with another face....

I have learned a close identity with all,
Yet am by nothing bound that I become.

This mood or experience, of a "secret harmony" cannot be one of emotional coldness. Of course it is rare. In *The Bliss of Brahman*, the poet cries out the joyful wisdom, the epiphany:

All Nature is taught in radiant ways to move,
    All beings are in myself embraced.
O fiery boundless Heart of joy and love,
    How art thou beating in a mortal's breast!

The fiery boundless Heart dwells paradoxically, in "the spirit's calm nothing can move". Familiar with the cosmic mysteries, the poet knows the strivings of the man within, and what these point to or reveal:

There is a need within the soul of man
    The splendours of the surface never sate;
For mind and life and their glory and debate
    Are the slow prelude of a greater theme.
A sketch confused of a supernal plan,
    A preface to the epic of the Supreme.

The Hidden Plan gives us a clearer indication of thate pic of man:

However long the night's hour, I will not dream
That the small ego and the person's mask
Are all that god reveals in our life scheme
The last result of Nature's task.

A greater presence in her bosom works:
Long it prepares its far epiphany;
Even in the stone and the beast the godhead lurks,
A bright Persona of eternity.

It will burst out from the limit traced by Mind
And make a witness of the prescient heart;
It shall reveal even in the inert blind
Nature, long veiled in each inconscient part,

Fulfilling the occult magnificent plan,
The worldwide and immortal spirit in man.

Elsewhere, as part of the knowledge or experience:

Each sight is now immortal with Thy bliss;
My soul through the rapt eyes has come to see;
A veil is rent and they no more can miss
The miracle of thy world-epiphany.

From these examples one should not imagine that the poet is lost in some *O altitude*! No, these are, what he has called elsewhere, "open realisations". In Sri Aurobindo's view or experience "All life is Yoga". And life as he sees it is not without its note of laughter, a merry twinkle. The world would have gone to blazes without a sense of humour, he had written in one of his letters. Here is a proof, the humour of the holy, tweaking the nose of the self-deceived spiritual gymnast:

He said, "I am egoless, spiritual, free",
Then swore because dinner was not ready.
I asked him why. He said, "It is not me,
But the belly's hungry god who gets unsteady."

I asked him why. He said, "It is His play,
  I am unmoved within, desireless, pure,
I care not what may happen day by day,"
  I asked him, "Are you very sure?"

He answered, "I can understand your doubt.
  But to be free is all. It does not matter
How you may kick and howl and rage and shout,
  Making a row over your daily platter.

To be aware of self is liberty,
Self have I got and having self, am free"

In *A Dream of Surreal Science* the fun can be quite deadly. Gently twisting—a contrast to the heavier gait of the poetry of the middle period—naturalism and determinism the sonnet hints, darkly, at the liquidation of the world at the hands of insane and irresponsible scientists:

One dreamed and saw a gland write Hamlet, drink
  At the Mermaid, capture immortality.
A committee of hormones on the Aegean's bank
  Composed the *Iliad* and the *Odyssey*.

A thyroid mediating almost nude
  Under the Bo-Tree saw the eternal light
And, rising from its mighty solitude,
  Spoke of the Wheel and eightfold Path all right.

A brain by disordered stomach driven
  Thundered through Europe, conquered, ruled and fell
From St. Helena went, perhaps, to Heaven.
  Thus wagged on the surreal world, until
The scientist played with atoms and blew out
  The universe before God had time to shout.

Another humorous piece is the delightful *Despair on the Staircase*:

Mute stands she, lonely on the topmost stair,
An image of magnificent despair;

The grandeur of a sorrowful surmise
Wakes in the Pargeness of her glorious eyes.
In her beauty's significant pose I find
The tragedy of her mysterious mind.
Yet is the stately, grandiose, and full of grace.
A musing mask is her immobile face
Her tail is up like an unconquered flag;
Its dignity knows not the right to wag.
An animal creature wonderfully human,
A charm and miracle of fur-footed Brahman,
Whether she is spirit, woman, or a cat,
Is now the problem I am wondering at.

The poet of the "charm and miracle of fur-footed Brahman" is a mystic with a difference.

Another surprise in Sri Aurobindo's poetry is his concern with and insight into the work of politics, especially with the totalitarian menace, which he had anticipated in his sociological essays. *The Human Cycle.* He had no illusions on the score and in his letters during the war years he had made his position perfectly clear. "The Dwarf Napoleon", or the Nazi *avatar* is mordant and pitiless, like Ananke:

Behold, by Maya's fantasy of will
A violent miracle takes sudden birth,
The real grows one with the incredible...
The puny creature would bestride the earth
Even as the immense colossus of the past....
A headlong spirit driven by hopes and fears,
Intense, neurotic with his shouts and tears,
Violent and cruel, devil, child and brute,
The screaming orator with his strident tongue,
The prophet of a scantily fixed idea.
Plays now the leader of the human march....
But if its tenebrous empire were allowed
Its mastery would prepare the dismal hour
When the inconsicent shall regain its right,
And man who emerged as Nature's conscious power,
Shall sink into the deep original Night

Sharing like all her forms that went before
The doom of the mammoth and the dinosaur....
A tortured channel, not a happy vessel,
Drives him to think and act and cry and wrestle.
Thus driven he must stride on conquering, all,
Threatening and clamouring, brutal, invincible,
Perhaps to meet upon his storm-swept road
A greater devil—or thunderstroke of God.

The poet does not judge the agent, "a tortured channel" or the situation in terms of conventional ethics but as the workings of destiny, as, to use his own words, "the hammer of a new creation." In their own way, these perverts know their role well enough. The Children of Wotan do not suffer from any lack of knowledge. Asked: What is the end of your armoured march, O children of Wotan? They answer, exultantly their self-appointed task and well-laid strategy:

"We mock at God, we have silenced the mutter of priest at the altar
Our leader is master of Fate, medium of her mysteries.
We have made the mind a cypher, we have strangled thought with a cord
Dead now are pity and honour, strength only is Nature's lord.
We build a new world-order; our bombs shout Wotan's peace.
We are the javelins of Destiny, we are the children of Wotan,
We are the human Titans, the supermen dreamed by the sage,
A cross of the beast and the demoniac with the godhead of power and will,
We are born in humanity's sunset, to the Night is our pilgrimage.
On the bodies of perishing nations, and the cry of the cataclysm coming,
To a presto of bomb and shell and the aeroplane's fatal humming,
We march, lit by Truth's death-pyre, to the world's satanicage.

A shorter poem, in a totally different key, is *Cosmic Man.* The sensitivenes to the world situation is a mark of this modern mystic, who is no recluse from life. His vision includes the victims of aerial bombing and can sing even in affliction:

I look across the world and no horizon walls my gaze;
I see Paris and Tokyo and New York.

I see the bombs bursting on Barcelona and on Canton streets.
Man's numberless misdeeds and rare good deeds take place
    within my single self.

I am the beast he slays the bird he feeds and saves,
The thoughts of unknown minds exalt me with their thrill.
I carry the sorrow of millions in my lonely breast.

But not to cover to defeat or sentimentality. On the contrary, Sri Aurobindo is the poet of Man the Master:

Nature in me one day like Him shall sit
Victorious, calm, immortal, infinite.

The hope is supported by his firmly held vision of human possibility or evolution. As for the antinomies of existence, the source of recurring defeat and disillusionment, these are not unknown to him. Few know better that:

In the Inconscient dreadful dumb Abyss
    Are heard the heart-beats of the infinite.
The insensible midnight veils His trance of bliss,
    A fathomless sealed astonishment of Light.

All in all Aurobindean poetry provides a new image of man. None has dug deeper into the buried self and come up with a more inclusive, integral vision. In the end art, like religion and philosophy, has perforce to answer the old riddle: What is man? Is "Man, the Thinking Animal" the poet tells us:

A trifling unit in a boundless plan
Amidst the enormous insignificance
Of the unpeopled cosmos fire-wheel dance
Earth as by accident engendered man.

A creature of his own grey ignorance,
A mind half-shadow and half-gleam, a breath
That wrestles, captive in a world of death,
To live some lame brief years. Yet his advance,

Attempt of a divinity within,
A consciousness in the inconscient Night,
To realise its own supernal Light.
Confronts the ruthless forces of the Unseen.

Aspiring to Godhead from insensible clay,
He travels slow-footed towards the eternal day.

While a poem like this may seem to depend overly on statements and perhaps a theory of life, Sri Aurobindo is too much of a poet to forget the delight-self, the *ananda-purusha,* the key to the Indian life-style. In a near-*Vaishnava* poem, but suitably altered to chime with his world-view, he celebrates Time's voyage towards beauty and bliss :

Because Thou art all-beauty and all-bliss,
My soul blind and enamoured yearns for Thee,
It bears Thy mystic soil touch in all that is
And thrills with the burden of that ecstasy.

Behind all eyes I meet Thy secret gaze
And in each voice I hear Thy magic tune;
Thy sweetness haunts my heart Through Nature's ways;
Nowhere it beats now from Thy snare's immune.

It loves Thy body in all living things,
Thy joy is in every leaf and stone;
The moments bring Thee on their fiery wings;
Sight's endless artistry is Thou alone.

Time voyages with Thee upon its prow.
And all the future's passionate hope is Thou.

Neither nostalgia nor indulgence in a private dream, the poem expresses that higher possibility which is the deeper truth of man's aesthetic being, a possibility which no true civilization can afford to ignore. It is not only the living truth of man but his destiny. Only to the extent that one earns this vision has one lived. "The Infinite Adventure" is man's perilous voyage of self-discovery, yet bright with hope :

On the waters of a nameless Infinite
My skiff is launched; I have left the human shore.
All fades behind me and I see before
The unknown abyss and one pale pointing light.
An unseen Hand controls my rudder. Night
Walls up the sea in a black corridor,—
An inconscient Hunger's lion plaint and roar
Or the ocean sleep of a dead Eremite.

I feel the greatness of the Power I seek
Surround me; below me are its giant deeps.
Beyond, the invisible height no soul has trod.
I shall be merged in the Lonely and the Unique.
And wake into a sudden blaze of God,
The marvel and rapture of the Apocalypse.

But a merger is not enough. The new Rishi, his mind fixed upon great and distant things, will sail further and "light the suns that never die". That will be the theme of his next book, *Savitri,* and its epic exploration of the cosmic waters in search of the hidden wisdom or truth. In every sense a testament, only Sri Aurobindo—"the explorer and mariner on a secret ocean without bourne"—could have written it, and he has:

The ordeal of the veiled Initiate,
The hero soul at play with Death's embrace,
Wrestler in the dread gymnasium of Fate
And sacrifice a lonely path to Grace.

VII

All Sri Aurobindo's works lead up to *Savitri: A Legend and a Symbol.* He had been at work upon the poem for years, made several revisions. A work by itself unlike all others, was the author's own considered view. Yet he was fully aware that, for a long time to come, the appeal of the poem might be limited. Among other reasons it is the inability of the divided modern consciousness to experience and unify different levels of reality that explains the lack of response. The easiest way out of the difficulty is to describe, that is to dismiss, the poem as philosophical. The charge might have some ground when applied to his earlier writings, but not now. The theme, the legend or the story of a faithful wife who brings back to life her dead husband, is familiar. Then where does the difficulty come in? The difficulty arises out of the subjective or symbolic dimension given to the story. The absence of outward action, the prolonged interior dialogues, the massive flashbacks, the timeless stance, call for 'another breathing'* But the symbol, symbol of what? The poem, which is its own best commentary, makes that clear. Its inner motive is one with the motive of all art: immortality. As Sri Aurobindo phrases it: "The end of Death, the death of Ignorance". It is not an allegory, a philosophy or a doctrine but experience that Sri Aurobindo is concerned with. Indeed, there lurks about the poem, and his long labour upon it, a prophetic note of the shape of things to come. Psychologically viewed, he *had* to write it, the "inner epic' of which he had spoken in *The Future Poetry*. In the words of K.D. Sethna, "To create a poetic mould equally massive and multiform as *The Life Divine*...such a task is incumbent on one who stands as the maker of a new spiritual epoch. Scattered and short pieces of poetry cannot build that sustained *Weltanschaung* required for putting a permanent stamp upon the times. Nothing except an epic or a drama can—*Savitri* is, from every angle the right corelate" to Sri Aurobindo's total effort and status as a poet, its crown jewel. In the body of this single poem he has revealed or restored a whole world, of transvalued values. Come what may, he will be known as the poet of *Savitri*.

As it is, not many have read the poem or read it aright. Even those who are well up in the Aurobindean lore fight shy of the poem or tend to reduce it to some kind of a sacred canon instead of coming to it first as poetry. Little attempt has been made so

* Rilke's phrase; Poetry, he said, called for "another breathing", an idea tantalisingly analogous of the yogic hypothesis.

far to relate it—"the poetry of tomorrow", as the Mother once said—with world literature or to stress its significance for the future of consciousness and man. The poem no doubt demands a discipline of its own, a capacity for subjective experience and the Mysteries, at least of the symbolic imagination. This capacity the modern mind has more or less lost, else looks upon the loss itself as progress. This explains better than anything else the lack of interest and interpretation. The inward look has grown alien to us and *Savitri's* reader soon finds himself on another terrain, an "adventurer and cosmologist of a magic earth's obscure geography," "the explorer and mariner on a secret ocean without bourne." The obscure calms and the secret ocean are of course not without but within. Also, and this is remarkable, whatever happens within lights up and is related to the outside. That is, not only is the inner voyage real in itself but it makes real everything else in the life we lead on the surface. *Savitri's* unfailing capacity to clarify existence puts every other poet into the shade. By its side there is no poetry that does not appear a little superficial.*

Roughly, there are two journeys in the book—of father and daughter. The first makes possible the incarnation of the heroine ("a world's desire compelled her mortal birth)," the second prepares the resurrection of Satyavan : "Built is the golden tower, the flame child born." Between these two journeys there are differences, but in both the archetypal worlds or levels of the Self have been encountered or 'realised'. Sri Aurobindo has added a new dimension to our development, enlarged the doors of perception beyond belief. But in order to receive we need to be the poet's equal and that is not easy. Few of us will claim the poet's stance and sustaining power:

A colonist from immortality....
A skyward being nourishing its roots
On sustenance from occult spiritual founts
Climbing through white rays to meet an unseen Sun.

---

* See "However various the *donnees* of literature the basic question is, and will remain : what is Man ?" Georg Lukacs, *The Meaning of Contemporary Realism*, p. 19. This is where Sri Aurobindo easily triumphs over others.

As for the story or the legend, it is too simple to be missed. But one does not read Sri Aurobindo's *Savitri* for the story but for what lies behind, the symbol. And what may that be, the system of occult correlations, "the reading of the text of without from within?"

> Efforts that would shatter the struggle of mortal hearts
> Pursued in a royalty of mighty ease.

A subjective poem, *Savitri,* demands a different order of seeing and sensibility, an inwardness that is rare. To many it will appear as abstruse and obscure, at best philosophising. Sri Aurobindo—who had once said he was "never, never a philosopher"—does not believe in taking away the poet's right to think, but he does not accept philosophy *qua* philosophy in poetry as necessary or a mark of superior virtue. But in *Savitri* he is not engaged in versifying doctrine, esoteric or otherwise. What he is doing is quite different, he is giving the ground plan of reality, the cosmic order, on many interrelated levels as he has seen and known it. Considering that he was dealing with the order of the worlds ("The World Stair") and the corresponding hierarchy in the consciousness of man the poem could not have been plainer. In fact, nothing is more striking than the poem's visionary and interpretative power, which some have mistaken as a prosaic element. Sri Aurobindo is at once a master of experience and exegesis, and it should not be too difficult for the right reader to find out that *Savitri's* encycolpaedic of symbols is best understood in terms of the multiple unity of the Self. If this is unacceptable the reader had better leave the poem aside. The loss will be his, also the responsibility.

As Krishnaprem put it so well : "*Savitri* is neither subjective fantasy nor yet mere philosophical thought, but vision and revelation of the actual structure of the inner cosmos and of the pilgrim of life within its sphere—the Stairway of the Worlds reveal itself to our gaze—worlds of Light above, worlds of Darkness beneath —and we see also over-encircling life ("kindled in measure and quenched in measure") ascending that Stair under the calm unwinking gaze of the Cosmic Gods who shine forth now as of old. Poetry is indeed the full manifestation of the Logos, and when, as here, it is no mere irridescence dependent on some special standpoint, but the wonderous structure of the mighty cosmos, the 'Adored One', that is revealed, then in truth does it manifest its full, its highest grandeur."

Also, as he adds : "Such poetry can be written either in the early days before the rise to power of self-conscious mind or when the particular cycle has run its course and life establishes itself once more in the unity beyond, this time with the added range and power that has been gained during the reign of mind. It is an omen of the utmost significance and hope that in these years of darkness and despair such a poem as *Savitri* should have appeared." How one wishes that the literary pundits had shown as much understanding of the poem's motif and manner! *Savitri* may need a little effort but it is worth the carriage. After all, the poem is addressed to us, to "the powers that sleep unused within man". Here a whole lost tradition or language has come alive in a modern idiom, and nothing is more authentic than its images and metaphors, and what these point to. With its integral image of Man, and of a profound awareness of human destiny, seen against the stark background of an intense inner drama without pause or cease, concentrating centuries of development, here is an inner drama, the inner epic of Man. Except for the insensitive and the allergic there is no escape from the poem and its "harmonic order of the self's vastitudes," "the structured visions of the cosmic self". This many-levelled exploration of the order of the cosmic self is the poem's inalienable background, and its free gift to all who are able or willing to claim it. Like his own Aswapathy, the poet is our Representative Man, for sometime "One life is charged with earth's destiny". At some level of being we are all involved in the poem's action, *engage*. Does this stupendous subjectivity of approach and treatment mean that the action of the poem is wholly static? On the contrary things are always happening, even if the events are psychic rather than physical. Its action does not take place 'out there', to 'other' people. Both events and *dramatis personae* are within us. We are its locale and our lives its grand theatre. As Sri Aurobindo is careful to indicate, the poem's action takes place in the inner of soul-space, soul-scene, in "a larger self that lives within us, by ourselves unseen." It is part of the poem's achievement that it makes the larger self and the unseen realities vivid presences and the reader feels "His self's infinities begin to emerge." The poem is a continued evocation in depth.

But the psychological, subjective or occult emphasis should not make us forget the human side of the poem and the protagonist. The appeal of certain passages not too few, is a fact of immediate experience. Even if the action, the plunge into the inner realms (not the nether worlds only), the long encounter and debate with Death and Nothingness, is seen under the aspect of a cosmic drama or myth, the poem's main theme is love, may be love of a rarer birth. Sri Aurobindo calls it in the opening book the drama of "Earth, Love and Doom". The drama unrolls itself through a psychological rather than a time sequence. The "endless moment" is also for ever—again, a symbol rather than a legend. The symbolic content and enrichment are Sri Aurobindo's very own, a sign of superior sensibility and his affiliation with the seer-poets of old. Here is poetry such as the Rishis wrote or might write. From which it follows that the poem's basic or real theme is "the soul's search for lost Reality", or immortality, to which the poet restores its original meaning.

In spite of the tremendous range of explorations, the core of the poem is dramatic, depending on a supreme change, challenge and choice. A death followed by a debate or encounter, a crisis provides the backdrop of the 'inner epic'. The order of the worlds gives the background its depth and incredible massive reality, not as an imaginary or imagined decoration but of the very substance of one's enlarging experience. No wonder the action involves the fate of man rather than of this or that man. And the finale? The poet is explicit on the issue. The drama of destiny can have but one denouement:

The end of Death, the death of Ignorance.

This may sound eschatological. But in truth it is a dramatic myth set against a cosmic background. A single gonglike sentence at the end of Book I, Canto I, is enough to set the pace:

This was the day when Satyavan must die.

Satyavan's death is not the end but the beginning of the encounter, reminiscent of Orphic archetypes that the mind can never forget or disown, archetypes that return or resurrect at every crisis. What is involved in the poem's myth is the deepest longing of the heart and the imagination (and more than imagination, if the evidence of the poem is any proof). As we read it we have a feeling that an ancient Mystery— "The sun-word of an ancient Mystery's sense"—is being enacted before our mind's eyes. How bare and original the confrontation can be the reader will see through nearly half the length of a fairly long poem. The hint had been dropped early that:

> The soul's debate with embodied Nothingness
> Must be wrestled on a dangerous dim background:
> Her being must confront its formless Cause,
> Against the universe weigh its single self....
> In the world's death-cave uphold life's helpless claim
> And vindicate her right to be and love.

Later, when Savitri sticks to her choice to marry the doomed Satyavan, Narad anticipates the turn of events, her solitary wager with destiny:

> A day may come when she must stand unhelped
> On a dangerous brink of the world's doom and hers,
> Carrying the world's future in her lonely breast,
> Carrying the human hope in a heart left sole
> To conquer or fail on a desperate verge....
> Where all is won or lost for man.
> In that tremendous silence lone and lost
> Of a deciding hour in the world's fate
> In her soul's climbing beyond mortal time
> When she stands sole with Death and sole with God
> Apart upon a silent and desperate brink
> Alone with her self and death and destiny
> As on some verge between time and Timelessness
> Where being must end or life must build its base,
> Alone she must conquer or alone must fall....
> Cry not to heaven, for alone she can save.

Nothing could be plainer and, to the eye of vision, more prophetic. This, then, is the stark issue: of "self and death and destiny." There are also numerous collateral issues, martyrdom, for instance. Why does, why need Satyavan die and how is his death "the spirit's opportunity"? For such as who are looking for autobiographical undertones, is the poet to be identified with Aswapathy or with Satyavan, or both? Perhaps we shall never wholly know, unless we too dare to go along the ancient path, the path of "the mysterious sacrifice." Incidentally, the following passage comes as close to a deeply felt rationale of the Crucifixion as one may hope to get from a non-Christian imagination. A half-veiled autobiographical hint but adds to the Mystery*:

He who would save the world must share its pain:
This he shall know who obeys the grandiose urge.
The great who come to save this suffering world
And rescue out of Time's shadow and the Law,
Must pass beneath the yoke of grief and pain....
The son of God born as the son of Man
Has drunk the bitter cup, owned God's debt,
The debt the Eternal owes to the fallen kind.
His will has bound to death and struggling life
That yearns in vain for rest and endless peace.
Now is the debt paid, wiped off the original score.
The Eternal suffers in a human form,
He has signed salvation's testament with his blood;
He has opened the doors of undying peace.
The deity compensates the creature's claim,
The creator bears the law of pain and death ;
A retribution smites the incarnate God.
His love paves the mortal's road to heaven:
He has given his life and light to balance here
The dark account of mortal Ignorance.
It is finished, the dark mysterious sacrifice.

But martyrdom is incomplete; by itself part of a deeper mystery, it points to resurrection. An allied theme of the poem, on which the entire action hangs, is resurrection, the resurrection of Satyavan, the soul of the world, *Telos*. Not defiance of the Law, not personal desire, but Grace alone can do the miracle, some

* One wonders why the Eighth Book, the Book of Death was left incomplete by the poet.

descent of the Supreme. This exactly is what Savitri, the Eternal Feminine, the World Mother, cast in a new role, represents. Fate shall be changed by an unchanging will, the World Mother had assured the aspiring Aswapathy. And to Death Himself, Savitri, her deputy, throws the deathless challenge:

> I am stronger than death and greater than my fate;
> My love shall outlast the world, doom falls from me
> Helpless against my immortality,
> Fate's law may change, but not my spirit's will.

Thus the epic moves beyond tragedy, but not in terms of a sentimental family reunion. Rather is it a prelude to the coming of a new order, a new life or race when

> The Spirit shall look through Matter's gaze
> And Matter shall reveal the Spirit's face....
> The mighty Mother shall take birth in time
> And God be born into the human clay
> In forms made ready by your human lives.

The apocalyptic strain should not make us overlook the fact that *Savitri* is primarily a poem of love and Sri Aurobindo a poet of love. This is true not only of Book Five, called the Book of Love, but of the poem as a whole, its major motive. Let a few excerpts show. To the young heroine:

> Here with the suddenness divine events have,
> Repeating the marvel of the first descent,
> Changing to rapture the dull earthly round,
> Love came to her hiding death.

Later, when Savitri's father sends her out to seek "the unknown lover" he speaks of both the agony and ecstasy of love:

> Depart where love and destiny call your charm.
> Venture through the deep world to find thy mate.
> For somewhere on the longing breast of earth,
> Thy unknown lover waits for thee unknown.
> Then shall you grow like vibrant kindred harps

One in the beats of difference and delight,
Responsive in divine and equal strains,
Discerning new notes of the eternal theme.
One force shall be your mover and guide,
One light shall be around you and within;
Hand in strong hand confront Heaven's disguise, life;
Challenge the ordeal of the immense disguise.

But when she returns and speaks of her choice of Satyavan who has but one year to live, the disconsolate parents try to dissuade her. This is what she says, the very spirit of woman:

"My father, I have chosen. This is done....
I have discovered my glad reality
Beyond my body in another being:
I have found the deep unchanging soul of love....
My spirit has glimpsed the glory for which it came.
My eternity clasped by his eternity
And, tireless of the sweet abysms of love time,
Deep possibility always to love.
This, this is the first, last joy and to its throb
The riches of a thousand fortunate years
Are a poverty....
If for a year, that year is all my life.
And yet I know this is not all my fate
Only to live and love a while and lie."

To Death's repeated importunities to cease from the hope and the vain attempt to have Satyavan back to life this is what she says, thrice:

And silently the woman's heart replied;
"Thy peace, O Lord, a boon within to keep
Amid the roar and ruin of wild Time
For the magnificent soul of man on earth.
Thy calm, O Lord, that bears thy heads of joy."

And passionately the woman's heart replied:
"Thy energy, Lord, to seize on woman and man,
To take all things and creatures in their grief
And gather them into a mother's arms."

Then all the woman yearningly replied:
"Thy embrace which rends the living knot of pain,
Thy joy, O Lord, in which all creatures breathe,
Thy magic flowing waters of love,
Thy sweetness give to me for earth and man."

Compassionate, "a wonderful mother of countless souls," but not cowering, she hurls at the dread Lord of Death her *mahavakyas,* the great words : *I am, I love, I see, I act, I will.* And, when, finally, she has won her heart's desire, what does she tell her amazed, awakened husband? Only this:

"Let us go through this new world that is the same.
For it is given back, but it is known,
A playing-ground and dwelling-house of God,
Who hides himself in bird and beast and man,
Sweetly to find himself again by love,
By oneness."

That 'sweetly' is a master touch. Of such is the kingdom of the "eternal bridegroom and the eternal bride." To read *Savitri* as it ought to be read, is to be present at the marriage of time and eternity, the bridal of Spirit and Matter. It is to be born anew, level after level

He stood alone on a high roof of things
And saw the light of a spiritual sun.
Aspiring he transcends his earthly self,
He stands in the largeness of his self new-born
Redeemed from encirclement by mortal things
And moves in a pure free spiritual realm
As in the rate breath of a stratosphere.

When poetry can do that, what more does one ask for? As Raymond Piper put it: "We know that we must resort to the art of poetry for expressing to the fullest possible artistic limits, the yearning and battles of mankind for eternal life....I venture the judgment that *Savitri* is the most comprehensive cosmic poem ever composed. It ranges symbolically from a primordial cosmic void, through earth's darkness and struggle, to the highest realm of spiritual existence and illumines every important concern of man through verse of unparalleled massiveness, magnificence and metaphorical brilliance. *Savitri* is perhaps the most powerful artistic work in the world for expanding man's mind." Anyone who has read the poem with an open mind will agree. The first thing to do, we repeat, is to read it, as it should be read, "this Legend of the Past that is a Symbol of the Future." As one reads it, at every step the reader will find that the poet is there to help him. And when that happens, all else will be added into him.

VIII

No one who goes through the Aurobindean corpus can deny his claim to be counted among world poets. As for the yogic life, the Wisdom of the East, that too does not entail any abandonment ro weakening of the poetic impulse. On the contrary, it helped to bring in a new tone and range, characteristic of the author. While his earlier works might be looked upon as accomplished and promising, the later poetry opens up a new world and a new language. True, the philosophic strain is too pervasive to disappear at once or wholly but in the main it is vision rather than reflection that is the mark of the later yogic and mystical poetry. "Out of thought we must leap to sight." Or, as he says elsewhere in *Savitri:*

> And with a silver cry of opening gates
> Sight's lightnings leaped into the invisible.

It is a pity that, in spite of the fairly explicit statements, a poem built on such foundations should remain unappreciated, inaccessible to the many, even to poets. This is surprising, since even when "staring at the frontiers of the infinite" there is nothing deliberately difficult or obscure about Sri Aurobindo's poetry. Nor is it a blank infinite. More than that, it is subtly related to what is happening here and now. The poetry is, as he sees it, all a part of a living whole, a "complete existence." In *The Future Poetry* he had noted: "To find our self and the self of things is not to go through a rarefied ether of thought into *Nirvana*, but to discover the whole greatest integral power of our complete existence." It is this totality and the unification of fields, *bhumis,* that distinguishes Sri Aurobindo from merely idealising poets. It is a mistake to look upon this reconciling and fusing vision and its interpretative power as a prosaic element. On the contrary, it is the mark of a superior organisation in which our rising experience explains itself as a "self-luminous mystery."

And it is throughout balanced. The outward balance is the index of an inward grace or victory, beyond the sphere of sorrow. Whatever happens, there is:

> A deep spiritual calm no touch can sway
> Upholds the mystery of the Passion-play.

The serenity and authenticity of such soul-states and their poetic nuances are an addition to the world's poerty. To an unprejudiced mind their relevance for the renewal of man ought to be obvious. Sri Aurobindo's mature poetiy marks an ontological discovery and triumph. Briefly, he has helped us to get rid of the false view of man which has dominated history for the last four hundred years or so. And this widening, liberating experience, his "self-discovery's flaming witnesses", he has freely shared with us. *Savitri* remains a challenge and an opportunity to enter into the "kingdom of the seer." One can only wonder at the discipline that must have gone to its making, and the stupendous recovery of reality that the poem celebrates:

> Lifting the heavy curtain of the flesh
> He stood upon the threshold serpent-watched,
> And peered into gleaming endless corridors,
> Silent and listening in the silent heart
> For the coming of the new and the unknown.
> He gazed across the empty stillnesses
> And heard the footsteps of the undreamed Idea
> In the far avenues of the Beyond.
> He heard the secret voice, the Word that knows,
> And saw the secret face that is our own.

The recovery of revelation of "the secret face that is our own" brings in the world of the adept and the yogi, a world of pure perception into the modern consciousness. This opens a new possibility for a subjective, hieratic poetry, subjective but profoundly real: "A self-discovery that could never cease." It is a discovery which all of us have to make, one way or the other, if we are to be human. In his *Cosmic Art of India,* Radhakamal Mukherjee has pointed out that the image of Man in the art of India reflects the moods, tensions and transcendences of his real Self or Being. Only the puerile positivist, allergic as well as ignorant, will deny the value of what Sri Aurobindo has called "*mantra* of the Real". Only in so far as we admit this possibility, and with this evidence before us there is little else one can do, can there be hope for poetry or hope for man. The hope of the race lies, as our poet-critic has said elsewhere, in "the fidelity of its intellect to the larger perceptions it now has of the greater self of humanity, the turning of its will to the inception of delivering forms of thought, art and social endeavour which arise from these perceptions and the raising of the intellectual mind to the intuitive supra-intellectual consciousness which alone can give the basis for a spiritualised life of the race and the realisation of its diviner potentialities."

If that is so, Sri Aurobindo's role as an awakener is beyond question. Not to see the truth for what it is to declare oneself insensitive:

> The gifts of the spirit crowding came to him;
> They were his life's pattern and privilege.
> A pure perception lent its lucent joy:
> Its intimate vision waited not to think
> It enveloped all Nature in a single glance,
> It looked into the very self of things...
> So might one fall on the Eternal's road
> Forfeiting the Spirit's lonely chance in Time
> And no news of him reach the waiting god;
> Marked 'missing' in the register of souls.

To read Sri Aurobindo is once more to believe, and more than that to be aware, aware on all levels. As for the ordeals that await the adventurer soul, few poets have known these more than the poet of transformation. Sri Aurobindo knows better than others how and why;

The Dragon of the dark foundations keeps
Unutterable the law of Chance and Death;
On his long way through Time and Circumstance
The grey-hued riddling neither Sphinx,
Her dreadful paws upon the swallowing sands,
Awaits him armed with the soul-slaying word;
Across his path sits the dim camp of Night.

It is an ancient secret: "None can reach heaven who has not passed through hell." (The descent into the underworld is known to all wayfarers.) It is out of the encounter with the "abodes of the dead" there rises the star of a new creation, tender and terrible:

O star of creation, pure and free,
Halo-moon of ecstasy unknown,
Storm-breath of the soul-change yet to be,
Ocean self enraptured and alone!

But alone is company enough, since the poet, a cosmic man, is one with the cosmic consciousness. Not only does he "carry the sorrow of millions in his lonely breast", but:

In rare and lucent intervals of hush
Into a signless universe he could soar
Packed with the content of formlessness
Where world was into a single being rapt
And all was known by the light of identity
And spirit was its own self-evidence.

Sri Aurobindo's poetry is a celebration of this self-evidence. Instead of "the settled anarchy of things" he has proposed a new centre of the creative self, a luminous totality, in brief, the New Being.

Not as something glimpsed hurriedly but as a steady and open realistaion. It is strongly held idea—more than an idea, a vision—of human evolution that distinguishes Sri Aurobindo's later poems. The experience has been expressed in a variety of ways, an encyclopaedia of insights, clear, consistent, rewarding:

I saw my soul a traveller through Time,
From life to life the cosmic way it trod.
Obscure in the depths and on the heights sublime,
Evolving from the worm into the god.

Again :

My senses change into golden gates of bliss.
An ecstasy thrills through touch and sound and sight
Flooding the blind material sheath's dull case
My darkness answers to his Call of Light.

From all this we should not hastily conclude that the poet is but an idealising agent wanting in a sense of the actual, a mistake frequently made. Sri Aurobindo has given every aspect of reality or experience its full share. "All is there, even God's opposites." As he once explained in a letter : The poem (Savitri) "expresses or tries to express a total and many-sided vision and experience of all the planes of being and their action upon each other." He who had written in *The Synthesis of Yoga* that "by contact with the facts of life art attains to vitality" would not himself play truant. A poet of the Apocalypse, he knows, better than others, the conditions needed for acquiring and stabilising the new poise or consciousness. The alchemist of consciousness does not quarrel with his material, is not easily put out by the so-called contradictions and difficulties in the evolutionary game or experiment. Indeed his whole labour, as poet and yogi, has been to mediate between the truth of life and the truth of the spirit. Poetry and art, he has told us, are born mediators between the immaterial and the material, the spirit and life. This cannot be done by working on or from the surface. The meeting of opposites is within and above, and in these poems, we are "called into the unborn skies." If this involves an inwardness of feeling or subjectivity that is as it should be. After all, as Sri Aurobindo is there to show, the ascent of poetry is the ascent to Self :

Only when we have climbed above ourselves...
The Ineffable shall find a secret voice.

The poet is that 'secret voice'. In fact Sri Aurobindo announces a new myth or symbol, of evolutionary change or the laws of our inner becoming. The poet of transformation, he looks forward to as he also makes possible, "the marriage of Earth and Heaven" when Matter shall be the Spirit's willing bride. In "Rose of God" we hear the poet say:

> Transform the body of the mortal like a sweet
> and magical rhyme;
> Bridge our earthhood and heavenhood, make
> deathless the children of Time.

This theme or mode Sri Aurobindo has made his own, without sacrifice of contemporaneity. This he has done by renewing the archetypal tradition of poetry as *prajna* or *mantra,* the intuitive or inspired Word, *Vak* or Logos. The role is entirely in keeping with the rest of his life and works. If his major prose works are an intellectual statement of his deeper experience, the later poetry, and the whole of *Savitri,* is an intimate, inevitable correlate of that poetic vision, of the return of the Rishi, which he had announced or anticipated in *The Future Poetry*. At the moment this poetry of genuine insight and awareness might seem to be outside the main stream of modern poetry. But the illusion cannot last. When the antics of the absurd, the strategies of the sophisticate have become curiosities of cultural decadence, poetry such as Sri Aurobindo's might come into its own and provide the needed relief and restitution. "How shall the wounded be well?" "Only by understanding their illness." And where shall we find a greater *Kaviraj** than Sri Aurobindo, not merely the poet of knowledge but of Love?

> Love must not cease to live upon earth,
> For love is the bright link twixt earth and heaven
> Love is the far Transcendant's angel here,
> Love is man's lien on the Absolute.

When Savitri has finally gained her soul's wish, and her husband has been restored to life, a bewildered sage asks her to explain the miracle. To this:

---

* The king of poets. The word also means a physician or healer.

Low she replied,
"Awakened to the meaning of my heart
That to feel love and oneness is to live
And this the magic of our golden change
Is all the truth I know or seek. O sage."

In another poem, "World Game", the god, no ascetic, tells the goddess the rationale of creation thus:

Then shall life he thy arms drawing thy own clapsed
 to thy breast's rapture or calm peace,
With thy joy for the spirit's immortal flame and
 thy peace for its deathless base.
Our eyes meeting the long love shut in deep eyes
 and our being held fast and one,
I shall know the game was worth the toil
 whose end is thy divine embrace.

IX

What is true of the enduring arts of India is true of the mature poetry of Sri Aurobindo's: a recovery of the human whole. The present age of troubles, frustration, and atomised living may find in its varied symbols and unified vision a profound promise and affirmation, of the reality of Being and Becoming in their cosmic or occult range and depth. A Vyasa of the inner life, Sri Aurobindo is a pointer to that change of consciousness, that apocalypse of the archetype, which every crisis in world history brings a little nearer. An *uttarsadhaka,* Sri Aurobindo stands for a renewal of modern man and a cure for the blight he suffers from "thrust down from completeness", The healing is in terms of the cognitive and delight self, *vijnana* and *ananda purusha.* In the unity of the most modern with the most ancient may be found the key to the future, the return to the roots, the revolution of the Word : "But tranquil, but making easy. The steep ascent to God." Or shall we say, the self? Reading this poetry one feels as if

The Word was near...
Of which the darkened universe was the robe,

No more existence seemed an aimless fall.
Extinction was no more the sole release.
The hidden Word was found, the long sought clue,
Revealed the meaning of the spirit's birth
Condemned to an imperfect body and mind
In the inconscience of material things
And the indignity of mortal life.

Heidegger has reminded us echoing, without knowing, the Vedic idea—that genuine poetry is the establishing of Being by means of the world and that what the poet names is holy. "Poetry is the act of establishing by the word and in the word. What is established in this manner ? The Permanent and the holy." If that is so, Sri Aurobindo's poetry needs no other justification. Though our present literary fashoins obscure such a possibility, is it so small a thing to have established the New Being with the help of poetry, the 'overhead' poetry of the peaks?

Piercing the limitless unknowable.
Breaking the vacancy and voiceless peace,

The words of the poet are worlds:

On peaks where Silence listens with the still heart
To the rhythmic metres of the rolling worlds,
He served the sessions of the triple fire;
On the rim of two continents of slumber and trance
He heard the ever unspoken Reality's voice
Awaken revelation's mystic cry,
The birth-place found of the sudden infallible word
And lived in the rays of an intuitive sun.

If and when the modern crisis of indentity is over that will be the time to read Sri Aurobindo again, in a new light. Then we shall learn again, with amazement and gratitude, that which can never be wholly forgotten—the truth of our larger self that lives within us by ourselves unseen:

A deathbound littleness is not all we are;
Immortal our forgotten vastnesses

Await discovery in our summit selves,
Unmeasured breaths and depths of being are ours.
Even when we fail to look into our souls
Or lie embedded in earthly consciousness,
Still have we parts that grow towards the light.
In moments when the inner lamps are lit
And the life's cherished guests are left outside,
Our spirit sits alone and speaks to its gulfs:
A wider consciousness opens then its doors;
Invading from spiritual silences
A ray of limitless Glory stoops awhile
To commune with the seized illumined clay
And leave its huge white stamp upon our lives.
These signs are native to a larger self
That lives within us by ourselves unseen.

Drawing the harmony of the higher spheres, Sri Aurobindo has recovered for us the joy and the knowledge the unbounded experience of the cosmic self that lives within us, "by ourselves unseen." He has established poetry where it belongs—in the self. Thus he is a poet *per se*, poet of poets.
Sri Aurobindo had once said that he had been first and foremost a poet and a politician, only later he became a yogi. Yes, and when he became yogi he also became first and foremost among poets, Rishi who aspired to live poetry as well as write it. Leader on the inner roads, "beyond the mind's imaginings."

A seer, he has entered the forbiddden realms
A magician with the omnipotent wand of thought,
He builds the secret uncreated worlds,
Armed with the golden speech, the diamond eye,
His is the vision and the prophecy;
Imagist casting the formless into shape,
Traveller and hewer of the unseen paths,
He is the carrier of the hidden fire,
He is the voice of the Ineffable,
He is the invisible hunter of the light,
The Angel of mysterious ecstasies,
The conqueror of the kingdom of the soul.

Sri Aurobindo's Poetry as the Mantra of the Real

S.K. PRASAD

It is clear from the study of *The Future Poetry* that Sri Aurobindo would have us remember, from the first, the true which is also the highest aim and essence of poetry. "What is the highest power we demand from poetry; or,—let us put it more largely and get nearer the root of the matter,—what may be the nature of poetry, its essential law...?"[1] This is the fundamental question he would have us solve, first and last. All else can but follow this primary purpose. If we wish to make the best of poetic activity, we must first know "its spirit, its inner aim, its deeper law,"[2] for knowing this also means knowing the very highest possibility and use of poetry. It is this knowledge which will save both the writer and the reader of it from falling into false traps and side issues which lie on the path even here. What is more, taking our stand firmly on this vantage point we may gain a quite full view of the entire range, mode and purpose of this form of human expression and also develop a more catholic, comprehensive and enlightened attitude towards it than is usually the case with us. But above all it is through this means, more than any other, that we are able to see, says Sri Aurobindo "how out of this arises the possibility of its use as the *mantra* of the Real."[3]

"The *mantra* of the Real"—it is this phrase which, according to him, embodies the highest achievement of poetry. Indeed,

1. *The Future Poetry*, p. 12.
2. *Ibid.*, p. 13.
3. *Ibid.*, p. 12.

if we accept the truth that poetry is essentially an activity and expression of the spirit, the soul, and if the innate bent of the soul is towards the Divine Truth, the Divine Delight and the Beauty, in brief, an intimate and all-vibrant experience of the Divine Reality, it follows naturally that the very ultimate stage of the poetic achievement or realisation can be reached only when the poet is able to sing out to us in words, clear and bold, "the *mantra* of the Real." Now what is *mantra*? Ordinarily, it is translated into English words 'incantation' or 'magic'. Indeed, there are critics in the West who from ancient times have not only looked upon poetry as a sort of incantation or magic but also felt and stated that the highest reach of poetry is attainable only when its words and rhythms and images and ideas are all dissolved or subtly transformed through some mysterious power into a form of incantation; and thereby acquire an irresistible, haunting Power over the hearer's or reader's mind. The experience may be said to go back to the very earliest times of human history and appears to have become fairly articulate in the platonic days, for when Plato spoke of the persons who were "possessed by the Muses" and composed poems as though they were "inspired" by some "frenzy", he was, in fact, referring to some such art of incantation into which poetry dissolved itself. As David Daiches says, referring to the Platonic conception of the poet, "The poet was a possessed creature, not using language in the way that normal human beings do, but speaking in a divinely inspired frenzy."[4] It was at any rate in this frame of mind or consciousness that the prophetic poets delivered the word of God. This was a common enough notion in the early stages of civilization. Such a view of the poet Plato suggests, first, in a passage in his *Phaedrus*, and later develops at great length in his *Ion,* where the poet is presented as the inspired rhapsodist through whom God Himself speaks. He is generally represented as a man lacking in art,...and even any volition of his own, a passive vehicle merely. Says Socrates to Ion, "The gift which you possess...is not an art, but...an inspiration; there is a divinity moving you, like that contained in the stone which Euripides calls a magnet—all good poets, epic as well as

---

4. Quoted in Daiches, *Critical Approaches to Literature*, London, 1959, p. 6.

lyric, compose their beautiful poems, not by art, but because they are inspired and possessed—the poet is a light and winged and holy thing and there is no invention in him until he has been inspired and is out of his senses, and the mind is no longer in him, when he has not attained to this state, he is powerless and is unable to utter his Oracles...the poets are only the interpreters of the Gods by whom they are severally possessed."[5]

Now though the word "incantation" or "magic" is not used here, yet we may safely assume it to be implied by Plato from the way in which a poet, supposed to be "possessed" by some "power divine" or by the Gods is described as composing his beautiful poems so as to cast a kind of spell upon his audience. According to this conception, the poet's activity is taken to be one of casting a spell or magical effect upon the audience, for the time being at any rate, through the medium of the word he utters. And this may be taken to be equivalent to his uttering an incantation or "*mantra*", specially when he sings as if pos-possessed by some "divine power", and, therefore, it is not he who sings or speaks but "god himself is the speaker,"[6] through him. If, as we shall see soon, some of the distinctive features of *mantric* poetry are that it should aim at setting up a direct relationship or communication between the gods or the divine powers above and the poetic soul, and through him the listener's or reader's soul, below, and that the effect of the poetic utternace of such an experience is to cast everybody concerned under some potent, mysterious, haunting spell or charm so that at the highest or intenseset point of the working of this charm, everything else is forgotten and only the vibrant fusion of the human and divine souls becomes effectively real, it may be safely supposed that the kind of inspired, incantatory, "frenzied" expression by the poet to which Plato refers comes sufficiently close to the *mantric* expression in poetry, according to the ancient Indian tradition.

It is significant that in the earliest stages of human civilization when "the poet and the priest were united originally in the same person" and "the poet was he who was conscious of the world of spirit as well as that of sense, and was the ambassador of the

5. *Ibid.*, pp. 7-8.
6. *Ibid.*, p. 7.

Gods to men," we had some of the ideal conditions in which poetry could best flourish as *mantra.* And it is accepted both in the East and the West that this kind of poetry is the poet's highest achievement and it was in this kind of poetic composition that he came to be looked upon as the "seer" or Rishi. But as soon as the functions of the poet and the priest begin to be separate, and still later on in human history, when the poet as the "seer" becomes secondary to the "maker", and his office is reduced to that of the entertainer from that of the teacher, we naturally perceive an inevitable decline in the production and appreciation of poetry as *mantra.* What is more, it appears, as civilization and sophistication advance and we reach the modern intellectual and scientific age, the disapperance of the *mantric* poetry seems to be almost complete.

However, even in modern times we have some English critics like Abercrombie and C. Day Lewis who once again remind us of this important and high function of poetry, and, thereby, seek to restore, as far as possible, the incantatory power of poetry.

"What, then", asks Abercrombie, "is the first thing which we require of all poetry, not merely in order to be great, but to exist at all?"[7] And quite at once he replies, "I will call it, compendiously 'incantation' the power of using words so as to produce in us a sort of enchantment; and by that I mean a power not merely to charm and delight, but to kindle our minds into unusual vitality, exquisitely aware both of things and of connexions of things."[8] This power of incantation is not at all a matter of technique or craftsmanship, continues Abercrombie, and yet it is in and through the quality of words, first of all, and more than anything else, that the critical mind will be able to lay hold on this peculiar power of incantation which is the hall-mark of all true and great poetry. But then, as he says, "we do not require an absolute enchantment in every phrase we read, even in the finest poetry."[9] Nevertheless, the poets have an art of making us expect the magical phrase; and when it comes, it casts its enchantment over the whole surrounding texture of language.[10] Indeed, as he says further, "unless it does come,

---

7. *The Idea of Great Poetry,* 1926, p. 18.
8. *Ibid.*
9. *Ibid.*
10. *Ibid.*, pp. 18-19.

and come often to keep our minds invigorated by its release even from the common words, of uncommon energy of meaning, we begin to murmur: "This may be very sincere and painstaking, but it is not poetry."[11] Abercrombie, thus, makes it quite clear that the very essential and primary power of a true poet is the power of discovering "the magical phrase" and of "keeping our minds invigorated by its release, even from common words, of uncommon energy of meaning." And in order to reinforce his point, and drive it concretely home to our understanding he gives us a few very well-chosen, even familiar illustrations from Chaucer, Herrick, Shakespeare, and Giles Fletcher. When we go through these we get a clear and concrete notion of what he means by this power of incantation or enchantment in poetry. A single example of it from Shakespeare's *Julius Caesar* will be sufficient here for our purpose. It is the night of prodigies in Rome and Casca whose mind is already agitated by thoughts of treason tells us how that night he met on the way a lion, "who glazed upon me and went surly by." "There was never", comments Abercrombie, "any other lion quite like that. And the sight of its mysterious demeanour has been made over to us in perpetuity. The very sense of Casca's appalled encounter is absolute in us; Shakespeare's art has so enchanted us, that we become, for a moment, what he became."[12]

Abercrombie's argument is that by means of "the magical phrase," the incantatory word, the poet seeks to recreate, and not merely describe, the state of mind in which he found himself at that moment in the reader himself. It is something like a vigorous, vital transference of the state of mind from one person to another, i.e. from the creator to the recipient. Then there is another important thing which happens, as a result of it, at the same time. Says Abercrombie, "There are, naturally, infinite occasions for the poet's incantation; but its purpose is always the same. It may be giving us simply a moment of sensation: but it will make the moment individual, exquisite, unique...the poet's words not only make the whole fact start alive in our mind's; they are electric with the subtle distinction of the moment in which the fact occurs, stored with those delicate and

---

11. *Ibid.*, p. 19.
12. *Ibid.*, p. 21.

profound reverberations which make the fact unique. For the facts we are speaking of are experiences; and experiences are always unique: they occur in some particular person's mind, in some particular sequence of other experiences."[13] And exploring the matter thus Abercrombie leads us on to what he takes to be the poet's chief business. He says, "Whatever the nature of his topic, the poet's business is always the same. He must, out of subtly adjusted sound and sense of words, contrive such a texture of intensities and complexities of meaning, of unsuspected filaments of fine allusion and suggestion, as will enable those gossamers to capture and convey into our minds just those fleeting, gleaming qualities of experience which elude the hold of everyday straightforward language. For these are the very qualities which give to each moment of experience its unique distinction; and the words that can securely convey them are magical words, for they are truly creative."[14]

To Abercrombie, therefore, the poet's real creative power lies in the ability to discover and get hold of those magical words and phrases by force of which he is able to communicate, nay directly transmit to the reader, the unique, individual, exquisite, vibrant experiences occurring at a particular moment in his own particular individual mind. The poet's power of incantation lies, thus, in creating a unique, individual, vibrant psychological state in the reader or listener by means of words and phrases which Abercrombie calls "magical". Its process or mode is verbal no doubt but the aim is to induce a particular, unique state of mind in which the peculiar individual experience of the creative poet is easily and directly transmitted to the recipient's mind with all that subtle "texture of intensities and complexities of meaning, of unsuspected filaments of fine allusion and suggestion" which inevitably lies embedded in the core of every unique experience of men. And this "magical infection of our minds with the poet's mind by means of language, is the first thing," says Abercrombie "poetry must be capable of, in order to exist at all" and therefore, to accept the incantation—re-creation in us of another man's experience is to make our first acknowledgement of the presence of poetry."[15]

13. *Ibid.*, pp. 21-23.
14. *Ibid.*, pp. 23-24.
15. *Ibid.*, pp. 24-25.

Though C. Day Lewis is not so detailed in the exposition of the incantatory or magical power of poetry as Abercrombie, yet his brief observations are no less germane to our purpose, inasmuch as he, too, believes that poetry has "its roots in incantation" and that "its effect has always been to create a state of mind...."[16] And although the modern times seem to be quite alien to the growth of poetry which "has its roots in incantation," yet he does not consider the situation to be so bleak as to lose hope altogether. On the contrary, even in this age of science and propaganda the magical poetic power can assert itself and ultimately triumph against all odds making use of those very properties which seem to be alien to the creation of poetry. "Poetry", as he says, "was born from magic: it grew up with religion: it lived through the age of reason"[17] and there is no reason why it should "die in the century of propaganda."[18] Indeed, it is according to him, not "death, perhaps, but a self-defensive cataleptic trance"[19] in which it seems to be fallen today. And though it would appear that it has hardly any hope of "making itself heard in such a pandemonium of slogans, national anthems, headlines...straight talks, loudspeakers, manifestos, monkey business, madhouse gossip and high-explosive ideals"[20] and it would seem that in a scientific age "the flower of poetry must wither,"[21] yet it need not be so, inasmuch as "it is possible for poetry", C. Day Lewis continues to say, "to steal the thunder of science, to absorb these trivial business incantations and turn them to its own uses."[22]

When we now turn to Sri Aurobindo's interpretation of poetry as *mantra,* we find that in his large spiritual utterance, the whole incantation particularly, as interpreted by Abercrombie and C.Day Lewis, falls quite short of the potencies and depths and complexities of meaning which lie packed in the Sanskrit word *mantra.* And no wonder, for it is the rich ancient Vedic sense and usage and not in accordance with the Western conception of either

16. *A Hope for Poetry*, 1945, p. 30.
17. *Ibid.*
18. *Ibid.*
19. *Ibid.*
20. *Ibid.*, p. 26.
21. *Ibid.*
22. *Ibid.*, p. 30.

ancient or modern times that he interprets the term to us. He takes the *mantra* "as the highest intensest revealing form of poetic thought and expression"[23] "and in this he has the sanction of the Vedic poets themselves. As he says, "what the Vedic poets meant by the *mantra* was an inspired and revealed seeing and visioned thinking attended by a realisation, to use the ponderous but necessary modern word, of some inmost truth of God and self and man and Nature and cosmos and life and thing and thought and experience and deed. It was a thinking that came on the wings of a great soul rhythm, *chhandas*. For the seeing could not be separated from the hearing; it was an act. Nor could the living of the truth in oneself which we mean realisation, be separated from either, for the presence of it in the soul and its possession of the mind must precede or accompany in the creator or human channel that expression of the inner sight and hearing which takes the shape of the luminous word. The *mantra* is born through the heart and shaped or massed by the thinking mind into a chariot of that godhead of the Eternal of whom the truth seen is a face or a form. And in the mind too of the fit outward hearer who listens our word is a real *mantra*; the sight of the inmost truth must accompany the hearing, the possession of the inmost spirit of it by the mind and its coming home to the soul must accompany or follow immediately upon the rhythmic message of the word and the mind's sight of the Truth. That may sound a rather mystic account of the matter, but substantially there could hardly be a more complete description of the birth and effect of the inspired and revealing word, and it might be applied, though usually on a more lowered scale than was intended by the Vedic Rishis, to all the highest outburst of a really great poetry. But poetry is the *mantra* only when it is the voice of the inmost truth and is couched in the highest power of the very rhythm and speech of that truth. And the ancient poets of the Veda and Upanishads claimed to be uttering the *mantra* because always it was this inmost and almost occult truth of things which they strove to see and hear and speak and because they believed themselves to be using or finding its innate soul rhythms and the sacrificial speech of it cast up by the divine Agni,

---

23. *The Future Poetry*, p. 280.

the sacred Fire[24] in the heart of man. The *mantra*, in other words, is a direct and most heightened, and intensest and most divinely burdened rhythmic word which embodies an intuititive and revelatory inspiration and ensouls the mind with the sight and the presence of the very self, the inmost reality of things and with its truth and with the divine soul-forms, the Godheads which are born from the living Truth. Or, let us say, it is the supreme rhythmic language which seizes hold upon all that is finite and brings into each the light and voice of its own infinite."[25]

The quotation had to be given in full so that the *mantra*, as it is to be truly understood, should be clearly and variously driven home to us. It is doubtful whether anybody else has defined or described it better and more fully than Sri Aurobindo. And here is a poetically vivid and precise and revealing description of the way in which it operates upon the recipient of the *mantra*:

> As when the *mantra* sinks in Yoga's ear,
> Its message enters stirring the blind brain
> And keeps in the dim ignorant cells its sound;
> The hearer understands a form of words
> And, musing on the index thought it holds;
> He strives to read it with the labouring mind,
> But finds bright hints, not the embodied truth;
> Then, falling silent in himself to know
> He meets the deeper listening of his soul:
> The word repeats itself in rhythmic strains:
> Thought, vision, feeling, sense, the body's self
> Are seized unalterably and he endures
> An ecstasy and an immortal change;
> He feels a Wideness and becomes a Power
> All knowledge rushes on him like a sea:
> Transmuted by the white spiritual ray

---

24. The Western reader may get some idea of this sacred fire from the following lines of Matthew Arnold:

> "We cannot kindle when we will
> The fire which in the heart resides,
> The spirit bloweth and is still,
> In mystery our soul abides;"

25. *Ibid.*, pp. 280-81.

He walks in naked heavens of joy and calm,
Sees the God-face and hears transcendent speech....[26]

It is rather strange that no classical, well-known literary critic has considered it necessary to refer to the kind of poetry known as the *mantra.* All possible arguments and counter-arguments have been advanced to explain *Rasa* (aesthetic taste), *Alankara* (embellishments or figures of speech), *Dhvani* (suggestion), *Guna* (excellence), *Dosha* (faults) etc., and all possible subtleties demonstrated to enumerate these as well as the types of drama, poetry, style, hero, heroine etc., but nowhere does one come across in classical Sanskrit literary criticism, composition which was long known as the *mantra* in the Vedic and Upanishadic poetry. Probably it was because the very connotation of the word *Kavi* or poet had undergone a radical change during the period of classical Sanskrit and, as Sri Aurobindo says, it came to be applied in classical Sanskrit to "any maker of verse or even of prose", but "in the Vedic it meant the poet seer who saw and found the inspired word of his vision."[27] And as the Sanskrit literary critics mostly belonged to and concerned themselves with the period of classical Sanskrit, so they hardly looked upon the poet as a "seer who saw and found the inspired word of his vision," or even bothered to explore the possibility of the kind of poetry which "embodies an intuitive and revelatory inspiration and ensouls the mind with the sight and presence of the very self, the inmost reality of things and with its truth and with the divine soul-forms of it..." Nevertheless, this serious lacuna in Sanskrit literary criticism is something inexcusable. For Sri Aurobindo, however, who, from the first, looks upon poetry with the same vision and outlook as it was regarded in the Vedic times, and declares in unambiguous terms that "the true creator of poetry, as also its true hearer, is the soul," it was inevitable that he should not only think of *mantra* as the highest and greatest poetic utterance but also give us as clear and convincing a rationale of it as is possible for the human mind to understand. The fact is that the *mantra* can never be a product of the human mind, however great and brilliant, nor is it accessible even to the

26. *Savitri*, Book IV Canto III, p. 426.
27. *The Future Poetry*, p. 39.

highest poetic imagination as we usually understand it. It is the product of what Sri Aurobindo calls the "Overmind." The *mantra*, he says, "...As what comes from the Overmind inspiration. Its characteristics are a language that says infinitely more than the mere sense of the words seems to indicate, a rhythm that means even more than the language and is born out of the Infinite and disappears into the Infinite and the power to convey not merely some mental, vital or physical contents or indications or values of the thing it speaks of, but its value and figure in some fundamental and original consciousness, which is behind them all."[28] That is to say, it is something essentially mystical and spiritual, although it need not always operate upon what we usually take to be spiritual things and experiences or the Divine. On the contrary, it is concerned with the realisation "of some inmost truth of God and self and man and Nature and cosmos and life and thing and thought and experience and deed." That is to say, its subjects and their range are unlimited. It may "seize hold upon all that is finite:" only it "brings into each the light and voice of its own infinite." As he says at another place, "To arrive at the *mantra* he (i.e. the poet) may start from the colour of a rose, or the power or beauty of a character, or the splendour of an action, or go away from all these into his own secret soul and its most hidden movements."[29] The starting point may be, therefore, anything which belongs either to the outer or the inner or any supraphysical, transcendental world. But "the one thing needful is that he should be able to go beyond the word or image he uses or the form of the thing he sees, not be limited by them, but get into the light of that which they have the power to reveal and flood them with it until they overflow with its suggestion or seem even to lose themselves and disappear into the revelation."[30] That is to say, the poet of the *mantra* must be able to penetrate the very soul of the thing or image or word and invariably reveal the very "inmost reality of things." However, the ultimate result of the mantric experience is, as in the case of Plato's "possessed" or "frenzied" rhapsodist or Abercrombie's creator of incantation" or "enchantment", the discovery of the

---

28. *Letters*, III Series, p. 97.
29. *The Future Poetry*, p. 48.
30. *Ibid.*

potent, luminous, vibrant word. And the discovery of such a word is not something mental or imaginative but an actual seeing of it. As Sri Aurobindo tells us again, the poet-seer sees and finds "the revealing word not merely the adequate and the effective, but the illumined and illuminating, the inspired and the inevitable word, which compels us to see also."[31] And yet the whole process operating behind such a discovery of the "luminous inspired and inevitable word" is a complex and suitable one and keeps the whole integral being of the poet as well as the hearer engaged. For, though the *mantra* is visibly, almost physically received in the form of words, yet it is not a pack of words only. The words are but the interfused embodiments of "an inspired and revealed seeing and visioned thinking," attended by realisation of the inmost reality of the thing concerned. For the seeing is "revealed" and the thinking "visioned" and what is more, the thinking comes "on the wings of a great soul rhythm;" and the seeing could not be separated from the hearing; it is "one act." And all these various subtle swift acts of our receptive organs are actually realised experiences. As K.D. Sethna says, quoting a compendiously felicitious and luminously revealing line from Sri Aurobindo's *Savitri* "Sight's sound-waves breaking from the soul's great deeps"[32]—which is itself a striking example of *mantric* utterance—,... "the poet's act of seeing is simultaneously an act of hearing. They are not two processes really—the sight-substance comes fused with the sound-form, the vision is its own word, the right-manifesting word which is not just "transmissive" but "incarnative" embodying with a living intimacy and concrete directness the gleaming stuff and stir of the soul's revelatory contact with reality."[33] We, thus, find that at least three main activities or processes must get involved, compounded and fused together here before the "seen" or "revealed" word would become a real *mantra*. The sight of the "inmost spirit of it by the mind and its coming to the soul must accompany or follow immediately upon the rhythmic message of the Word and the mind's sight of the Truth." That is to say, it is but a well-integrated soul, dynamic on all its instrumental faculties and

31. *Ibid.*
32. *Savitri*, Book IV Canto IV, p. 435.
33. *Mother India*, Pondicherry, April 1955.

organs as well which can become the fit medium of the *mantric* expression and the true creator of the *mantric* poetry. As such, the turth which we get from the *mantra* is not merely some local, particular truth of the thing or experience visibly expressed but some force or form of the Truth itself, the very Supreme Reality. That is, indeed, the very essence of the *mantra*, and it is this which, above everything else, not only distinguishes it from all other kinds and qualities of poetry but raises it to the highest level of human utterance. Moreover, the process of its birth is not something purely human for there is the direct and simultaneous working and intervention by the Divine Power. That is why Sri Aurobindo says that the *mantra* in poetry is "that rhythmic speech which, as the Veda puts it, rises at once from the heart of the seer and from the distant home of the Turth."[34] It is obviously a dual movement linking the human with the ultimate Reality. For the purpose in the *mantra* is, as suggested before, to reach up to some integral truth above, through the word, the divine movement, the form of thought proper to the reality which, as Mr. Cousins[35] excellently says, "lies in the apprehension of a something stable behind the instability of word and deed something that is a reflection of the fundamental passion of humanity for something beyond itself, someting that is a dim foreshadowing of the divine urge which is prompting all creation to unfold itself and to rise out of its limitations towards the Godlike possibilities."[36]

This is the fundamental motive and impulse behind the birth of the *mantra*—to reach out to, and lay hold on, "a something stable behind the instability of word and deed."

As regards its mode of expression, Sri Aurobindo tells us that three things are simultaneously indispensible. The *mantra*, particularly the poetic expression of the deepest spiritual reality, is only possible when three highest intensities of poetic speech meet and become indissolubly one, a highest intensity of rhythmic movement, a highest intensity of verbal form and thought-substance, of style, and a highest intensity of the soul's

34. *The Future Poetry*, p. 11.
35. It was James Cousins's book *New Ways in English Literature*, which originally prompted Sri Aurobindo to come out with the series of articles in *The Future Poetry*.
36. *New Ways in English Literature*, p. 11.

vision of truth. All great poetry comes about by a union of these three elements; "it is the insufficiency of one or another which makes the inequalities in the work of even the greatest poets; and it is the failure of some one element which is the cause of their lapses...But it is only at a certain highest level of the fused intensities that the *mantra* becomes possible."[37]

And when, thus, as a result of these triple simultaneous movements of the highest intensity it becomes possible, it strikes upon our ear and consciousness with a music which is of the utmost spiritual resonance. "It is where the metrical movement remains as a base, but either enshrines and contains or is itself contained and floats in an element of greater music which exceeds it and yet brings out all its possibilities, that the music fit for the *mantra* makes itself audible."[38] Indeed, it is "the triumph of the spirit over the difficulties and limitations of its physical instrument." Naturally it is not with the help of just the physical ear that we can really listen to such a celestial music. On the contrary, its listener seems to be "that eternal spirit whom the Upanishad speaks of as the ear of the ear, he who listens to all hearings; and 'behind the instabilities of word and speech' it is the inevitable harmonies of his own thought and vision for which he is listening."[39] That is to say, in the ultimate stage of the experience, the inner spiritual listener attending to that "greater music" discovers that 'it is the inevitable harmonies of his own thought and vision for which he is listening.' Thus in the *mantra* the human soul below gets most harmoniously and completely identified with the eternal spirit above.

Similarly, its verbal style is also of an extraordinary, superhuman nature, and hardly subject to any rule or particular form of expression. Outwardly it may have quite a variety of forms and styles but the real pressure comes from what is spiritually known as the Word itself for the original home of Truth sends down its own verbal form and the physical instruments of human expression have only to achieve the capacity and power of unhindered transmission. The verbal intensity with which the *mantra* is inevitably filled, says Sri Aurobindo, "belongs to no

---

37. *The Future Poetry*, p. 30.
38. *Ibid.*
39. *Ibid.*

particular style, depends on no conceivable formula of diction. It may be the height of the decorative imaged style as often we find it in Kalidasa or Shakespeare; it may be that height of bare and direct expression where language seems to be used as a scarcely felt vaulting-board for a leap into the innate; it may be the packed intensity of language which uses either the bare or the imaged form at will, but fills every word with its utmost possible rhythmic and thought suggestion. But in itself it depends on none of these things; it is not a style, but poetic style itself, the Word; it creates and carries with it its elements rather than is created by them. Whatever its outward forms, it is always the one fit style for the *mantra*."[40]

Such being some of the graspable facts about the *mantra*, it is evident that it is the very "highest inspiration" which can call it forth : "the intrinsic word, the spiritual mantra."[41] Also we must not confuse the *mantra* with any philosophic, intellectual truth and knowledge. It is not, as Sri Aurobindo says, "in its substance of form poetic enunciation of a philosophic truth." On the contrary, it is "but the rhythmic revelation of intuition arising out of the soul's sight of God and Nature and the world and the inner truth-occult of the outward eye of all that peoples it, the secrets of their life and being."[42] It is "the voice of the inmost truth and is couched in the highest power of the very rhythm and speech of that truth."[43] And "at the highest he, i.e. the poet, himself disappears into sight; the personality of the seer is lost in the eternity of the vision, and the Spirit of all seems alone to be there speaking out sovereignly its own secrets."[44] We could not have a more precise and concise and pregnant description of the *mantra* than this. Born out of this "soul sight," ultimately in the *mantra* "the personality of the seer is lost in the eternity of the vision." Prof. V.K. Gokak rightly says, "this disappearance of the seer in his vision is more significant than the negative capability, the annihilation of the poet's identity which Keats describes in one of his letters or the

40. *Ibid.*, p. 38.
41. *Letters*, III Series, p. 77.
42. *The Future Poetry*, p. 46.
43. *Ibid.*
44. *Ibid.*

'depersonalisation' that T.S. Eliot speaks of."[45]

The poet of the *mantra* is, thus, essentially an inspired spiritual being through whom "the Spirit of all seems to be there speaking out sovereignly its own secrets." Here, too, as Prof. Gokak says in the same article, we must not confuse this "Spirit", that is to Sri Aurobindo a shining Reality and not a mere figure of speech, with some Romantic vision of Nature who according to Arnold, takes the pen from Wordsworth's hand in the most moving passages and seems to write herself. Still we may feel inclined to think that the *mantric* poet, being ultimately the child of such a Spirit, is like the inspired rhapsodist through whom God Himself speaks, as pointed out by Plato. But this, too, is merely a superficial resemblance, for whereas the inspired rhapsodist of Plato's description is a man lacking in art and even any volition of his own,—"the mind is no longer in him; when he has not attained to this state, he is powerless and is unable to utter his oracles...," as Plato said,—the poet of the *mantra*, though outwardly passively and silently open to the Word, the Spirit, the home of Truth above, is, nevertheless, inwardly a fully conscious, dynamic integrally attuned spiritual being himself, and what is more, is at the greatest and intensest possible spiritual heights of luminous creative seeing, hearing and utterance. It is no "frenzy" or "madness" which seizes hold upon him and though he, too, becomes, for the time being a being "possessed" by some mysterious occult power, he is not thrown into some cataleptic trance but remains fully conscious spiritually within, and, for that reason, is able to transmit the very "inmost truth of God and self and man and Nature and cosmos and life and thought and experience and deed." Also, his range of seeing and hearing and expression is all-comprehensive and not confined merely to things usually known as divine. And whatever the inmost truth of the thing seen or heard, it becomes at once a matter of self-realisation, a part and parcel of his inmost spiritual experience. That is why, the *mantra* he utters comes to exercise so much power over his listener or reader. As Sri Aurobindo points out, "The Vedic poets regarded their poetry as *mantras*, they were the vehicles of their own realisations and could become vehicles of realisation for others."[46] Being illuminations of the

45. *Mother India*, Pondicherry, October 1953, p. 6.
46. *Letters*. III Series, p. 292.

Word, the Light, they could immediately touch the deepest spiritual chords of one's being. They were instruments of an extraordinary occult power and could cause unusual occult experiences in the recipient too, if properly received and recited. The Vedic and Upanishadic *mantras* are, therefore, not words but concealed, packed powers. You repeat them in the true manner and spirit—the true manner and spirit depending upon the status of being you have reached—and the occult force hidden in them surrounds and seizes hold upon you from all sides like a living presence and begins to cause illuminations and realisations in you, too, in consonance with your capacity for receptivity.

It is, thus, clear from the above observations that it is the highest and intensest utterance of one's deepest possible spiritual experience or realisation which alone can take the form and substance of *mantra.* Here, therefore, the three important factors involved are all spiritual—the truth seen, heard and realised in its own appropriate verbal rhythmic and imaged form, the creator-seer of such a truth and the moved illumined recipient-hearer or reader of it. These three factors combine together to give the *mantra* of our Indian conception—the Vedic and Upanishadic conception, to be more exact—that unique quality and power which it usually possesses, and separate it so sharply from the "inspired" poetry of the ancient Greek, Platonic conception and the poetry of verbal and psychological "incantation" of the modern Abercrombiesque or C. Day Lewis's conception.

Sri Aurobindo's Wit and Humour

NIRODBARAN

MANY years ago, a Bengali littērateur said, "It is a pity Sri Aurobindo has no humour." Perhaps, he made a mental comparison with Tagore and lamented this deficiency in Sri Aurobindo who was otherwise great in many fields. He is not to be blamed for his ignorance, for Sri Aurobindo, even to his disciples in the very early thirties either because of his life of seclusion or of his reserved nature, had the reputation of being majestically serene, but not a smiling *Avatar*. Dilip had to hunger for the flicker of a smile during the three *Darshan* days of the year when he appeared before his disciples. Sri Aurobindo had to console him in letter after letter that he did smile at him! Even during his political days, Nevinson remarked about him, "The most dangerous man in India, who never smiles," which Sri Aurobindo amended later on by adding, "but who always jokes." He also said, "How could I smile when I was made to preside over a meeting?"

It was after Dilip had settled in the *Ashram* and I had taken my permanent place that Sri Aurobindo's hidden humour began to come out and flow in cascades through our correspondence. In the pre-*Ashram* days of the twenties his wit regaled the few inmates during the "Talks" but it remained unrecorded and therefore unknown to the public. In a book like *Kārākāhini* or in a comic drama like *The Viziers of Bassorā* his humour has burst like a 'Champagne bottle'. These prove that wit and humour were an essential ingredient of his nature. Only they remained quiescent and waited for an opportune moment to erupt. As to why we, Dilip and I, worked as the catalytic agents and were at the same time recipients of this heavenly laughter, he alone knows.

Meanwhile, voicing the general impression of the *sadhakas* re-received at the *Darshana*, I wrote to him that his Himalayan austerity and grandeur took our breath away, and got this answer, "O rubbish! I am austere and grand, grim and stern! every blasted thing I never was! I groan in an un-Aurobindonian despair when I hear such things. What has happened to the common sense of all of you people? In order to reach the Overmind it is not at all necessary to take leave of this simple but useful quality. Common sense by the way is not logic (which is the least common-sense-like thing in the world), it is simply looking at things as they are without inflation or deflation—not imagining wild imaginations—or for that matter despairing 'I know not why' despairs."

Sometime later, I took up this point and wrote, "You thrashed me for calling you grave and austere at *Darshan* time. But see, when we do *pranam* to the Mother sitting by your side, how seraphically she smiles while your noble self, Sir, being near, appears far away at some Olympian height! It is difficult to discern the gravity or jollity of a face at such a distance! I suppose, our conception of the gods was formed from such a vision." He replied, "Neither gravity nor jollity, but a large, easy, quiet amiable condition. The gods can't be amiable?"

This was the tone he often used with me in our long and massive correspondence on yoga, literature, politics, medicine, ete. etc., I sparred with him as between equals, played verbal duals, poked fun at 'tail of the Supermind', challenged his ideas about yoga, verging at times on blasphemy. Instead of being offended at my impudence he rewarded me with gentle raillery, Shavian playfulness, Homeric laughter of the Gods and Shakespearean lightning spontaneity of wit, either in a single word, in a line, a passage or even in a punctuation mark! Any circumstance, situation, tragic or comic sparked off his comic Spirit and set us into rollicking laughter. In my battle of wits with him, even in my own field of medicine, I could never score a single point. When I thought that I had at last cornered him, it was I who was floored at the end, but it was very sweetly done. Apropos of this, he wrote to Dilip, "I castigated or fustigated Nirod not from displeasure nor even 'more in sorrow than in anger,' but for fun and also from a high sense of duty! For that erring mortal was bold enough to generalise from his very limited experience and impose it as a definite law in yoga, discrediting in the process my own immortal philosophy! What then could I do but to jump on him in a spirit of genial massacre?"

'Fun' is the word. Oh, what fun! Buried under an 'avalanche of correspondence' dealing with physical or psychological 'troubles' light or serious, of about 200 inmates every night for 8-9 hours, plunged on the other hand in the 'subconscient mud' or in world-problems during the day or soaring in the supramental sky, his spirit was yet like a god's looking at the turmoils of the universe with a vast equanimity, compassion and divine levity. When I asked him where was the hidden spring from which his inexhaustible humour gushed out, he replied cryptically, "Raso vai sah!"[1]

He once remarked to Dilip, I believe: "Sense of humour? It is the salt of existence. Without it the world would have got utterly out of balance; it is unbalanced enough already—and rushed to blazes long ago."

Without further abstract dissertation, let me quote examples of his humour from our correspondence, relying mainly on my own letters.

I shall start with quotations from Dilip's letters: the first one is rather long, but extremely delicious! Dilip writes,"... Gurudev's secretary brought me a telegram to Gurudev which read : 'Wire permission for your Darshan on the fifteenth of August. Dilip, my friend, will recommend me—Aurobindo,' On the margin was written in Gurudev's handwriting: 'Please recommend and enlighten'"

It was just that little query which happily, made the wicked goddess—*Dushta Saraswati*—fall 'plump' and perch on my irreverent tongue. I dashed off then and there a Bengali poem which I sent up to Gurudev hoping against hope to draw him out. Here is an English translation of my wicked burlesque:

> You ask me Guru, who is this Aurobindo who desires to come
> To have your blessing on your birthday? I would rather now be dumb.

1. **"He is indeed the Delight." (*Upanishad*).**

> Because, I find, I know four personalities distinct and great
> Who are your namesakes and so wonder how to place this candidate!
>
> So I'll recount the deeds of each still graven in my memory,
> For your Supramental may shed light where I grope rayless hopelessly!

Dilip goes on in this vein, but I refrain from further quotations in order to wait on the Guru's reply which is also quite long. I shall extract some portions out of it. Sri Aurobindo answers: "Dilip, your epic of the four Aurobindos is luminous, informing and hair-raising!...His address? How in the name of the wonderful am I to know? His address in the telegram is 'Aurobindo, Bombay,' just as mine might be 'Aurobindo, Pondicherry...' although he is Aurobindo, Aurobindo does not know him from Adam. However, what I am doing is to send you his reply-paid telegram form and shove my responsibility on your shoulders. You will decide this according to the ripe wisdom of your many Aurobindonian experiences. Whether you wire 'come and be blessed' or 'stay where you are in your Eden'—is your shout. I back out. To sum the matter up in two far-flowing Alexandrine couplets:

> Tell him, by wire: 'come on' with a benignant nod,
> Or leave him journeying to the devil or to God
> Decide for the other Aurobindo what you please,
> This namesake-flooded Aurobindo leave at ease."

Then he continues in prose sparkling with laughter and light tracing the genesis of his own name. He ended the letter on this note: "Your, 'epistolary frivolity' was all right. There is laughter in the kingdom of Heaven, though there may be no marriage there."

I recommend the perusal of the whole letter in Dilip's *Sri Aurobindo Came to Me.*[2]

Next, Dilip was like me often a subject of the Man of Sorrows. At such times he would resort to hard *tapasya* as a quick means

2. First Edition, p. 318.

of realisation. In one of those crises he wrote, "O Guru...I propose —subject to your approval—a diastic prescription for my long-suffering unconvalescing self:

Number one—I will give up tea: I love it.
Number two—I will do without cheese: I like it.
Number Three—...I will start periodic fasts.
Number four—Will forswear hair-oil and shave my head.
Number five—I will sleep without the mosquito-curtain which I fear, will be the most difficult of all fears because I have never been able to hail the crooning of the mosquito as a lullaby.

Sri Aurobindo's reply: I stand aghast as I stare at the detailed proposals made by you! Fastings? I don't believe in them, though I have done them myself. You would really eat like an ogre afterwards. Shaved head? Great heavens! Have you realised the consequences? I pass over the aesthetic shock to myself at *Darshan* on the 24th November from which I might never recover —but the row that would rise from Cape Comorin to the Himalayas! You would be famous in a new way which would cast all your previous glories into the shade. And just when you are turning away from fame and all the things of the ego! No, too dangerous by half. Sleep without the mosquito-net? That would mean no sleep, which is as bad as no food. Not only your eyes would become weak, but yourself also—and, to boot, gloomy, grey and gruesome—more gruesome than the Supramental of your worst apprehensions! No and No again."

Then giving examples of 'pure fun, just unqualified laughter and mirth,' Dilip writes, "I had a friend whom we called Bindu. He wrote to Gurudev a long letter besieging him with a number of world-shaking questions to which the reply came in due course:

"'Bindu, Good heavens! But what! But when! But which!...'"
One day Bindu prevailed upon Sri Aurobindo to cook for him and the Mother what we call *prasād.* Sri Aurobindo ate a little of it whereupon Bindu penned him a disconsolate letter. "'Gurudev,'" he wrote, "'Nalina brought me back the dishes. I was stunned to find that you had hardly touched them. I am deeply pained, sorely disappointed, utterly dejected and mortally wounded, and cannot imagine why you are so unsympathetic to me.'"

Gurudev wrote back a sweet letter of solace:
"'Bindu!

Don't be absurd! Our sympathy towards you is profound and perfect, but it cannot be measured by our sympathy towards your eatables. We, usually, just taste the *prasad* people send to us; sometimes we take more but never when it is very sweet or very extraordinary. Of your vermicelli pudding we could well speak in the language of the passionate address of the lover to his beloved: 'O sweet! O too too sweet!' And the stew was extraordinary, albeit of another world—so much so that if I tasted the first forkful with anxiety, the second was with awe, after which I ventured no farther into these unknown countries....'"

Space forbids me to quote more extensively from Dilip's correspondence. I am sure our Bengali litterateur will now humbly withdraw his objection and admit Sri Aurobindo's name in his gallery of humour! Further examples that follow from my correspondence will make him erect a statue of Sri Aurobindo and adore him as a great wit. In my correspondence, "When he sparred with his doctor-disciple, assuredly another side of his nature found expression," Dilip writes, "Albeit I find it difficult to label....All the same, I may not be far out if I say that what expressed itself through this letters to Nirod was his love of raillery oscillating between a Shavian playfulness and a Ramakrishnonian badinage."

I shall classify the instances into four types: medical, spiritual, poetic and general; and they will be rather short to bring out their abundance and variety.

Myself: Guru, my big photo requires Sanjiban's treatment. Permission solicited.

Sri Aurobindo: What? which? where? how? what disease? what medicine wanted?

Myself: (Trying to shed some light), I send you your big photo, it is your photo that would be drawn by Sanjiban.

Sri Aurobindo: You are always plunging me into new mysteries. If it is a photo, how can it be drawn by anybody? And what is the tense, connotation and psychological and metaphysical annotation of 'would be'[3] here?

Myself: I am pained when I hear people saying—after all

3. Word indistinct.

Pondicherry has brought X to this?

Sri Aurodindo: Why can't they say he has acquired a godlike *samata*? Don't you remember the *sloka*—A Brahmin, a cow, an elephant, a dog and an outcaste are all the same to the sage? So X can embrace even actors—hope, he will stop short of the actresses, though.

Myself: Really, Sir, you have caught a magnificent fellow for supramentalisation, what?

Sri Aurobindo: Well, sir, in the Supramental world all kinds will be needed, I suppose. Then why not a supramental ass?

Myself : (I sent my photograph and asked him) What do you think of this snap,—a Mussolini gone morbid? Anyhow, it looks as if you have at last succeeded in putting some intellect into this rigid brain-box of mine!

Sri Aurobindo: Good heavens, what a gigantic forehead they have given you! The Himalayas and the Atlantic in one brow! also, with the weird supramental light upon it! Well, well, you ought to be able to cross the Ass's Bridge with that. Or do you think the bridge will break down under its weight?

Myself: But really, Sir, I never expected you to take my 'overnight' so literally...you could have allowed for a little exuberance in metaphor, surely?

Sri Aurobindo: Don't understand your deep expressions—you did not mean that it would happen rapidly and suddenly? 'Overnight' in English means that...May I ask, very humbly, what you did mean, if not a sudden and rapid development into a great *sadhak*?

Myself: Tomorrow, by the way, I am going to burst a little. *Attention*!

Sri Aurobindo: Eh, what? Burst? which way? if you explode, fizz only—don't blow up the *Ashram*.

Myself: I can't resist the temptation of disturbing your Sabbath, Sir, here is a poem. The forceps were indispensable, but I hope it will be an 'Angel'!

Sri Aurobindo: It is not bad at all—can be accorded the 'order of merit.' Traces of the forceps are visible. But if you go on, probably the forceps will not be indispensable.

Myself: Two English poems from N enclosed. Your correction and opinion, please.

Sri Aurobindo: All right, I think. Re-reading it, I find it

tres joki. Congratulations to myself and Nishikanta with Nirod Talukdar in the middle.

Myself : By the way, you didn't like my poem or you hesitate to call it mine because of so many corrections by N?

Sri Aurobindo: It was very good! mixed parentage does not matter, so long as the offspring is beautiful.

Myself : What thinkest Thou of this anapaest poem, Sir, Written by my humble self? Pray, does it stir Any soft feelings in Thy deep within Or touch not even Thy supramental skin?

Sri Aurobindo: So soft, so soft, I almost coughed, then went aloft To supramental regions where rainbow-breasted pigeons Coo in their sacred legions—

N.B. This inspired doggerel is perfectly private. It is an effort at abstract or surrealist poetry, but as I had no models to imitate, I may have blundered.

Myself : You referred to "circumstances being exceptional" as regards my early success in English versification. But how are they exceptional?

Let me know
How'tis so,
A dullard like me
Bursting like the sea,
With the heart of the Muse
Makes his rhythm fuse?

Sri Aurobindo:

You are opening, opening, opening
Into a wider, wider scopening
That fills me with a sudden hopening
That I may carry you in spite of gropening
Your soul into the supramental ropening.

I often used to suffer from attacks of cold and boils and appealed to Sri Aurobindo to cure me of these petty nuisances. Once I wrote: My brain is now less hampered by the body's indisposition.

My boil has burst and as you see
From the depression I am free!
Thanks, Guru, thanks to thee!

Sri Aurobindo: Yes, I got irritated last night by your persistent boiling and put a gigantic Force which, I am glad to see burst the little boil.

Thank God for that!
Free from boil,
At poems toil
Laugh and grow fat.

Myself : You actually propose 'Laugh and grow fat' though laughing never makes fat!

Sri Aurobindo: You oppose one of the most ancient traditions of humanity by this severe statement. But your statement is mistaken even according to Science. We are now told that it is the activity of certain glands that makes you thin or fat. If glands, then why not gladness?

Another day: Guru,

My head, my head
And the damned fever—
I am half dead!

Sri Aurobindo: Cheer up! Things might have been so much worse. Just think if you had been a Spaniard in Madrid or a German Communist in a concentration camp! Imagine that and then you will be quite cheerful with only a cold and headache. So,

Throw off the cold,
    Damn the fever,
Be sprightly and bold
    And live for ever.

Myself: Nose boil boiling down; terrible headache, fever too. Feeling fed up, Sir!

Sri Aurobindo: Cellular bolshevism probably.

Myself: What's cellular bolshevism?

Sri Aurobindo: Bolshevism of the cells surging up against the Tsar (yourself). Also the Bolsheviks carry on their propaganda by creating communistic 'cells' everywhere, in the army, industries,

etc. You don't seem to be very up in contemporary history.
Myself: No medical cases today.

Sri Aurobindo: Hello! Golden Age come or what? No—for R's pain is kicking cheerfully again. It is telling her 'your Nirod's potions and things indeed! I just went because I took the fancy. I go when I like, I come when I like. Doctors—pooh!'

Myself: Shall we turn a deaf ear to the patient's complaints?

Sri Aurobindo: What complaints? Micturition and phosphates? Tell him to learn to economise his phosphates instead of squandering them and he will become healthy and strong as a tiger.

Sri Aurobindo: Well, I don't know why, but you had the reputation of being a fierce and firebrand doctor who considers it a sin for patients to have an illness; you may be right, but tradition demands that a doctor should be soft like butter, soothing like treacle, sweet like sugar and jolly like jam.

Myself: Please ask Mother to give some blessings to this hopeless self.

Sri Aurobindo:*R/ Vin Ashriv m VII
Recept. Chlor. gr XXV
Aqua jollity ad. lib
Tinct. Faith m XV
Syr. Opt. z.s.s.
12 doses every hour
(Signature)

Myself: 12 doses—every hour—these tinctures and vinums?

Sri Aurobindo: Twelver doses—every hour (one each hour. Plagiarised from your language, sir).

Myself: And who will pay the cost?

Sri Aurobindo: Gratis—for the poor.

Myself: Arjuna was stupefied, horrified, flabbergasted by seeing the *Vishwarup* of Krishna whom he thought of as friend, guru, play-mate. Could I for a moment play all these pranks on you if I saw your *Vishwarupa*? No, Sir, I am satisfied with you as Sri Aurobindo pure and simple.

Sri Aurobindo: But that was because the *Vishwarup* was enjoying a rather catastrophic dinner, with all the friends and

---

*Vin. Ashirv=vinum Ashirvadam.
Recept. chlor=Chlorate of Receptivity.
Syr. Opt.=Syrup of optimism.

relations of Arjuna stuck between his *danstrani karalani*. My *Vishwarup* has no tusks, Sir, none at all. It is a pacifist *Vishwaurp*.

No objection, I only suggested that . don't know who this Sri Aurobindo pure and simple is. If you do I congratulate you.

Myself: I am obliged to sleep out for a few days because of repairs; the whole building is smelling of lime, lime, lime!

Sri Aurobindo: If you want to be a real yogi go on sniffing and sniffing at the lime till the smell creates an ecstasy in the nose and you realise that all smells and stinks are sweet and beautiful in the sweetness and beauty of the Brahman.

Myself: ...No chance for me! *Kismet,* Sir ! What to do?

Sri Aurobindo: ...Not at all, Sir, Mind, Sir, mind. Madam doubt, Sir, Madam doubt! Miss Material Intellectualism, Sir! Aunt Despondency, Sir! Uncle self-distrust, Sir.? Cousin, self-depreciation, a Sir! The whole confounded family, Sir!

Sri Aurobindo: But why hug despair without a cause—Dilipian or other? Come to your senses and develop a Nirodian jollity instead (not necessarily Mark Taplygan, though that is better than none). Laugh and be fat—then dance to keep the fat down—that is a sounder programme.

Myself: I understand your protesting against 'great' or 'big' *sadhaks*; but why against 'advanced' *sadhaks*? It is a fact that some are more advanced than others.

Sri Aurobindo: Advanced indeed! Pshaw! Because one is 3 inches ahead of another, you must make a class of advanced and non-advanced? Advanced has the same puffing egoistic resonance as 'great' or 'big'. It leads to all sorts of sutpidities, *rajasic* self-appreciating egoism in some, *tamasic* self-depreciating egoism in others, round-eyed wonderings why X an advanced *sadhak*, one 3 inches ahead of Y, should stumble, tumble or fumble while Y, 3 inches behind X, still plods heavily and steadily on, etc., etc. Why, sir, the very idea in X that he is an advanced *sadhak* (like the Pharisee 'I thank thee, O Lord, that I am not as other unadvanced disciples') would be enough to make him fumble stumble and tumble. So one more of that, Sir, no more of that.

Well, I believe I have well-documented my thesis and proved to the last button that Sri Aurobindo was not only an *avatar* of *Life Divine* but an *avatar* of Humour too. And mind you, all these letters were the spontaneous outbursts without a moment's reflection in the midst of his enormous correspondence every night. Those who are interested in more of these delicious feast, can read my *Correspondence Part II* which consists only of humour.

Having enjoyed this treat, I hope people will not swing to the opposite extreme and murmur, "What kind of a yogi is he who indulges in such levity?"

The Literary Criticism of Sri Aurobindo

S. NAGARAJAN

SRI Aurobindo is known all over the world as a philosopher and yogi, and many, whose literary judgement I respect, consider him a great poet also. But Aurobindo's literary criticism does not seem to be equally well-known, at least in departments of English Studies in our universities, if my own experience is any guide. I had occasion recently to supervise, in the course of my official duties at my university, a doctoral dissertation on the problems of the Indian writer in English, and it was planned that one of the chapters of the dissertation should deal with modern Indian literary criticism concerning English Literature. When I began the formal and systematic reading on the subject required for the role of a conscientious supervisor of doctoral dissertations, I became more clearly aware of the uneasy feeling that I had before of the paucity of original and significant literary criticism in our country concerning English literature. I felt depressed naturally, and I began to wonder why our long study of English literature had not produced any Indian school of literary criticism. Was there something wrong with our aims and motives of study, or with our methods of teaching? Was it because in spite of our proud familiarity with English, we did not really develop any inwardness, as Dr. F.R. Leavis would demand, to the English language, so essential to the making of a critical judgement? Was it because we had somehow—it is not necessary to go into the history now, Sri Aurobindo has himself done so in his *The Renaissance in India*—lost our sense of values, and were therefore merely puzzled and bewildered by the new literary experience that confronted us in English, and we never quite, in our depths as it were, got over its alien culture? There may be something in these several reasons for the absence of an Indian school of literary criticism, but there had been (and still is) an Indian response, a critical response, to English literature. It had not taken the form of an Indian school of literary criticism, but it had resulted in a great flowering of the literatures in the regional languages of the country. Anyone who looks into the dreary eassays of Elizabethan Literary Criticism—the only exceptions that I can make are those of Sidney and Ben Jonson—for evidence of the critical reception of the Renaissance in England would come away sadly disappointed wondering whether there had been any Renaissance at all. For the Renaissance, you must go especially to the English dramatic literature of the age.

But, it may be asked, is not this desire to have an Indian school of criticism, a form of provinciality which surely it is time those who have pretensions to any sort of intellectual awareness, got away from? Matthew Arnold, you will recall, was distressed when they began to talk of an American literature. All literature, at least all literature written in English, is one, he said, whether it is trans-atlantic or Cis-atlantic in origin. Is there any justification except in one's enslavement to the idea of nation or to one's moment in history, for an Indian school of literary criticism? Such a school, if it ever comes into existence, must eventually seek and obtain its sanction not from the Indian nationality of its members or its publishers, but in the uniqueness of its achievement, of its contribution to the world's vision of English literature and the values of English literature. Otherwise, it had better not be another chorus of confusion at the Tower of Babel.

It was with thoughts and feelings of this sort that I came to read the literary criticism of Sri Aurobindo. That criticism is to be found for the most part in *The Future Poetry*, (published originally as a series of articles in the *Arya*, 1917 to 1920; in book form in Pondicherry in 1953)' and in the third series of his *Letters* (Bombay 1949). Sri Aurobindo, as I acknowledged at the outset, is pre-eminently a philosopher and yogi, and his views not only on poetry, but on other subjects as well, cannot be properly understood except in the larger context of the general philosophical system that he has expounded, most notably in *The Life Divine*. Since he has written a considerable amount of verse and drama, including a vast epic, his literary views need to be related to his literary practice also. Obviously in a brief exploratory paper such as this, all these requirements cannot be fulfilled, and I must content myself with merely indicating the nature of the importance of Sri Aurobindo's work as a literary critic and with outlining the need for a detailed study.

Perhaps the best way of indicating this importance would be to look at some of his particular judgements. One could take one's examples either from *The Future Poetry* or from the *Letters*. Since the essays in the former were ally finished in 1920, it is in the *Letters*, written some ten or fifteen years later, that one comes across Aurobindo's judgements on post-Victorian authors such as Lawrence, Shaw, Wells, Chesterton and Galsworthy. There are several letters which touch on Lawrence briefly. They all seem to have been written between 1933 and 1937, for the dates are not always clearly mentioned, but one has the impression that Huxley's collection of the Lawrence letters had not been out long. Sri Aurobindo confesses that he has not read much of Lawrence, and for criticism that deserves public notice, something more ample and considered would be necessary. In spite of these hesitations, he feels that Lawrence's poetry has too much importance and significance to be a passed over lightly.[1] During those early years, the appreciation of Lawrence, you will recall, was by no means so general as it became later. Sri Aurobindo, for all his slight acquaintance with Lawrence, shows a very acute understanding of what Lawrence was trying to do in his poetry. Let me quote:

> "Lawrence had the psychic push inside towards the Unknown and Beyond at the same time as a push towards the vital life which came in its way. He was trying to find his way between the two and mixed them up together till at the end he got his mental liberation from the tangle though not yet clear knowledge of the way—for that I suppose he will have to be born nearer the East or in any case in surroundings which will enable him to get at the Light."[2]

---

1. *Letters*, Series, III, p. 320.
2. *Ibid.*, p. 314.

The phrase "vital life" which occurs in this quotation needs a word of explanation. Sri Aurobindo holds that Reality is omnipresent *Sat-Chit-ananda* (Existence-Consciousness-Bliss). Inherent in this Reality is a force, a universal energy which we can see all round us in the world. This force or energy is a conscious energy. The *Sat-Chit-ananda* is responsible for the creation of the phenomenal world. Creation takes place with the aid of this energy, according to a definite plan or law.

> "The world is therefore not a figment or conception in the universal mind, but a conscious birth of that which is beyond mind into forms of itself. A truth of conscious being supports these forms and expresses itself in them, and the knowledge corresponding to the truth thus expressed reigns as a supramental truth-consciousness (*rtachit*). To this supreme truth-consciousness, Sri Aurobindo has given the name Supermind..."

> "It (the Supermind) is the link between *Sachchidananda* and the finite world...The Supermind as an infinite principle of creative will and knowledge, organizing real ideas into a perfect harmony before they are cast into the mental-vital-material mould, is the creater of the worlds."[3]

The vital life is a stage in evolution whose ultimate goal is the realization of the Supermind. To seek to realize the perfection of life is to seek it on the wrong, because penultimate and temporary, level. Sri Aurobindo points out in another letter that ego-centricity is the very nature of our present life, and there is only one way in which one can escape from it:

> "It is only by finding something deep within or above ourselves and making *Laya* (dissolution) of the ego in that, that it is possible. It is what Lawrence saw, and it was his effort to do it that made him 'other' than those who associated with him—but he could not find out the way. It was a strange mistake to seek it in sexuality; it was also a great mistake to seek it in the wrong end of the nature."[4]

3. H. Chaudhury and F. Spiegelberg (ed.), *The Integral Philosophy of Sri Aurobindo*, London, 1960, pp. 40-41.
4. *Letters*, Series III, p. 322.

The same acuteness of perception and the same firmness of evaluation are seen in Aurobindo's remarks on Lawrence's poetry: Sri Aurobindo had not read a great deal of it—he had his yoga, after all, to occupy his time with, but he perceives clearly enough what Lawrence was about. Lawrence, he writes,

> "wanted to get rid of the outward forms that for him hide the Invisible and arrive at something that would express with bare simplicity and directness some reality within...The idea is to get rid of all over-expression, of language for the sake of language, or form for the sake of form, even of indulgence of poetic emotion for the sake of the emotion, because all that veils the thing in itself, dresses it up, prevents it from coming out in the seizing nudity of its truth, the power of its intrinsic appeal. There is a sort of mysticism here that wants to express the inexpressible, the concealed, the invisible...The idea of Lawrence is akin: let us get rid of rhyme, artifices which please us for their own sake and draw us away from the thing in itself, the real behind the form. So suppressing these things let us have something bare, rocky, primarily expressive."[5]

For someone who had confessedly not read much of Lawrence or given the matter deliberate thought, these remarks are astonishingly perceptive. Sri Aurobindo goes on to cite an example from a Lawrence poem and concludes that Lawrence did not succeed. Perhaps it would have been truer to say that Lawrence did not *always* succeed, and perhaps Sri Aurobindo would have made the necessary discriminations if he had read more of Lawrence and had been writing of him for a public audience. (His remarks in *The Future Poetry* seem based firmly on wide reading in the particular author who is being discussed at the moment). Sri Aurobindo seems to attribute Lawrence's failure to Lawrence's giving up all form, as "form" is generally understood. Those who take a more favourable view of Lawrence's poetry[6] have argued that Lawrence's successes and failures both arise from the same source: his poetic theory, "the faith that if a thing is

---

5. *Ibid.*, pp. 317-318.
6. Gamini Salgado, *The Collected Poems of Lawrence*, The Criterion Quarterly, VII, p. 391.

only intensely enough felt, its mere expression in words will give it satisfactory form." The theory of course is not novel; it has affinities with Wordsworth's experiments in the *Lyrical Ballads,* with Hazlitt's theory of "gusto" and Hopkins's theory of "inscape." Sri Aurobindo's view seems to be that Lawrence's vision could have been more powerfully expressed in a closer-knit language and metre. Sri Aurobindo was not against new and free forms nor did he doubt that they could succeed. But he held that the new vision, the aim of expressing reality without the intervention of any distorting medium could be realized better, not by discarding entirely the old forms of expression but by striving for an ever closer integration of poetic form and poetic vision. To put the matter in the terms of the controversy between Wordsworth and Coleridge, metre is not, need not, and ought not to be, a superaddition to a poem. The art of poetry has been in existence for a long time—long enough to have built up some resources whose flexibility and range it is at least worthwhile trying out before discarding them. What these resources can achieve when they are well employed is the minimization of whatever it is that interfers with the reception of experience in its pristine purity. A total elimination of these interferences is not possible; for a permanent total elimination one must go to yoga; for a temporary one, mescalin will do; so we are told. In this limitation, poetry is rather like the wireless set. Even the radio advertised widely in India as the set for a connoisseur cannot totally eliminate all disturbance. The medium of expression for pure experience is silence, not language, not even that of poetry. Experience cannot be transmitted; it can only be experienced; in language, however, transparent we may make it, there is always some climbing down. We may make it as small as we can, but it remains, a stubborn fact. The poetry of love, it is obvious, is not love; it is love talked about, love hinted at. Every honest poet tries to reduce the distortion of experience to the minimum. Certainly one must polish the crystal as much as one can, but the white of the white crystal is also a colour. Of course in speaking thus solely of the distortions of experience caused by language, we assume that the experience is itself not distorted at the very source—the perceiving mind. Sri Aurobindo would demur that it is a large and unwarranted assumption; we assume that the perceiving agent is free from the limitations of egoism. The poet lives still on the evolutionary stage of the mind, and is not yet a spiritual seer:

> "But he represents to the human intellect the highest point of mental seership where the imagination tries to figure forth and embody in words its intuition of things, though that stands far below the vision of things that can be grasped only by spiritual experience.... Yet the Rishi or Yogi can drink deeper of Beauty and Delight than the imagination of the poet at its highest can conceive. The Divine is Delight and it is not only the unseen Beauty that he can see, but the visible and the tangible also has for him a face of the All-beautiful which the mind cannot discover."[7]

The highest poetry is the poetry in which one can experience the vision of the *rishi*. Sri Aurobindo argues that such poetry is the speech of what he calls the Overmind. The Overmind is different from the Supermind, and Sri Aurobindo himself explains the difference thus in one of his letters:

> "By the Supermind is meant the full Truth-Consciousness of the Divine Nature in which there can be no place for the principle of division and ignorance, it is always a full light and knowledge superior to all mental substance or mental movement. Between the Supermind and the human mind are a number of ranges, planes or layers of consciousness—one can regard it in various ways— in which the element or substance of mind and consequently its movements also become more and more illumined and powerful and wide. The Overmind is the highest of these ranges; it is full of lights and powers; but from the point of view of what is above it, it is the line of the soul's turning away from the complete and indivisible knowledge and its descent towards Ignorance....In the Supermind, mental divisions and oppositions cease, the problems created by our dividing and fragmenting mind disappear and Truth is seen as a luminous whole. In the Overmind there is not yet the actual fall into Ignorance, but the first step is taken which will make the fall inevitable."[8]

7. *Letters*, Series III, p. 300.
8. *Ibid.*, Series I, p. 116.

When it is said that the poetry of the Overmind is the highest poetry, *mantra,* it does not necessarily mean that the poetry which emanates from other levels of consciousness, other stages of evolution, is poetically inferior.

> "The poetic value, the perfection of a line, does not depend on the plane from which it comes but on the purity and authenticity and power with which it transcribes an intense vision and inspiration..."[9]

The characteristics of the speech of the Overmind are a language that says infinitely more than the mere sense of the words seems to indicate, a rhythm that means even more than the language and is born of the infinite and the power to convey not merely some mental, vital or physical contents or indications or values of the things it speaks of, but its value and figure in some fundamental and original consciousness which is behind them all.[10] There are further elaborations of what he means by Overmind poetry in other letters also.

> "The Overmind is essentially a spiritual Power. It embraces beauty and sublimates it, it has an essential aesthesis which is not limited by rules and canons, it seems an universal and eternal beauty while it takes up and transforms all that is limited and particular. It is, besides, concerned with things other than beauty or aesthetics. It is concerned especially with truth and knowledge, or rather with a wisdom that exceeds what we call knowledge; or its turth goes beyond truth of fact and truth of thought, even the higher thought which is the first spiritual range of the thinker. It has the truth of spiritual thought, spiritual feeling, spiritual sense and at its highest the truth that comes by the most intimate spiritual touch or by identity. Overmind in all its dealings puts truth first....a limited, aesthetical, artistic aim is not its purpose."[11]

To distinguish this note of the Overmind, Sri Aurobindo confesses, is not easy, no rules can be given for it. The business

9. *Letters*, Series III, p. 95.
10. *Ibid.*, p. 97.
11. *Ibid.*, pp. 99-100.

of the critical intellect, no doubt, is to appreciate and judge, but it can do so rightly only if it learns to see and sense inwardly and interpret. The mere critical intellect not touched by a rarer sight can do little here.[12] A rule of thumb, such as that the Overmind poetry takes a transcendent view of things, is worse than useless; it encourages bad, self-deceived poetry. Sri Aurobindo does give many examples of what he considers Overmind poetry ("In the dark backward and abysm of time;" "Those thoughts that wander through eternity," and perhaps, "The winds come to me from the fields of sleep") but at the end of a lengthy analysis and description, he admits that to detect the Overmind touch in poetry, we must ourselves have had some experience, however fleeting, of that level of consciousness. Further, it is easy to mistake the merely grand and noble for the poetry of the Overmind. For instance, we may think that Milton often achieves the Overmind note but "though Milton's architecture of thought and verse," says Sri Aurobindo, "is high and massive, there are usually no subtle echoes there, no deep chambers, the occult things in man's being are foreign to his intelligence, for it is in the light of the poetic intelligence that he works. He does not stray into 'the mystic cavern' of the heart."[13] As things are with man's evolution, today Overmind poetry occurs in intermittent flashes in the midst of other poetry, bringing in new tones, new colours, new elements but as yet it does not change radically the stuff of the consciousness with which we labour.[14] Whether it produces great poetry or not depends on the extent to which it manifests its power and overrides rather than serves the mentality which it is helping. At present it does not do that sufficiently to raise the poetry that is being written to full greatness.

After explaining what Overmind poetry consists in, Sri Aurobindo goes on to consider how it works on us, its aesthesis.

> "By aesthesis is meant a reaction of the consciousness, mental and vital and even bodily, which receives a certain element in things; something that can be called their taste, *Rasa,* which passing through the mind or sense or both, awakens a vital

12. *Ibid.,* p. 100.
13. *Ibid.,* pp. 118-19.
14. *Ibid.,* p. 120.

enjoyment of the taste, *Bhoga*, and this can again awaken even the soul in us to something yet deeper and more fundamental than mere pleasure and enjoyment, to some form of the spirit's delight of existence, *Ananda*. It brings a *Rasa* of the word and sound, but also of the idea, and through the idea of the things expressed by the word and sound and thought, a mental or vital or spiritual image of their form, quality, impact upon us, or even, if the poet is strong enough, of their world essence, their cosmic reality, the very soul of them, the spirit that resides in them as it resides in all things. Poetry may do more than this, but this at least it must do to however small an extent or it is not poetry."[15]

Aesthesis is of the very essence of poetry; its parent is universal *Ananda*. Universal *Ananda* (Bliss) is the artist and creator of the universe, witnessing, experiencing, and taking joy in its creation. Its highest manifestation is ecstasy. Ecstasy is the sign of a return toward the original or supreme *Ananda:* that art or poetry is supreme which can bring us something of the supreme tone of ecstasy. Ecstasy is the experience of intense consciousness, intense being, intense delight in existence. As aesthesis enters the overhead planes it becomes pure delight. The duties and conflicts of existence that plague us on the lower planes leave us, and there is a consciousness of universality. It sees that all things have their meaning and significance which the mind does not see, for the mind is only concerned with a surface vision.

Sri Aurobindo is perfectly aware that the real problem for the critic—and the perfect critic is a *Sadhaka*—a spiritual practitioner—is to recognize the aesthesis of the Overmind. The Overmind has after all to use a language made by mind, not by itself. It can only strain and intensify this medium and try to heighten, deepen and enlarge it;[16] of course for one rare line of genuine, authentic Overmind poetry, there will be a hundred surrogates. It is difficult to distinguish the poetry of the Overmind, admits Sri Aurobindo, unless one has lived in the light oneself. If this admission of the rarity of critical genuis is a limitation in Sri

---

15. *Ibid.*, pp. 122-23.
16. *Ibid.*, p. 152.

Aurobindo's aesthetic poetry, he seems willing enough to accept it cheerfully. "Really", he says, "it is only the few that can be trusted to discern the true value of things in poetry and art."[17] Or again: "It is not the opinion of the general mass of men that finally decides; the decision is really imposed by the judgement of a minority and elite which is finally accepted and settles down as the verdict of posterity; in Tagore's phrase, it is the universal man, *vishvamanava,* or we might say the Cosmic Self in the race, that fixes the value of its own works."[18] He hopes for his own part that this verdict will not consign his *Savitri* to the waste-paper basket!

Finally, there is the question: What is the importance of poetry in Life? Poetry is not a major means for the realization of the Divine. To claim that it is, would be, says Sri Aurobindo, a gross exaggeration. He explains his position thus:

> "The word has power—even the ordinary written word has power. If it is an inspired word, it has still more power. What kind of power or power for what depends upon the nature of the inspiration and the theme and the part of the being it touches. If it is the Word itself, as in certain utterances of the great Scriptures, Veda, Upanishad, Gita, it may well have a power to awaken a spiritual and uplifting impulse, even certain kinds of realization. To say that it cannot contradicts spiritual experience."[19]

The illumination gained by means of poetic vision or the experience of such vision differs from the yogic realization in not being permanent. Poetry is a step towards the Real says Sri Aurobindo —an answer which is in harmony as much with Aristotle's most unmystical *Poetics* as with the traditional view of the Indian rhetorician that the experience of poetic *rasa* is akin to the experience of the *Brahman*[20]. When such descriptions of the function of poetry are offered, we must not forget that they apply to the highest poetry. All poetry is *mantra,* but the highest poetry is the *mantra* of the Real, says Sri Aurobindo.

17. *Ibid.*, p. 263.
18. *Ibid.*, p. 273.
19. *Sri Aurobindo on Himself and on the Mother*, p. 293.
20. *The Life Divine*, pp. 136-137.

What I have been trying to do in this rather brief paper is to give you some idea of the particular judgements of Sri Aurobindo and of his general literary theory so that the nature and importance of his work as a literary critic may be appreciated sufficiently to encourage further study. His literary theory, as I said at the beginning, is really part of "the life divine." It was not of course mere theory for him—nor is it for his followers. It is a *sadhana*, spiritual practice pursued unremittingly with dedication, faith and perseverance. To attempt an estimate of this theory of literature without some experience of the *sadhana* is perhaps risky; we would be, of course, well within our rights, as students of literary criticism, in taking the risk. My own study of the theoretical aspects of Sri Aurobindo's metaphysics is, however, far too sketchy at the moment to qualify me for the task of a concluding estimate. I shall instead bring this account to a close with a few tentative observations on the estimate offered by a more competent scholar and student of Sri Aurobindo than I can claim to be. In a very interesting paper on "Western Thought and Indian Aesthetics,"[21] Professor V.K. Gokak has suggested that the impact of Western thought on Indian aesthetics found its fulfilment in Sri Aurobindo. "Coleridge's mantle fell on him", says Professor Gokak. A detailed investigation of this line of thought should prove instructive. Coleridge, it will be recalled, distinguished between the poetry of fancy and the poetry of the imagination. "The Imagination," wrote Coleridge, "is that reconciling and mediatory power which, incorporating the reason in images of the sense and organizing (as it were) the flux of the senses by the permanence and self-circling energies of the reason, gives birth to a system of symbols." The Imagination is not a separate faculty of the mind, but rather a completing power that works through and by means of the entire mind. Coleridge distinguished between understanding and reason. The Understanding was concerned with receiving and organizing sense-experience. But there were also certain forms and laws of nature (Plato regarded these as the only reality) that could be perceived directly by the reason. The Imagination incorporated the direct insights of reason with the images of the understanding, and the product was a symbol. Hence a symbol was a very different

---

21. H. Passin, (ed.), *Cultural Freedom in Asia*, 1956, pp. 96-108.

creation from an allegory. "An allegory is but a translation of abstract notions into a picture-language—which is itself nothing but an abstraction from objects of the senses." Coleridge continues:

> "On the other hand, a symbol is characterised by a translucence of the special in the individual, or of the general in the special, or of the universal in the general; above all, by the translucence of the eternal through and in the temporal. It always partakes of the reality which renders intelligible; and while it enunciates the whole, abides itself as a living part in that unity of which it is the representative."[22]

With this we may compare Sri Aurobindo's explanation of a symbol.

> "There is a considerable difference between symbolism and allegory....Allegory comes in when a quality or other abstract thing is personalized and the allegory proper should be something carefully stylized and deliberately sterilized of the full aspect of embodied life so that the essential meaning or idea may come out with sufficient precision or force of clarity....A symbol expresses on the contrary not the play of abstract things or ideas put into imaged form, but a living truth or inward vision or experience of things, so inward, so subtle, so little belonging to the domain of intellectual abstraction and precision that it cannot be brought out except through symbolic images—the more these images have a living truth of their own which corresponds intimately to the living truth they symbolize, suggests the very vibration of the experience itself, the greater becomes the art of symbolic expression."[23]

There is obviously a correspondence here though I am not sure that Coleridge's thought has been carried further in a sense which would perhaps justify speaking of Coleridge's mantle on Sri Aurobindo's shoulders; there is of course no reason why Sri Aurobindo should wear anybody's mantle except his own ! But equally I think there are differences also which make further

22. Coleridge, *The Statesman's Manual*
23. *Letters*, Series III, p. 85 ff.

investigation necessary. Sri Aurobindo believes that at present Overmind poetry comes to us only in stray flashes of single lines. Coleridge does not seem to think of imaginative poetry (which, incidentally, he looks for in the poem as a whole and not in a series of striking lines) as poetry that we may expect to achieve only in the future when man has evolved to higher stages of consciousness. Secondly, the idea of evolution occupies a key place in Sri Aurobindo's system, and though it is present in Colerdige, how he intended to link it with his poetics, I do not know. Coleridge wrote in *Biographia Literaria*:

> "The highest perfection of natural philosophy would consist in the perfect spiritualization of all laws of nature into laws of intuition and intellect. The phenomena (the material) must wholly disappear, and the laws alone (the formal) must remain. Hence it comes that in nature itself the more the principle of law breaks forth, the more does the husk drop off, the phenomena themselves become more spiritual and at length cease altogether in our consciousness...The theory of natural philosophy would then be completed when all nature was demonstrated to be identical in essence with that which in its highest known power exists in man as intelligence and self-consciousness."[24]

In the third place, Coleridge left his "deduction of the imagination" incomplete, and it is worth investigating how far Sri Aurobindo's poetics harmonizes with and completes Coleridge's pioneer efforts. Such a study, if it is undetaken by a scholar who is well-versed in Western and Indian literature and aesthetics and who is also trained in logic and metaphysics, should help us in making a definitive estimate of Sri Aurobindo's achievement and in assessing the possibility that I touched on at the beginning of this paper, of an Indian school of literary criticism. It should also help us in deciding what we can take from Sri Aurobindo's thoughts that will serve less exalted mortals toiling at more mundane levels. We cannot all be Sri Aurobindos. One can at a pinch get an English governess, or if the creature is extinct,

---

24. Coleridge, *Biographia Literaria*, Everyman's Library, chapter XII, p. 146.

a respectable substitute, to look after one's lisp and toddle. One can get sent to school in England. One can even become a fine classical scholar. One can, and this more easily than the rest I have enumerated, pass independent India's surrogates for the I.C.S. examination and horse riding. One can, finally, get involved in terrorist activities for which independent India, especially Bengal, provides ample independence. But to discover a Pondicherry (now part of India) and sit tight at one's *sadhana* for forty years may be more difficult; certainly it is inconvenient. No, we cannot all be Sri Aurobindos. To hear the Overhead note—to distinguish the genuine from the so-like-the-genuine—in poetry requires (Sri Aurobindo, alas, is quite clear on this point) yogic vision, and confining myself to my own habitat strictly in Poona, University Departments of English suffer from an acute shortage of *yogis*. But perhaps I am being too pessimistic. There may be some foreign aid for this shortage also.

The Yoga and Philosophy of Sri Aurobindo

ARAVINDA BASU

SRI Aurobindo once said that he was first a poet, then a patriot. We can say in a similar vein that he was first a yogi and then a philosopher. Indeed, his world-vision is a statement in rational terms of his own personal yogic experiences. He took to yoga in 1904 and had many experiences which confirmed for him the claims made by yoga. Practice of *Pranayama* made his brain full of light, *prakashamaya,* and also resulted in a greater capacity for writing poetry. Sri Aurobindo himself has said that before he started *Pranayama* he could write only a few lines at a time, but afterwards the flow of poetry increased appreciably. This kind of experience showed him the truth of *Prana,* the vital force, its functions and how it could be increased and utilised to better purpose[1]. In a letter written in Bengali to his wife, Shrimati Mrinalini Devi in 1907, Sri Aurobindo said that a madness had seized him. It was that if God existed, he must have his direct vision, for he believed that if God did exist, there must be a way directly to see Him. He pointed out that the scriptures of Hinduism had shown the path and that he was following it. What convinced him of the truth of these scriptural writings was the fact that definite statements were made about signs and changes in the body and mind that the recommended discipline would bring about. And Sri Aurobindo could see those signs and changes in his own body and mind[2]. He wrote in 1918, "Our idea was the thinking out of a synthetic philosophy which might be a

1. *Sri Aurobindo on Himself and the Mother,* p. 123.
2. *Sri Aurobinder Patra* (in Bengali), p. 7.

contribution to the thought of the new age that is coming upon us." The spiritual experience and the general truths on which such an attempt could be based were already present to us, otherwise we should have had no right to make the endeavour at all."[3]

Sri Aurobindo's first great yogic experience, however, was almost overwhelming. In December 1907 when Sri Aurobindo was in Baroda, Lele, a Maharashtrian yogi, asked him to watch thoughts coming from outside into the mind and to reject them. Only after three days this discipline resulted in the experience of *Nirvana.* The mind felt completely silent without any function whatsoever. There was the indubitable and unquestionable experience of a reality abiding in its own right, in which all phenomenal seemed to exist but which itself was not in anyway related to them. There was no sense of a pure 'I', it was not the experience of the One-Self, the *Atman.* The Reaility could only be referred to as 'That.' "Now to reach *Nirvana*", says Sri Aurobindo, "was the first radical result of my own yoga. It threw me suddenly into a condition above and without thought, unstained by any mental or vital movement; there was no ego, no real world—only when one looked through the immobile senses, something perceived or bore upon its sheer silence the world of empty forms, materialised shadows without any substance. There was no one or many even, only just absolutely That, featureless, relationless, sheer, indescribable, unthinkable, absolute, yet supremely real and solely real. This was no mental realisation, nor something glimpsed somewhere above,—no abstraction,—it was positive, the only positive reality—although not a spatial physical world, pervading, occupying or rather flooding and drowning this semblance of a physical world, leaving no room or space for any reality but itself, allowing nothing else to seem at all actual, positive or substantial."[4] Sri Aurobindo has a poem called *Nirvana* which describes this experience thus:

All is abolished but the mute Alone
The mind from thought released, the heart from grief
Grow inexistent now beyond belief ;

3. *Arya,* July, 1918, pp. 763-764.
4. *On Yoga II, Letters on Yoga* Tome I, 1969, p. 47.

There is no I, no Nature, known-unknown
The city, a shadow picture without tone,
Floats, quivers unreal; forms without relief
Flow, a cinema's vacant shapes; like a reef
Foundering in shoreless gulfs the world is done.

Only the illimitable Permanent
Is here. A peace stupendous, featureless, still,
Replaces all,—what once was I, in It
A silent unnamed emptiness content
Either to fade in the Unknowable
Or thrill with the luminous seas of the Infinite.[5]

Sri Aurobindo has said that the reality can be experienced in various ways. This is because the Reaility itself has many aspects and also because human nature is infinitely varied. Seekers after spiritual truth do not have the same capacity, the make-up of their nature varies, temperaments differ. Besides, the mental consciousness which is the chief instrument of Yoga has many levels and the experiences will be different according to the level on which the soul dwells. It must also necessarily make a choice of approach, because it has not got the power of integral realisation. Indeed one can go farther and say that in the soul itself there may already be the stamp of a spiritual destiny which determines the course of its progress and fulfilment

Though Sri Aurobindo accepts different types of experiences, he says he is not bound to accept also the mental philosophies based on them. Thus even though he himself had the experience of *Nirvana*, the extinction of the ego and, it would appear of the Self too, and the reducing of the world to a mere materialised shadow which is at the base of the philosophy of an ineffable Permanent Reality or that of the static Self and the doctrine that the world is an illusion, Sri Aurobindo refuses entirely to accept Buddhist philosophy or *Mayavada*. We may note in passing that his experience of *Nirvana* did not include that of the Self. In this respect it may be described as more radical than that from which Shankara's philosophy arises. It seems to

5. *Collected Poems and Plays*, Vol. II, 1942, p. 298.

me that it would not be wrong to say that this experience is nearer the Buddhist perception. True, Buddhism speaks in terms of the *shunya*, the Void, and Sri Aurobindo refers to that as the sheer supreme sole reality. But Sri Aurobindo has always held that the Buddha himself and Buddhism, excepting one or two extreme schools, believed in a Permanent as supreme reality. Buddha says in Udana VIII[6] that this world is a flux, things here are constructed mixtures of different elements, nothing is pure, on the other hand there is something which is outside the flux, Permanent, unmixed and unconstructed pure; if, adds Buddha, there were no such reality, it would not be possible to go beyond this world and attain *Nirvana*. Sri Aurobindo has always taken the view that the '*Asat*' of the Buddha is not a nullity, a mere nothing, but a transcendent reality which goes beyond our conception and experience of even the highest, the most abstract Existence. "Buddha, it must be remembered, refused always to discuss what was beyond the world. But from the little he said it would appear that he was aware of a Permanent beyond equivalent to the Vedantic *Para-Brahman*, but which he was quite unwilling to describe." And again, "Actually when we examine closely the Nihil of certain philosophies, we begin to perceive that it is a zero which is All or an indefinable infinite which appears to the mind a blank, because mind grasps only finite constructions but is in fact the only true Existence."[7]

Non-being is the Reality's affirmation of its freedom from its aspect of the free base of universal existence which is the same as *Sat* and *Atman*, Existence and Self. When the Taittiriya Upanishad says that *Sat* was born out of *Asat*, Sri Aurobindo understands it to mean what we have just said above. He is not unaware that Chhandogya Upanishad rejects the idea of the birth of Being out of Non-Being. But he says that if Non-Being is understood as he interprets it, then there is no difficulty.[8] In spite of the fact that Buddhism speaks in terms of Non-Being or *shunya* and Shankara's acosmic *Adwaita Vedanta* in those of Being and Atman: Sri Aurobindo identifies the two in certain respects. For example, the Absolute in neither of the two schools

6. *On Yoga, Letters on Yoga*, Tome I, p. 59.
7. *The Life Divine*, New York, 1949, p. 29.
8. *Op. cit.* pp. 28-29.

individualises itself, and therefore individuality is an obstacle to *Nirvana* or *Mukti* and has to be shed."[9]

We have said above that according to Sri Aurobindo there are different levels of the mind, of which the higher ones can be described as spiritualised when they shed all their own activities and receive knowledge, peace, power, delight, etc. from the Spirit. Though the medium still remains mind, it is not mind as we know it. When the spiritualised mind is the medium of the perception of the One Self, it reduces all multiplicity to a mere appearance and loses itself in that One; then we have the *Vedantic* experience. But such spiritualised mind may seek to go farther ahead and reduce the self to Non-Being. "For behind the *sad-atman* is the silence of the *asat* which the Buddhist Nihilist realised as the *shunyam*..."[10] Sri Aurobindo himself comments on this passage thus: "The passage in *The Yoga and Its Objects* is written from the point of view of the spiritualised mind approaching the supreme Truth directly, without passing through the supermind or disappearing into it. The mind spiritualises itself by shedding all its activities and formations and reducing everything to a pure Existence, *sad-atman,* from which all things and activities proceed and which supports everything. When it wants to go still beyond, it negates yet further and arrives at conceivable to mind, speech or defining experience. It is the silent Unknowable, the *Turiya* or featureless and relationless Absolute of the monistic *Vedantists*, the *shunyam* of the nihilistic Buddhists, the *Tao* or omnipresent and transcendent Nihil of the Chinese, the indefinable and ineffable Permanent of the *Mahayana*".[11]

Sri Aurobindo's great experience of *Nirvana* was in a real sense the true beginning of his Yoga. He not only did not stop with this experience, but without losing it, he had on the basis of it and in it a series of most powerful experiences which led to an entirely new *weltunschuung*. As he himself says, "I lived in that *Nirvana* day and night before it began to admit other

9. *On Yoga II*, 1, p. 64: "According to both Buddha and Shankara liberation means *laya* of the individual in some transcendent Permanent that is not individualised—so logically a belief in the individual soul must prevent liberation while the sense of misery in world leads to the attempt to escape."

10. *Op. cit*., p. 61.

11. *Ibid.*

things into itself or modify itself at all and the inner heart of experience, a constant memory of it and its power to return remained until in the end it began to disappear into a greater Super-consciousness from above. But meanwhile realisation added itself to realisation and fused itself with this original experience."[12] As an illustration we can quote from a poem, entitled *Liberation,* of Sri Aurobindo in which he speaks of the One Being and also of its Bliss. We may note in passing that in the letter quoted above on *Nirvana*? Sri Aurobindo adds: 'I, cannot say there was anything exhilarating or rapturous in the experience, as it then came to me,—but what it brought was an inexpressible Peace, as stupendous silence and infinity of release and freedom," Now here is the poem:

I have thrown from me the whirling dance of mind
And stand now in the spirit's silence free;
Timeless and deathless beyond creature-kind,
The centre of my own eternity

I have escaped and the small self is dead;
I am immortal, alone, ineffable;
I have gone out from the universe I made
And have grown nameless and immeasurable.

My mind is hushed in a wide and endless light,
My heart a solitude of delight and peace,
My sense unsnared by touch and a sound and sight,
My body a point in white infinities.

I am the one Being's sole immobile Bliss;
No one I am, I who am all that is.[13]

The next landmark in Sri Aurobindo's yogic life was his experience of the omnipresent Divine, of Vasudeva, while he was in jail. Whatever he saw, whatever he touched, all that he tasted was Sri Krishna. To quote from his own description:

"....He (God) made me realise the central truth of the Hindu religion. He turned the hearts of my jailors to me and they

12. *op. cit.* p. 47.
13. *Last Poems*, 1952, p. 6.

spoke to the Englishman in charge of the jail, 'He is suffering in his confinement, let him at least walk outside his cell for half an hour in the morning and in the evening.' So it was arranged, and it was while I was walking that his strength again entered into me. I looked at the jail that secluded me from men and it was no longer by its high walls that I was imprisoned; no, it was Vasudeva. It was Narayana who was guarding and standing sentry over me. Or I lay on the coarse blankets that were given me for a couch and felt the arms of Sri Krishna around me, the arms of my friend and lover. This was the first use of the deeper vision He gave me. I looked at the prisoners at the jail, the thieves, the murderers, the swindlers, and as I looked at them I saw Vasudeva, it was Narayana whom I found in these darkened souls and misused bodies."[14]

Naturally, his world-view changed radically. It was no longer possible to see the world as a materialised shadow, a mere false appearance which nevertheless persists in falsely appearing forever. "At an early stage," Sri Aurobindo continues to say in his description of the experience of *Nirvana*, "the aspect of an illusionary world gave place to one in which illusion[15] is only a small surface phenomenon with an immense Divine Reality behind it and a supreme Divine Reality above it and an intense Divine Reality in the heart of everything that seemed at first a cinematic shape or shadow. And this was no re-imprisonment in the senses, no diminution or fall from supreme experience, it came rather as a constant heightening and widening of the Truth; it was the spirit that saw objects, not the senses and the Peace, the Silence, the Freedom in Infinity remained always, with the world or all worlds only as a continuous incident in the timeless eternity of the Divine."[16] And again, "Now, that is the whole trouble in my approach to *Mayavada*, *Nirvana* in my liberated consciousness turned out to be the beginning of

---

14. *Uttarpara Speech*, 7th edition, 1968, pp. 7-8.
15. Sri Aurobindo adds here in a footnote: "In fact it is not an illusion in the sense of an imposition of something baseless and unreal on the consciousness, but a misinterpretation by the conscious mind and sense and a falsifying misuse of manifested existence."
16. *On Yoga*, pp. 47-48.

my realisation, a first step towards the complete thing, not the sole true attainment possible or even a culminating finale. It came unasked, unsought for, though quite welcome.

I had not the least idea about it before, no aspiration towards it, in fact my aspiration was towards just the opposite, spiritual power to help the world and to do my work in it, yet it came—without even a 'May I come in' or a 'By your leave'. It just happened and settled in as if for all eternity or as if it had been really there always. And then it slowly grew into something not less but greater than its first self. How then could I accept Mayavada or persuade myself to pit against the Truth imposed on me from above the logic of Shankara?"[17]

We have already observed that though Sri Aurobindo does not accept the whole philosophy of either Buddhism or the Vedanta as interpreted by Shankara, he nevertheless acknowledges the experiences behind them and the great practical contributions they make to spiritual life. Indeed, he says that the real gist of the Buddha's teaching is not the petty idea of escape from the ego and the suffering of the world "but an impersonality and a void calm within, outwardly doing the works of Love, Truth and Righteousness."[18] And about the Buddha himself he says, "The Non-Being permits the Being, even as the Silence permits Activity. By this simultaneous negation and affirmation, not mutually destructive but complementary to each other like all contraries, the simultaneous awareness of conscious Self-being as a reality and the Unknowable beyond as the same Reality becomes realisable to the awakened human soul. Thus was it possible for the Buddha to attain the state of *Nirvana* and yet act puissantly in the world, impersonal in his inner consciousness, in his action the most powerful personality that we know of as having lived and produced results upon earth."[19]

And though Sri Aurobindo's own path is not that of the ascetic, he pays high tribute both to it and the experience supporting it. "For an age out of sympathy with the ascetic

---

17. *Op. cit.*, p. 48.
18. *The Life Divine*, p. 30.
19. *Op. cit.*, pp. 29-30.

spirit—and throughout all the rest of the world the hour of the Anchorite may seem to have passed or to be passing—it is easy to attribute this great trend (asceticism) to the failing of vital energy in an ancient race tired out by its burden, its once vast share in the common advance, exhausted by its many-sided contribution to the sum of human effort and human knowledge. But we have seen that it corresponds to a truth of existence, a state of conscious realisation which stands at the very summit of our possibility. In practice also the ascetic spirit is an indispensable element in human perfection and even its separate affirmation cannot be avoided so long as the race has not at the other end liberated its intellect and its vital habits from subjection to an always insistent animalism."[20]

However, Sri Aurobindo's own vision of things is more realistic and comprehensive. He calls his system a realistic *Adwaita* as distinguished from the traditional *Adwaita Vedanta* which, he says, bisects existence into Self and not-Self. After paying tribute to the ascetic outlook in philosophy and the ascetic spirit in life, Sri Aurobindo states his own position. "We seek indeed," says he, "a larger and completer affirmation. We perceive that in the Indian ascetic ideal the great *Vedantic* formula, 'One without a second', has not been read sufficiently in the light of that other formula equally imperative, 'All this is the Brahman'. The passionate aspiration of man upwards to the Divine has not been sufficiently related to the descending movement of the Divine leaning downwarrd to embrace eternally Its manifestation. Its meaning in Matter has not been so well understood as Its truth in the Spirit. The reality which the *Sannyasin* seeks has been grasped in its full height but not, as by the ancient *Vedantins* in its full extent and comprehensiveness."[21]

The utter silence of the mind which Sri Aurobindo achieved in the incredibly short period of three days only was never again broken. It remained always at the background of his consciousness which acted out of the silence. The mind as such never functioned again. His intellectual genius was used as

20. *Op. cit.*, p. 24.
21. *Sri Aurobindo on Himself and The Mother*, 1953, pp. 135-136.

an instrument for the communication of truths beyond the mind to people who still have to approach philosophical and spiritual truths through the mental consciousness. And all that he wrote—and it is more than a lifetime's work for an expert scholar to read all of it—came, as he himself once said, 'directly from above to the tip of the pen'. When Sri Aurobindo says that 'Silence permits the Activity,' that Being by its inherent Force supports the Becoming, it must be out of this experience of his own. In a letter to the present writer Sri Aurobindo said "Realisation of the silent inactive *Brahman* is no bar to the dynamic side of the yoga, often it is the first step. One must not associate it with attachment to inertia. The silent *Brahman* is attached to nothing...I had the realisation of sublime *Nirvana* first. There was complete *cittavrtti nirodha,* entire silence. Then came the experience of action not my own, but from above. One has to grow into it unless it comes easily."[22] So all his activity was a result of a descent of Will from above. One is reminded of the *Gita's* descrption of a yogi "*sarvarambhaparityagi,* one who has given up all initiative and yet is engaged in doing good to all creatures, *sarvabhutahite ratah.*" Now here we have a basis of Sri Aurobindo's doctrine that *Sat,* existence, which is Consciousness, is also *Shakti*, Consciousness-Force. It is by virtue of this Consciousness-Force inherent in the Reality that *Tat*, 'That', is also *Sat,* He and Deva, the supreme Deity. In Sri Aurobindo's view *Brahman* is not only the base, source and material of the universal existence but also a giver of the sanction for universal activity and at the same time the Lord and Master of that activity. *Brahman* is *Atman*, Self who supports the world-becoming by its mere presence and as its foundation; it is the Soul, *Purusha* who sanctions the work of *Prakriti* without himself being active in it, it is also *Ishwara* which is the active Lord and Master of creation, but who is yet free from his own activity and freely witnesses and sanctions the same cosmic expansion of his own inherent Force. which he controls and deploys.[23]

These are the three basic aspects of *Brahman* in relation to the world. The fundamental idea that there are different aspects

22. *Ibid.* pp. 24-25.
23. The reader is referred to the Chapter 'Brahman, Purusha, Ishwara' *The Life Divine.*

of the supreme Reality is found in many classical works of spiritual philosophy in India. The *Isha Upanishad,* for example, describes the Self as 'That which is bright, bodiless, without scar of imperfection, without sinews, pure, unpierced by evil.' The Upanishad also speaks of the same Reality as, 'It is He who has gone abroad.'[24] In the *Gita,* according to Sri Aurobindo's interpretation, the supreme Divine has three aspects, the *Kshara Purusha,* the *Akshara Purusha* and the *Purushottama.* The first is the Reality in the flux of the world and all creatures, the second is immutable and aloof from all movements of *Prakriti,* the third reconciles in his being the mutable and the immutable *Purushas,* their apparent contradiction is resolved in this supreme-aspect of the super-personal Person who is both unmoving and moving and yet transcends these two formulations of his self-existence.[25] To take another example, the *Bhagavata Purana,* states that the knowers of Reality say that it is non-dual consciousness, *jnanam advayam,* which is termed *Brahman, Parmatma* and *Bhagavana.*[26] The *Bhagavata* clearly asserts that this non-dual Consciousness is both static and dynamic. The book is full of terms like *Chit-,Shakti, Yoga-Maya, Atma-Maya,* etc. And the distinction between the three aspects of Reality is determind by whether or not the consciousness-force is manifest and if it is, whether it is partially or fully so. Thus the reconciliation of the inactive Self with the Self that moves is not an innovation of Sri Aurobindo. The School of Bengal *Vaishnavism* has raised a great system of philosophy on the basis of this assertion of the celebrated *Purana. Brahman* is, according to *Mahaprabhu* Chaitanya and his followers, that aspect of the Reality in which Conscious-Force is not in the least manifest, it represents mere existence, *sat. Paramatma,* the Great Self, has a lower aspect of the Conscious-Force manifest in him, which he utilises in creating the world. It is a lower aspect of Conscious-Force because it is Maya, the power of Ignorance, in which the element of consciousness is not manifest. *Bhagavan* is the highest aspect of the Reality in which *Svarupa-*

---

24. Verse 8, Sri Aurobindo's translation, *Isha Upanishad,* 3rd edition, p. 5.
25. See *Essays on the Gita,* Chapters, 'The Three *Purushas*', 'The Supreme Divine' 'The Two Natures.'
26. I. 2. 11.

sakti, own-force, inherent in the supreme Lord, is completely and perfectly manifest. This is not the power that creates the world but *Bhagavan*'s Energy for loving and enjoying love. Love splits itself into the Lover and the Beloved, Krishna and Radha which are not two separate realities, *dvaita,* but *yugala,* biume, one-in-two, two-in-one. Sri Aurobindo, I think, would agree with the basic idea of this classification, though his arrangement of the categories would be different. We find in the *Tantric* systems also the clear acceptance of both the static and the dynamic aspects of reality. In the Trika Philosophy, for example, *Shiva* and *Shakti,* are the same reality, considered respectively as *Prakasa,* illumination or consciousness and *vimarsa,* the power of integral self-knowledge of *Shiva* as the all-inclusive One, identical with everything. The universe is a becoming of *Shakti* and its basis is *Shiva.* Here again we may observe that Sri Aurobindo would agree with the fundamental stand-point of monistic *Tantric* philosophy though he would not accept the arrangement of categories in them.

Apart from the idea of Reality being static and dynamic, there is another angle from which different aspects of *Brahman* can be delineated. Sri Aurobindo speaks of the transcendent, the universal and the individual aspects of the Divine. In its original and native status *Brahman* is beyond the Universe and cannot be spoken of as the Self, which is the base and source and material of creation. But since in Sri Aurobindo's experience the Reality becomes everything, he accepts the idea of *Brahman* as the Self of the Universe, which manifests itself as a plurality of the individual self. These individual selves are centres of the Self's self-knowledge, self-action and self-enjoyment. The individual is nothing but the Absolute in essence, it is not a separate reality, and on the highest level of consciousness it knows itself as the universal Self and transcendent *Brahman* and at the same time a focal point of these two, deliberately brought about for the purpose of universal manifestation. The *Gita,* describes the *jiva* as an eternal portion of *Purushottama.* It also says that *Para-Prakriti* has become the *jiva.* And *Para-Prakriti,* according to Sri Aurobindo's interpretation, is the dynamic aspect of consciousness and force of *Purushottama.* The word portion is an image and in spiritual and philosophical thought represents individuality assumed by the Absolute.

Sri Aurobindo certainly believes in a diverse pattern of relationships between the individual and the Absolute. "The Divine is always 'One' that is 'Many'. The individual spirit is part of the 'Many' side of the One, and the psychic being is what it puts forth to evolve here in the earth-nature. In liberation the individual self realises itself as the One (that is yet Many). It may plunge into the One and merge or hide itself in its bosom that is the *laya* of the *Adwaita*; it may feel its oneness and yet as part of the Many that is One enjoy the Divine, that is the *Dwaitadwaita* liberation; it may lay stress on its Many aspect and be possessed by the Divine, the *Visishtadwaita* or go on playing with Krishna in the eternal Vrindavan, the *Dwaita* liberation. Or it may, even being liberated, remain in the *Lila* or manifestation or descend into it as often as it likes. The Divine is not bound by human philosophies—it is free in its play and free in its essence."[27]

"Yoga means union with the Divine—a union either transcendental (above the universe) or cosmic (universal) or individual, or, as in our Yoga, all three together. Or it means getting into a consciousness in which one is no longer limited by the small ego, personal mind, personal vital and body but is in union with the supreme Self or with the universal (cosmic) consciousness or with some deeper consciousness within which one is aware of one's own inner being and of the real truth of existence."[28]

We see from the above quotations that Sri Aurobindo accepts the possibility of the merging of the individual soul in such a way that it loses itself in the Self or the Absolute. But it is equally possible to unite the soul with the active Self so completely that it can feel an active identity with everything in the universe. "I see perhaps or feel in myself or as myself first the eternal Presence and afterwards only can extend the vision and sense of this greater self of mine to all creatures. Then I see the world in me or as one with me. I perceive the universe as a scene in my being; the play of its processes as a movement of forms and souls and forces in my cosmic spirit; I meet myself and none else everywhere".[29] One is reminded of the pratyabhijna philosophy

27. *Lights on Yoga*, 1948, pp. 30-31.
28. *op. cit.* p. 16.
29. *The Synthesis of Yoga*, 1951, p. 131.

according to which the ultimate destiny of the individual soul is to recognise itself as the Absolute and through that recognition realise its identity with everything. *'Mamedam Vibhavam Sarvam'* 'all this is my glory' '*ahameva sarvam,* I am indeed all. While *Shiva,* which is the name of the Absolute in the Pratyabhijna philosophy is pure illumination, *prakasa,* it is also at the same time a power of integral self-reflection as universal 'I', one with everything. *Shiva* and *Shakti* are the two sides of the same identical reality. While *Shiva* is transcendent, it is also as *Sakti* immanent in the universe in which it assumes several forms and also is hidden as individual soul which by progressive spiritual knowledge recognises itself as the Absolute, *Shiva,* which is known as *Paramashiva,* the perfect harmony of *Shiva* and *Shakti.* Though Sri Aurobindo was not familiar with this philosophy, something of this experience is expressed in the following poem called "The Indwelling Universal:"

"I contain the whole world in my soul's embrace:
  In me Arcturus and Belphegor burn
To whatsoever living form I turn
  I see my own body with another face.

All eyes that look on me are my sole eyes;
  The one heart that beats within all breasts is mine,
The world's happiness flows through me like wine,
  Its million sorrows dreamy agonies.

Yet all its acts are only waves that pass
  Upon my serve: only for ever still,
Unborn I sit, timeless, intangible;
  All things are shadows in my tranquil glass.

My vast transcendence holds the cosmic whirl;
  I am hid in it as in the sea a pearl.[30]

We shall see later that this tripartite distinction of the transcendent, universal and individual divine is central to Sri Aurobindo's philosophy and yoga. Without anticipating much now we may briefly point out that Sri Aurobindo envisages the emergence of the divine man on this earth as the goal of creation. The Knowledge and Will, the evolution of which is essential for this

30. *Last Poems,* 1952, p. 2.

emergence, is inherent in the transcendent, manifest in the universal and will evolve in the individual. Thus for the understanding of Sri Aurobindo's philosophy the nature of the individual has to be firmly grasped.

The Self-manifestation of *Brahman* as the universe presupposes a self-veiling on the part of the spiritual reality. If the Absolute does not in some way give up its absoluteness, the world of relations cannot come into being. It is true that the Reality is One without a second but it is equally true that all this is the *Brahman*. The unity of the Reality must be to some extent shrouded before the many can emerge. This self-veiling is a deliberate act on the part of *Brahman*.

The becoming of the One is imaged by Sri Aurobindo as a descent. The Spirit through different levels of descent becomes Matter. There are in the main four lines of descent. When we regard Being as substance, we can think of its descent as the involution in different types of substance till it assumes a material form, seizable by the senses. The spirit as consciousness also descends through different levels of decreasing Light till it becomes the senses. *Ananda*, the self-existent delight of existence by descent becomes distorted as pleasant or painful reactions to stimuli and the absence of it, as pleasure, pain and insensitivity. And then the transcendent Divine affirming itself as cosmic Self reproduces itself as it were spiritually in and as different individual selves. But the individual self does not in Sri Aurobindo's view descend into the world in which we live, move and have our being. In the process of descent infinite consciousness translates itself into the infinite faculty of knowledge. And it is in the world of knowledge that self manifests itself as individual self. The world of knowledge is full of infinite potentialities waiting to be manifested. The individual self there knows everything as the same identical Reality which by its inherent Force has become a world of variety. But the unity is the central reality and diversity only its manifestation. Each individal self knows that it is the ultimate Self and that each other individual self is the same. Each self is conscious that it is an expression of the basic Truth. Thus there is no ignorance yet and thus no separation. For discrete realities to emerge from the state of existence where diversity is only an expression of unity which is the dominating principle, the separative outlook must be develcped. What is contained in unity is seen to be different from it as it were. This perception of a distinction between the unitary consciousness and its own contents hardens into a separative outlook and this is ignorance.

The individual self does not itself descend into the world of ignorance but projects a portion of itself into it. This is what Sri Aurobindo calls the psychic being or soul. It is a deputy of God in this world, a spark of the Divine Flame. It supports the mental, vital and physical being and nature secretly from behind. It is this soul which continues to exist after physical death and takes a new body when it is ready for further evolution. While Sri Aurobindo accepts the doctrine of rebirth, he gives it a new orientation from the point of view of the evolution of soul. In Sri Aurobindo's view rebirth does not merely provide opportunity to exhaust one's *karma* nor is it caused by past *karma* only. It is not that this element of the traditionl doctrine of rebirth has no place in Sri Aurobindo's theory of rebirth. But the main point is not that the soul is reborn to reap the rewards of the good actions or suffer unplesant consequences of bad actions of past life or lives. This is an external mechanism; the inner significance of rebirth is that the soul is given repeated opportunities to evolve in such a way that it can attain spiritual fulfilment. Sri Aurobindo even goes to the length of saying that the fruits of past *karma* cannot occur unless the soul gives its consent to it.[31] In point of fact it is extremely difficult for the soul to assert itself sufficiently to nullify the effects of *karma*. Nevertheless it can be done if the soul learns to unify all its acts of will and concentrate them on making *karma* unproductive of its effects. Anyway what we would like to point out here is that the evolution of the soul is the central arch of Sri Aurobindo's philosophy.

It would be rather pointless for the psychic being to come down to the world only to return to the pure spiritual world from which it came and thence to unite itself with God or even identify itself with the Absolute. Needless to say that sooner or later the soul will seek self-knowledge and if it is destined to have a comprehensive experience, it will seek God-knowledge too. Sri

31. *op. cit.*, 'The soul in man is greater than his fate', *Savitri* Book XI Canto I, p. 315. see also Sri Aurobindo's, *The Problem of Rebirth.*

Aurobindo never tires of saying that this world is undoubtedly one of Ignorance. We do not know the true nature of the world, nor do we know ourselves, our true being and true nature. But Ignorance in our Yogi-philosopher's view is not an original power of creating unrealities and illusions, but it is a development by limitation from Knowledge. From the point of view of the descent of consciousness it is knowledge hiding itself partially; from that of the ascent of consciousness, it is developing knowledge. We have spoken above of the third poise of the Supermind, its projecting and apprehending activity in which it looks at an aspect of itself as if it were an object other than itself. Ignorance arises from this apprehending status and function of the Supermind. It results in a division of consciousness leading on to a separation in being. As already mentioned above, the dynamic Reality descends along two lines, those of consciousness and being. Consciousness by progressive involution becomes the senses and lower down the Inconscient which is an amorphous mass of existence in which all is involved and from which all will evolve. The formation of matter, the release of the life-force in matter, the emergence of mind in living matter are steps in the onward and upward march of consciousness imprisoned in the inconscient towards an overt manifestation of itself. In this process Ignorance is an intermediate stage. It is not entirely devoid of consciousness though it is not knowledge. It is half-light and half-shadow. The soul has to shed this burden of ignorance and recover the knowledge inherent in it. It may or may not be able to obtain the total experience and realisation of Reality of which it is a spark but it does come to know that it is not the body, life or mind or a combination of these three but a spiritual substance.

But if the soul comes to the world only for this, it is not easily seen why it should have done so at all. Would it not be, asks Sri Aurobindo, more reasonable to think that the soul comes into the world to do something not only in the world but for the world or rather for God in the world? In other words the world is not merely a vale of soul-making but itself the field of the manifestation of the Spirit. The aspiration of the soul in Sri Aurobindo's view should be in two directions,—towards the Spirit, and towards a transformation of matter, life and mind which, though manifestations of the Spirit, are unspiritual in their actual nature. The world was created precisely because the Divine wants to manifest himself openly and integrally in something which for all practical purposes is entrely opposed to his own nature. What is involved must evolve and the instruments of the Spirit in Matter, Life and Mind emerge and be organised. And the individual is the pivot of this evolution. That is why, says Sri Aurobindo, "In the practice of Yoga there is a great dynamic difference in One's way of dealing with these three possible realisations (Transcendental, Cosmic and Individual). If I realise only the Divine as that, not my personal Self which yet moves secretly all by personal being and which I can bring forward out of the veil, or if I build up the image of that Godhead in my members, it is a realisation but a limited one. If it is Cosmic Godhead that I realise, losing in it all personal self, that is a very wide realisation, but I become a mere channel of the universal Power and there is no personal or divinely individual consummation for me. If I shoot up to the transcendental realisation only, I lose both myself and the world in the transcendent Absolute. If on the other hand my aim is none of these things by itself but to realise and also to manifest the Divine in the world bringing down for the purpose a yet unmanifested power—such as a Supermind,—a harmonisation of all three becomes imperative. If I have to bring it down and from where shall I bring it down—since it is not yet manifested in the cosmic formula—if not from the unmanifest Transcendent, which I must reach and realise? I have to bring it into the cosmic formula and, if so, I must realise the cosmic Divine and become conscious of the cosmic self and the cosmic forces. But I have to embody it here, —otherwise it is left as an influence only and not a thing fixed in the physical world, and it is through the Divine in the individual alone that this can be done.

"These are elements in the dynamics of spiritual experience and I am obliged to admit them if a divine work has to be done."[32]

If until Sri Aurobindo re-discovered the Supramental Truth-Consciousness this vision had not been vouchsafed to any yogi, it is because even the highest and the most complete yoga has had to use the mental consciousness in its approach to the reality.

---

32. *Riddle of the World*, pp. 77-79.

The result has been that while great spiritual experiences and realisations have been attained, they have nonetheless been incomplete in the last analysis. Each yogi, each great spiritual genius sees one or may be more than one side of the absolute Truth but not all of its aspects. Buddha speaks of the *shunya*, Shankara of the static, featureless Self intolerant of all duality, Ramanuja asserts the truth of the personal God with infinite features and qualities and with matter and soul qualifying it, the *Tantrik* systems make out that the Reality is dynamic and that the expansion of its Self-Force becomes the world with everything in which *Shiva* is intimately identical. Which of these visions is wrong and which right? But for Sri Aurobindo each of these is correct but not entirely so. His life's work was to realise a perfect harmony of complete knowledge, perfect devotion and utterly dedicated will and then to raise this realisaton to a level higher than the mental, to wit, the supramental. For there in that higher level of consciousness is the key to the world-enigma. It is the supermind which manifested the world out of the Absolute and is the secret principle and power of its existence and of our own physical, vital and mental being and nature and the force behind their evolution. And the supermind is the only thing that can bring to man the integral realisation of God and the complete manifestation of the Divine in man's being and nature.

Now we can understand the significance of the soul's descent from the world of Knowledge into the world of Ignorance. The purpose is, first, to realise the Divine integrally by the supramental consciousness, to acquire the infallible Will which is the other aspect of the same consciousness, then to discover the supreme Knowledge-Will involved in matter and to help in its release and evolution in matter, life and mind. The certain result is their transformation. New instruments of the Spirit must be evolved in matter so that greater and greater splendours of the Divine can be manifested here on earth. "Mind attains its self-fulfilment," says Sri Aurobindo, "when it becomes a pure mirror of the Truth of Being which expresses itself in the symbols of the Universe; Life, when it consciously lends its energies to the perfect self-figuration of the Divine in even new forms and activities of the universal existence."[33] And we may add, matter

33. *The Life Divine*, American Edition, p. 72.

finds its self-fulfilment when it becomes fully aware of the spiritual substance of which it is now a dark formation but of which it is destined to become a luminous figure., then

"The spirit shall look out through Matter's gaze
And Matter shall reveal the spirits face."

Though the individual is the indispensable means of spiritual evolution, it is not for the sake of the individual as such. The integral yoga of Sri Aurobindo is integral in more than one sense. The all-complete development of the individual, the attainment of a perfection that is whole and comprehensive,—perfection of the soul, mind, life and body, —is the foundation of the total achievement of Sri Aurobindo's yoga. He asserts that there is a social and a national soul and even a soul of humanity. Indeed it is God himself who supports the individual, the society, the nation and mankind as a spiritual being of different dimensions behind each of these manifestations of himself. And conscious Nature's intention is to bring these different types of souls into the front. Sri Aurobindo envisages a spiritual society in which the soul of the commune will be the presiding deity of its collective life. Individuals will be considered and treated primarily as developing souls and not merely as economic and political animals come together for the fulfilment of material and vital needs. The diverse types of interests of the individuals and those of the society will not clash but will be complementary. Similarly, the soul of a nation will be awakened in such a way that all its deepest potentialities will begin to be realised in a harmonious manner. The nation will not be guided by its ego in conflict with other national egos. A fundation will be laid for constructive cooperation between nation and nation because they will be guided by the intimate perception of their respective souls, the way of seeing being intuitive and direct. And however much the present facts may point in the other direction, the soul of humanity will also emerge. Men all over the world will come to feel a strong religious worshipful sentiment for humanity. A spiritual religion of humanity, based upon a strong and effective sense of the vital need for the unity of all mankind, is the hope for the future of the world. Sri Aurobindo has discussed in detail the psychological laws of social evolution and of

34. *Savitri*, Book XI, Canto I, 1957, p. 331.

the movements which bear witness to Nature's attempts at forging human unity in his two books, *The Human Cycle* and *The Ideal of Human Unity*. And to get a full understanding of his views of the evolution of man who is at once a portion of God and part of mankind, we really need to study with all the attention we can command, his classical works, *The Life Divine*, *The Synthesis of Yoga, The Human Cycle* and *The Ideal of Human Unity*. Together they expound in a most inspiring manner the ideal and the process of the Divine's utter manifestation in the world on different levels of Life, the life Divine.

"Thus shall the earth open to divinity
And common natures feel the wide uplift,
Illumine common acts with the spirit's ray
And meet the deity in common things.
Nature shall live to manifest secret God,
The Spirit shall take up the human play,
This earthly life become the life divine."[35]

35. *op. cit.*, p. 333.

Essential Elements in Sri Aurobindo's Thought

ASTER PATEL

In this very brief paper, we wish to make an attempt to consider a few of the essential elements of the philosophy and yoga of Sri Aurobindo *in terms of contemporary understanding*, rather than in terms of their affiliation to the concepts and values of the Indian tradition in general. Not that tradition and modernity are totally distinct, for history, ensures continuity and nowhere is this continuity so powerfully present as in the work of Sri Aurobindo. In fact, tradition is so carried forward and further enriched by contemporary experience as to present a view of the whole in the perspective of historicity. What then are these elements that we wish to consider.[1]

Aurobindo takes all experience to be real—inner or outer. He has a sort of an innate feeling that nothing that forms part of the totality of human experience can be unreal. The role of philosophy is, firstly, to seek an enlargement of the limits of experience and, subsequently, to interpret this wealth of experience in terms of appropriate identification, right characterisation and complex inter-relationship. Thus philosophy has a strictly experimental basis. No doubt, before the validity of an experience can be accepted, there has to be a firm ground of discrimination, scrutiny, control. But given these exigencies of method, all experience must be taken to be real and considered worthy of philosophical interpretation and meaning. In respect

1. Indra Sen, Preface to *The Philosophy of Sri Aurobindo*, by R.M. Sharma, Meerut, pp. IX-X.

of this essential attitude of Sri Aurobindo, says an Indian philosopher who has been a disciple of long standing: "He has a sort of innate sentiment that all experience must be real. Nothing that is experience, that is a fact of experience, can be unreal. The essential problem is to identify the quality and the degree of reality present in the experience, and to relate it correctly to other experiences."[2]

It is interesting to observe here that in respect of the contemporary scene in the Western world, the noted French Philosopher Mr. Jean Wahl, says that it is essentially characterized by a seeking for "an enlargement of the field of experience, an expansion of our mode of knowing."[3]

Given this basic attitude, Sri Aurobindo assigns limit to his investigation, which is marked by a perpetual reaching out for new ranges of experience. These ranges succeed one another in a *qualitative* progression in terms of totality and integration and the highest of these is termed, by him, the Supermind. Thus experience is distinctly multi-dimensional. But this differentiation does not imply an absolute plurality, it reveals itself only as the concrete content of an organic totality. This totality is, for Sri Aurobindo, the primary fact; the differentiation is the secondary but necessary fact of experience. The various levels of differentiation correspond to an ascending scale of values—from that of discrete plurality to that of progressive unity, culminating in total integration. These levels of experience correspond to the realms of matter, life, mind and supermind. Between the last two, there exists a whole hierarchy of intermediate domains delineated as the higher mind, illumined mind, intuitive mind and overmind. The inter-action of these different levels with one another within the framework of the organic totality and their relationship to the whole have been presented by Sri Aurobindo with luminous insight.

It would be useful to remark here upon Sri Aurobindo's methodological concern in the interpretation of this experience. He formulates it succinctly in these words: "Our means of knowing must be appropriate to that which has to be known."[4]

---

2. *Ibid.*
3. *Jean Wahl, Vers le concret*, Paris.
4. *The Life Divine.*

Thus he visualises a whole ascending range of faculties of knowledge that correspond to the different levels of reality that are sought to be interpreted. These extend from sense-perception and reason to an integral intuition, which can seize the whole in a single unified perception. This possibility of integration of our means of knowing in a supreme faculty of cognition, which can know the totality as well as the differentiation present within it is foundational to the philosophy of Sri Aurobindo. It is interesting to note that the very faculities of cognition are considered in the perspective of possible growth. Our present status is not a final term; it is only an intermediate stage.

This brings us to a point of great importance. How to characterise this organic totality to which we referred earlier? Sri Aurobindo affirms and this is central to his philosophy, that it is an evolving fact.

The various levels of experience are linked together by means of an ascending order of evolution—from the realm of matter to life, from that of life to mind, from mind to spirit. But how does this ascension proceed, what is the exact nature of its process? This ascension from one level to another takes place by means of a triple action of the force of consciousness—that of widening, heightening and integration. Thus each level is taken up into the next higher one and there assimilated and transformed. Evolution is consequently an integrative process. It implies, in fact, a two-fold movement, the first being an inverse process of involution by means of which each successive level of experience gets involved in the antecedent one and is present therein as potentiality. The evolution of each term out of the precedent one remains otherwise inexplicable.

On the subject of evolution, Sri Aurobindo evinces a very characteristic initial attitude. He feels a profound attraction for the dimension of the prospective in evolution, for the indefinitely richer possibilities of the future that await man, the newer and vaster ranges of experience that can become accessible to him. This exploration of the prospective, of the ranges of experience that lie ahead, their characterisation, the means of reaching out to them and actualising them—this latter is an important point and we shall return to it further on—this is what Sri Aurobindo essentially seeks to do. Since this is the real burden of his total thought and experience, we shall consider it at some length.

Firstly, how does Sri Aurobindo characterise this dimension of the prospective? He does so in terms of *qualitatively* newer levels of experience—each successive level possessing a progressively greater integration of knowing, feeling and willing. The mental level of experience, which is our present possession, is characterised by an essential division in the personality and its functioning, even though there is present at this level a very definite and persistent seeking for wholeness. But this seeking for wholeness arrives at a slow fruition only in the ranges of experience beyond that of the mental level, which Sri Aurobindo discerns in the dimension of the prospective. It is this *qualitative* change in the level of the experience towards which all evolution tends, a change which points to the possibility of arriving at a state of whole-being, whole-knowledge, whole-power.

It is interesting to observe here that this pre-occupation with the future, a future which is not so much a temporal category but is symbolic of a further evolutionary reach of newer and higher levels of experience that can be attained, is the dominant characteristic of contemporary thought, however, variously it may be formulated or in however incipient a manner. This ascendancy of the future over the human spirit, a kind of a polarisation of attention on this particular dimension, a reaching out towards the 'not-yet-there', the urge to actualise it—these seem to be, philosophically, the most powerful attitudes prevalent today. And of all philosophers, no one seems to embody them as does Sri Aurobindo. These find expression not only in the creation of a complex and consistent system of thought but, what is more pertinent, in the fact that he also elaborates a distinct psychological discipline that can help man to actualise this range of future possibility. In fact, this emphasis on the 'practical', the word being given its widest significance, or to use a richer Indian equivalent, 'realisation' in fact of experience and qualitative growth of consciousness, is the most attractive and uplifting aspect of Sri Aurobindo's entire philosophy. To know is the first indispensable necessity but thus to know that knowledge remains not merely conceptual but is embodied in the totality of the being as a fact of concrete experience. This truth is firmly embedded in the Indian tradition generally and it finds in the philosophy of Sri Aurobindo a very powerful formulation in terms of contemporary understanding. It is interesting to note that the schools of existentialist thought in the West lay a similar emphasis on the primacy of the 'practical' but the term is given a different connotation.

It is interesting to observe here that Prof. Julian Huxley among Western philosophers, feels specially drawn to, what we might call, the 'practical' dimension of the problem. He states that once it is recognised that the attainment of a new *quality* of consciousness is the true and final goal of man, we would need to create "a science of human possibilities" to help us work out the long process of psycho-sociological evolution that lies ahead. The expression "a science of human possibilities" is most intriguing! Sri Aurobindo feels for this a very special attraction and elaborates in this connection a psychological discipline of growth and evolution of the individual, which he terms *Integral Yoga*. This is a fresh creation but which offers, at the same time, a synthesis of the essential elements of the traditional disciplines of yoga. It has a very special relevance for the contemporary consciousness—in the matter of terminology, methodology and philosophical basis of the entire discipline. This is largely due to the fact that the *Integral Yoga* rests within the framework of a philosophy of evolution. For Sri Aurobindo affirms that the evolution of the individual can be pursued only by remaining faithful to the processes that evolutionary nature has herself pursued in her movement upward. The two are co-terminous one with the other. The difference between them being that the latter takes place subconsciously, whereas the former can proceed in a conscious and deliberate manner, thus greatly accelerating the course of the movement. These processess of evolutionary nature, i.e, the triple action which leads to the growth of consciousness—that of widening, heightening and integration—are systematised into a psychological discipline of the individual self-development. It is interesting to remark upon the relevance of this discipline to the essential content of Huxley's expression "a science of human possibilities."

In fact, the feeling that a deliberate and methodised effort should be made towards self-enrichment and self-exceeding has become steadily more pervasive. For, with the appearance of man in the course of evolution, the product of the process becomes the agent of the process: the active participation of the individual in carrying the movement further becomes essential. On this point, there is a wide consensus of opinion amongst contemporary philosophers but the question of real importance remains to be put: *how* is this participation to be effected? A mere statement made on the subject is hardly adequate: a way must be found to make this possible. Here Sri Aurobindo alone provides the answer, an answer that is being passionately sought by modern man. This incorporation, within the framework of a philosophy of evolution, of a psychological discipline that aims at the growth and evolution of the individual is one of the very special features of his approach to the subject as a whole. Its implications are far-reaching.

There is a final point we would like to refer to.

This synthesis of the theoretical and the practical standpoints, philosophy and yoga, metaphysical statement of the problem and practical method which aims at the resolution of the problem—is, for the contemporary consciousness, the most fascinating aspect of Sri Aurobindo's entire work. Merely 'to know' has proved inadequate, as is clearly borne out by the present period of cultural upheaval and crisis through which we are passing. There is now an imperative 'need to become' that which we know: knowledge must needs become a fact of concrete experience. Philosophy and a corresponding psychological discipline that can actualise the truths of the former in concrete experience, are the twin necessities for modern man. This two-fold expression of the philosophical urge has been a persistent feature of the Indian traditon in general. It finds at the hands of Sri Aurobindo a fresh and powerful formulation in terms of contemporary perspective and aspiration. Tradition and modernity come together in a perspective of wholeness.

To bring our short paper to a conclusion, we would like to state that what Sri Aurobindo essentially communicates to us is a rare optimism about the future destiny of man—a future towards which he tends, knowingly or unknowingly. He offers us also the possibility of doing so in full awareness of both the process and the goal and of making of this movement forward a fully conscious endeavour. This optimism does not call for merely a facile acceptance but requires a kind of a spiritual heroism, that gives us the courage to feel out for the future that is to be and to make an attempt to actualise it. Sri Aurobindo's is a veritable philosophy of the prospective; the prospective in the process of actualisation. It is both philosophy and yoga.

Sri Aurobindo's Evolutionary Philosophy

Y. MASIH

THE western process philosophy yoked to the ancient wisdom of Indian sages has given rise to the integral philosophy of Sri Aurobindo. Again Sri Aurobindo's personal experience of political struggle against the British rule has made his philosophy earthy. However, Sri Aurobindo is still too much ahead of his times and the world will have to wait till it becomes ripe enough for receiving the message of this great son of India.

The present article has three parts. Part I deals with those portions of the western process philosophy which have relevance for appreciating Sri Aurobindo's integral philosophy. Part II is concerned with the Indian tradition in which Sri Aurobindo's evolutionary philosophy is deeply soaked. Part III proposes to assess the relevance of Sri Aurobindo's philosophy for contemporary India.

I

The evolutionary philosophy has been popularised by the idealists and since the publication of Darwin's *Origin of Species* in 1859 and *The Descent of Man* in 1871 it has become the predominant feature of speculative philosophy. In the wake of biological discoveries Henri Bergson a French Jew, advanced the philosophy of creative evolution. He posited *elan vital* as the Reality which is a pure motion without anything that moves, and, is creative along divergent routes of its advance. The life force moves backwards and forward. Matter is nothing but *elan vital* in inverse direction. That the Reality which is essentially creative is also regressive in inverse direction is reflected in Sri Aurobindo's doctrine of matter as 'secret God' or veiled divinity, in contradiction of the *mayic* view of the world. Bergson in his earlier writings, *Creative Evolution, Matter and Memory*, gave the impression that *elan vital* is unceasing creativity without any end or goal. However, in his final view in *Two Sources of Morality and Religion,* Bergson held that the supreme task of *elan vital* is to create creators or gods (pp.201,202,275). He also held that through technology man would so much mechanise matter that it would be made to serve the higher ends of man. This would be called the spiritualisation of matter. In contrast, Sri Aurobindo's doctrine of the divinisation of matter is more direct in as much as he talks of the transformation of matter under the impact of supramental consciousness. Again, Sri Aurobindo's evolutionary process is goal-oriented from the start. Sri Aurobindo's integral philosophy not only includes creative process, but also lays stress on the emergence of new qualities in the forward stride of the divine creative pull. This key-notion of emergence is fully worked out by the two British philosophers Llyod Morgan and the Jewish philosopher Samuel Alexander.

Samuel Alexander, posits space-time continuum with its nisus towards deity as the supreme reality. Space-time is pure motion without anything which moves. However there is an urge within it by virtue of which this pure motion rises above its source. In due course matter is the first to arrive, containing within it something which was not explicit at the stage of *S-T*. But the evolved matter does not remain static. It is further caught up in the creative throw and in the fullness of time gives birth to life, and Life in its turn gives rise to Mind. Should the nisus stop at Mind? The fact that the mind is infected with the drive of self-transcendence shows that the emergence evolution is destined to go beyond Mind. The language of Alexander is that the whole of the universe is caught up with its nisus towards deity. The deity is higher than the highest emergent known to us. The deity is always to be and can never be fully actualised or exhausted in the highest conceivable rung of the evolutionary ladder. For the emergence of any supervenient quality, according to Alexander, the whole of the universe must be caught up in the creative frenzy. Once the supervenient quality emerges all the elements in the body of the new emergent get transformed. This thought is also included in Sri Aurobindo's theory of the transformation of the mental, vital and physical processes in the birth of the mind of light, of course independently of Alexander's writings. For example, with the emergence of mind, according to Alexander, the physico-chemical elements within the body and all its vital elements specially of the brain work in a holistic way, which otherwise they do not. In like manner Sri Aurobindo also talks of the transformed workings even of the constituent cells of the body as soon as supramental consciousness will descend into the human structural frame. A crucial question arises with regard to the emergent evolution of Alexander. What makes the emergent emerge? Alexander would say the whole process is natural and spontaneous and the ongoings of the universe have to be accepted with 'natural piety.' Llyod Morgan would say that it is God who makes the emergent emerge. Here the ingressive evolution of Alfred North Whitehead is significant.

Whitehead starts with point-instants (akin to S-T of Alexander) and eternal objects (akin to the Ideas of Plato) and together they break forth into novelties. But the universe is not a self-regulative process according to Whitehead. God is the ultimate principle of concrescence. Actual entities by prehending and by being prehended by other actual entities are forever freshly organised for the ingression of eternal objects which are the forms into which the world creativity is cast under the directive agency of God. In like manner, according to Sri Aurobindo man must prepare himself with the help of yogic exercise for receiving the supramental consciousness. Along with the yogic push there is the pull of the supramental consciousness for the emergence of the supermind in the earthy frame. Nay, according to Aurobindoian, the supreme sacrifice of Sri Aurobindo himself like the Vedic sacrifice of *Purusha* itself (*Rg. X*-90; 6) has already brought the supermind into the earthy existence. In accordance with the Lamarckian theory (adopted by Bernard Shaw) human beings with the help of Aurobindoian Yoga should prepare the way for the birth of the supramental race. But the last sentence stands in need of further elaboration, otherwise it would not go much beyond Alexander, Llyod and Whitehead. In Sri Aurobindo' philosophy the western process metaphysics has been powerfully assimilated into the ancient Indian tradition of *yogic* contemplations to which we can turn now.

II

From the time of Indus Valley Civilization which antedates the advent of the Aryans in India there has been in vogue the cult of meditation. Jainism and specially Buddhism have perfected the practice of *Dhyanas, Samadhis* and *Yogic* trances. What could be the rationale of this practice? It can be conjectured that the spirit of enquiry and the sense of conquest drove the Indians to find a way of getting themselves established in their Being in the face of threats of nature, society and intra-psychic disturbances. As technology and science were not sufficiently developed they could not conquer nature. Again, as the means of collective and social agitation against the socio-political powers were not at the disposal of the people, so they could not stabilise themselves in the face of social ills. But surely the world inside could be conquered. What the moderners have not been able to achieve even now the ancient Indians could realize. They devised the means of gaining psychological control of themselves to a remarkable degree. The whole psychological control followed from the following assumptions:

1. *Ajnana, Samsara, Karma and Moksa* are the four cardinal principles of life.
2. *Karmas* under the influence of nescience are at the root of births, and life in nescience is full of sufferings, i.e., under the threat of non-being (physical, moral and spiritual).
3. This state of sufferings, called bondage is beginningless. Yet they assumed as a piece of daring adventure of thought that there is an eternal state of bliss which can be won through the systematic use of yoga.
4. The final state of liberation dawns upon the realisation that the body, matter and the world are all absolutely extraneous to the real nature of the *jiva*. Illusoriness of the world and the eternal state of liberation are the two aspects of the same realisation.
5. The release can be won by the individual when he attains to the discriminative knowledge. This knowledge does not

mean pure cognition, but an integral attitude of viewing all things as unreal, and discerning the underlying Reality behind the fleeting show of things.

Sri Aurobindo not only perfected the way of yoga, but also introduced newer assumptions in his integral philosophy. As opposed to the older assumptions Sri Aurobindo accepted the reality of the world and the world of matter, life and mind, that is the world revealed by science. He also accepted the social challenge and the task of changing the socio-political structure of the world. Formerly, according to the doctrine of *jivanmukti* or *bodhisattva*, the released soul in this earthly frame could preach the right way and through his example a *jivanmukta* was expected to lift the fallen masses into greater awareness and consequent effort of reaching their final goal. Even Radhakrishnan thought that the life of a *jivanmukta* was a sufficient guarantee against social ills. Most probably he must have been disillusioned now. Sri Aurobindo claimed that the world events can be controlled by yogic means.

> "In his retirement Sri Aurobindo kept a close watch on all that was happening in the world and in India and actively intervened whenever necessary, but solely with a spiritual force and silent spiritual action...."

Again, the following two statements of Sri Aurobindo can be quoted here:

> "When I concentrate, I work upon others, upon the world, upon the play of forces."

> "I have always said that the spiritual force I have been putting on human affairs, such as the War, is not the supramental but the overmind force,...."

Whether one accepts this claim or not, but this is the most consistent view to take with regard to the life of *jivanmukta*. It appears to me absurd that a *jivanmukta* can be the Prime Minister of India or of any country for spiritualising socio-political activities.

Again, Sri Aurobindo held, after the spirit of the Western idealists, that the matter *is* the *absolute* in its otherness. Matter is life, otherwise it could not have given birth to life and Life *is* Mind, otherwise mind could not have come out of vital forces. Nay, Sri Aurobindo has the plan of divinisation of matter and vital forces to subserve spiritual goals. Not only Sri Aurobindo rejects the *mayic* doctrine concerning the illusoriness of the world, he hopes to attain physical immortality even with this body transformed under the spell of yoga.

> "Never in the past has there been any vision of the thoroughly divinised body, immune even from accidents, as the external support for an integrally divine manifestation. If that vision put forth by Sri Aurobindo is not NEW, and revolutionary NEW at that, tell me what significance the words NEW has!"

Here the body is supramentalised and not simply spiritualised. The two processes not only differ in degree but in kind. Ancient sages, according to the Aurobindoite, stopped at the process of spiritualisation: Sri Aurobindo goes beyond to the stage of divinisation of the earthy existence.

The stages of spiritualisation are Higher Mind, Illumined Mind, Intuition and Overmind. Under the attraction of the Supermind, the earthy man is pulled up to the stage of Overmind. But the imperfection is never totally got rid off. However, there is another process, according to Aurobindoite yoga through which the Supermind ingresses into the earthy frame and transforms the mental, then the vital processes and finally overcomes the physical elements of the body. This is the final stage of the mind of Light,...the complete divinisation of the material, vital and mental processes. Here the yogi leaves behind every trace of nescience. The light in the beginning may be restrained, but one moves from the less to the greater light till finally all is light and this light is in all. This is the stage of the descent of the supramental consciousness into the earthy man.

> "A divinised being on earth is one in whom not merely the mental and vital consciousness but also the physical instrument

has been changed into divine and therefore fully illumined and immortal and immune substance."

III

First, I do not believe that in an intellectual community of the world any sharp distinction can be made between Indian and non-Indian philosophies. One can however choose between Ancient and Contemporary traditions, between the heritage of wisdom and the current value of science, technology, socialism and secularism. Moderners do not accept any one path of absolute perfection. Life always oscillates between the two extremes of Being and non-Being according to them. I for my part choose science, tehnology, socialism and secularism. From this stand Aurobindoism is not quite relevant to the needs of the masses. Yet the Aurobindoian tradition also contains an eternal truth for the discerning eye. Life will oscillate between these two extremes.

I dogmatically assume that man's chief end of life is not to become immortal in his physical frame. My reason for saying so is very much akin to the arguments of Bernard Bosanquet in favour of adjectival view of individuality in contrast to the substantial theory accepted by A. Seth Pringle-Pattison. Later on in his own way the adjectival view has been powerfully held by the poet philosopher George Santayana. For me it is enough if a man has lived in devotion and dedication in accordance with the best insight available to him. Such a man might grant that there are heights greater than his own, but his own climb is all that he can scale. Sri Aurobindo has certainly plumbed the depth and scanned the heights for which posterity will remember him, but lesser goals have to be achieved no less if humanity has to march further. And this lesser goal is of socialism.

Sri Aurobindo's integral philosophy is grand and vast, but it is a metaphysics. Metaphysics for me is not nonsense, but it is the deeper poetry of the soul evoking larger intellectual horizons and opening new perspectives and visions. But it can claim no scientific knowledge and cognition. It is enough if it succeeds in elevating people by its conceptual symphony. Take the case of Supermind.

What is the evidence for the reality of the Supermind? Nothing beyond this that emergents emerge and that there is within man an urge for his own self-transcendence. But this fact is as much compatible with the naturalism of Alexander, theism of Llyod Morgan, Whitehead's God as the principle of concrescence, holistic theory of Smuts, Jung and a number of American psychologists, not to speak of Indian sages who maintain that there is an inner urge in each *jiva* to regain his lost lustre and omniscience. True, an Aurobindoite would adduce his yogic experience in support of the truth of his metaphysical claims. However, any truth to be acceptable for a modern man must ultimately rest on repeatable, shareable and communicable ordinary experience of man, and not on any extraordinary experience induced in him by virtue of psychic change and suggestibility. But yogic experience has its own logic. It alone bestows authenticity and genuineness in each man in gaining his personal stability in relation to all kinds of threats to his Being. The scientific public experience and yogic experience can be interwoven, but one cannot be assimilated to the other.

Freud, Jung and Sri Aurobindo think that social improvement can come about by improving the individual. This stand is consistent with the age-old tradition of the Indian sages who started with the dictum of self-conquest. But society is the life-blood of each individual. In a socialist pattern of society the individuality is preserved and is yet transcended. Socialism gives meaning to each individual by using and harnessing it in the service of the whole State and the State itself is shaped through an ever increasing evaluation of its moves by a society of intellectuals. Thus the evolution of an individual is a matter of the State and the society of vigilant intellectuals. Is Sri Aurobindo's Yoga useless in a socialist State?

The Yoga of Sri Aurobindo can be used for gaining stead-fastness to the individual's efforts for gaining the socialist ideal. As it stands in India, socialism can come only through a change of mental outlook of Indians concerning food, sex, caste and scientific technology. Every socialist feels staggered at the stupendous task before him. In India the protagonists of socialism do little to bring about socialism. In the face of capitalisitc pattern of economy, feudal means of gaining and using political power, a socialist feels frustrated, thwarted and his spirit dwindles down.

Here Yoga would strengthen his resolve and would energise his efforts in the task of building a heaven on earth. There is also another point with regard to any evolutionary scheme of things and this point one misses in Sri Aurobindo.

Yoga and all its marvellous achievements and depths were brought about in India some 2500 years ago when a number of spiritual explorers were seized with the creative frenzy of attaining self-perfection. Look at Makkhali Gosal, Purana Kasyapa, Ajit-késa-Kambal, Sanjaya-Velatthiputta and so on. They differed a lot amongst themselves. But they all practised penance and were seized with the ideal of self-perfection. In the same way supramental consciousness can dawn only if a vast number of people be seized with the creative throw for becoming a New Being. How can such a social consciousness be created on such a large-scale? Only when society has reached a state in which everyone gets according to his needs and works according to his abilities. When the task of living each day is reduced to the minimum and when the duration of leisure is increased to the maximum, then and then alone man will get an opportunity of rising upwards. Only at this stage there will be the heightening of the holistic drive in each man to become a thing of supreme value.

Lastly, to my thinking there is no necessity of becoming immortal. Socialised individuals informed and transformed by the rich stimulation of the whole man by the socialist educational system can experience things which ae now beyond the imagination of even fiction-writers and novelists of the present time. If there is going to be an invasion of supramental consciousness, then it is possible in such a state of socialism. The Yoga of Sri Aurobindo requires the precondition of social efforts at self-effacement, individual dedication and devotion to the ideal of social well-being. For this reason I believe that Sri Aurobindo and his Yoga are too much ahead of the time.

The Epiphany of Human Fellowship

V. MADHUSUDAN REDDY

In Sri Aurobindo's vision of the perennial unfoldment of time, history or *Geschichte,* becomes an apocalypse. It is identified with an upward movement, a saga of the endless manifestation of the Absolute in space-time continuum. Sri Aurobindo's philosophy of history is not based on certain mere metaphysical pre-suppositions although it has an explicit metaphysic. It is a part of his total vision of Truth,—an outcome of his integral experience of Reality as a whole. The concept of an integral Absolute is central in Sri Aurobindo's philosophy. The spiritual Infinite and the Eternal—*Sachchidananda,* is the basis, the beginning and end of all existence. This supreme Reality has three eternally real poises—the supra-cosmic transcendence, the cosmic universality and the unique separate individuality, which are equally essential and fundamental. This Absolute has the double aspects of dynamic consciousness and that of passive or silent consciousness. The first aspect represents the free infinite self-creation in terms of multiplicity, mobility and activity. Whereas the second represents its illimitable, stable, eternal immobility. Though each of the three primal aspects of *Sachchidananda,* have their own self-determinates, namely, *Atman, Purusha* and *Ishwara* of *Sat*, *Maya, Prakriti* and *Shakti* of *Chit,* and love, joy and beauty of *Ananda*, *Sachchidananda,* the supreme Reality is not bound or limited by them in its plenary and original freedom. The *Brahman* has the power of infinite self-variation, self-limitation and self-absorption. It is the will of *Brahman* formulating itself through these triple powers that creates the multiple worlds. The central force which is wholly responsible for the creation of the universe is the "all-containing, all-originating, all-consummating Supermind," the supreme Truth-consciousness, *Sachchidananda*. "The Truth-consciousness is everywhere present in the universe as an ordering self-knowledge by which the One manifests the harmonies of its infinite potential multiplicity."[1] The Supermind therefore is "Being moving out into a determinative self-knowledge which perceives certain truths of itself and wills to realise them in a temporal and spatial extension of its own timeless and spaceless existence."[2] It is thus that the Divine Consciousness "creates in itself all things by a movement of its consciounsness-force and governs their development through a self-evolution by inherent knowledge-will of the truth of existence or real-idea which has formed them."[3]

Sachchidananda or the supreme spiritual reality, Supermind or the self-ideative and self-creative Truth-consciousness and the evolutionary progression or the progressive manifestation of the supreme Reality in the universe are the three basic concepts of Sri Aurobindo's integral philosophy. It is upon these fundamentals that his entire historical and political thought-structure is based. History as viewed from the surface "teaches us nothing; it is a confused torrent of events and personalities or a kaleidoscope of changing institutions."[4] The real sense of all this constant change often seems to have been missed by the historians. History, for Sri Aurobindo, is the progressive revelation of the secret Godhead in the soul and life and humanity. It is the dynamic fulfilment of the Eternal in Time, the concretization of the supreme Reality, the Absolute in terms of evolving multiplicity. Nature is then, in its essence, a spiritual power of the Divine which is eternally trying to His will and purpose.

The purpose of cosmic evolution is the progressive manifestation of the supreme Spirit and the consequent total spiritual transformation of the individual through the liberation of his entire being from ignorance and inconscience. Man is essentially an *eternal* individual, a spiritual self, whose ultimate destiny is the

1. *The Life Divine*, 1943, p. 159.
2. *Ibid.*, p. 175.
3. *Ibid.*, p. 155.
4. *The Ideal of Human Unity*, 1950, p. 2.

realisation of a gnostic consciousness and the spiritualisation of his terrestrial life. The family, the clan and the tribe are all based on vital foundations and have their origin in the vital needs of human nature. These invariably impose on the individual their mechanical interests and rough immediate convenience, compel him into their moulds and hardly allow him to be in the true sense *manusya, Purusha,* soul or spirit capable of evolving into a highest perfect being. Like the family, the society also is a vital, but a competitive and cooperative ego, for the primal law and purpose of a society, community or nation is to seek its own self-fulfilment :

> "The reason is the same; for this too is a being, a living power of the eternal truth, a self-manifestation of the cosmic Spirit, and it is there to express and fulfil in its own way and to the degree of its capacities the special truth and power and meaning of the cosmic Spirit that is within it. The nation or society, like the individual, has a body, an organic life, a moral and aesthetic temperament, a developing mind and a soul behind all these signs and powers for the sake of which they exist. One may see even that, like the individual, it essentially is a soul rather than has one; it is a group-soul that, once having attained to a separate distinctness, must become more and more self-conscious and find itself more and more fully as it develops its corporate action and mentality and its organic self-expressive life."[5]

Sri Aurobindo distinguishes an organic society from a rational society in as much as the former arranges the modes of its cooperative behaviour and social interaction with reference to "the general sense and instinct or intuition of the group-life" and the latter is governed by planned and deliberate calculation and rational organisation. In rational societies, group-life tends to become more and more self-conscious, but self-consciousness, according to Sri Aurobindo, finds its fullest development not in reason-based political norms but in a cosmic consciousness. Learning and science, economics and politics, culture, religion and aesthetics are only aids to life, and are no part of its very

5. *The Human Cycle*, pp. 39-40.

substance. "Life itself is the only object of living."[6]

The ancients recognised the great importance of the primary activities—the social, political, economic and cultural; yet, these were not their chief business. They regarded life as an occasion for the development of the rational, the ethical, the aesthetic and the spiritual being.

> "Greece and Rome laid stress on the three first alone, Asia went farther, made these also subordinate and looked upon them as stepping stones to a spiritual consummation. Greece and Rome were proudest of their art, poetry and philosophy and cherished these things as much as or even more than their political liberty or greatness. Asia too exalted these three powers and valued inordinately her social organisation, but valued much more highly, exalted with a much greater intensity of worship her saints, her religious founders and thinkers, her spiritual heroes. The modern world has been proudest of its economic organisation, its political liberty, order and progress, the mechanism, comfort and ease of its social and domestic life, its science, but science most in its application to practical life, most for its instruments and conveniences, its railways, telegraphs, steamships and its other thousand and one discoveries, countless inventions and engines which help man to master the physical world. That marks the whole difference in the attitude."[7]

The ideals of modern society are merely the physical good and vitalistic well-being of the individual and the collectivity and almost merely or principally exists for the maintenance, comforts, vital happiness and political and economic efficiency of the species. Its primary impulse of life is essentially individualistic and makes family, social and communal life a means for the greater satisfaction of the vital individual.

A true society will regard man not as a mind, a life and a body, but as a soul incarnated for a divine fulfilment upon earth, not only in heavens beyond, which after all it need not have left if it had no divine business here in the world of physical, vital and

---

6, *Ibid.*, p. 195.
7. *Ibid.*, p. 195-96.

mental nature."[8] Life, mind and body will therefore be regarded neither as ends in themselves nor as mortal members but as instruments of the soul, 'the yet imperfect instruments of an unseized divine purpose.'

"It will believe in their destiny and help them to believe in themselves, but for that very reason in their highest and not only in their lowest or lower possibilities. Their destiny will be, in its view, to spiritualise themselves so as to grow into visible members of the spirit, lucid means of its manifestation, themselves spiritual, illumined, more and more conscious and perfect. For, accepting the truth of man's soul as a thing entirely divine in its essence, it will accept also the possibility of his whole being becoming divine in spite of Nature's first patent contradiction of this possibility, her darkened denials of this ultimate certitude, and even with these as a necessary earthly starting-point. And as it will regard man the individual, it will regard too man the collectivity as a soul-form of the Infinite, a collective soul myriadly embodied upon earth for a divine fulfilment in its manifold relations and its multitudinous activities. Therefore it will hold sacred all the different parts of man's life which correspond to the parts of his being, all his physical, vital, dynamic, emotional, aesthetic, ethical, intellectual, psychic evolution, and see in them instruments for a growth towards a diviner living. It will regard every human society, nation, people or other organic aggregate from the same standpoint, subsouls, as it were, means of a complex manifestation and self-fulfilment of the Spirit, the divine Reality, the conscious infinite in man upon earth. The possible godhead of man because he is inwardly of one being with God will be its one solitary creed and dogma."[9]

A truly spiritual society swears by liberty for it is in complete freedom that human society grows towards the possibility of spiritualisation. The spiritual aim will recognise not only the freedom of the individual to grow in his own strength but also allow science, thought, philosophy, religion and art to seek truth

---

8. *Ibid.*, p. 281.
9. *Ibid.*, pp. 281-282.

dispassionately, without prepossession, prejudice or prejudgement and to realise the unity of God with Truth, Good and Beauty. "But meanwhile they must be left free even to deny God and good and beauty if they will, if their sincere observation of things so points them. For all these rejections must come round in the end of their circling and return to a larger truth of the things they refuse. Often we find atheism both in individual and society a necessary passage to deeper religious and spiritual truth: one has sometimes to deny God in order to find him; the finding is inevitable at the end of all earnest scepticism and denial."[10]

As the individual is soul incarnate for a divine fulfilment upon earth, so also the collectivity a soul-form of the Infinite. There should therefore be no antagonism in their aim and practice. The truth of a self-assertive, vital, egoistic and self-fulfilling individual is as one-sided and partial as the concept of a totalitarian social collectivity. A harmonious and integral synthesis of the two which envisages and promotes perfect individuality and perfect reciprocity will be the ideal law of the individual and of social development.

Ours is an age of evolutionary crisis. Human civilisation itself seems to be on trial. Accordng to Sri Aurobindo mankind has arrived at a critical stage of its destiny. This crisis is symptomatic of the cosmic crisis. It is indicative of the insufficiency and inadequacy of our vital and mental instruments to deal with the complicated and complex problems of human nature and society. There is the need of a higher power, the Supermind, the need for a new race of men and a new supramentalized humanity to fulfil the purpose of creation:

> "Our destiny may be the conversion of an original animal association into a community of the gods. Our progress may be a devious round leading from the easy and spontaneous uniformity and harmony which reflects Nature to the self-possessed unity which reflects the Divine."[11]

To fulfil such a destiny the immediate thing that has to be achieved is the spiritualization of politics, economics and the sociology

10. *Ibid.*, p. 284.
11. *The Ideal of Human Unity*, p. 17.

of human behaviour. This can be achieved only by the transmuting power of Truth consciousness. The ideal of rationalization is not bad in itself, but without a refounding of life on the basis of the individual's innate divinity it will be hopelessly inadequate for the task of establishing the Kingdom of heaven upon earth. It is the integral supramental knowledge alone that can transform art, science and life into living symbols of a higher and more perfect life. A supraphysical, supramental knowledge, says Sri Aurobindo, is necessary for the completion and fulfilment of physical knowledge. Any over emphasis on the powers of mechanical reason, science or political-economic institutional devices such as democracy, communism and socialism will inevitably lead to the assertion of the communal ego, to psychological suppression or to the mechanical compression of life or to unhealthy indoctrination and coercion. These scientific and rational systems may promise efficiency, order and organisation but only at the cost of the freedom of the individual, individual initiative and diversity. Human intellect is incapable of harmonizing freedom and order. Their synthesis can be realized only by the supermind.

Humanism and humanitarianism too are not the ideal solutions for, in a way, they are vain efforts of the sentimental idealist at synthetic eclecticism,[12] and only glorify the empirical man. So also the movements of ethical idealism and religious theology are inadequate, for divine life cannot be based on the social and pragmatic canons of divergent ethical and religious systems but would be the realisation of the inner spiritual truth of life. Religions, no doubt, exercise a great socializing and moralizing influence on human society, but often compromise with the lower parts of life and cannot insist on the inner change of the whole being. Though they originate in the superconscious experience of great spiritual geniuses, religions, through the passage of time, accumulate a lot of local and communal historical traditions, tend to become credal and formal, and are left incapable of universal acceptance. Only in the radical change of inner consciousness lies the real and perfect solution. The political, the economic, the humanist, the international, the institutional, the ethical and religious solutions are all inadequate for the

12. *Bases of Yoga* p. 50.

purpose of global human fellowship for they are all partial. The real solution lies in the overcoming of animal propensities and physical-vital tendencies, in the spiritual efforts for collective liberation, in the total spiritual and supramental transformation of human nature. This means the transformation of the sensational, vital and physical nature, the spiritualization of the mental being. A total and radical change of human nature with the power of Truth-consciousness alone can solve the terrestrial problems of man. It is this transformation of human nature that would lead to the establishment of an ideal society—a spiritualised society.

Looking at the panorama that the evolutionary history of human civilisation unfolds, indeed, we see great creative epochs in various cultures when men as well as masses lived on the luminous crest of their consciousness and gave to themselves and to posterity a rich legacy of cultural and spiritual output. These have been the periods of the outflowerings of the human genius, of intensity of aspiration and breadth of vision. The Periclean age in ancient Greece and the Age of Augustus in Rome are such times which epitomised the gains of European civilisation. Between them they embraced a world of light and power, brought a new understanding, a fresh outlook and a re-evaluation of life in terms of a new consciousness. Their gains can be matched only with those of the Renaissance, the most represntative movement of this kind which really gave a new birth to Europe and brought to the world the modern epoch of science. The Romantic Revival is another outstanding example of a similar creative phenomenon which evoked in the hearts of millions 'more vibrant living and powerful perceptions' and kindled in their hearts a new sensibility and new aspirations. With the French Revolution we see the manifestation of a force mighty and terrible in its transformation, which changed the very character and nature of society and brought in the bourgeois culture. And in more recent times the Russian Revolution has ushered in the socialistic era. In India too, her historic struggle for independence was 'a mighty evocation of both Light and Power' and carried a deeper import, the spiritual awakening and regeneration of mankind. "These larger human movements are in a sense anonymous. They are not essentially the creation of a single man as are some of the well-known religious movements.

They throw up great aspiring souls, strong men of action, indeed, but as part of themselves, in their various aspects, facets, centres of expression, lines of expansion. An Augustus, a Pericles, a Leo X, a Louis XIV, or a Vikramaditya are not more than nuclei,....centres of reference round which their respective epoch crystallises as a peak culture unit. They are not creators or originators; they are rather organisers. A Buddha, a Christ or a Mohammed or even a Napoleon or Caesar or Alexander are truly creators; they bring with them something—some truth, some dynamic revelation—that was not there before. They realise and embody each a particular principle of being, a unique mode of consciousness—a new gift to earth and mankind."[13]

It is in and through these great souls and these movements that the destiny of human society has been shaped through the centuries. These have been the two limbs of our evolutionary process. The Light descends through great souls, the enlightened individuals, consolidates itself in small centres few and far between, then spreads its gains among larger sections and groups and finally vast masses are touched and moved by it. This then has been the pattern of the cultural and spiritual development of human race. In our times, all movements social, political, economic, or spiritual are practically world-wide and encompass all nations and peoples. The world is fast becoming one compact, homogenous and organic society. This widening movement in the outer world is linked up with the inner progress of mankind, its spiritual history. It is the ascent of the human spirit towards the summits of his highest status and existence, his spiritual desitny. The beginnings of the soul-perception in the West are found in the Hebrew Old Testament, but the purest ray of the inner consciousness is installed only by the Christ and the need for the spiritual personality firmly established. And the task of materialisation of the Spirit on a large-scale and the remodelling of human society in spiritual terms was left to the other great Semitic Revolution that of the great Arab Master Mohammed. This complete curve of human progress, the picture of the whole evolutionary process is fully epitomised in India. Among her greatest epochs of spiritual induction and more intense rapid evolution have been those of the Vedic, Upanishadic, Dharshanic,

---

13. Nolini Kanta Gupta, *The March of Civilization*, pp. 6-7.

Puranic, Bhagavata and the Tantric. It is thus that the Light descends and establishes itself in everwidening circles until it slowly inhabits the world and possesses the entire humanity. Such is the process of 'canalisation, materialisation and fixing upon earth and in the physical being of the increasing powers of the Light.'

The appearance of the Greeks on the scene of European civilisation marks a new and definite turn in the history of human evolution. For the Minoan or Creatan civilization, Egyptian or Chaldean, are not merely chronologically old but psychologically different from the Hellenic culture. They were more instinctive and intuitive, more clairvoyant and mythopoeic in their approach to life, whereas Hellas brought in the luminous Reason, the logical faculty which helped man to mediate between the perceptual and the intuitive world, and to have an increasing control over material Nature. It is this formative power of the Mind which is the cornerstone of the great edifice of all scientific progress. It is Reason again which provided the inspiration and framework for all subsequent revolutions in Europe. In India and China too, we meet such characteristic movements. The Vedas represented an age of vision and revelation, *sruti*; it was these and the myth and the parable that moulded the life of the people. It was only in the Upanishadic age that the first rays of Reason are seen illuminating the peaks of Mind. And descending through the *Mahabharata* and the *Brahmanas* the Mind of Reason flowered in full vigour in the great Buddhistic illumination and the philosophical systems. It may be noted here that the Buddha was almost a contemporary of Socrates and Confucius. The Mind, therefore, is the luminous bridge between the two leaves of human experience—the spiritual, the occult and the intuitive on one hand and the physical, material and the sensuous on the other.

But, nonetheless, spirituality should not be looked upon as only the product of the ancient or medieval times and that science is a product of higher illumination and therefore has stolen a march over it. This crude and categorical formulation of the achievements of science and spirituality into two separate domains is the greatest misfortune of our times, for this only empties them of their deeper and all-embracing import. What we need today, more than ever before, is an all-comprehending and satisfying fulfilment, an internal truth and realisation that would embrace our total existence Man has always had a double aspiration, one of ascent into the transcendent world of Spirit, a world of truth, beauty, goodness and harmony and the other of descent into the mystery of the physical and material world. This double aspiration has found its expression, though in varying degrees in all the cultures and continents of the world. Science and spirituality are not only not incompatible with each other but are integrally one. It is in the realisation of such a synthesis of the two that lies our supreme destiny. The vision and experience of the spiritual is as necessary as our knowledge which gives us the hold upon the physical realities in the making of our new destiny, of the luminous future of humanity. For the supreme Reality is not only static Consciousness but dynamic Force; it is creative conscious energy. It is *that* as well as *this* fundamentally and integrally. It is the vision of the supracosmic Truth that gives Science its total sense and significance; it is the detailed grasp of the workings of material Nature that gives the Spirit its hold upon the esoteric process of cosmic evolution, and fulfilment.

"A global view of humanity is becoming more and more insistent, unavoidable and inevitable. It is being forced upon the normal consciousness of mankind so that the ordinary life itself has to be conducted and lived according to the demands of that view."[14] This is because primarily humanity is one and mankind as a whole is a single organism, and this underlying unity progressively manifests itself in outer unity and harmony. Today, more than any time in recorded history, this sacred fact of existence seems to insist on its manifestation as a concrete reality.

Nature constantly moves between two poles of life, the individual and the aggregate, seeking an integration and harmony between them. Between the individual and the totality of mankind Nature seems to introduce a series of lesser aggregates which act 'partly as aids and partly as barriers to the final unity.' This graduation results in a great complexity, for Nature does not destroy these smaller aggregates once the larger are successfully formed but keeps them in order to serve her passion for variety, richness and multiformity. She only seems to efface the dividing lines between them and so modifies the nature of

14. *Ibid.*, p. 55.

the smaller entities that they freely allow, promote, and even contribute to her creating of the larger unity. And this has confronted humanity with the most difficult problem of seeking accord between the interests of the individual and the immediate aggregate on one hand and the needs and interests of the latter and the growth of the larger whole on the other.

The goal of Nature is to help man learn to fulfil himself in the fulfilment of Mankind, by expanding his ego out of its attending limitation and eventually losing it in something superior and greater which it now tries to represent. The State is a means for common human development and therefore not an end in itself. Man, primarily, lives by the community for he needs it to develop himself individually as well as collectively. The State can only provide all necessary conveniences for his progress and remove all the obstacles in his way. Instead, any attempt on the part of the State to control the cooperative activity of the community and to clamp on the individual needless checks and restrictions would only result in a monstrous machinery crushing out the freedom, initiative and creative growth of the individual. All collectivist societies tend to immolate the individual to a communal egoism and envisage and seek unduly to subordinate him and create a static communal order that is dead set against all creative growth. It is, therefore, that in the present conditions the State is incapable of bringing about a healthy unity of mankind. This will be possible only when mankind develops into a self-conscious collective soul capable of subordinating mechanical means to the inner and creative growth of the human being. The development of a spiritualised humanity, and not an organised and mechanical human existence is the goal of evolution. Any attempt at the political, economic and administrative unification of humanity must, therefore, be preceded by the strong idea and conviction of a moral and spiritual oneness. If it is a living principle of national oneness that binds together the people of a nation, then a more dynamic and conscious principle of spiritual oneness is required to hold the peoples of the world in a common human fellowship.

The fruitful consequences of the French Revolution, reinforced by the revolutionary ideals of an organised national state in Germany and the Russian Revolution have together contributed not a little to the recent idea of a federation of free nations, the parliament of man, a world union. Undoubtedly, such a free association and unity of free nations must be the ultimate goal of our political development and until it is realised the nations and governments of the world must be subject to constant changes and even revolutions. However far mankind may be from this ultimate ideal of a federation of free aggregates it is worthwhile that it moves in the direction of the unfoldment of the moral and spiritual progress of the race that would ensure a just and healthy social, political and economic foundation as a part of the preparation and eventual fulfilment of its higher destiny.

This 'gospel of philosophic anarchism' missioned to reassert man's revolutionary faith in individual freedom and free self-fulfilment, perhaps may invoke the assistance of a new and superior religious and spiritual revolution hiterhto unknown to human history. For, all great and enduring movements, cultural and political, social and economic have sought their sustenance and appeal from deeper sources of spiritual experience. This supra-national aggregate of free people, it can be presumed, would combine the vivacity of spiritual life present in the Vedic and Upanishadic times with the general vividness of life and dynamic force of culture and creation of the early Greek and Roman civilisations.

If this new unification is in the very nature of things as a compelling urge, then conscious humanity must, through a constant, living and vigorous striving, evolve an enduring framework or scaffolding within which the new edifice might arise, as well as consolidate this aspiration as part of the vital and mental habits of the race. There should therefore precede a long intellectual preparation and a vital urge supported by an inner passion and the hope to achieve this new happiness for mankind by breaking up the present basis of things and reconstructing a new scheme of collective life. The present individualistic basis of society has to be replaced by an increasing collectivism founded on liberty, equality and the ideal of fraternity wherein the individual is helped to new ethical and social advancement and fulfilment. The two World Wars have in their wake ushered in a new precipitative force into the channels of human thinking. and made intellectuals the world over feel the necessity of an immediate international co-existence. But the mass of men are ruled in their actions not so much by an ideal as by their interest.

What is needed is a great outburst of a massed and dynamic idealism and creative human hope that can release into the earth atmosphere forces and factors capable of bringing about the needed transformation. The new consciousness of world unity must eliminate the bases of national egoism, hungers, cupidities and self-assertions, abolish national armies and all the causes of conflicts, explosions, wars and catastorphies and lay hold upon much purer roots of action of individuals, communities, races and nations in a mighty bid towards the total transmutation. As respect for the individual liberty and free growth of the personal being is harmonised with respect and consideration for the needs, natural growth, solidarity and organic perfection of the collectivity in an ideal State, so also national liberty, free national growth and self-realisation must be progressively harmonised with the solidarity, unified growth and perfection of the human race in an ideal aggregate of all humanity.

However, utopian the ideal may be, it would be worthwhile to know the ideal and the best method to achieve that ideal. To bring about such an ideal unification of mankind, peoples all over the world my be allowed to form themselves into large organised and harmonious groupings according to their natural divisions, of locality, race, culture or other convenience—free and natural groupings which would leave no room for internal discords, repressions or revolts. Simultaneously attempts may be made at the formation of large or small administrative and economic confederations as a possible means of habituating peoples of different races, traditions and cvilisations to live together in a common political family which promotes the principle of variation in a large measure.

Through the centuries Nature has brought about a great change, a change which in principle represents the evolution of society from a natural and organic state to rational and mechanically organised developing community. Science, Commerce and rapid communications have not contributed a little to this consummation of a common mental existence. The idea of World-Union therefore seems to be growing in the very consciousness of humanity and have its roots in the very necessity of this new common existence. To have the psychological assent, the moral authority and the active support of all its member nations, such a World-Union must in its constitution and character conciliate the sentiments and interests of the different sections of mankind representing the leading social, political, cultural ideas of the time. A World-Union or a Parliament of Free Nations can come into existence only when all the member nations and particularly most of the leading nations consent to total disarmament which again is possible when national egoisms are eschewed.

Once nationalism is subordinated to a cosmopolitan human fellowship only the much too important differences of culture and race threaten to linger for a longer period. But here too science, powerful as it is in the enforcement of uniformity of thought, life and method, is sure to succeed in minimising these differences. Also because of the constant meeting of the minds of the Orient and the Occident a common world outlook and culture will be the most natural outcome and the race sense too will be removed by the closer intellectual, cultural, and physical intercourse which is inevitable in the future. Unity is at the very basis of all existence which the evolving spirit in Nature steadily realises through diversity and complexity at the surface. In fact life exists by diversity; that is why every individual, every group however similar with the others is by some principle of variation unique. But uniformity and artificial regulation is not the law of life. A perfect order comes from within; it is the outflowing of inner nature.

The idea of a religion of humanity was born in the minds of the forward looking rationalists of the eighteenth century who tried to substitute it for the formal spiritualism of ecclesiastical Christianity. Positivism, humanitarianism, philanthropy, democracy, socialism and pacifism, have been among its chief by-products. As a result mankind came to be worshipped as a godhead and the progress and service of human life became the chief preoccupation of its protagonists in place of the family, the state and the nation. And war, physical or moral cruelty, capital punishment, oppression and exploitation came to be treated as crimes against this new gospel. The body, life and heart of man were to be held sacred and their service supreme. This great idealism was always faithful to the values of human life and existence. This gospel of the religion of humanity will exercise on the vast majority only a modifying influence and can never entirely prevail upon individual, class or national egoisms and leave the field still open to the arrogant and brutal adversary, unless it becomes the absorbing aim and passion of mankind as a whole. This can be accomplished only when the inner human nature and the inner way of living are radically changed.

If the integral unity of mankind has to be realised, the present idea of the religion of humanity must spiritualise itself and become the general inner law of the life of the human race. Today, more than ever before, nations are thrown together in an increasing closeness of common interests which makes old divisions superfluous. Moreover, the forces of a common uniting sentiment—a cosmopolitan, international sentiment, are steadily, growing stronger and effective. Taking advantage of these forces and the evolutionary pressure of circumstances leaders of mankind must set themselves to the supreme task of organising human life towards the creative unification of the race. The alternative is a lingering suicide, a total annihilation of the human race. Respect for the human individual and the natural human groupings, love of liberty, a sense of human oneness are all the essential components of the religion of humanity. Such a religion does not refer to a single system of thought or a particular creed and a universal religion or outward dogma. Freedom and variation of self-expression is the very essence of spiritual life. By a religion of humanity is therefore meant "the growing realisation that there is a secret Spirit, a divine Reality, in which we are all one that humanity is its highest present vehicle on earth that the human race and the human being are the means by which it will progressively reveal itself here. It implies a growing attempt to live out this knowledge and bring about a kingdom of this divine spirit upon earth. By its growth within us oneness with our fellowmen will become the leading principle of all our life, not merely a principle of cooperation but a deeper brotherhood, a real and an inner sense of unity and equality and a common life."[15] This is the truth of our being and our existence: and towards the realisation of such 'a free inner variation and a freely varied outer expression' that mankind should progressively move.

To evolve such a conscious human fellowship embodying the higher and wider ranges of consciousness and integrating the achievements of all the cultures and peoples of the world into an

15. *The Ideal of Human Unity*, p. 378.

intimate unity and harmony, seems then to be the secret purpose and end of Nature. The various modes of consciousness developed by man, namely, the occultism of Egypt, the moral fervour and spirit of righteousness of the Hebraic genius, the sweetness and light of the Hellenic mind, the Roman genius for law and government and organisations, the aesthetic sensitivity of the Japanese and the spirituality of India and such other elements must integrally combine their forces and emerge to build up this great godhead of humanity. Humanity as a race will then present the figure of perfect unity in diversity with an overall harmony and integration as its foundation. Mankind, if it has to survive and evolve and move towards its destined goal, will have to establish a living contact with the enduring and fundamental principles of existence,—the eternal springs of inner life, and progressively weld them into the outer life. The human race will gain a new meaning and significance and rejuvenate and revitalise itself only when it learns to aspire for a higher and fuller life in the spirit.

As in the individual or in the homogenous aggregate, in the entire human race too a spiritual cosmic principle seeks to express and manifest itself. Being the only self-conscious species, humanity shall have justified its existence through its constant search for self-fulfilment through the progressive manifestation of the soul's light in and through its manifold body. Such is its great mission and its greater destiny. This is possible only when it can develop an integrated soul personality and formulate its outer existence in the light of this deeper life and consciousness.

Sri Aurobindo's views, in this regard, are very definite and clear. He envisaged the transformation of man and his material existence on earth. The total spiritual transformation of humanity is not only possible but inevitable. Bare mental and moral powers are wholly inadequate to this great task of the reclamation of human nature. It can be accomplished only with the supreme creative power of the Spirit, the Truth-consciousness, which is not only up there above, but is here below and within Matter. This very nature of Matter makes its transformation inevitable and its destiny luminous and fulfilling. The hope of humanity lies in the growing number of men and women who will realise this truth and seek to develop it in themselves.

Man in Transition

R. R. DIWAKAR

EVOLUTION now is an accepted concept so far as the modern elite are concerned. There are bound to be shades and interpretations as to what evolution of man means, what stage he has reached and what awaits him in the future.

Nietzsche, Bernard Shaw and some others projected the Superman idea. Bergson, the French philosopher, opined that intuition would be the guide of man in future instead of his instincts, emotions and his vacillating reason, which always thinks in alternatives. Chardin has stated that man has already passed from the geosphere and biosphere and is now in the psychosphere. He has speculated about the next step.

The title of this small article is from Sri Aurobindo. Man is in transition—from animal, through man, to the life divine, is the course of evolution. *Homo Novo* is shaping within the shell of *Homo Sapiens*. That 'homo novo' of Sri Aurobindo would however be so different from Nietzsche's Power-Superman, and such other ideas as robots, automatons, computor man etcetera, that the main characteristic would be divinity and not mere humanity. The new race would be Truth-conscious straight away, and love, harmony, beauty, health—physical, mental, and moral, would be the hall mark. That would give man the power to transform and transmute even gross matter for purposes of living an illumined life in higher dimensions.

As we analyse the stage of evolution in which the present-day humanity is living, we find that it is a stage in which there is a combination of *anna* (physical), *prana* (vital), and *mana* (mental). Very few of us have had the privilege of peeping into the higher states of consciousness; but we are all familiar with *anna*, the material body, which may be said to be 99 per cent physics and chemistry. Almost every part of the body responds to physical and chemical laws. That is *anna*. But without vitality (life) the body is but a corpse, a mechanical thing. This vitality is supplied by *prana*. It assimilates things from outside, it grows and gives scope for consciousness to manifest itself. But that part of consciousness which is manifesting itself in us is only the mind, the mind which is analytical, the mind which looks at things and defines, the mind which is conscious of the individuality rather than of the integral being, the mind that sees divisions, classifications and separateness everywhere.

But Sri Aurobindo and the Mother have given to humanity a great call to rise above this stage of our mental development. If we continue to be in this stage, it is impossible for us to outgrow the evils of this stage of development. It will possibly be like the physical body which is eternally getting ill, getting medicines, getting cured for the time being, but never being wholly healthy and immune from all disease. We must aspire to be born with bodies which can never be ill. What we require today is not merely a healing balm here and there, not merely a small flickering flash of light for a time and then again a lapse into darkness, but we want a *jyoti*, a flame which burns in our own hearts forever like the inner light which Buddha called *atmadipa* (lamp of the soul). I think it is here and in this respect that the value of the path shown by Sri Aurobindo and the Mother is utmost. Let us remember that we are not merely bodies with souls inside them but that we are primarily souls who have bodies as vehicles for onward journey to the eternal.

The main thing in us is our consciousness. It is from that point of view that the *Gita* declares that the soul is indestructible. The *Gita* does not stop there. There is something higher and eternal in us and that is the most important part of us. The *Gita* says that there is *Paramatma* also in us along with the *Atman*. *Paramatma* is not somewhere in the temple, somewhere in the books, somewhere, in the *mantras* of the *Vedas* or any other religious book. It is in this body that the *Paramatma*, the *Paramapurusha*, the Super-Conscious, is living, is recognisable, is realisable and that can be done by human efforts.

In this perspective, I think, we have to cast a glance at the eternal stream of life that has been flowing for millions and millions of years on the surface of this earth. After millions of years life, evolving through numerous forms, came to a stage which was preliminary to that of humanity. That stage is called the stage of the anthropoids. Nobody had dreamt that suddenly there would be a leap from the stage of other animals to that of the anthoropoid stage. Possibly if the anthropoids had held a conference among themselves and thought about their future and if one of them had the audacity to say, 'Well, we are not going to stop there, a stage is going to come when a human being far higher and different from us with superior powers, with better consciousness, with potentialities of higher progress will be born,' possibly the conference would have passed a resolution of condemnation, or, if they had a mental hospital, that prophetic ape would have been sent to that hospital! But that stage did come and we are today human beings, human beings with certain individuals amongst us who already show that there is likely to be a better and higher stage also which can be reached possibly by meditation, possibly by yogic endeavour. That stage is certainly going to be something which is far higher than the stage we are living in today. It might be that most of the people will say, 'What have we to do with that stage? It may be after millions of years when that may happen. We are busy with our day-to-day problems, problems of bread and butter, problems of accommodation, and so many other problems.' Sri Aurobindo would say, it is exactly to find a permanent solution to these problems that we have to attempt to rise to a stage which is far higher than the present one. If it is on account of the inherent weakness of human nature or of its defects that humanity is suffering then certainly those weaknesses, those defects cannot vanish by merely administering temporary remedies. We want immunity from these weaknesses; if that is the quest of humanity, then it is only through an internal evolution by which the human mind will function better, will function on the plane of synthesis rather than of analysis, on the plane of harmony rather than of discord, on the plane of love than of hatred, on the plane of peace rather than of war, on the plane of *Panchshila* (coexistence etc.) rather than of crooked diplomacy, on the plane of peaceful and co-operatve existence rather than of military pacts. If our mind persists in thinikng in terms of hatred, of selfishness, of individuality, of diplomacy, of cheating each other how are we going to find a solution for breaking this vicious circle. War will not be a solution, wars have not been solutions. All of them have failed and have led to future and more destructive wars.

If that is the case, it is clear that the main defect lies in our present basic mental make-up. If that is to improve, we have to lift the level of our minds. If love is to rule instead of hatred, if peace is to rule instead of war, then our minds must be thinking in terms of peace and love at one and act always accordingly. It should not be the privileg only of a few saints and seers and sages to think and act in terms of love, peace and brotherhood. It should be possible to bring into existence a whole race whose normal life is conducted on the lines of those of saints.

Every man and woman must now begin to make an effort, and that effort should lie in the direction which Sri Aurobindo and the Mother have pointed out. Let us not think only in terms of India's glorious past or something that has passed away. Let us not be defeatists and say, 'Well, there is no future for us.' Why do we always think that everything good has happened in the past, as if India has lost the power to create anew and to initiate creative thoughts and to teach ourselves and humanity a lesson? Let us survey the last fifty years of India's life and India's contribution to the world of thought, to the world of spirituality, to the world of higher and better ways of living and to the ways of love and peace. I think we have contributed very richly in these matters. It might be that very many creative chemists and physicists have not been born in India! but physics and chemistry are not everything. Physics and Chemistry and their highest achievements are not going to solve the problems of life.

If human problems have to be solved, they can be solved only by a thorough research into our inner *Atmic* (spiritual) powers, as also by research into Atomic power. Then there has to be a complete synthesis of the knowledge of *Atmic* and Atomic powers so that a real harmonious way of life is evolved. Atomic power is only one side, the outer side of power and *Atmic* power is that which can control, command and regulate the Atomic power. Almost everything can be used for good or for evil. If human beings are to use the Atomic power for their own good, for the good of humanity, for the good of our future generations, it is the culture of our inner being, our souls, our consciousness alone which can do it.

I think Sri Aurobindo and the Mother have unfolded before us a vast vista. They are the prophets of future humanity. They have declared that a new stage, a new and higher dimension of consciousness can and will be reached and we have to strive after it. May be some people will say that they are merely dreaming and that kind of dreaming has nothing to do with the present-day humanity and that it is nothing but hallucination. But I think that their ideas and thoughts, their contribution to human experience, and also to the ways of *sadhana* are to be assessed in the perspective of the whole trend and progress of humanity. If seen in that perspective we shall find that a very rich contribution in recent times has been made by Sri Aurobindo and the Mother. I think they have taken us beyond merely the mental world to a higher and superior world of elevated consciousness. They have asserted that a new stage is going to come; they have asserted also that stage can be expedited by humanity by great endeavour. The stage that humanity has already reached is not merely that of consciousness. We have risen far above that. We are today self-conscious. That self-consciousness has given us the power of introspection; that introspection has enabled us to perceive what is wrong and what is right with us, where lies our strength and where our weakness. That introspection also gives rise to the discovery of our aspiration to hasten our progress towards perfection. Such aspiration is '*utsa*' (rise above) which pushes us upward, urges us to go onward. That is the eternal fire (*agni*) mentioned in the *Vedas*. Sri Aurobindo and the Mother have made us see that this aspiration of ours has a meaning. It is not mere wishful thinking: it is not merely a dream or a hallucination. The writer of the Upanishads said long long ago, '*Asato ma sadgamaya*,' lead me from falsehood to truth; '*Tamaso ma jyotirgamaya*,' lead me from darkness to light; '*Mrityorma amrtam gamaya*,' lead me from death to immortality. This has been the eternal aspiration of man.

I think it is Sri Aurobindo who has said in very apt words, 'Yoga is conscious evolution.' Since the very birth of life on this planet, various species have been evolving by what may be termed as the process of unconsciousness evolution. Even if any species or human being wants to stop, he cannot stop; just as a child grows when it is an infant, say, two years old, without having any conscious aspiration to grow, we have also been growing, developing and evolving. The eternal and vital urge of evolution is carrying us farther. What is expected of us, conscious beings, self-conscious beings, of us who are conscious of our aspiration, conscious of the potentiality of being able to contribute to evolution? An earnest effort to evolve further is expected of us and that effort lies in the direction of what Sri Aurobindo and the Mother have pointed out.

We are all manifestations of the infinite 'unconscious' of C.G. Jung. However, small and however humble we might be, we participate in the mighty urge of volution and the mighty stream of life. A single drop of water in the ocean is infinitesimal when compared to the ocean, but then it has all the qualities and all the essentials of the ocean itself. So, let us become more and more conscious of the urge of evolution and of our potentiality and let us try to carry ourselves forward by the guidelines of Sri Aurobindo and the Mother and with the help of the light that they have held for us.

India's past has been rich in all respects, there is absolutely no doubt. Her sons and daughters have shown their capacity to reach great heights and achieve mighty things in all human activities, political and cultural, social and philosophical. But then the one message that permeates the atmosphere of India is spirituality, the experience of the oneness of consciousness or spirit. The *Rishis* and *Munis* and sages, hundreds of them all over India, have spoken in different languages, but the spiritual message that they have given is one and the same. The spirit is one and indivisible and it is higher than matter in the sense that we are to reach spiritual heights through matter and thus transcend and conquer matter. It is not merely a question of regaining the balance that we might have lost. Equilibrium, equanimity is all right. The *Gita* itself has said that *Brahma* is wthout any blemish and at the same time is *Sama*, the very essence of equanimity. But I think there is a stage which is beyond this, I mean the stage which is not merely *Sama* but which has the positive quality of blissfulness or *Dhanyabhava* (fulfilment) or *Lila-bhava* (sportiveness); that is the stage of consciousness where, whatever may be happening, it is experienced as *Lila* or eternal sport. The Spirit as well as its manifestation are but the two aspects of the one energy or *Shakti*. I think that it is in those terms that we are called upon by Sri Aurobindo and the Mother to make a supreme effort to reach the highest stage. Let us not be bound by the bodily laws; there are higher laws by following which we go beyond to a new dimension. We have to be adventurous in this matter.

I am sure that before Patanjali wrote his *Yoga Sutras*, hundreds of people must have experimented and attempted to reach higher stages of consciousness and attain *Samadhi*. Hundreds must have gone mad as even today many people go mad, when they miss the way. But then after all those experiments, the path that they have found out, the *Yoga* system, is the greatest contribution of Indian culture to the world. If it is a question of comparing our metaphysics, philosophy and religion on the one hand, and the teaching and system of yoga, along with its latest phase the synthesis of yoga, I think, possibly the contribution of yoga is far greater. Many other countries have contributed in the field of metaphysics and philosophy, but there is practically no other country in the world which has sysmtematically probed into the laws and secrets of our consciousness, its powers, its depths, its widths, its heights, and tried to work out a system by which this *atmic* (spiritual) energy can be purified, controlled, conserved, concentrated and lastly surrendered to the *Paramatman* with a view to be identified with that Supreme Cosmic Power, so that thereafter one may act merely as an instrument, '*Nimittamatram bhava*;' Krishna asked Arjuna, who are you, what are you? Krishna told him, "You are but a clod of earth or a speck of dust, you are nothing more. You might be the greatest archer in the world, but then think for a while, identify yourself with the Supreme Power, then see what you are. You are but an intrument of the Cosmic Power." Krishna asked him therefore to be consciously an instrument of God It is in that direction that we have to progress. Sri Aurobindo's integral yoga is a distinctly forward step in the evolution of the system of yoga It has now thrown open to us the path which, if we trust with awareness, with ambition and aspiration, we shall be contributing to the great task that Sri Aurobindo and the Mother took up years ago.

Science and Vedanta

D.S. KOTHARI

"Is Brahman the cause? Where are we born? Whereby do we live; and whither do we go?...Should time, or nature, or necessity, or chance, or the elements be considered as the cause, or he who is called the pursha?"

—Svetasvatara Upanishad

"Life, Life, Life, I hear the passions cry; God, God, God, is the soul's answer. Unless thou seest and lovest Life as God only, then is Life itself a sealed joy to thee."

—Sri Aurobindo

ERWIN Schroedinger, a most distinguished physicist, and even greater as a natural philosopher, who received the Nobel Prize for his epochal contribution to modern theoretical physics, writes: "A hundred years ago, perhaps, another man sat on this spot...Like you he was begotten of man and born of woman. He felt pain and brief joy as you do. *Was* he someone else? Was it not you yourself? What is this self of yours?...What clearly intelligible *scientific* meaning can this 'someone else' really have?...Looking and thinking in that manner you may suddenly come to see, in a flash, the profound rightness of the basic conviction in *Vedanta...This,* as we know, is what the Brahmins express in that sacred, mystic formula which is yet really so simple and so clear: *Tat twam asi,* this is you. Or, again, in such words as "I am in the east and in the west, I am below and above. *I am this whole world.*"

And he continues: "It is the vision of this truth (of which the individual is seldom conscious in his actions) which underlies all morally valuable activity. It brings a man of nobility not only to risk his life for an end which he recognises or believes to be good, but—in rare cases—to lay it down in full serenity, even when there is no prospect of saving his own person."

Schroedinger expressed these profoundly daring (certainly so in the western cultural milieu) and deeply moving thoughts in his essay, *Seek for the Road.* He wrote this a few months before his discovery of wave mechanics, a landmark in the history of twentieth century physics. The essay was first published with another, *What is real*?, in 1961, under the title, *My View of the World,* thirty-five years after it was written. (The English translation of the German original was brought out by the Cambridge University Press in 1964).

This reference to Schroedinger serves to emphasize the profound relevance, in the present age, of the Indian philosophic thought, and more recently of the great contribution of Sri Aurobindo. The Upanishads ask questions at the deepest level of our existence and with a daring and earnestness that is as inspiring as it is matchless and incomparable. Take for example the opening stanza of the *Kena Upanishad*: "By whom missioned falls the mind-shot to its mark? By whom yoked docs the first life-breath move forward on its paths? By whom impelled is this word that man speak? What god set eye and ear to their workings?" It is therefore not surprising if we find a kind of creative resonance between the spirit of the Upanishads and that of modern science, particularly its most fundamental part, theoretical physics. The limitations of language, of words, in dealing with basic questions of existence (e.g. what am "I"?) was long recognised by the Upanishad thinkers. The recent developments in physics have forced us to recognise the inherent limitation of language in describing atomic phenomena. P.A.M. Dirac, one of the most original physicists of our times and a Nobel Prize winner says: "The new theories, if one looks apart from their mathematical setting, are built up from physical concepts which cannot be explained in terms of things previously known to the student, which cannot even be explained adequately in words at all. Like the fundamental concepts (e.g. proximity, identity) which everyone must learn on his arrival into the world, the newer concepts of physics can be mastered only by long familiarity with their properties and uses." The radically new situation in physics, symbolized by Niels Bohr's *principle of complementarity* can help us, in a sense, to understand somewhat more easily the thoughts of the Upanishads, but we shall not pursue this subject here.

There is an upsurge in science and technology as never before. The extraordinarily rapid growth of science in the last three hundred years has proved immensely fruitful, successful, beyond all expectations. And yet, as never before, there is a sense of inner disquiet, a restlessness of the soul, that is deeply disturbing. It is increasingly affecting the youth, especially in countries most advanced in science and industrialisation.

Science is *universal*. This is a fact of observation, and a most inspiring one. The laws of motion which describe the trajectory of a falling stone serve also to describe the motion of the moon, and other planets. This terrifically important discovery in science, and in man's intellectual history, was made by Newton barely three hundred years ago. To take another example of the universality of science, the atoms on our earth are *identical* with those in the sun and the stars, near and distant as revealed by observation and analysis of the light received from them. A central theme of science has been that every advance in science has re-inforced its universality.

Despite the very severe limitations of space and time to which man's body (which includes the *brain*) is subject to, man's *mind* is capable of "understanding" the physical universe. The realm of the mind is not circumscribed by the realm of the body. Not only that. The mathematical description of nature at the fundamental level has turned out to be astonishingly simple and beautiful. Indeed, a physical theory which is "mathematically beautiful" is likely to prove closer to nature, more successful and fruitful, than one which is mathematically ugly. Sir James Jeans exclaimed that God appears to be a pure mathematician.

The most significant and basic characteristic of science is doubtlessly the *objectivity* of science. (Universality is a fruit of science, but objectivity is its seed, its foundation). Science and objectivity are inseparable. We take it as axiomatic that a scientific "explanation" can contain no reference to, no intervention by, any supernatural agency, benevolent or malicious. In natural science there is no place for anything which does not satisfy the rigid criteria of logical reasoning. It is concerned with only "facts" that can be verified by experiment and observation. This demands that description of facts and theories in science should be unambiguously communicable from one person to another. Progress in science contributes to, and depends on, precision of "language." In this context "language" includes mathematics. Mathematics is necessarily precise and unambiguous. It is this which gives to mathematics a supreme place in science.

It is important to recognise that the objectivity of science, now taken as self-evident, has been achieved only gradually with the development of science over the centuries. When Newton explained the motion of the planets on the basis of his law of gravitation, he was unable to account for the stability (over a long period of time) of the solar system. He invoked, therefore, intervention by God to restore from time to time stability to the system (against the planets' mutual gravitational interactions). It was the French mathematician-astronomer Laplace who, nearly a hundred years later, availing of the advances in mathematics, since Newton, proved that the solar system was stable. When Napoleon asked Laplace why there was no reference to God in his astronomical treatise, Laplace answered that he found no need for it. To Newton intervention by God to prevent disruption of the solar system was a point in favour of his gravitation theory. It revealed directly (scientifically?) the living presence of God. To take another example, again from Newton, to account for the indivisibility of atoms, he wrote in his great work on *Optiks* that no earthly power could set atoms as under because God had made them indivisible. But an "explanation" (which involves the idea of purpose of any kind) is completely *objectiv*, not projection. This is its basic axiom. The greatest achievement of modern science, its most profound success, is the growth and strengthening of man's conviction, his *faith* in science, in reason.

It is the modern man's faith that what is not within the reach of reason today, will come within its reach some day, if man *can* continue his strivings, undeterred and undaunted. There are no barriers that science may not one day penetrate. Science is *autonomous*. In a sense, the replacement of 'God' of Newton's *Principia* and *Optiks* by 'Faith in Reason' is the meaning of the autonomy of science. There is a *certain* similarity in the concept of the autonomy of science and the *Samkhya* concept expounded in the Upanishads. An illuminating exposition of the *Samkhya* is given by Sri Aurobindo in his Essays on the *Gita* (the Chapter on the Determinism of Nature).

The objectivity of science makes it truly and effectively, a cooperative enterprise which can be shared by all men. Dogmatism of any kind whatsoever is not admissible in science. Dogmatism is *subjective*. Its ultimate basis is *personal* belief, not reason or argument. Dogma is *personal,* science is *public*. Dogmatism and objectivity are a flagrant contradiction. The cooperative enterprise of science has been amazingly successful, far more than any other enterprise of man. But the *objectivity* of science is not without its price—and a very big price. It imposes a vital and most far-reaching limitation to which we now turn.

Science by excluding *subjectivity* cannot, even in principle, deal with our thoughts, feelings, emotions, with subjective experience of any kind. It excludes 'I'. The exclusion is total. Our feelings—pain, joy, or what not—are inherently incapable of unambiguous communication. Even if I succeed in expressing in words some particular feeling or emotional state of mind, there is no proof, there *can* be no proof, that these words will produce within you an identical "feeling". "I", consciousness, mind, or soul, or whatever name we may give to subjectivity (or to any aspect of it), has no place in science. We should note that what is excluded is the *mind* and not, of course, the *brain*. Brain can be investigated objectively; and recent developments in electronics have provided powerful techniques. The *objectivity* of science excludes from it "I", its *autonomy* excludes from it "God". Science is a deeply inspiring pursuit of objective truth; but its domain is by definition *incomplete*. Science is objective; but faith in science and in the pursuit of science demands a *subjective* decision. It is a *moral* quality. (In the *Samkhya* a distinction is made between *atma* (individual soul), and *ahamkar*, *buddhi* and *maan*, we use the word *mind* to include all these 'entities').

For a moment let us go back to the basic distinction between *brain* and *mind*. Brain is objective, mind subjective. When, for instance, sound waves impinge on our ears, the pressure changes of sound waves produce electric currents in the nerve fibres which from the ear reach the brain. How do these electric currents in the brain transform in the mind into *sensations* of sound? The same applies to other sensations. Science provides no answer to this riddle, the riddle of all riddles? The point to appreciate is that science by its very nature, its very objectivity, can give no answer. Science does not, and cannot, deal with sensation, and thought. To quote Sir Charles Sherrington, one of the greatest physiologists of our times (*Man on his Nature,* Cambridge University Press, 1951, p 228-257): "The mental is not examinable as a form of energy. That in brief is the gap which parts psychiatry with physiology...Thoughts, feelings and so on are not amenable to energy (matter) concept. They lie outside it. Therefore they lie outside Natural Science...In some ways this is embarrassing for biology. Biology as its name says, is the study of life...Natural science has studied life to the extent of explaining away life as any radically separate category of phenomena...there is no radical scientific difference between living and dead...But though living is analysable and describable by natural science, that associate of living, thought, escapes and remains refractory to natural science...Our mental esperience is not open to observation through any sense-organ...Mind, for anything perception can compass, goes therefore in our spatial world more ghostly than a ghost. Invisible, intangible, it is a thing not even of outline, it is not a "thing." It remains without sensual confirmation, and remains without it for ever."

At this point, if not earlier, the question is bound to arise that if *mind* is outside science, then, how does it create science. All experience, everything without exception, is fundamentally a personal experience: it is subjective. When you and I look at a tree there is no conceivable way of determining that my *sensation* of "green" is the same as yours. That your perception and mine of a given thing is the same has no clear, no objective, meaning. How is objective knowledge then possible? This is not an easy thing to explain. The basic point is that an objective statement is not and cannot be, about one *single* sense impression (say, my sensation of red colour produced by a flower), but it expresses always some relation between *two* sense impressions. My sense impression of red may be (or may not be—who knows?) different from yours, but it is a verifiable, objective statement that two given flowers are of the same colour or they are not. This simple example can be readily generalized. The essence of the matter is that objective, communicable statements become possible when we consider pairs of sense impressions—not about *single* sense impressions. This is called the *principle of objectivation.* It is this which is the basis of the objectivity of science. "The fact that by comparing pairs communicable, objective statements are possible, has an immense importance because it is the root of speaking and writing, and of the most powerful instrument of thinking, of mathematics." (Max Born, *My Life and My views*, 1968, Chapter Five "Symbol and Reality)."

The conclusion that mind is outside the realm of objective science is extremely uneasy and tantalizing. How can anything, in principle, be outside science? What could be more "natural" than to assume that mind has evolved from matter, an accompaniment of the evolution of the brain, as a part of the long process of organic evolution. However, if the methodology of science is carefully analysed, there seems to be no escape from the Sherrington-Schroedinger conclusion that mind, by its very nature, cannot be described in objective scientific terms. Another consideration in support of this view is based on recent developments in mathematical logic. It is of great interest, and is fundamental but subtle. Let me quote from the Nobel Prize Lecture (December 1969) by M. Delbruck (Scientific World, Vol. 14, p. 15, 1970): "....our friends the (mathematical) logicians have made it clear to us long ago that in any but the simplest languages we must distinguish between an "object language" and a "metalanguage." The word "truth," and thus all discussion of truth, must be excluded from the object language if the language is to be kept free of antinomies. There then follows the strange result that there must be sentences that are true but not provable."

And he says: "Thus, even if we learn to speak about consciousness as an emergent property of nerve nets even if we learn to understand the processes that lead to abstraction, reasoning, and language, still any such development presupposes a notion of truth that is prior to all these efforts and that cannot be conceived as an emergent property of it, an emergent property of a biological evolution. Our conviction of the truth of the sentence, "The number of prime numbers is infinite," *must be independent of nerve nets and of evolution,* if truth is to be meaningful word at all." (italics added).

If the mind is not a "thing", and if it cannot be described in terms of space and time, then the concept of *separate* minds—as many minds as there are bodies—has no clear meaning. The idea of separation implies localisation in space, and is therefore not applicable to mind: mind is not a "thing". This leads irresistibly to the grand Vedantic concept of ONE MIND. We shall return to this presently.

If the mind is *not* a "thing", how can it interact with the body which *is* a "thing." If the mind cannot interact with the body, cannot influence its activity, how can an individual be held responsible for his acts, the actions of his body? If my mind (my thoughts) does not influence the movement of the pen in my hand, *who* is writing this sentence? On the other hand, if the mind does influence and determine the actions of the body, *how* is such interaction possible? How can an entity not describable in terms of space and energy interact with matter and influence its motion. How do drugs—and there are plenty of them and available in increasing abundance— affect the state of the mind, if there be no interaction between matter (drugs) and mind? Do "I" have any influence, any control over my actions, or is everything my body does (all actions are performed by the body) determined precisely by the *equations of motion* which completely specify the motion of (all) material things? Is free-will a reality or is it an illusion? And if free-will has no reality, then moral responsibility, compassion, repentance and the like have little meaning. *All this totally defies understanding.* The phenomenal progress in science in our times has only served to deepen the mystery of the mind-body interaction. It has made the situation more disquieting than ever before.

We may recall two recent articles in the *New Scientist*. Professor D.M. MacKay (*New Scientist* 2 July 1970) argues against determinism, whereas Professor John Taylor (*New Scientist* 30 September 1971) reaches the opposite conclusion. His thesis is that brain research is yielding increasing evidence in favour of determinism and against the concept of free-will. Mind is only a "shadow."

We may also refer to the book, *The Interpretation of Nature and the Psyche*: C.G. Jung, Synchronicity, an acausal connecting principle; and W. Pauli, the influence of archetypal ideas on the scientific theories of Kepler; Routledge and Kegan Paul, London, (1955). Jung says that the *sychronicity principle* advanced by him may help to "clear up the body-soul problem." He says: The "absolute knowledge" which is characteristic of synchronistic phenomena, a knowledge not mediated by the same organs, supports the hypothesis of a self-subsistent meaning, or even expresses its existence. Such a form of existence can only be transcendental, since, as the knowledge of future or spatially distant events shows, it is contained in a psychically relative space and time, that is to say in an irrepresentable space-time continuum." (p. 124).

An interesting schematic representation of the physical-psychical situation which Jung presents, after discussion with Pauli, is (p. 137)

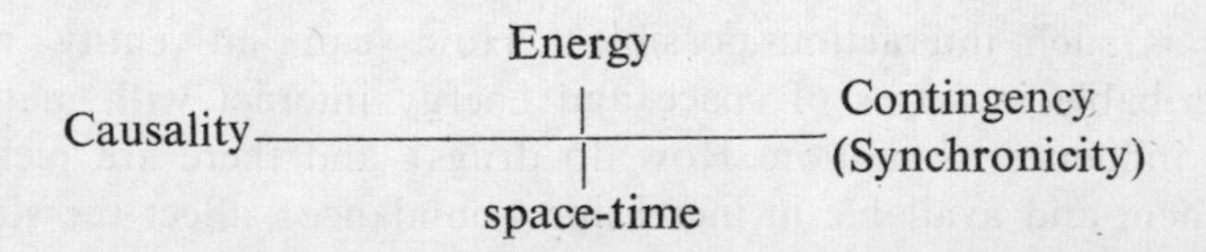

Synchronicity deals with phenomena that are inexplicable not merely because the cause is unknown, but for them a "cause is not even thinkable in intellectual terms."

The mind-body paradox is as alive as ever. It is deeply disturbing and at the root of much of the restlessness and frustration affecting man's spirit today. It is in this sense that Sri Aurobindo is so relevant to the contemporary situation.

In the word of Erwin Schroedinger the only "solution" to the unfathomable mind-body paradox, "in so far as any is available to us at all, lies in the ancient wisdom of the Upanishads."

The human body, like that of any other animal, is composed of atoms and molecules. The molecular organisation is extraordinarily complex and many of its features it would take a long time to unravel. Yet the basic "chemical units" are the same throughout the whole range of living organisms, animals and plants. These are twenty aminoacids and four types of nucleotides. This is a demonstration of an evolutionary process which, starting with simple atoms and molecules, has over some thousand billion years led to the present plant and animal kingdoms. In terms of complexity of organisation there is nothing (in the known universe) even remotely comparable to the human brain.

The recent far-reaching discoveries in molecular biology serve to provide beginnings of a framework for description, in physical terms, of the evolutionary process. The view is re-inforced that the source of evolution is random fluctuation, over billions of years, operating at the molecular level. This operates in combination with the extraordinary fidelity (stability) of the mechanism of duplication of genes (macro-molecules) responsible for transmission of hereditary characteristics from one generation to another. All this is explicable in terms of physics and chemistry. Jacques Monod has emphasized in his recent extremely fascinating and thought-provoking book (*Chance and Necessity—An Essay on the Natural Philosophy of Modern Biology* (1970), p. 110) that "....chance *alone* is at the source of every innovation, of all creation in the biosphere. Pure chance, absolutely pure but blind, at the very root of the stupendous edifice of evolution: this central concept of modern biology is no longer one among other possible or even conceivable hypotheses. It is today the *sole* conceivable hypothesis, the only one compatible with observed and tested fact. And nothing warrants the supposition (or the hope) that conceptions about this should, or even could, be revised." This is a grand affirmation of the objectivity and autonomy of science. A scientific study of biological evolution reveals, can reveal, no underlying purpose—no underlying design or goal towards which evolution is moving or directed. It could not be otherwise, as we have repeatedly emphasised. No considerations of purpose, divine or human, nothing which implies value judgments, can enter the gateway of objective science. The exclusiveness is total: Science by its very axioms is objective, not projective. If we ask: What *purpose* do the stars in the sky serve? the answer of astronomy is: The stars serve no purpose what ever. In the realm of objective science any other answer would be an absurd answer.

What we know about living organisms is not much, but we know enough to be able to conclude that the *human body is a machine*. It is so beyond question, subject to the laws of physics and chemistry which make no distinction at all whether the atoms are parts of a living body or dead matter. Equally, one cannot deny the incontrovertible direct experience that the motions of his or her body are under his or her control. My body is a "machine," but "I" control its movements. Any other assumption would be unacceptable, unreasonable to most people. Let us assume as undisputed the two facts that (1) my body is a machine and (2) its motions are under my control. From these two "facts" what is the inference we can draw which would not be contradictory to science—not violate its basic axiom of objectivity and autonomy? The only possible inference (as Schroedinger observes) is that every mind that has ever said or felt "I" is the person (if any) who controls the 'motions of the atoms,' controls the universe, according to the Laws of Nature. This is the Vedanta formula: *self=SELF**

The formula, self=*SELF* is simple as a formula, but how to comprehend it and activate it in one's life. What is the way? Says Sri Aurobindo (in the concluding chapter of the *Essays on the Gita*): "Follow...the law of your *Swadharma*, do the action that is demanded by your *Swabhava* whatever it may be. Reject all motive of egoism, all initiation by self-will, all rule of desire, until you can make the complete surrender of all the ways of your being to the Supreme...A supreme presence within you will take up your *Yoga* and carry it swiftly along the lines of

*Modern Physics, to which Schroedinger made such a crucial contribution, provides a helpful analogy. An electron, in fact, any physical entity on the atomic scale, shows both *particle* and *wave* properties. The two concepts, particle and wave, are sharply opposed to each other—one contradicts the other. The strange thing, totally unexpected, is that in the description of atomic phenomena both the concepts are essential: the two concepts provide complementary description. Nature is so made that an experimental arrangement designed to test the particle aspect automatically excludes an experimental arrangement to test the wave aspect. The two experimental conditions are mutually exclusive. Every act of observation is accompanied by a certain "disturbance" which cannot be eliminated and which is inherent in the nature of things. This is spoken of as Heisenberg's principle of uncertainty. It is this uncertainty principle which accounts for the mutual exclusion of experimental arrangements for investigation of wave and particle properties.

An appreciation of the complementarity of the relation, *self-SELF* (the complementarity of the *many* and the ONE) cannot be achieved within the framework of objective knowledge. It needs its equivalent of the "principle of uncertainty."

your *Swabhava* to its consummate completion. And afterwards whatever your way of life and mode of action, you will be consciously living, acting and moving in him and the Divine Power will act through you in your every inner and outer motion. This is the supreme way because it is the highest secret and mystery and yet an inner movement progressively realisable by all. This is the deepest and most intimate truth of your real, your spiritual existence."

The Next Great Religion?

R. RAMANUJAM
and
KENNETH L. WOODWARD

In each of the world's great religions, there are myths that anticipate the dawn of a new age for all mankind. Among some Hindus today, there is a growing conviction that the new age has already arrived through the life, thought and spiritual discipline of Sri Aurobindo, the Indian mystic, philosopher and poet who died in 1950 and whose system of "integral yoga" is now winning converts, throughout Europe, Asia and the U.S. Indeed, some students of Oriental thought believe that Sri Aurobindo's spiritual vision and discipline may blossom into the first new religion of global scope since the rise of Islam thirteen centuries ago.

When he died at the age of 78, Sri Aurobindo left behind a nucleus of disciples in Pondicherry, where the master's work is carried on by 1,800 devotees who live in India's largest, *ashram,* or spiritual community. The *ashram's* most ambitious project is Auroville, a new city five miles away on the Bay of Bengal, where 300 citizens from all over the world are building a self-sufficient city-state (maximum planned population: 50,000) based entirely on the principles of Sri Aurobindo. Presiding over both the *ashram* and the new city is "the Mother"—French-born Mira Richard, now 94, whose spiritual powers are reputed to be at least as great as those of Sri Aurobindo himself.

Sri Aurobindo's life work began with a career in politics. After earning a classics degree at Cambridge, he returned to India and

---

*Text of the article which appeared in the *Newsweek*, November 20, 1972.

plunged into the fight for independence from Britain. As the leader of an extremist faction of nationalists in Calcutta, he advocated armed insurrection and other steps more radical than those later espoused by Mahatma Gandhi. Sri Aurobindo was eventually jailed for his activities, and a year in prison turned him from politics to mysticism. Like other Hindu mystics, his initial goal was to attain spiritual union with *Brahman,* the "supreme principle of life," through the rigorous discipline of yoga. Step by step, he mastered the traditional forms of yoga: *jnanayoga* (knowledge), *bhaktiyoga* (devotion) and *karmayoga* (work). Later, he synthesized all three into a new system of *purna* (integral) yoga. But personal union with *Brahman* was not enough.

Unlike other Hindu mystics, Sri Aurobindo wanted to transform the material world, not escape it. To his integral yoga, he added, an evolutionary vision of the world which, much like the theories of the late Jesuit mystic Pierre Teilhard de Chardin, anticipated the eventual "spiritualization" of this earth. On Nov. 24, 1926, Sri Aurobindo told his disciples that he had "realized the Overmind"—the first step toward harnessing the "divine consciousness" to the forces of human evolution. Once a pilot community of disciples was properly prepared, he believed, the full "supramental consciousness" would descend, thus paving the way for a world community of spiritualized men.

With Sri Aurobindo's death, the task of drawing down the supramental consciousness fell to Mira Richard. The beautiful wife of a French diplomat, she met Sri Aurobindo in 1914, and he soon concluded that she embodied the traditional Indian ideal of the "Divine Mother." On the same day that Sri Aurobindo realized the Overmind, Mira took charge of the *ashram* of Pondicherry, and she has supervised the master's disciples ever since.

On Feb. 29, 1956, the Mother announced to the community at Pondicherry that "this evening...I knew and willed in a single moment of consciousness that 'the time had come'... Then the supramental light and consciousness rushed down upon earth in an uninterrupted flow." Thus disciples were not at all surprised when, fourteen years later, Apollo 12 astronaut Charles Conrad observed during his return from the moon an inexplicable light "as big as Venus" flashing steadily from a point "down from Burma and east of India."

The Mother has turned the *ashram* into a bustling, disciplined "spiritual university" that, in this centennial year of Sri Aurobindo's birth, is reaching out for disciples in India and around the world. With the approval of Indian Prime Minister Indira Gandhi, the *ashram* has opened hundreds of "Sri Aurobindo's Action" centers throughout India in an effort to spread the master's radical plans for social reconstruction. In addition, the *ashram* has published 30 volumes of Sri Aurobindo's writings, including his 23,000 line poem "Savitri", which describes the struggle to unite divine consciousness with the processes of history.

In the West, *ashrams* and Sri Aurobindo centers devoted to world unity have been established in almost every major European city and in a half-dozen U.S. cities from New York to San Francisco. Currently, more than 30 American colleges have booked lectures by Udar Pinto, a disciple who is making his first appearance outside the Pondicherry *ashram* in 35 years. "We do not want to start another religion," Pinto told a recent conference at Cornell University. "We want to go above religions."

Nowhere is this goal more evident than in Auroville, which the Mother founded in 1968. Politically, Auroville is recognized by India as an international city-state, and its efforts to become "the cradle of the new world" are symbolized by a lotus-shaped marble urn containing the soil of 120 nations.

To its residents, Auroville offers a blend of discipline and freedom. The Mother personally scans photographs of each applicant for signs that he or she is prepared to become "a willing servitor of the divine consciousness." After a year of apprenticeship, those who choose to remain at Auroville must surrender all their belongings, for the Mother regards private property as an obstacle to unity. Aurovilians are expected to avoid the use of drugs, alcohol, tobacco—and sex. But "if a couple has not gone beyond sex," the Mother says, they may have relations and even raise children.

The Mother believes that everything in Auroville—as in man—ought to be organically related. All crops, called "Aurofood," are grown without chemical fertilizers or insecticides. Architecturally, the Mother has planned the city with separate residential, cultural and industrial zones linked by parks and pedestrian causeways (automobiles are forbidden). At the center, citizens have carved out a vast crater, where they are building a huge golden sphere for the *Matrimandir,* or "Temple of the Mother."

Even the most optimistic Aurovilians think it will take another quarter-century to complete their city. By then, the Mother will presumably be dead. Even so, her disciples are confident that her spirit will remain incarnate among them. Last March, the Mother reported another vision in which she saw her own body transformed into a unisexual being with no stomach or genitals. Her disciples take this vision as a sign that the Mother is the harbinger of a new age in which humanity will sustain—and reproduce—itself by spiritual powers alone.

The Mother is confident that the new age has already arrived. "The signs are evident," "but they can be seen only by those who have the new consciousness."

Whatever happens to the Mother, Auroville seems to be well on its way to becoming the center of a new world religion. "In my view," says U Thant, former Secretary-General of the United Nations and a student of Sri Aurobindo's work for some 40 years, "he was one of the greatest spiritual leaders of all time." By combining Eastern spirituality with a Western sense of history, Sri Aurobindo offers a structured philosophy geared to the hope for a united world community. "Sri Aurobindo's legacy," says City University of New York Philosophy Professor, Robert McDermott, "is a uniquely promising attempt to spiritualize human institutions without institutionalizing the spirit."

A Select Bibliography

C.P. VASHISHTH

ACHARYA, K D
Guide to Sri Aurobindo's philosophy.
Pondicherry: Divyajivan Sahitya; 1969

ADVENT. Vol. 1—; 1944—
Pondicherry: Sri Aurobindo Ashram. *Quarterly*

ARYA. 1914-21
Pondicherry. *Weekly*

ARYAN PATH. Vol. 1—; 1930—
Bombay. *Monthly*

AUROBINDO (1872-1950)
Bases of Yoga. Ed. 6.
Pondicherry : Sri Aurobindo Ashram. 1952; 133 p.

— Brain of India. Ed. 4.
Calcutta: Arya Publishing House. 1948; 31 p.

— Collected poems and plays. 2 v.
Pondicherry : Sri Aurobindo Ashram. 1942

— Complete Works. 30 vols.
Pondicherry : Sri Aurobindo Birth Centenary Library. 1970-72.

— Doctrine of passive resistance. Ed. 2.
Pondicherry: Sri Aurobindo Ashram. 1952; 88 p.

— Elements of Yoga.
Pondicherry: Sri Aurobindo Ashram. 1953; 120 p.

— Eric: A dramatic romance.
Pondicherry: Sri Aurobindo Ashram. 1960; viii+102 p.

— Essays on the Gita.
Pondicherry: Sri Aurobindo Ashram. 1953; 580 p.

— Foundations of Indian culture.
Pondicherry: Sri Aurobindo Ashram. 1959; 449 p.

— Future evolution of man: The divine life upon earth. Comp. by P B Sant-Hilaire.
Pondicherry: Sri Aurobindo Ashram. 1963; 156 p.
— Future poetry.
Pondicherry: Sri Aurobindo Ashram. 1953; 406 p.
— Hour of God.
Pondicherry; Sri Aurobindo Ashram. 1970; 112 p.
— Human Cycle
Pondicherry: Sri Aurobindo Ashram. 1949; 334 p.
— Ideal of human unity. Rev ed. 2.
Pondicherry: Sri Aurobindo Ashram. 1950; 400 p.
— Ideal of Karmayogin. Ed. 6.
Calcutta: Arya Pub. House. 1945; vi+65+13 p.
— Ideals and progress—essays: Evolution. Ed. 4.
Pondicherry: Sri Aurobindo Ashram. 1951; 71 p.
— Ilion; An epic in quantitative hexameters.
Pondicherry: Sri Aurobindo Ashram. 1957; 178 p.
— International value of art. Ed. 4.
Pondicherry: Sri Aurobindo Ashram. 1953; 61 p.
— Kalidasa. Ed. 2
Pondicherry: Sri Aurobindo Ashram. 1964; 128 p.
— Life divine.
Pondicherry: Sri Aurobindo Library. 1949; 1040 p.
— Life, Literature, Yoga; some new letters. Rev ed.
Pondicherry: Sri Aurobindo Ashram. 1967; 278 p.
— Meditations on Savitri (Poetry) 4 vols.
Pondicherry: Sri Aurobindo Ashram. 1960-64;
— Mind of light.
New York: E P Dutton & Co. 1953; 118 p.
— More light on Yoga. Ed. 2
Pondicherry: Sri Aurobindo Ashram. 1953; 138 p.
— Perseus the deliverer.
Pondicherry: Sri Aurobindo Ashram. 1955; 146 p.
— Phantom hour: A story.
Pondicherry: Sri Aurobindo Ashram. 1951; 22 p.
— Renaissance in India. Ed. 4.
Pondicherry: Sri Aurobindo Ashram. 1951; 77 p.
— On Veda.
Podicherry: Sri Aurobindo Ashram. 1956; v+671 p.
— On Yoga. Rev & Enlarged Ed.

Pondicherry: Sri Aurobindo Ashram. 1969;
— Practical guide to integral Yoga. Ed. 2.
Pondicherry: Sri Aurobindo Ashram. 1958; 428 p.
— Prince of Edur. (An incomplete play).
Pondicherry: Sri Aurobindo Ashram. 1961;
— Rodogune.
Pondicherry: Sri Aurobindo Ashram. 1958; 162 p.
— Savitri: A legend and a symbol. Ed. 4.
Pondicherry: Sri Aurobindo Ashram. 1970; 839 p.
— Significance of Indian art.
Pondicherry: Sri Aurobindo Ashram. 1947; 103 p.
— Social and political thought.
Pondicherry: Sri Aurobindo Birth Centenary Library. 1970; 111 p.
— Speeches. Ed. 3.
Pondicherry: Sri Aurobindo Ashram. 1952; 154 p.
— Synthesis of Yoga.
Pondicherry: Sri Aurobindo Library. 1948; 283 p.
— Vasavadatta: A dramatic romance.
Pondicherry: Sri Aurobindo Ashram. 1957; 154 p.
— Views and reviews: Philosophical studies reprinted from the *ARYA*. 1914-20; Ed. 2.
Madras: Sri Aurobindo Library. 1946; iv+88 p.
— Viziers of Bassora; a dramatic romance.
Pondicherry: Sri Aurobindo Ashram. 1959; 202 p.

BAIG, M R A
In different saddles.
Bombay: Asia. 1967; 359 p.

BANDEMATARAM. Vol 1—, 1906—
Calcutta: *Weekly*

BANERJEE, SIDDESWAR
Short treatise on '*The life divine*'.
Pondicherry: Sri Aurobindo Ashram. 1956;

CHANDRASEKHARAM, V
Sri Aurobindo: Three essays.
Madras: Personal Bookshop. 1961;
— Sri Aurobindo's The life divine: A brief study. Ed. 2.
Madras: Sri Aurobindo Library. 1946; 105 p.

CHATTERJEE, JULSIDAS
Sri Aurobindo's integral yoga.

Howrah: The author
CHAUDHURI, HARIDAS
Philosophy of integralism; or, the metaphysical synthesis inherent in the teachings of Sri Aurobindo. Ed. 2.
Pondicherry: Sri Aurobindo Ashram. 1967; viii+4+181+5 p.
CHAUDHURI, HARIDAS and SPIEGELBE, R G, *Eds.*
Integral philosophy of Sri Aurobindo.
London: George Allen & Unwin. 1960; 350 p.
DAS, ADHAR CHANDRA
Sri Aurobindo and the future of mankind.
Calcutta: Calcutta University. 1934; xvii+130 p.
— Sri Aurobindo and the modern problems.
Calcutta: General Printers and Publishers. 1958; x+192 p.
DATTA, CHARU CHANDRA
Culture of India as envisaged by Sri Aurobindo.
Bombay: Bharatiya Vidya Bhavan. 1960; 152 p.
DESHMUKH, CHINTAMAN D
Sri Aurobindo relics enshrinement celebrations..
In *Mother India* Vol 9 (12) : 6-16. January 1958.
DIWAKAR, RANGANATH RAMACHANDRA
Mahayogi Sri Aurobindo: Life, discipline and teachings. Ed. 4.
Bombay: Bharatiya Vidya Bhavan. 1967; xxxiv+300 p.
GANDHI, KISHORE H
Social philosophy of Sri Aurobindo and the new age.
Pondicherry: Sri Aurobindo Society. 1965; ix+273 p.
— Letters of Sri Aurobindo on poetry & literature.
Bombay: Sri Aurobindo Circle. 1949; 350 p.
— Lights on life problems: Aurobindo's views on important life-problems.
Bombay: Sri Aurobindo Circle. 1950; 230 p.
GHOSE, CHINMOY
Infinite: Sri Aurobindo.
Pondicherry: Sri Aurobindo Ashram, 1956; iii+45 p.
GHOSH, JYOTISH CHANDRA
Life work of Sri Aurobindo.
Calcutta: Atmashakti Library. 1929; vii+186 p.
GODIN, HUGUETTA
Auroville—a twentieth century utopia becomes reality. In *National Herald* (supplement)

3rd March 1968; 3 p. columns 6-8.

GOKAK, V K

Sri Aurobindo
In *Mother India* vol. 3 (13): 15 August 1951.

— Sri Aurobindo: A sketch of his life and work.
In *Mother India* vol. 14(3); 57-60 April 1962;

— Sri Aurobindo and aesthetics.
In *Mother India* vol. 5(9): 3-11 October 1953; vol 5(10/11) Nov/Dec 1953; Vol 5(12): 18-23 January 1954; Vol 6(4) : 14-18 May 1954; vol 6(5): 18-22 June 1954; Vol. 6(6) : 15-18 July 1954.

GUPTA, NOLINIKANTA

Collected Works. 2 vols.
Pondicherry: Sri Aurobindo Ashram. 1970-71; 406; 376 p.

— Yoga of Sri Aurobindo (based on talks with the Mother) 11 parts.
Pondicherry: Sri Aurobindo Ashram. 1943-71;

GUPTA, NOLINIKANTA and AMRITA, K

Reminiscences.
Pondicherry: Sri Aurobindo Ashram.

GUPTA, RAMESHWAR

Eternity in words: Sri Aurobindo's Savitri.
Bombay: Chetan Prakashan. 1969; 194 p.

INDRA SEN, *Comp*

Integral education in the words of Sri Aurbondo and the Mother; selected from their writings.
Pondicherry: Sri Aurobindo Ashram. 1952; 93 p.

— Message and mission of Indian cutlure: Extracts from the writings of Sri Aurobindo.
Pondicherry: Sri Aurobindo Ashram. 1951; 61 p.

— Science and culture: A selection of passages from the writings of Sri Aurobindo and the Mother.
Pondicherry: Sri Aurobindo Ashram. 1951; vi+116 p.

KAPILA SASTRY, T V

Lights on Veda.
Pondicherry: Sri Aurobindo Ashram. 1961; vi+89 p.

KARAN SINGH

Prophet of Indian Nationalism: A Study of the political thought of Sri Aurobindo Ghosh. 1893-1910.
London: George Allen & Unwin. 1963; 163 p.

— Prophet of Indian nationalism: A study of the political thought of Sri Aurobindo Ghosh. 1893-1910.
Bombay: Bharatiya Vidya Bhavan.

KAUL, H K
Sri Aurobindo: A descriptive bibliography.
Delhi: Munshi Ram Manohar Lal. 1972; xxvii+222 p.

KESHAMURTI
Sri Aurobindo—the hope of man.
Dipti Publications.

LANGLEY, G H
Sri Aurobindo, Indian poet, philosopher and mystic.
Johnson. 1949;

LOVING HOMAGE
Calcutta: Sri Aurobindo Prathamandir. 1958.

MADHUSUDAN REDDY, V
Auroville: City of the future.
In *Deccan Chroncile.* 21st July 1968; p. 4

MAITRA, S K
Introduction to the philosophy of Sri Aurobindo.
Pondicherry: Sri Aurobindo Ashram. 1965; 71 p.
— Studies in Sri Aurobindo's philosophy.
Banaras: Banaras Hindu University. 1945; viii+160 p.

MITRA, S.K.
Resurgent India.
Allied Publishers. 1964;

MITRA, SISIR KUMAR
Liberator—Sri Aurobindo; India and the world.
Bombay: Jaico Publishing House. 307 p.
— Sri Aurobindo and his Ashrama.
Shantiniketan: Visva Bharati. 1940. 12 p.

MOTHER INDIA Vol 1—; 1949—
Pondicherry: Sri Aurobindo Ashrama. *Monthly*

MOTWANI, KEWAL, *Comp;*
Aurobindo on social sciences and humanities for the new age: An anthology.
Calcutta: Longmans Ltd. 1962. 204 p.

MUKHERJEE, Haridas and MUKHERJEE, Uma
Sri Aurobindo and the new thought in Indian politics.
Calcutta: Firma K L Mukhopadhyay. 1964; 393 p.
— Sri Aurobindo's political thought.

Calcutta: Firma K L Mukhopadhyay. 1958. 188 p.

MUNSHI, K M
Sri Aurobindo.
In *Advent* vol 8(4); 302-5. November 1951
— Sri Aurobindo—an appreciation.
In *The Hindustan Times*. December 6, 1950

NANDKUMAR, PREMA
A study of 'Savitri'.
Pondicherry: Sri Aurobindo Ashram. 1962; xx+568 p.

NANDI, S K
Aurobindo on art and utility.
In *Searchlight* (Magazine Section). 11 May 1969; 1 p, columns 4-8.

NARAYAN PRASAD
Life in Aurobindo Ashram.
Pondicherry: Sri Aurobindo Ashram. 401 p.

NIRODBARAN
Correspondence with Sri Aurobindo.
Pondicherry: Sri Aurobindo Ashram 1954; 191 p.

PANDIT, M P
Life behind life.
Pondicherry: Sri Aurobindo Ashram. 1965; 142 p.
— Lights from Sri Aurobindo.
Pondicherry: Dipti Publications. 1970; 217 p.
— Readings in Savitri. 3 parts.
Pondicherry: Dipti Publications. 1969-70.
— Sadhana in Sri Aurobindo's yoga.
Pondicherry: Sri Aurobindo Ashram. 1962.
— Sri Aurobindo: Studies in the light of his thought.
Pondicherry: Sri Aurobindo Ashram. 1957; 247 p.
— Teachings of Sri Aurobindo.
Madras: Aurobindo Study Circle. 1959.

PIONEER of the Supramental age: Sri Aurobindo the enshrinement and the future.
Pondicherry: Sri Aurobindo Ashram. 1958.

PURANI, A B
Evening talks with Sri Aurobindo.
Pondicherry: Sri Aurobindo Ashram. 1959.
— Lectures on Savitri: Lectures delivered in the United States.
Pondicherry: Sri Aurobindo Ashram. 1967; 107 p.

— Savitri: An approach and study. 3rd impression.
Pondicherry: Sri Aurobindo Ashram 1970; 397 p.
— Studies in Vedic interpretations on the lines of Sri Aurobindo.
Varanasi: Chowkhamba Sanskrit Series. 1963;
— Sri Aurobindo's vedic glossary.
Pondicherry: Sri Aurobindo Ashram 1962; x+103+426 p.

RAJENDRA PRASAD
August 15, Sri Aurobindo's birthday.
In *Mother India* vol 14(7): 6 August 1962.

REGE, P S
Savitri and Avalokita.
Bombay: Thackers. 1969; 182 p.

RISHABHCHAND
Divine collaborators.
Pondicherry: Sri Aurobindo Ashram. 1960;
— In the Mother's light. 2 parts.
Pondicherry: Sri Aurobindo Ashram.
— Integral yoga of Sri Aurobindo. 2 parts.
Pondicherry: Sri Aurobindo Ashram. 1953-1955.

ROY, ANILBARAN
Sri Aurobindo and the new age. Ed. 2.
Pondicherry: Divyajivan Sahitya. 1965; 175 p.
— The world crisis: Sri Aurobindo's vision of the future.
London: Allen & Unwin. 1947; 157 p.

ROY, DILIP KUMAR
Sri Aurobindo came to me.
Pondicherry: Sri Aurobindo Ashram. 1952.

SEETHARAMAN, M V
Studies in Sri Aurobindo's dramatic poems.
Pondicherry: Sri Aurobindo Ashram. 1967; 99 p.

SETHNA, K D
Sri Aurobindo: The poet.
Sri Aurobindo International Centre of Education, 1970.
— Vision and works of Sri Aurobindo.
Pondicherry: Sri Aurobindo Ashram.
— Sri Aurobindo on Shakespeare.
Pondicherry: Sri Aurobindo Ashram. 1965; 131 p.

SHARMA, RAM NATH
Philosophy of Sri Aurobindo (Thesis)
Lucknow: Bharatiya Prakashan Mandir. 1960; xvi+192 p.

SRI AUROBINDO and the Mother on Education.
Pondicherry: Sri Aurobindo Ashram. 1960.

SRI AUROBINDO INTERNATIONAL CENTRE OF EDUCATION Handbook.
Pondicherry: Sri Aurobindo Ashram. 1960; 142 p.

SRI AUROBNDO on himself and on the Mother.
Pondicherry: Sri Aurobindo Ashram. 1953; 782 p.

SRI AUROBINDO PATHAMANDIR ANNUAL. Vol. 1–; 194—
Pondicherry: Sri Aurobindo Ashram. *Annual*

SRINIVASA IYENGAR, K R
Sri Aurobindo. Ed. 2.
Calcutta: Arya Publishing House. 1950; 404 p.

SRIVASTAVA, R S
Sri Aurobindo and the theories of evolution.
Varanasi: Chowkhamba Sanskrit series.

TAGORE, RABINDRANATH
Salutation to Sri Aurobindo.
Perkins. 1949.

TAN YUN SEN
Sri Aurobindo—a homage. Ed. 3.
Madras : Sri Aurobindo Library. 1950; 66 p.

TEHMI, *Tr.*
Satprem: Sri Aurobindo or the adventure of consciousness.
Translated from French.
Pondicherry: Sri Aurobindo Ashram. 1968 395 p.

VARMA, SHARADA PRASAD
Sri Aurobindo.
Surat: Yugantar Karyalaya. 1961.

VARMA, VISHWANATH PRASAD
Political philosophy of Sri Aurobindo.
Bombay: Asia. 1960; xiii+471 p.

WORLD UNION GOODWILL Vol. 1, 1961.
Pondicherry: Sri Aurobindo Ashram. *Quarterly*.

INDEX